D0363208

"The authors comprehensively outline effective approaches to marketing and selling innovations – important topics that have limited coverage in most of the existing texts on entrepreneurship. They have also done an excellent job in highlighting the two key elements of successful technology entrepreneurship, by emphasising both the processes needed to validate the market for the developed innovation/technology, and how to actually design the 'winning business model'." – *Olli Kuivalainen, Professor, International Marketing, Lappeenranta University of Technology, Finland*

"Evers, Cunningham and Hoholm meet a particularly important need here by providing students with the knowledge as well as practical tools required to transform scientific and technological research or ideas into business opportunities with the aim of establishing high-growth ventures. Given a context where high-growth technology start-ups are viewed as significant to economic recovery and growth, and universities – as producers of knowledge – are assumed to take a more central position in the innovation system of a nation or region through commercialisation activities, this book is very well placed. It is a comprehensive, insightful and significant resource for those wishing to learn about the process of technology entrepreneurship." – *Majella Giblin, Ussher Assistant Professor in Entrepreneurship and Innovation, School of Business, Trinity College Dublin, Ireland*

"This book is immensely comprehensive and superbly pulls together and applies a panoply of management frameworks to the 'process' of creating technology ventures in a way I've not seen before." – *Jeff Skinner, Executive Director of the Deloitte Institute of Innovation and Entrepreneurship, London Business School, UK*

"Reading *Technology Entrepreneurship* is a must for the students and scholars of entrepreneurship and the creators, guardians, policy makers and supporters of technology. Evers, Cunningham, and Hoholm have recognized the duality of entrepreneurship and technology and have written a book that bridges the divide between the two disciplines to bring them well within the easy grasp of engineers, scientists and inventors who aspire to commercialize their new ideas, new findings and inventions in a marketplace where many new technology-based products and services compete for the end user's discriminating eye for high value. The 12 well-structured and very clearly written chapters of the book cover all the influential and detracting factors that all agents, including those in the scientific and creative, entrepreneurial and business, and policy formulation communities, need to have at their fingertips to ensure success. This volume's rich combination of pedagogical, structural and informative components provides the concepts, tools and methods that concerned agents need to have, even if they are not currently and directly involved with technological entrepreneurship." – *Hamid Etemad, Professor, Desautels Faculty of Management, McGill University, Canada*

Technology Entrepreneurship

Bringing Innovation to the Marketplace

Natasha Evers
Lecturer in Marketing, J.E. Cairnes School of Business & Economics,
National University of Ireland, Galway

James Cunningham
Director of the Whitaker Institute and Senior Lecturer,
J.E. Cairnes School of Business & Economics,
National University of Ireland, Galway

Thomas Hoholm
Associate Professor, BI Norwegian Business School, Oslo, Norway

First published 2014 by
PALGRAVE MACMILLAN

Palgrave Macmillan in the UK is an imprint of Macmillan Publishers Limited, registered in England, company number 785998, of Houndmills, Basingstoke, Hampshire RG21 6XS.

Palgrave Macmillan in the US is a division of St Martin's Press LLC, 175 Fifth Avenue, New York, NY 10010.

Palgrave Macmillan is the global academic imprint of the above companies and has companies and representatives throughout the world.

Palgrave® and Macmillan® are registered trademarks in the United States, the United Kingdom, Europe and other countries

ISBN: 978–1–137–02010–9

This book is printed on paper suitable for recycling and made from fully managed and sustained forest sources. Logging, pulping and manufacturing processes are expected to conform to the environmental regulations of the country of origin.

A catalogue record for this book is available from the British Library.

A catalog record for this book is available from the Library of Congress.
Printed in China

Seán, Catherine, Cillian -
Daoibhse an saothar seo – Le grá mór, Mam.

Sammi

Camilla, Sebastian, Rasmus, Oliver and Linus:
Thank you for keeping up with me.

Contents

List of Figures

List of Tables

Preface

The knowledge and skills required to transform scientific research into commercial innovation is commonly termed as "technopreneurship". Local regional development can be driven by "technopreneurs" (Venkataraman, 2004; Lee and Wong, 2004). Technopreneurs are scientists, lab technicians, engineers and technologists who utilise their technical knowledge and know-how to establish business ventures. The EU's *Europe's 2020 Growth Strategy for Innovation* (http://ec.europa.eu/europe2020) and changes in the US Patent application processes as well as support at national levels to encourage entrepreneurship have meant that entrepreneurship, and particularly technology entrepreneurship, is to the fore for policy-makers, support agencies, venture capitalists, technology transfer professionals and academic entrepreneurs.

The past two decades have witnessed a dramatic increase in investment in technology entrepreneurship. The translation of discovery, development and diffusion of technological innovations at the national level has become a part of the innovation and economic agenda for every developed economy in Europe against the background of increased uncertainty and competition of Asian economies and China. Transfer of knowledge and technology, encompassing intellectual property, from higher education institutions (HEIs) and Public Research Organisations (PROs) has been articulated in the EU Innovation Scorecard. The founding of small, start-up firms developing inventions and technology with significant potential commercial application is critical to the success of the "smart economy", which all European states aspire for. Such processes can be referred to as technology entrepreneurship.

> Technology entrepreneurship is defined as "an investment in a project that assembles and deploys specialised individuals and heterogeneous assets that are intricately related to advances in scientific and technological knowledge for the purpose of creating and capturing value for a firm". (Bailetti, 2012, p. 5)

The ability to connect specific knowledge and a commercial opportunity requires a set of skills, aptitudes, insights and circumstances that are distributed neither uniformly nor widely (Venkataraman, 1997). In creating a new venture, scientists, engineers and technologists can be involved in both the invention and the commercialisation–exploitation phases (Grandi and Grimaldi, 2005); thus, they need both specific scientific knowledge and business skills.

There is a critical knowledge and skills deficit amongst the science and technology community to commercialise technological discoveries arising from their research and industry experience. Many technical entrepreneurs are "in love" with their product and tend to forget about thinking how to build a business around it. Often this leads to business plans with very convincing technology and product descriptions but with no sign of how it will create value for customers and owners, and how to organise the business in order to capture (a share of) the economic value in order to profit from it. Research shows clearly how companies within the same industry may have very different ability to capture economic value from their business model.

At the individual and group level, a key challenge is how to translate promising technologies into a stream of economic returns for their founders, investors and employees. In other words, the main problem is not so much invention but commercialisation (Gans and Stern, 2003). This book is focused on providing academic grounding and practical approaches that address the knowledge and skill deficit through a variety of pedagogical supports.

P.1 CORE AIMS OF THE BOOK

This book caters to pre- and post-experience students with technology-based backgrounds by providing them the knowledge and skills and practical approaches required to transform scientific ideas into commercial innovation for enterprise development. This book addresses the commercial agenda around issues of discovery, development and diffusion of technological innovations. It provides the reader with sufficient theoretical grounding as well as practical approaches and frameworks that assist with the transformation of scientific discovery for profit and/or social ends. In particular, a core aim of this book is to robustly address the marketing of technology – a critical area that is not well-covered in other texts on technology entrepreneurship. To address this knowledge gap, the authors have devoted four chapters (Chapters 7, 8, 9 and 11) to decisions most pertinently related to the marketing of technologies and marketing in high-tech ventures.

Specific aims of the book are to:

- Help students understand the entrepreneurial process for technology-based ideas and the appropriate diffusion and exploitation of intellectual property;
- Provide students with comprehensive insights into the specialised field of technopreneurship. This will provide a structured business planning process, from the "idea" stage to "market launch" and present best practices in raising finance and acquiring resources to bring commercial realisation to technological discoveries;
- Equip students with a sound appreciation of marketing, from opportunity validation, developing the value proposition, to formulating an effective

and feasible marketing strategy required to launch their innovation competitively in the domestic and international market space;

- Provide students with the knowledge and skills to transform technological invention into business concepts;
- Enable students to connect their specific knowledge to a commercial opportunity so they can actively lead and engage in the commercialisation–exploitation processes of their IP;
- Present the practical know-how to students so that they can commercialise and develop effective and implementable strategies for business modelling, prototyping, marketing and financing their technological discoveries sourced from industry, universities, public research institutions and in general;
- Offer students a framework for understanding the entrepreneurial process and expose students to the challenges faced by technology-oriented entrepreneurs;
- Educate students about the concept and application of dynamic tool of business modelling to configure the available resources to create unique customer value and capture economic and other value from this; and
- Guide students through real, short and long case studies, some of which have been authored by technology entrepreneurs themselves. They will expose students to challenges and realities of technology entrepreneurship.

Further, the book integrates both an academic and practitioner perspective of key approaches to dealing with the challenges involved in managing, commercialising and marketing technological innovation and new business development. It provides insights into the evaluation of the commercial feasibility of innovative research and critical innovation issues such as intellectual property, technology transfer and licensing. The book places a strong emphasis on development of the value proposition for the innovation and the business model as important business development and planning tools. The book devotes a full chapter to the mechanics of team organisation, leadership and cross-disciplinary nature of entrepreneurial teams in technology-based ventures.

A variety of case studies are included from North America, UK, Ireland, Scandinavia and Asia in technology-related sectors such as web-based technologies, green technologies, nano and biotechnology, material science, food processing, instrumentation and electronics and information technology.

P.2   KEY FEATURES OF THE BOOK

- *Marketing.* Part III is devoted to marketing and Chapter 11 especially examines international marketing decisions for the venture.
- *Market opportunity validation and market research.* Chapter 7 provides a comprehensive guidance on market opportunity validation and market research.
- *Innovation.* Chapter 9 takes the students through the process of how to develop their own value proposition for their innovation.
- *Business modelling and metrics.* Chapter 6 stresses on the importance of business modelling and business. It also identifies some key metrics

essential to test effectiveness of the business model and growth the venture.
- *Pedagogy and self-learning online material.* A coordinated and instructional pedagogical approach is delivered to ensure continuity and consistency in the development of each topic taking the idea to prototype and then to marketing stage. The book provides a route map for learners on when, how and what the business tools and frameworks are; guide templates can be found in the online companion website. This allows students to adopt a self-learning approach and instructors can draw on text as a resource to facilitate and support independent project assessments.
- *International case studies.* Case studies of high-tech companies at the end of each chapter as well as case examples embedded in chapters offer snapshots of high-growth sectors of engineering, sciences and IT sectors.
- *International entrepreneurship.* Chapter 11 is highly relevant for students as it helps understand internationalisation of new ventures and exploiting international opportunities.

P.3   ORGANISATION OF THE BOOK

The structure of the book is designed to provide a logical and structured approach for the readers to support their development and understanding of key themes, concepts and processes of technology entrepreneurship.

As illustrated in Figure P.1, the book consists of four parts (I–IV), with each part containing three chapters (totalling 12 chapters) that are supplemented with online material for each chapter. The book is designed to support both traditional lecturing format (12-week semester courses) as well as shorter more intensive formats (one-week courses). **Part I** provides the reader with an overview of contemporary policy and practice issues that impact technology entrepreneurship in key geographical regions and locations such

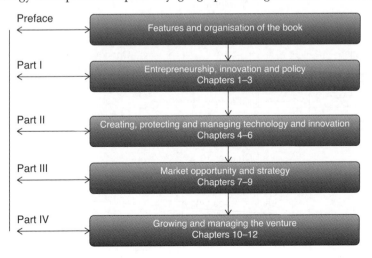

Figure P.1   Structure of the book

as Europe, United States, South Korea and Singapore. Chapter 1 examines how government policy and support influence sectoral entrepreneurship in areas of national and regional importance. Chapter 2 looks at the different mechanisms of technology transfer from higher educational institutions to business and society. Chapter 3 concludes by focusing on the individual entrepreneur or the entrepreneurial team in terms of the characteristics, motivations and barriers they face as they attempt to bring new innovations to the marketplace and in doing so create sustainable business that survive beyond the "valley of death".

Part II, III and IV then examine the issues and steps in the entrepreneurial process for high-tech entrepreneurs from creating and protecting their innovation to managing and growing the venture. Figure P.2 captures the key stages in the techno-entrepreneurial process and further identifies the corresponding chapters in the book related to each stage in the process.

Part II provides a systematic understanding of contemporary challenges facing engineers and scientists in managing, protecting and capturing value from their innovative ideas through the transformation into a viable business model. First, Chapter 4 introduces the reader to the concept and classification of innovation and innovation platforms and goes on to discuss their stages from concept development to prototyping. Chapter 5 then presents the fundamental and critical issues in intellectual property, such as

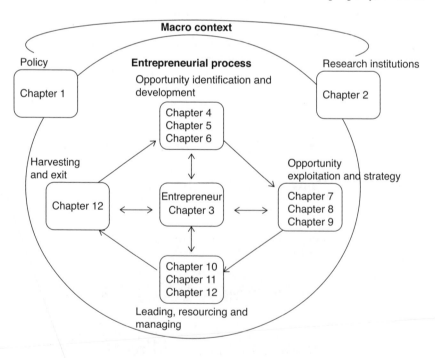

The techno-entrepreneurial process

managing IP, assessing its value, and patent application processes. Chapter 6 discusses the dynamic tool of business modelling and the business plan as an important outcome of business model development followed by most effective metrics for measuring business growth.

Part III addresses the role of marketing in the venture and captures comprehensively the nuts and bolts of marketing for high-tech ventures. Chapter 7 begins with market research and market validation processes. In Chapter 8 the commercialisation routes are explored followed by the importance of sales pitching for initial investor funding. Chapter 9 outlines the steps involved in developing the value proposition, and in designing and formulating marketing strategies to deliver it.

Part IV looks at growing and managing the venture for sales growth, expansion and financial viability, with specific focus on three core areas. Chapter 10 addresses managing teams, leadership and organisational culture. Chapter 11 looks in detail at the internationalisation of a new venture. Chapter 12 examines how financial capital is sourced and managed to grow the business and equally ensure the venture is financially viable and can deliver a profitable return for the founder and investors.

P.4 STRUCTURE OF EACH CHAPTER

Each chapter has a number a pedagogical features designed to support the learning experience of non-experts who are new to this domain area. Each chapter begins with a chapter synopsis and we have designed the text such that each chapter covers three core issues. In doing so, we provide clear guidance to learners, by way of an overall framework, accessible writing style and illustrative examples throughout each chapter. Each chapter includes an end of chapter case study that provides course leaders a basis for group discussion and exercises. Each chapter is structured as follows:

- Learning objectives
- Chapter structure
- Core chapter themes
- Chapter summary
- Case study
- Revision questions
- References
- Further reading and resources
- Glossary of terms

P.5 SUMMARY OF CHAPTERS

Chapter 1 starts with exploring the environmental context that helps technology entrepreneurs create new businesses and innovate. It first outlines the triple helix approach, which has influenced national policy approaches in global economies. The reader is then introduced to some of

the important policy initiatives in key regions that support entrepreneurship and innovation, e.g. European Union (EU), United States, Australia
and South Korea. The chapter then discusses direct and indirect impacts on
innovation. Chapter 1 concludes by forecasting some macro future trends
that will have an impact on technology entrepreneurs and discusses the
case of Reinshaw Diagnostics Ltd. This case illustrates the complexities and
challenges of technology-based entrepreneurship, the importance of technology and newness and how environmental conditions can have a positive influence for technology-based firms.

Chapter 2 explains how universities are embracing research commercialisation or what is termed more broadly as *third-mission activities*. It
explores the theoretical debates of the mission activities and outlines some
key technology transfer mechanisms relevant to technology entrepreneurs,
which include patents, licensing and company formation – start-ups and
spin-offs. Chapter 2 concludes by examining the stimulants and inhibitors
to technology transfer. The case study on the Allergy Standard Ltd company
provides insights into the entrepreneurial journey from new idea inception
through to international marketplace success. The case further highlights
the role of campus-based and external support as well as the importance of
environmental conditions.

Chapter 3 explores three areas with respect to technology entrepreneurs and new technology ventures. It begins by exploring the different
definitions of entrepreneurship and then examines how technology entrepreneurship is different from other types of entrepreneurship. To explore
the commonalities and differences, the focus is turned to examining the
characteristics of technology entrepreneurs and entrepreneurs. Chapter 3
concludes by outlining the psychological characteristics, motivations and
entrepreneurial intent of entrepreneurs and technology entrepreneurs.
The case on Rovio Entertainment, the creators of Angry Birds, reinforces
the difference between technology entrepreneurship and other forms of
entrepreneurship. The novelty of the game and the technology platform
created an addictive and simple offering that gained worldwide attention
and significant growth as a new technology firm.

Chapter 4 introduces the core issues and central ways of understanding
innovation and innovation processes. It presents the variety and complexity
of innovation as well as some of the main challenges related to managing
innovation. The chapter provides insights into the concepts and classifications of innovation and innovation platforms Next, it discusses how
innovation processes are organised and managed, from idea development
stage to prototyping of the innovation lifecycle. The chapter then identifies key challenges for organising and managing innovation processes
and provides some suggestions for overcoming them. Finally, Chapter 4
addresses technology diffusion process of moving innovations through
commercialisation into widespread use. The end of chapter case study,
Salma, tells the story of biotechnical innovation in the food industry from
research project, via product development to marketing. It illustrates the
typical crooked path of innovation processes, and how dead-ends may
spur new ideas that eventually lead to success in the market.

Chapter 5 presents fundamental and critical issues faced by technology entrepreneurs with regard to intellectual property. While many are familiar with some of the basic concepts of intellectual property, e.g. patents, copyrights or trademarks, for the first-time entrepreneur, managing intellectual property can take on the aura of a full-blown crusade. Assessing intellectual property, its value and whether or not it is important to a startup can seem like a minefield. This chapter unravels some of the conundrums and mysteries associated with the unique cross-disciplinary skills at the interface of business, law and technology required to manage intellectual property (IP). The chapter covers four main themes. It explores how scientists, engineers and technological researchers think and act in creating and capturing IP. It then highlights the legal issues in protecting IP and provides a comparison of legal perspectives in the different geographical territories, namely the United States, Europe and Asia. It then provides an investor's and entrepreneur's perspective in evaluating IP and how it can be used to create value. It also takes a looks at the commercialisation process and how technology entrepreneurs marshal resources in exploiting IP, either licensing it or transforming it into a successful new venture, which is covered in more depth in Chapter 8. The chapter concludes with a case outlining the challenges presented in the realm of nanotechnology.

Chapter 6 emphasises the development of business concepts and business models for testing and learning how to create a profitable match between customer values, production factors and income factors. Business model innovation has become an important way to get ahead of competitors in today's globalising and increasingly connected world. The final chapter of this section includes the business plan as an important outcome of business model development, followed by most current metrics for measuring business growth. First, the chapter highlights the need for opportunities to be developed into *business concepts* consisting of products/services, and what value they will create in the market (value proposition). Second, it argues that the iterative development of a viable *business model* helps configure the available resources in order to create unique customer value (value proposition) and how the company will capture economic and other values from this. Third, it outlines the importance of the business plan and the components of business plans. Finally, the chapter explains how to develop metrics for measuring growth and business model performance. The end of chapter case study in this chapter is on Spotify, Inc. The Swedish music streaming service has taken a strong position in many countries with a potentially disruptive service, showing that people are willing to pay for user-friendly and socially oriented online services.

Chapter 7 presents the key analytical tools for inventors to conduct the Market Validation Process (MVP) for high-tech ventures to ensure the product or service is entering a valid and sustainable market. MVP helps assess the market worthiness of ideas that are based around incremental, radical or disruptive innovations. This chapter also introduces the learner to the marketing ecosystem and presents the necessary frameworks for carrying out a market ecosystem analysis for a new technology. It presents the key processes available for testing their business concept and distinguishes between the nature and dynamics of customer and business markets for conducting customer analysis. Finally, it details the key marketing research techniques needed to carry out the validation process for both consumers and business markets. The end of chapter case on Skype highlights the importance of environmental factors using the marketing eco-system analysis for the strategic development of the company.

Chapter 8 addresses two crucial areas of commercialisation of innovation: first, decisions relating how best to commercialise IP to generate revenue, and second, planning the initial pitch to attract initial investment to develop the commercial idea further. In most cases, innovative technological ideas require further technical development (and hence funding) to successfully commercialise them in the marketplace. As the IP and patenting issues have been addressed in Chapter 5, this chapter outlines possible commercial options available for commercialising IP. In examining the topic of commercialisation of intellectual property, we will consider *five* fundamental questions, namely: WHY would an individual or organisation consider commercialising IP? WHICH geographical market(s) and customer segments should be addressed? WHEN should an individual or organisation commercialise their IP? HOW should they commercialise their IP? WHO should lead the commercialisation effort? Second, the chapter explores the idea of pitching for investment in order to raise the requisite funds for commercialising a given technology. Technology entrepreneur, Dr. Brian Kelly, co-founder and former CEO of Celtic Catalysts Ltd, takes us through the challenges he encountered in commercialising his IP to the actual pitching of the technology to investors.

Chapter 9 presents the key processes and analytical tools for inventors to conduct, design, implement and manage effective marketing strategy for a new technology. It discusses a step-by-step process that will help inventors develop a value proposition for their innovation in response to a validated market opportunity. The chapter also discusses identification of target customer markets (as discussed in Chapter 7). It then addresses the tactical decisions related to designing a marketing programme that will help an individual or organisation deliver value proposition and position it correctly in the minds of their target customers. It outlines the different marketing approaches for both consumer and business to business marketing markets and the importance of "solution" selling processes and customer relationship building. Finally, this chapter highlights the marketing plan as a key output underpinning their marketing design and implementation plans required to deliver an effective marketing strategy to target customers. The HMS case illustrates how a high-tech Swedish company focuses on customer segmentation and business relationships to market its network card designed for OEM (Original Equipment Manufacturers) for a diverse range of industrial application across different industry sectors.

Chapter 10 addresses managing teams, leadership and organisational culture within a business as new ventures need to integrate and combine their technologies with excellent leadership and manage of human talent. In high-tech ventures, knowledge is embedded in the intellectual capital created by people. A core task for the entrepreneur is to design and execute effective management and to leverage the intellectual capital embedded in human resources, both inside and outside the organisation, as well as lead and nurture an organisational mindset and culture towards growth and success. The end of chapter case study, Meltwater Ltd., is about a highly successful ICT venture providing software-as-a-service (SaaS) monitoring of news and social media for companies and organisations. Its success is partly based on their focus on recruiting and building a strong sales-oriented organisation culture, to an extent that is somewhat unusual for a technology venture.

The rapidly changing global business environment, economic integration and advances in technology and communications have created unprecedented opportunities for small firms looking to extend their sales activities beyond the domestic market. **Chapter 11** hence introduces international entrepreneurship and presents an overview of how a new firm internationalises as a means for growth and expansion. Pursuing an international market development strategy involves seeking new markets by selling its innovation to customers outside its own domestic market. This chapter unravels the complexity of internationalisation by providing the learner with a comprehensive insight into the necessary knowledge, skills and techniques to gain an appreciation of the nature of and issues that affect international marketing decisions of new and growing high tech ventures. Specifically, it informs the learner of the internationalisation process and the type of decisions that need to be carefully considered for launching their technology into the global markets. It provides the learner with a cohesive and integrated understanding of how a firm can achieve and sustain international competitiveness in dynamic and globally driven high-tech markets through developing and managing strategic attributes. It further raises some of the key issues for conducting and managing business negotiations in a cross-cultural context. The founder and CEO of Irish global medical device company writes about his company Aerogen and how he internationalised it to becoming a global market leader of electronic nebuliser products that are used in acute care facilities in 65 countries throughout the world.

Chapter 12 provides the tools to evaluate whether or not an idea is worth pursuing. It applies financial theory to the decision-making process in planning a new venture. While many textbooks on entrepreneurship focus on institutional financing issues, such as sources of finance and valuation, the focus of this chapter is on using finance in the strategic decision-making process. While good ideas are a dime a dozen, it is much harder to find good people with an eye for detail to implement them. Entrepreneurs, therefore, need to have the financial literacy if they are to turn their visions into a reality. Entrepreneurs need to be comfortable with *investment decisions* and *financing decisions*. This chapter looks at the centrality of maximising value to the entrepreneur. It outlines how finance and its sources are intrinsically linked to the new venturing process from inception of an idea to harvesting of the investment. It gives the learner an insight into the key operational imperatives for planning a new venture such as funding, cash-flow and profitability. The chapter underpins the importance of relating classic financial theory to the practice of new venturing, leading to better financing and investment decisions and a higher success rate for a new enterprise. End of chapter cases details Facebook IPO and takes us through the financing and growth stages of this social media giant.

P.6 REFERENCES

Bailetti, T. (2012) "Technology Entrepreneurship: Definition, Overview and Distinctive Aspects", *Technology Innovation Management Review*, February: 5–12.

Gans, J.S. and Stern, S. (2003) "The Product Market for 'Ideas': Commercialization Strategies for Technology Entrepreneurs", *Research Policy*, 32: 333–350.

Grandi, A., and Grimaldi, R. (2005) "Academics' Organizational Characteristics and the Generation of Successful Business Ideas", *Journal of Business Venturing*, 20(6): 821–845.

Venkataraman, S. (1997) "The Distinctive Domain of Entrepreneurship Research: An Editor's Perspective", in J. Katz and R. Brockhaus (eds), *Advances in Entrepreneurship, Firm Emergence and Growth*, Vol. 3, Greenwich, CT: JAI Press.

Venkataraman, S. (2004) "Regional Transformation through Technological Entrepreneurship", *Journal of Business Venturing*, 19: 53–167.

Lee, S. H. and Wong, P. K. (2004) "An Exploratory Study of Technopreneurial Intentions: A Career Anchor Perspective", *Journal of Business Venturing*, 19: 7–28.

Acknowledgements

Natasha Evers wishes to acknowledge the research assistance of Ms. Gabriela Gliga and her contribution of case studies for inclusion in Chapters 7 and 8.

James Cunningham wishes to acknowledge the research assistance and support of Brendan Dolan and Dr. Grace Walsh for her contribution of case studies for Chapters 1 to 3. He also acknowledges the funding support from the Irish Social Science Platform as part of the Programme for Research in Third Level Institutions Cycle 4, administered by the Higher Education Authority and co-funded by the European Regional Development Fund (ERDF).

Thomas Hoholm wishes to thank his colleagues Stein Bjørnstad, Jon Erik Svendsen and Ranvir Rai, who have generously shared their insights on entrepreneurship and education over the years. His students in entrepreneurship, innovation and new venture creation classes at BI have participated actively in developing and testing designs for learning. In addition, Casey Trahan Carney was incredibly helpful in the last phase of preparation of this manuscript.

The authors collectively would like to acknowledge the substantial contributions of Cormac McMahon and Brian Kelly and wish to thank and acknowledge all our case study contributors: Grace Walsh, Svante Andersson, Casey Trahan Carney, John Power, Vibeke Møller Isachsen, Tom Ove Grønlund, Eythor Ivar Jonsson,Tor Grønsund, Robert Wentrup, Patrik Ström, Stein Bjørnstad, Martin Hannibal, Gabriela Gliga, Neil Ferguson, Breda Kenny, Rod McNaughton, Michelle Devaney and Stein Bjørnstad for his contribution towards business plan online material for Chapter 6.

The authors would like to give a special thanks to our publisher Martin Drewe and his team at Palgrave Macmillan, whose absolute professionalism and continued support made this task a lot easier!

This publication was grant-aided by the Publications Fund of National University of Ireland Galway / Rinneadh maoiniú ar an bhfoilseachán seo trí Chiste FoilseachánOllscoil na hÉireann, Gaillimh.

The editor and publishers wish to thank the following for permission to reproduce copyright material: American Marketing Association for Figure 11.2, reprinted with permission from "A framework for analysis of strategy development in globalizing markets" in *Journal of International Marketing*, published by the American Marketing Association, C. A. Solberg, 1997, Volume 5, Issue 1, Figure 1, p.11; BDRC Continental Limited for Figure 12.4, from BDRC Continental, *SME Finance Monitor: Q3 2011:*

Developing a Deeper Understanding (November 2011); Emerald Group Publishing Limited for Figure 11.6, from N. Evers, "International new ventures in 'low tech' sectors: a dynamic capabilities perspective" in *Journal of Small Business and Enterprise Development* (2011) Volume 18, Issue 3, pp. 502–528, © Emerald Group Publishing Limited, all rights reserved; Getty Images for the image in Case Box 12.2, David Paul Morris/Getty Images News/Getty Images; Higher Education Funding Council for England for Table 2.2, adapted from HEFCE (2012) UK universities contribute to economic growth, 23 July, http://www.hefce.ac.uk/news/newsarchive/2012/news73740.html; Joe Dermody for 'Innovation vouchers a success story for firms and colleges' in *Irish Examiner*, 3 September 2010; NUI Maynooth for Figure 5.5, from *Guide to Commercialisation at NUI Maynooth*, Rev5 – 01/04/11, Figure 2, p.16; Orpen Press for Figure 11.1, adapted from N. Evers, "Factors influencing new venture internationalisation: a review of the literature" in *Irish Journal of Management* (2011), Volume 30, Issue 2; Pearson Education Ltd. for Figure 6.1, adapted from S. Hollensen, *Global Marketing*, 5th Edition, Figure 4.1, p.105. © Pearson Education Limited 2001, 2011; Pearson Education Ltd. for Table 11.3, adapted from S. Hollensen, *Global Marketing*, 5th Edition, Table 7.1, p.238. © Pearson Education Limited 2001, 2011; Pearson Education Ltd. for Figure 12.6, after C. Walsh, *Key Management Ratios*, 4th edition, © Pearson Education 2008; Pearson Education, Inc. for Figure 9.9, from Mohr, Jakki, J.; Sengupta, Sanjit; Slater, Stanley, *Marketing of High-Technology Products and Innovations*, 3rd edition, ©2010, printed and electronically reproduced by permission of Pearson Education, Inc., Upper Saddle River, New Jersey; Taylor & Francis Ltd. for Figure 6.3, adapted from N. Evers and C. O'Gorman, "Improvised internationalization in new ventures: The role of prior knowledge and networks" in *Entrepreneurship and Regional Development* (2011) Volume 23, Issue 7–8, reprinted by permission of the publisher (Taylor & Francis Ltd., http://www.tandf.co.uk/journals); Tomasz Tunguz for Table 6.2, adapted from Your Startup's 10 Most Important Metrics, from omtunguz.com/your-startups-10-most-important-metrics/; Publications Office of the European Union for Figure 5.2, adapted from European Commission (2003) *Intellectual Property: Good Practice Guide*, p.6. © The European Commission.

Notes on the Authors

Natasha Evers is Lecturer of Marketing at the J.E. Cairnes School of Business & Economics at the National University of Ireland, NUI Galway. Her research and teaching interests include international entrepreneurship, international marketing strategies of SMEs and the commercialisation of innovation in new firms. She has published in international journals such as *Journal of International Marketing, International Marketing Review, Entrepreneurship and Regional Development, Journal of International Entrepreneurship, the International Journal of Entrepreneurship and Innovation Management, the Journal of Innovative Marketing and the Journal of Small Business & Enterprise Development.*

James Cunningham is the Director of the Whitaker Institute at NUI Galway and is a senior lecturer in strategic management at the J.E. Cairnes School of Business & Economics, NUI Galway. His research and teaching intersects the fields of strategic management, innovation and entrepreneurship. His core research interests focus on principal investigators, university research commercialisation, technology transfer offices strategy process, entrepreneurial universities, technology entrepreneurs new venture formation and academic entrepreneurship. His published in journals such *as Long Range Planning, Journal of Technology Transfer, Business Strategy Review* and he is an Editorial Board member of the *Journal of Technology Transfer*. Awards for this research include five best paper awards as well as national and international awards for case writing.

Thomas Hoholm is Associate Professor at the BI Norwegian Business School in Oslo, Norway. He is teaching entrepreneurship and innovation management, particularly focusing on entrepreneurial management, entrepreneurial growth, and the management of innovation in firms and industrial networks. He has been a visiting researcher at Lancaster University Management School and at UC Berkeley dept of Sociology. He has published in journals such as *Human Relations, Management Learning, European Journal of Innovation Management,* and *Industrial Marketing Management*. His book *The Contrary Forces of Innovation: An Ethnography of Innovation in the Food Industry* was published in 2011.

Notes on the Contributors

Cormac MacMahon is Dean of Business at Bahrain Polytechnic, a new higher education institution dedicated to developing enterprising and professional work-ready graduates within the Kingdom of Bahrain and wider GCC (Gulf Cooperation Council) region. He also serves as a representative on the Ebtikar Association, which provides a national platform for innovation through local and international collaboration. Cormac was a founding member of the accelerating campus entrepreneurship (ACE) initiative in Ireland, which aims to embed entrepreneurship within higher education for the development of entrepreneurial graduates. An engineer by background, Cormac has worked for several high-tech multinationals.

Brian Kelly is an entrepreneur, mentor and leader in the Irish life sciences industry. He has successfully founded and helped build innovative research-based, technology-driven companies in the life sciences and software industries. He has also worked with a number of early and mid-stage companies providing them with interim management, mentorship, advice and strategic oversight to support their growth and development. He has been involved (both as chairman and member) in numerous high level boards, taskforces and committees including being appointed by the Irish Prime Minister to the National Innovation Taskforce in 2009. He has chaired the University College Dublin Campus Company Development Programme and the Commercialisation Board of Trinity College Dublin's world-leading CRANN Institute.

Part I

ENTREPRENEURSHIP, INNOVATION AND POLICY

I.1 INTRODUCTION

Starting a new venture is a significant event in a person's life. Becoming an entrepreneur has become more socially accepted and is a legitimate career option in more societies. Becoming an entrepreneur has many positive outcomes for both the individual and society. One of the main benefits to society is the creation of wealth and jobs and the utilisation of the individual's knowledge. Entrepreneurs are distinguished by certain personal characteristics, such as the need for achievement and a type-A personality. Technology entrepreneurs and technology-based ventures provide significant growth opportunities for individuals but also carry great risk. Technology entrepreneurs have to bring a unique newness to the market in order to survive. Small incremental uniqueness may not be enough to succeed in hyper-competitive marketplaces. Technology is an inherent aspect in the conceptualisation of the new ideas and bringing them to reality.

With the rapid advances in science, growing market opportunities in convergent technology marketplaces and sustained levels of public and private investment in research and development means there are ample opportunities for technology-based entrepreneurs. Skills, knowledge and location are no longer significant barriers to setting up a technology-based venture. The increasing levels of educational attainment in many societies not only provide opportunities for technology entrepreneurs to attract the best talent but also means they are engaging with more sophisticated customers who have a more nuanced understanding of technology. The growth of smartphones over a short period of time is an indicator of this change. In peripheral regions, technology entrepreneurs can provide much needed employment, generate economic activity and help build a reputation for a region.

Universities and public research organisations have a significant influence on technology entrepreneurship and the creation of technology ventures. Universities are competing in a global marketplace for the best students, researchers and faculty. The more research-intensive that universities and

1

public research organisations are the more opportunities they will have to engage in technology entrepreneurship. Novelty is one of the defining characteristics of knowledge creation in universities and public organisations, and it is an essential ingredient for technology entrepreneurship. In addition to novelty, universities provide formal training in entrepreneurship as well as a location for informal interactions and the creation of networks – formal and informal. Such informal interactions provide opportunities for individuals to extend their own personal networks beyond their area of competence and expertise.

I.1.1   Understanding Context and Policy

In order to encourage technology entrepreneurs to form new ventures, the appropriate economic conditions are needed. Without favourable economic conditions, particularly with respect to growth, technology entrepreneur will not be inclined to take a risk and start a new technology venture. In our first chapter, we address the importance of innovation and entrepreneurship policy. Such national policies can shape and influence the decision-making process of technology entrepreneurs. Such issues as national public investment in research and development, the number of PhD students and availability of government supports, among many other factors, all have an influence in creating the conditions necessary for new venture formation. The triple helix approach (Etzkowitz, 2002) simply outlines the roles that government, universities and industry play in creating the conditions that shape knowledge, or what is now termed "smart based economies". We consider the roles played by these three actors.

With respect to policy, many more countries are investing in a range of activities and the outcomes of such investments are measured by the Innovation Union Scorecard and the Global Entrepreneurship Monitor. Each country tends to customise their policies and their implementation to suit national conditions. We have taken some policy perspectives from EU, the United States, Australia and South Korea to not only illustrate the differences in policy approaches being taken but also the commonality in exploiting the available resources – technological, human, antecedent industrial bases, etc. In reflecting on the differences and commonalities of policy approaches, we consider the impact of policy implementation as measured by different international comparison measurements. While these measures give an annual snapshot of progress regarding policy implementation, one should bear in mind that it takes years for countries to create the necessary conditions for technology entrepreneurship to flourish and grow.

I.1.2   University and Business Technology Transfer

Universities and public research organisations are at the fore in creating novelty and new knowledge. The challenge is creating the most effective and efficient technology transfer systems and mechanisms between universities, business and technology entrepreneurs. In Chapter 2, this is the central focus. We begin by exploring linear and non-linear models of technology transfer. With more open innovation system being adopted, non-linear models of technology transfer are becoming more prevalent. We then examine the technology transfer process and some common mechanisms – patents, licensing, company formation. Irrespective of the mechanism, the technology transfer can be a complex process as well as a costly one. Technology Transfer Offices within universities are charged with the responsibility of protecting and exploiting university intellectual property (IP). We also explore the stimulants and barriers to technology transfer at both macro and micro levels. From this we see that there are multiple factors that influence and shape technology transfer between universities, business and technology entrepreneurs.

I.1.3   Technology Entrepreneurship

In Chapter 3 we focus on technology entrepreneurs and ventures. You will see that entrepreneurs and technology entrepreneurs have many common characteristics. Some key differences emerging in defining technology entrepreneurs include company formation, the entrepreneurial process and the technology focus. While these may seem like nuanced differences, the core difference centres on the exploitation of a technology. The novelty of the technology will provide a strong basis for the survival of the new technology venture. Much research has been conducted on the distinctive, common characteristics of entrepreneurs. We focus and discuss opportunity recognition, perception and emotions, dealing with uncertainty, risk profile and appetite, resource appropriation, rewards and career and family context. Work experience, educational attainment and age are the personal characteristics that we consider. In concluding our understanding of technology entrepreneurship, we consider the motivations and intentions of technology entrepreneurs. Independence, control and achievement are strong motivating factors for technology entrepreneurs that we focus on. Through a short review of empirical studies of technology entrepreneurs, we note that they have a strong desire of achievement, they enjoy being on the cutting edge of their technology domain and that contextual factors influence their behaviour. We also highlight through citing some empirical studies the difference in personalities, the need for proactive public policies as well as the need to support the whole person – the technology entrepreneur.

Overall from Part I, you will see why environmental factors, policies, universities, technology transfer mechanisms, motivations, incentives, technology transfer barriers and stimulants as well as the individual characteristics of technology entrepreneurs shape, influence and matter in the creation of new technology ventures and the formation of technology entrepreneurs.

Chapter 1
SMART ECONOMIES, INNOVATION AND ENTREPRENEURSHIP

1.1 LEARNING OBJECTIVES

We begin this chapter and our book by exploring the environmental context that supports technology entrepreneurs in their efforts to create new businesses and to innovate. Entrepreneurs, through creating new businesses, contribute to the wealth creation in economies. We begin the chapter by outlining the triple helix approach, which has influenced national policy approaches in global economies in creating conditions that support technology entrepreneurship. We then turn our attention to reviewing some of the innovation and entrepreneurship policies being pursued by the European Union (EU), United States, Australia and South Korea. These policies vary in terms of how they support entrepreneurship and innovation but the common focus is on creating economic and environmental conditions for entrepreneurship to flourish, particularly technology entrepreneurship. From there we outline the impact of innovation and entrepreneurship policies on the various actors and economies. We then conclude the chapter by highlighting some macro future trends that will impact technology entrepreneurs.

After reading this chapter, you will be able to:

1. Explain the triple helix concept;
2. Outline some of the key policy initiatives in key regions that support entrepreneurship and innovation;
3. Describe the direct and indirect impacts on innovation and entrepreneurship policies; and
4. Discuss some future trends that will directly impact technology entrepreneurs.

1.2 CHAPTER STRUCTURE

The core elements of this chapter are as follows:

- Introduction
- Innovation and Entrepreneurship Policy

5

- • Triple Helix Approach
  - • Some Policy Perspectives – EU, United States, Australia and South Korea
- • Policy Outcomes and Impacts
- • Future Trends
- • Convergent Technology Spaces
- • Crowdfunding
- • Co-working Incubation
- • Chapter Summary
- • Case Study – Renishaw Diagnostics Ltd.
- • Revision Questions
- • Further Reading and Resources
- • References
- • Glossary of Terms
- • Appendix 1 and 2

1.3 INTRODUCTION

The global economy has seen significant changes since the banking crisis in 2008. Many economies have gone through large-scale austerity programmes to reduce deficits. This has resulted in higher levels of unemployment, less disposable personal income and recession. National government efforts have been focused on the implementation of austerity programmes, and some have also put in place stimulus initiatives designed to encourage growth and recovery. Job creation is at the core of policy initiatives to reduce unemployment levels and to generate new sources of economic growth. Investment in research and development through publicly funded sources coupled with private sector investment is now seen as vital in ensuring a recovery in the global economy. This investment in science and excellent research is also vital if economies are to sustain economic activities and flourish in the twenty-first century. Terms such as knowledge or smart economies have been used to describe economies where activity is centred on services, knowledge and highly trained and talented workers, as well as in developing young sectors such as biotechnology. The creation of new ventures and encouraging entrepreneurship are vital for economies to grow and create wealth. For this to happen, national governments need to consider having favourable economic and social conditions that enable those considering entrepreneurship to do so. Therefore, national policies help create environmental conditions that support entrepreneurship and provide potential investors with confidence in terms of their investments. For technology entrepreneurs in economies where there are ongoing investments in technologies, research and development is critical if their new ventures are to succeed in competitive international markets.

1.4 INNOVATION AND ENTREPRENEURSHIP POLICY

Innovation and entrepreneurship activities in an economy have positive economic benefits, particularly in employment, taxation revenue economic output and further investment in infrastructure. Over the last few decades, the roles and influence of key stakeholders involved in creating optimal economic and social condition for entrepreneurship has evolved. We are experiencing a more rapid pace of scientific development, further advances in Information Communication Technologies (ICT) and a more effective transition of research to the market place (Cunningham, 2008). These and other changes have influenced the nature of innovation and entrepreneurship polices that national governments adopt as entrepreneurs are vital contributors to wealth creation in economies. Many policies adopted by national governments have moved from industrial policies through to science and now innovation policies, which incorporate innovation and technology entrepreneurship as well as other forms of entrepreneurship. Dahlstrand and Stevenson (2007, p. 17) argue the need for holistic entrepreneurship policy and as this "...requires combination of entrepreneurship, SME, innovation, science and technology, education/university and regional policies...For example SME policies are often developed to help existing small firms, while entrepreneurship policies focus on individuals and their capacity (e.g., skills and motivation)".

1.4.1   The Triple Helix

One of the underpinning paradigms that have informed national innovation and entrepreneurship policies has been the triple helix approach (Leydesdorff, 2000). The triple helix approach attempts to understand the relationship and interaction between universities/public research organisations (PROs), industry and government and innovation (Godin, 2006). The dynamic interactions between these actors represent the true nature of innovation systems (Piekarski and Torkomian, 2005). Moreover, in this approach the university is seen as an influencer and actor in contributing to innovation and entrepreneurship. So what are the roles of universities, industry and government in the triple helix?

Universities: Universities have three core missions, that of teaching, research and what is now termed "technology and knowledge transfer" (see Chapter 2). At the heart of university activities is scientific excellence to create national or international leadership positions. These areas of excellence can be complimented by technology and knowledge transfer activities, which seek to take some of the outputs from research to be exploited for outcomes of public and private good. Technology Transfer Offices can play a key role in supporting the commercialisation of research. Many universities have moved to adopt many attributes of an entrepreneurial university, which Subotzky (1999) describes as "characterized by closer university-business partnerships, by greater faculty responsibility for accessing external sources of funding, and by a managerial ethos in institutional governance, leadership and planning". Etzkowitz (2003) describes this as: "Just as the university trains individual students and sends them our into the world, the Entrepreneurial University is a natural incubator, providing support structures for teachers and students to initiate new ventures: intellectual, commercial and conjoint". Universities are at the forefront of new technological and scientific developments and are core actors in global knowledge production systems. Their international research teams create environments that attract the best talent to undertake doctoral and post-doctoral research. Technological entrepreneurs benefit from entrepreneurial universities through access to talent, research that could be commercialised or incorporated into their product or service, and through formal linkages with universities, whereby they can connect with other sectors or companies for collaborative research and development projects. The intellectual and human capital generated by universities can have a direct and indirect impact on technology entrepreneurs. Etzkowitz and Leydesdorff (1997) best sum this up as: "The development of academic research capacities carries within itself the seeds of future economic and social development in the form of human capital, tacit knowledge and intellectual property".

Industry: Within the triple helix paradigm, industry can benefit from university engagement through exploiting research, hiring new talent and having access to international research networks. Moreover, industry can shape the research fields that national governments prioritise that is aligned with their near or long-term business needs. In some economies, governments have gone through a research prioritisation exercise designed to align research with industry needs so they can compete more effectively in international markets. R&D activities of large corporates support the development of a sector or cluster of activities within an economy. For example, Galway, a city in the west of Ireland is the fourth sub-critical location in the world for manufacturing of medical devices and an international cluster has developed over the last decade in medical technologies (see Giblin and Ryan, 2012). Local third-level institutions have supported the growth of this sector in the western region of Ireland through new programmes, establishment of international research programmes and recruitment of faculty.

Also, industry, through their interaction with national and local governments, put pressure on these bodies to ensure that they create environmental – economic, social and educational – conditions to enhance a firm's competitive positioning in international markets. For example, the British Chamber of Commerce that represents over 100,000 businesses across over 50 local chambers conducts policy studies in a variety of areas such as energy, government bureaucracy and transport to lobby the UK government about having an optimal environment for business. For technology entrepreneurs and new business creations, creating such an environment is vital to their growth and survival (see Chapter 3). Another role that industry plays is as co-investor in research within universities and PROs. Increasingly funding agencies are requiring research projects to have industry partners and some require financial investment as well as in-kind support. The forthcoming Horizon 2020 programme for the European Union will require more significant investment and collaboration between firms and academia.

Government: National governments, in terms of their economic and social policies, create the environmental conditions that make it attractive for new venture creation, for entrepreneurs and for supporting services, such as venture capitalists, to invest capital in the most efficient way possible. Mowery et al. (2004) argue that this is pivotal in supporting innovation and entrepreneurship and Etzkowitz (2002) suggests the role of government is expanding not only in relation to macro factors but increasingly to encompass the micro conditions of innovation. Corporate, personal taxation, levels of government administration, house prices, provisions of suitable office locations, public investment in education, access to transport linkages and a myriad of other macro and micro factors create these general environmental conditions. For governments, the level of entrepreneurship and new business creation is one of the measures of economic vibrancy. The World Bank (2013) notes: "Entrepreneurial activity is a pillar of economic growth. For evidence of the economic power of entrepreneurship, we need look no further than the United States, where young firms have been shown to be a more important source of net job creation than incumbent firms". In 2011, for example, there were 94,050 new limited company formations in Australia; 174,000 in Canada; 12,742 in Finland and 429,363 in the UK (see Work Bank http://www.doingbusiness.org/data/exploretopics/entrepreneurship#sub-menu-item-link).   Governments also play a role in providing public investment in system-wide education – pre-school to third-level. Educational policies and national curriculums are usually set by national governments. For example, the OECD conducts analysis of numeracy, literacy and science, which is collated based on data from 65 countries. The Programme for International Student Assessment (PISA) 2009 ranked Shanghia-China, South Korea and Finland as the top three countries in these student tests.

Another role that governments play within the triple helix is through public investment in research – through public research laboratories and higher level institutions. This public funding supports infrastructure, basic and applied research, human capital, doctoral students, senior researchers, etc. In the case of the Human Genome Project, for a US Government investment of $3.6 billion, 3.8 million jobs were created from 1998 to 2003, 310,000 jobs in 2010 and $796 billion generated in economic output. (Science Progress 2011).

1.4.2   Some Policy Perspectives from the European Union, United States, Australia and South Korea

The economic and policy supports at national levels play a role in creating the conditions for technology entrepreneurship and other categories of entrepreneurship. Technology entrepreneurs create economic wealth, employment and exploit further market opportunities. We have chosen the EU, United States, Australia and South Korean to give a sense of the different policy perspectives and initiatives that each have taken in creating economic conditions for entrepreneurship and innovation. The combination of policies and economic conditions are necessary for the development to technology entrepreneurs and new business ventures.

With increasing economic pressure on the EU countries and concerns about European competitiveness, the EU announced its *Innovation Union Strategy* in October 2010. The Innovation Union states that member states need to continue investment in education, RD& I and ICT; achieve greater collaboration between national systems of innovation; reform education systems to meet future demands; create a European Research Area for researchers; develop more effective innovations from research, removing barriers for entrepreneurs while building on strengths in design and creativity; and promote a more enhanced collaboration with international partners. For entrepreneurs, the European Comission (2010, p. 3) seeks to remove the barriers for entrepreneurs, including "better access to finance, particularly for SMEs, affordable Intellectual Property Rights (IPR), smarter and more ambitious regulation and targets, faster setting of interoperable standards and strategic use of our massive procurement budgets". In 2013, the EU announced major changes to its patent law to encourage entrepreneurs, innovators, inventors and Small and Medium Enterprises (SME's). By 2020, the EU estimates the 3.7 million jobs could be created based on a target of 3 per cent of EU Gross Domestic Product expenditure on R&D.

To support the realisation of the Innovation Union and the EU's Horizon 2020, it's Framework Budget for Research and Innovation will be used to ensure that Europe is at the scientific forefront and that it impacts on economy and society. The Horizon 2020 programme runs until 2020 and supports fundamental and applied research with a much stronger focus on innovation. The three pillars of Horizon 2020 are excellent science, industrial leadership and societal challenges (see Box 1.1). One of the key ambitions for the EU through Horizon 2020 is to create a European Research Area that involves: "...building a genuine single market for knowledge, research and innovation, enabling researchers, research institutions and businesses to circulate, compete and co-operate across borders". (EC, 2011, p. 12). Furthermore there will be opportunities for entrepreneurs to participate in a programme that connects them with researchers to 'spin-in' technologies as part of Eurostars. The Small Business Innovation Research Programme will allow entrepreneurs and SMEs to contribute to societal challenges by providing new approaches and innovations. Finally, for access to capital there will be a focus on how to work with member states and intermediaries to ensure entrepreneurs and SMEs have access to appropriate funding. In particular, according to the European Commission (2011, p. 10): "The equity facility will focus on early-stage investments, while having the possibility to make expansion and growth-stage investments in conjunction with equity facility under the Programme for the Competitiveness of Enterprises and SMEs". The culmination of these policy initiatives is to ensure that the EU and its member states are attractive for technology entrepreneurs to create new business ventures and the economic environment enables their ventures to grow and internationalise.

Box 1.1 Horizon 2020: Three Pillars

Excellence in Science: Excellent Science. This will raise the level of excellence in Europe's science base and ensure a steady stream of world-class research to secure Europe's long-term competitiveness. It will support the best ideas, develop talent within Europe, provide researchers with access to priority research infrastructure, and make Europe an attractive location for the world's best researchers.

Industrial Leadership: This will aim at making Europe a more attractive location to invest in research and innovation (including eco-innovation), by promoting activities where businesses set the agenda. It will provide major investment in key industrial technologies, maximise the growth potential of European companies by providing them with adequate levels of finance and help innovative SMEs to grow into world leading companies.

Societal Challenges: This reflects the policy priorities of the Europe 2020 strategy and addresses major concerns shared by citizens in Europe and elsewhere. A challenge-based approach will bring together resources and knowledge across different fields, technologies and disciplines, including social sciences and the humanities. This will cover activities from research to market with a new focus on innovation-related activities, such as piloting, demonstration, test-beds, and support for public procurement and market uptake. It will include establishing links with the activities of the European Innovation Partnerships.

Source: European Commission (2011) Horizon 2020 – The Framework Programme for Research and Innovation, COM (2011) 808 Final, 30 November 2011, pp. 4–5.

In the United States, the Obama Administration has published an *American Strategy for Innovation,* which has three areas of focus: investing in the building blocks of American Innovation, promotion of market-based innovation and catalysing breakthroughs for national priorities (see Figure 1.1). The intention of this strategy is the creation of jobs and growth. Specifically new initiatives include access to high speed wireless web access, patent reforms, clean energy technologies, and Start-Up America, which is focused on entrepreneurship: "The Administration launched the Start-Up American initiative with new agency efforts that accelerate the transfer of research breakthroughs from university labs; create two $1 billion initiatives for impact investing and early-stage seed financing, among other incentives to invest in high-growth start-ups; improve the regulatory environment for starting and growing new businesses; and increase connections between entrepreneurs and high-quality business mentors. Responding to the President's call to action around the national importance of entrepreneurship, private-sector leaders are independently committing significant new resources to catalyze and develop entrepreneurial ecosystems across the country". (White House, 2013). Like the EU policy initiatives, the objective is to create new ventures and an economic climate that encourage all categories of entrepreneurs, including technology entrepreneurs to set up new firms.

The Australian government published their innovation strategy entitled *Powering Ideas: An Innovation Agenda for the 21st Century* in 2009. Kim Carr (2009, p. iii) outlined this policy framework document as follows: "[T]his is a ten-year reform agenda to make Australia more productive and more competitive. Increasing our capacity to create new knowledge and find new ways of doing business is the key to building a modern economy based on

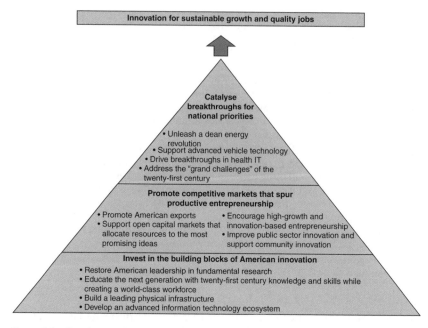

Figure 1.1 American strategy for innovation

Source: White House (2013) Strategy for American Innovation, http://www.whitehouse.gov/innovation/strategy/executive-summary.

advanced skills and technology. It is the key to success in this, the global century". Elements of the strategy include enhancing skills and research capacity, business innovation, public sector innovation, collaboration and governance. For entrepreneurs, the United States and EU strategies are about getting ideas to the market place as quickly as possible, using the private sector to support venture funding, reform of the patent system and improve innovation supports to create regional clusters and networks. The Australian objective, while designed to create new firms, is focused on making the Australian innovation system and economy more productive and competitive internationally.

South Korea is one of the leading innovating economies in the world and has a leading position in many technological fields. Park and Leydesdorff (2010) note: "Korean governments have focused on improving the university-industry relationships with the purpose of strengthening Korea's system of innovations". The 2008 *Science and Technology Plan* aimed at achieving a 5 per cent GDP investment in R&D by 2012. Changes in 2011, with the creation of the National Science and Technology Commission and the Intellectual Property Management Council, sought to strengthen South Korea's international leadership in innovation and entrepreneurship. The South Korean innovation and industrial model is centred around five elements: improving the investment climate, promoting regional economic growth, establishing an innovative R&D system, upgrading flagship industries and fostering new growth engines. The South Korean government has selected 17 new growth engine industries in green technologies, high-tech convergence and value-added services, which are maximised market opportunities aligned with market trends and increased levels of globalisation. The upgrading, for example, in semi-conductors within South Korea, the world's largest chip manufacturers, is now focused on developing new chip technologies. An element of the industrial model being pursued by South Korea is to enhance entrepreneurship through benchmarking "'best examples' of other countries to boost the entrepreneurial spirit of domestic firms" (MOTIE, 2011). Moreover, as Mittelstadt and Cerri (2009, p. 41) have noted, South Korea "... placed entrepreneurship and SME policy at the core of governmental action for over a decade. ... Although a myriad of programmes have been created for various SME categories, policy has mainly promoted innovative start-ups and supported industrial SMEs in upgrading their innovation potential". The South Korean approach to innovation and entrepreneurship is very targeted and focused on achieving international leadership in many technology fields. The combination of policy initiatives and public and private sector investments make South Korea an attractive location for technology entrepreneurs.

Finally, the desired primary outcome of national government and innovation policies is to increase the levels of entrepreneurship and innovation within economies that will have direct and indirect impacts. Technology entrepreneurs benefit from being in economies that have policy initiatives that are designed to mitigate any barriers they encounter and create enablers to allow them to create new ventures. How they achieve this differs but whatever entrepreneurship and innovation policies that national government adopt should focus on, as Lundström et al. (2008, p. 24) argue, "promoting role models, integrating entrepreneurship in the education system, reducing the time and cost of starting a business, increasing the percentage of science and engineering graduates, easing the intellectual property regime, fostering more cooperation between research institutes and entrepreneurs ... ".

1.5   POLICY OUTCOMES AND IMPACTS

One of the greatest challenges for governments and policy-makers is to evaluate whether their policy interventions and supports make a difference to all entrepreneurs and if they have an impact on broader internationally aggregated national data on innovation and entrepreneurship (see Table 1.1). This challenge is best summed up by Lundström et al. (2008, p. 24): "One of the challenges for Governments is to determine what actions or combination of actions will most appropriately address the salient direct and indirect barriers to achieving higher levels of entrepreneurship and/or innovation, given their idiosyncratic set of county contextual and structural circumstances". From a political perspective maintaining a high level of support for entrepreneurship and innovation can be difficult for governments to justify to citizens when there are cut-backs to other government funded services such as social welfare. Also, measuring of entrepreneurship by category can be difficult and international comparisons would require common measurement of activities.

Many organisations, public and private, are involved in the collection and analysis of data on innovation and entrepreneurship, and this data is being used for international comparative purposes. National governments use this comparative data to evaluate their national performance across a number of dimensions. Also, there is an increase in comparative analysis between leading trading unions such as the European Union and leading world innovation-oriented economies, such as the United States, China, Japan and South Korea, as depicted in Table 1.1. From this analysis completed by the Directorate-General for Innovation and Research, it is clear that the EU has to match and exceed the measured performance of the United State, China, Japan and South Korea for gross domestic expenditure on R&D (GERD) and R&D intensity. From Table 1.1, one can see the array of indicators that can be used to assess entrepreneurial and innovation performance.

Given the importance of innovation to the European Union, each year the Innovation Union Scorecard is published, which details the innovation leaders, followers, moderate innovators and modest innovators in Europe (see Table 1.2 for the 2013 Innovation Union Scorecard). The Innovation Union Scorecard uses a range of indicators in a national economy in relation to research and innovation performance for the 27 member state. Innovation indicators are presented per member state as well as an analysis of their strengths and weaknesses.[1] The Innovation Union Scoreboard 2013 reveals Sweden as the leading innovation performer with little change in innovation performance rankings, with innovative SMEs collaborating with others driving innovation performance. However, signs are emerging that an innovation performance gap is widening between member states. The danger is that over the coming years this gap could widen further, and it will be difficult for countries to close the gap, with more innovative countries accelerating and consolidating their performance. The Innovation Union Scoreboard (2013, p. 7) noted that "[t]he most innovative countries in the EU share a number of strengths in their national research and innovation systems, with a key role played by business activity and the higher education sector. The business sectors of all innovation leaders perform very well as measured by Business R&D expenditures and PCT patent applications. They also share a well-developed higher education sector as demonstrated by very high results of new doctorates graduates, international scientific co-publications and public-private co-publications with the latter also signalling strong linkages between industry and science".

Since the adoption of the Innovation Union in 2010 by all member states of the EU, the European Commission has undertaken further analysis that is reported in the Innovation Union Competitiveness Reports. Such analysis has focused on high-growth SMEs, new venture creation, conditions for business R&D, knowledge intensive services (KIS) and economic

Table 1.1 Summary table of indicators, 2009 with average annual growth (%), 2000–2009

	EU		United States		Japan		China		South Korea	
	2009	AAGR	2009	AAGR	2009	AAGR	2009	AAGR	2009	AAGR
		2000–2009		2000–2009		2000–2009		2000–2009		2000–2009
Gross domestic expenditure on R&D (GERD) millions of euro	236553	2.5	270733	2.4	113986	3.4	45151	17.7	21480	9.4
R&D intensity	2.01	0.9	2.77	0.4	3.44	1.8	1.54	6.9	3.37	4.6
Business expenditure on R&D (BERD) millions of euro	146905	2.1	196563	2.1	89436	4.1	33077	20.7	16188	10.2
Business expenditure on R&D (BERD) as % of GDP	1.25	0.3	2.01	0.0	2.70	2.8	1.12	9.6	2.54	5.4
Business expenditure by SMEs (0–249 employees), millions of euro	25235	6.6	30762	5.8	5496	7.6	:	:	4280	5.3
Business expenditure by SMEs (0–249 employees) as % of GDP	0.25	3.2	0.30	2.9	0.17	5.4	:	:	0.56	1.1
Inward R&D expenditure by foreign affiliates, millions of euro	38871	2.6	29892	3.0	4406	10.2	:	:	:	:

Conitnued

Table 1.1 Continued

	EU		United States		Japan		China		South Korea	
	2009	AAGR 2000–2009	2009	AAGR 2000–2009	2009	AAGR 2000–2009	2009	AAGR 2000–2009	2009	AAGR 2000–2009
Inward R&D expenditure as % of R&D expenditure by business enterprise	31.6	−0.4	14.3	1.2	5.1	5.2	:	:	:	:
Public expenditure on R&D (GOVERD + HERD) millions of euro	87275	3.2	63495	3.4	12073	0.7	22758	12.0	4984	7.0
Public expenditure on R&D (GOVERD + HERD) as % of GDP	0.74	1.7	0.65	1.3	0.69	−0.8	0.41	1.6	0.78	2.3
Investment in knowledge (R&D and Education), millions of euro	822588	1.8	930935	2.9	240224	1.9	:	:	74444	7.2
Investment in knowledge (R&D and Education) as % of GDP	6.6	−0.1	9.1	0.5	7.5	0.3	:	:	9.7	2.5

New doctoral graduates (ISCED 6), total	110073	3.7	63712	4.5	16296	3.7	:	:	9369	5.4
New doctoral graduates (ISCED 6) per thousand population aged 25–34	1.60	4.3	1.56	4.1	0.98	5.2	:	:	1.19	6.6
Number of researchers (FTE)	1504575	3.8	1412639	1.3	656676	1.9	1592420	10.9	236137	10.8
Number of researchers (FTE), per thousand labour force	6.3	2.9	9.2	0.3	10.3	1.2	2.0	9.9	9.7	9.3
Number of researchers (FTE) working in the private sector	707534	3.5	1130500	1.2	501077	2.2	1092213	15.1	185811	13.6
Number of researchers (FTE) working in the public sector	797040	4.0	282139	1.6	155599	1.2	500207	4.9	50326	3.1
Human Resources in Science and Technology aged 25–64	91554	2.9	:	:	:	:	:	:	:	:
Human Resources in Science and Technology aged 25–64 as % of labour force	40.1	1.9	:	:	:	:	:	:	:	:
New S&T graduates (ISCED 5A) with S&E orientation	586144	3.3	247147	2.0	114310	-0.7	:	:	:	:

Continued

Table 1.1 Continued

	EU 2009	EU AAGR 2000–2009	United States 2009	United States AAGR 2000–2009	Japan 2009	Japan AAGR 2000–2009	China 2009	China AAGR 2000–2009	South Korea 2009	South Korea AAGR 2000–2009
License and patent revenues from abroad, millions of euro	25137	2.3	62279	7.1	17474	13.0	:	:	:	:
License and patent revenues from abroad as % GDP	0.21	2.4	0.64	4.9	0.53	11.6	:	:	:	:
Community trademarks	60967	6.7	12877	-1.6	2081	7.6	811	49.2	:	:
Community trademarks per billion GDP (PPS€)	4.88	4.5	1.16	-3.6	0.62	6.3	0.13	35.4	:	:
Total number of scientific publications (fractional counting method)	469479	4.7	357837	3.5	92089	1.2	256495	20.7	39792	13.3
Scientific publications in the 10% most cited scientific publications worldwide	55557	5.9	58319	3.9	8122	2.2	14499	25.2	3231	13.9

Scientific publications in the 10% most cited scientific publications worldwide as % of total scientific publications of the country	11.6	1.4	15.3	0.0	8.3	0.7	7.0	4.7	8.5	0.6
PCT patent applications, total number	49545	4.3	49282	2.7	28970	15.0	6416	22.3	7227	20.5
PCT patent applications per billion GDP (PPS€)	4.0	1.9	4.3	0.3	8.3	13.2	1.1	10.8	7.0	15.1
Female PhD / doctoral graduates, total number	47741	4.9	32497	9.0	4499	4.5	:	:	2763	9.4
Share (%) of female PhD / doctoral graduates in total PhD / doctoral graduates	45.3	1.2	51.0	1.7	27.6	2.6	:	:	29.5	5.0
International scientific co-publications, total number	132412	9.6	117794	9.5	24064	7.4	37524	19.8	:	:
International co-publications as % of total publications	24.2	4.2	27.4	5.1	22.6	5.5	13.5	-0.5	:	:
PCT patent applications with co-inventor(s) located abroad	4719	2.3	5002	2.3	627	1.6	760	20.3	261	14.9

Continued

Table 1.1 Continued

	EU		United States		Japan		China		South Korea	
	2009	AAGR	2009	AAGR	2009	AAGR	2009	AAGR	2009	AAGR
		2000–2009		2000–2009		2000–2009		2000–2009		2000–2009
PCT applications with co-inventors located abroad, as % of total PCT patent applications	9.7	−0.5	11.1	1.7	2.3	−9.2	10.5	0.2	3.6	−2.0
Public-private co-publications per million population	36.2	2.7	70.2	0.9	56.3	0.3	1.2	24.6	:	:
Venture capital (early stage, expansion and replacement), millions of euro	10185	−8.1	12954	−19.2	:	:	:	:	:	:
Venture capital (early stage, expansion and replacement) as % of GDP	0.09	−9.7	0.13	−20.5	:	:	:	:	:	:
Cost of patent application and maintenance for SMEs, PPS€	167798	:	4413	:	6953	:	:	:	5509	:
Cost of patent application and maintenance for SMEs, per billion GDP (PPS€)	14.21	:	0.39	:	2.24	:	:	:	5.08	:

Health technology patents (PCT)	6798	4.1	10154	1.2	2277	8.0	540	-2.8	449	11.6
Health technology patents (PCT) per billion GDP (PPS€)	0.55	1.7	0.89	-1.1	0.65	6.4	0.09	-11.9	0.44	6.6
Climate change mitigation patents (PCT)	1195	16.9	551	16.9	744	28.7	115	35.6	89	30.3
Climate change mitigation patents (PCT) per billion GDP (PPS€)	0.10	14.2	0.05	14.2	0.21	26.7	0.02	22.8	0.09	24.4
Employment in knowledge intensive economic activitiesLicense and patent revenues from abroad, millions of euro as % of total employment	35.1	2.4	:	:	:	:	:	:	:	:
Medium and high-tech manufacturing exports, millions of euro	781149	5.4	522413	6.7	396343	7.7	544786	19.6	204299	11.1
Medium and high-tech manufacturing exports as % of total product exports	59.6	-0.3	59.1	-2.2	74.6	-1.6	56.0	1.2	71.2	-0.8

Continued

Table 1.1 Continued

	EU		United States		Japan		China		South Korea	
	2009	AAGR	2009	AAGR	2009	AAGR	2009	AAGR	2009	AAGR
		2000–2009		2000–2009		2000–2009		2000–2009		2000–2009
Knowledge intensive service exports, millions of euro	608223	7.8	153865	10.6	34418	12.8	38841	33.3	35703	24.2
Knowledge intensive service exports as %¨of total service exports	49.4	1.5	41.4	0.6	33.9	0.4	38.8	13.5	69.1	3.2
Contribution of medium-high and high-tech exports to the manufacturing trade balance as % of total manufacturing	5.1	:	5.4	:	12.2	:	:	:	3.5	:

Innovation Union Competitiveness Report 2011

Source: DG Research and Innovation http://ec.europa.eu/research/innovation-union/pdf/competitiveness-report/2011/data-and-statistics/key_indicators_summary_table.xls.

Table 1.2 Summary Innovation Union Scoreboard 2013

Innovation Leaders: Sweden, Germany, Denmark and Finland all show a performance well above that of the EU average.

Innovation Followers: Netherlands, Luxembourg, Belgium, the UK, Austria, Ireland, France, Slovenia, Cyprus and Estonia all show a performance close to that of the EU average.

Moderate Innovators: The performances of Italy, Spain, Portugal, Czech Republic, Greece, Slovakia, Hungary, Malta and Lithuania are below that of the EU average.

Modest Innovators: The performances of Poland, Latvia, Romania and Bulgaria are well below that of the EU average.

Source: European Union (2013) *Innovation Union Scoreboard 2013*, © European Union 2013.

competitiveness. Some interesting data from the Innovation Union Competitiveness Report 2011 is emerging about new business creation. In essence, there is a steady pattern of new business creation across the EU but lower than the US figures that have higher numbers of new venture creations in the high-tech sector (see Figure 1.2).

The Innovation Union Competitiveness Report (2011, p. 325) suggests: "The US business environment is more fertile for the growth of innovative firms. ... there is a 'sectorial' specificity: there are sectors, like biotechnology, internet, software, computer hardware and services and telecoms equipment, that evidence an above average share of R&D performed by young companies. They are called the 'young sectors'. For most of these sectors, the United States have a bigger share in their economy that the EU". Based on the implementation of the Innovation Union objectives and with the support of Horizon 2020, the expectation is that the EU will match if not surpass the US in terms of young sectors share in the EU economy. Consequently this opens up new opportunities for European technology entrepreneurs and some of the European structural reforms should create an attractive business environment that is even more supportive of technology entrepreneurs and young sectors. Moreover, the challenge for the EU is to encourage greater levels of entrepreneurship, which, based on 2011 data, is lower than USA and China, remembering that for " ... countries with the highest rates of entrepreneurial activity, there is a prevalence of the early stage over established business" (Innovation Union Competitiveness Report, 2011). Early stage businesses provide a clear indicator of potential future SMEs, and Finland, Romania, Cyprus, Ireland and Sweden have the highest rates of early stage entrepreneurship (Innovation Union Competitiveness Report, 2011, p. 33) (see Figure 1.3). Key barriers to entrepreneurship at an EU level include access to finance, administration complexities and access to start-up information. The fear of failure and the opportunity to start again were also reported as potential barriers to entrepreneurship (Innovation Union Competitiveness Report (2011)).

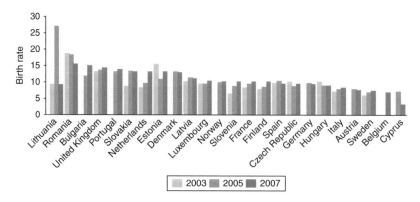

Figure 1.2 Birth rate of business enterprises[1]

Note
(1) The number of enterprise births divided by the number of active enterprises.

Source: European Commission, D-G for Research and Innovation (2011) *Innovation Union Competitiveness Report 2011*, © European Union, 1995–2012.

Data: Eurostat.

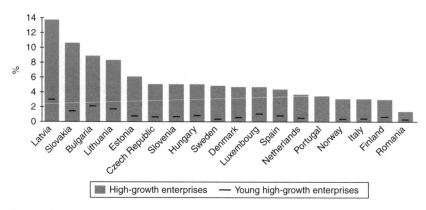

Figure 1.3 High-growth[1] and young high-growth[2] enterprises as % of total enterprises, 2007[3]

Notes
(1) Enterprises of more than ten employees with an average annual growth in employment of more than 20% per annum over a three year period.
(2) Enterprises up to five years old or more than ten employees with an average annual growth in employment of more than 20% per annum over a three year period. PT: Data are not available for young high-growth enterprises.
(3) LT, FI: 2005; BG, ES, NO: 2000.

Source: European Commission, D-G for Research and Innovation (2011) *Innovation Union Competitiveness Report 2011*, © European Union, 1995–2012.

Data: Eurostat.

The Global Entrepreneurship Monitor (GEM), established in 1999 as a partnership between London Business School and Babson College and a ten-country study, now has grown to be the world's largest annual assessment of entrepreneurial activities with 69 country studies in 2012. GEM has become one of the trusted sources of entrepreneurship data collection and analysis, covering attitudes, activities and growth aspirations. In their 2013 report, the GEM found positive attitudes toward entrepreneurs and that entrepreneurship education efforts need to be improved at primary and secondary level. GEM (2012, p.10) noted that "a high-growth oriented approach to entrepreneurship will create jobs and, in tandem, grow economies. Broad-based efforts to improve the labor market, increase the internal market and provide access to international markets can be more specifically addressed toward meeting the specific needs of entrepreneurs". GEM 2012 found that the age distribution of entrepreneurs varied per region and that ratio of female to male participating in early stage entrepreneurship also varied. In 2011, as part of the GEM project, Rhett Morris of the Centre for High Impact Entrepreneurship reported findings of a study on high-impact entrepreneurs who he defined as "individuals that launch lead companies with above average impact in terms of job creation, wealth creation and the development of entrepreneurial models". While only representing 4 per cent of total entrepreneurs that responded to the GEM surveys they found that entrepreneurs generated nearly 40 per cent of the job created, are driven to grow their income and have a global focus (Global Entrepreneurship Model, 2011).

1.6   FUTURE TRENDS

As we can see from the previous two sections, creating the appropriate economic conditions and policy initiatives to encourage entrepreneurship, and in particular technology entrepreneurs, is vital. The global economic crisis that began in 2008 has fundamentally challenged old business models and paradigms and has opened up new opportunities for technology entrepreneurs. There are many trends that we could look at here, but we decided to focus on three that we believe will influence technology entrepreneurship. These future trends are enabled by open innovation models of innovation and collaboration and have gained momentum in many sectors.

Convergent Technology Spaces: With rapid advances in many scientific fields, as established companies collaborate and co-invest in R&D outside their traditional areas of activities, supported by public research and infrastructure, they are presented with new market opportunities. From Section 1.4, we see that South Korea is making significant investments in convergent technology spaces. This might be, for example, an energy company and an ICT body collaborating to bring to the market new devices that monitor energy consumption. It may be a medical device company collaborating with a software company and other healthcare stakeholders in developing services that monitors patient health. In essence, different companies from different sectors converge on a common problem, seek ways to address it and develop an appropriate business model that shares the risk, cost and returns. In April 2013, President Obama launched the BRAIN Initiative (Brain Research through Advancing Innovative Neurotechnologies), which is a focused large-scale basic research effort on understanding the human mind and in doing so will present new opportunities to treat and prevent diseases such as Alzheimer's, schizophrenia, autism and epilepsy. President Obama (2013) outlined it as follows: "Imagine if someone with a prosthetic limb can now play the piano or throw a baseball as well as anybody else, because the wiring from the brain to that prosthetic is direct and triggered by what's already happening in the patient's mind. What if computers could respond to our thoughts or our language barriers could come tumbling down? Or if millions of Americans were suddenly finding new jobs in these fields – jobs we haven't even dreamt up yet – because we chose to invest in this project?" Such an initiative opens up significant technology-convergent opportunities. For example, IBM's Smarter Cities initiative seeks to use existing and new data in ways that improve city life and contribute to the growth of cities. This has meant that IBM increased its service offerings in public safety, energy and water, planning, environment, health and public administration and has opened up more opportunities for new services and collaborations. Moreover, current trends with Big Data, have opened up convergent technology opportunities for established businesses and technology entrepreneurs.

Crowdfunding: One of the major barriers for entrepreneurs as we saw in Section 1.6 is access to finance. For technology companies, access to early seed, high-risk capital can be even more difficult and has become even more challenging with the global recession. This has led to the development of different models where, in essence, investors come together in an organised manner to provide financial support to early stage companies, social entrepreneurs and other categories of entrepreneurs. Specific funds have been set up around this crowdsourcing concept. For example, crowdsourcing.org (2013) offers a wide variety of crowdsourcing products and in the finance space they offer "financial contributions from online investors, sponsors or donors to fund for-profit or non-profit initiatives or enterprises". Crowdfunding is an approach to raising capital for new projects and businesses by soliciting contributions from a large number of stakeholders following three types of crowdfunding models: (1) Donations, Philanthropy and Sponsorship where there is no expected financial return, (2) Lending and (3) Investment in exchange for equity, profit or revenue sharing". In April 2013, Impact Crowd, a Dutch-based crowdfunding company, sought crowd-sourced investments for Etiologics that transforms organic waste into sustainable nutrients. If the barriers to accessing finance continue, future refinements and new financial offers and services will need to be created to meet the demand.

Co-working Incubation: With changes in the working practices, new demands from entrepreneurs, and the growth of "young sectors", there has been a change occurring in the incubator landscape internationally. The incubator concept and the co-working space concept are converging, often based on private initiatives (e.g., property owners/estate management), but in some cases also transforming university incubators such as at the University of Oslo. Put simply: someone offering an arena for co-working and business incubation and acceleration. The economic basis is office rental by entrepreneurs. Activities includes an array of networking events, accelerator programs, competitions, lectures etc. Often less industrially specialised than other incubators, but the different co-working locations develop somewhat particular profiles, such as in new media and design or social entrepreneurship or early stage ventures or IT ventures. Many of them see themselves as networking hubs, and they may be very well connected to other similar hubs internationally (e.g., Berlin, London, Stockholm have large like-minded communities). Even some big companies have started putting a few of their people into these co-working spaces in order to keep track of what's going on, and tap into certain kinds of expertise. In 2012 Oslo had four new such co-working spaces, three of them were started by private persons (VCs and/or serial entrepreneurs), the fourth being the university incubator. One of the largest co-working spaces is Rock-Space in San Francisco founded by Duncan Logan in January 2011. The attraction of co-working spaces, according to Kreamer (2012), is: "1. They offer collaborative networks, built-in resources, and a dynamic ecosystem. 2. They foster innovation. 3. They make starting up a business simpler".

1.7   CHAPTER SUMMARY

We began the chapter by considering the role of government, industry and universities as part of the triple helix approach to innovation. We then turned our attention to the innovation and entrepreneurship policies in EU, United States, Australia and South Korea. From this we see that there is much commonality in terms of the outcome activities these policies are attempting to achieve, such as jobs, new business and wealth creation. We see that South Korea is investing in technology platforms with a view to keeping them in a leading international innovation position. While there is no specific data on technology entrepreneurship, our review of policy outcomes and impacts among EU member states shows the differences and emerging innovation and entrepreneurship gaps between member states. Data from the Global Entrepreneurship Monitor shows entrepreneurial vibrancy across 69 countries. The chapter concluded with a review of three future trends that will impact on technology entrepreneurs – technology-convergent products, crowdfunding and co-working incubation.

Case Study 1.1   Renishaw Diagnostics Ltd

Written by Dr. Grace Walsh, Duesto Business School, Spain.

Inception

In May 2007 Scotland's Strathclyde University launched D3 Technologies Ltd. to develop diagnostic tests and examinations that indicate genetic predisposition to diseases faster than existing technologies. D3 Technologies was formed by University's academics Ewen Smith, Duncan Graham and Karen Faulds, from the University's chemistry department, and life sciences entrepreneur Jim Reid. The firm's goal was "to exploit certain patents related to Surface Enhanced Raman Spectroscopy

(SERS) and to develop SERS for molecular diagnostics and trace detection" (www.renishaw.com, 1). The funding for this new venture was obtained from Renishaw PLC, a UK-based developer of high-tech measurement systems and FTSE-250 firm. In addition to providing finance Renishaw collaborated with Strathclyde researchers on developing and commercialising the diagnostic tools (www.scotsman.com). The investment deal, one of the Glasgow-based institutions biggest ever spin-out deals occurred in the form of £1.85 million in monetary assistance and also instrumentation support with a combined value of £5 million over five years, for which Renishaw received a 75 per cent stake in the spin-out. Part of the investment was also used by D3 Technologies to purchase the business and assets of the analytical business unit (ABU) operated by Mesophotonics Limited, a spin-out company of the University of Southampton, for £850,000. Renishaw, already a leading supplier of Raman instrumentation, has a vested interest in the progression of Raman spectroscopy and its application into new and developing markets (www.renishaw.com, 1).

Development

The merging of D3 Technologies and the Mesophotonics Ltd. ABU has resulted in a combination of complimentary products and this, in addition to the investment and mentoring by Renishaw, has given the company "the platform to develop new-generation products that give the potential to revolutionize medical and genetic testing" according to Dr. David McBeth, Strathclyde's director of research and innovation (www.scotsman.com). In January 2008, D3 Technologies was awarded a Strathclyde Enterprise Award, the award aimed at giving recognition to some of Scotland's most inventive businesses that have been supported by the University's enterprise network (www.renishaw.com, 2). Another honour was bestowed upon D3 Technologies in 2009 when the firm was shortlisted for the Scottish Enterprise Life Sciences Award). D3 Technologies' (www.renishaw.com, 3) University roots remained strong throughout the development of the firm with the founding professors remaining directors of the firm to this date (March 2013), and the firm's strong R&D focus continues to be a positive asset. In 2009 ITI Techmedia, part of an organisation that supports economic growth through market-driven R&D programmes, invested £7.9 million in a three and a half year R&D programme, and D3 Technologies Ltd. was one of a small number of R&D providers (www.innovationuk.org). The programme was funded with public finance, led by academics from multiple UK Universities and conducted in conjunction with numerous industry partners of which D3 Technologies was one (http://onlinelibrary.wiley.com). This highlights the strength of the triple helix and the lack of barriers to information-flow between industry, academia and government organisations.

Realisation

In February 2010 the firm's CEO, Professor Ewen Smith, stood down to focus on a new portfolio of products for the firm, and Mr David Burns was appointed new CEO. Shortly afterwards the company's name changed from D3 Technologies Ltd. to Renishaw Diagnostics Ltd (www.renishaw.com, 4). The investments of the previous years paid off in February 2011 when Renishaw Diagnostics Ltd. launched its first major product, the RenDx™ research-use-only multiplex assay system, which provides a marked improvement on existing screening methods (www.renishaw.com, 5). Shortly afterwards, in May 2011, the firm signed an exclusive licensing agreement to a patent on nucleic acid sequence identification (SERS beacons) from The University of Strathclyde, in a move that Professor Duncan Graham calls "another excellent example of technology transfer". According to Renishaw Diagnostics Ltd. CEO, David Burns, "the licensing of this patent will enhance our existing patent portfolio and allow us to develop new format molecular diagnostics assays in additional disease areas". However the collaboration signals more than a mere licensing deal, Dr McBeth believes it signifies a further strengthening of the University's relationship with Renishaw Diagnostics Ltd., and it is his hope that the license will underpin the company's growth and this in turn will create more highly-skilled jobs in the West of Scotland. Furthermore, Dr McBeth sees this as the beginning of a long and symbiotic relationship as he expects that they will develop several other research and knowledge exchange collaborations with Renishaw Diagnostics in the future (www.renishaw.com, 6).

Relationship

A key component of the success of this venture stems from the strong and overlapping relationship between the spin-out firm and the University of Strathclyde. Not only did Renishaw Diagnostics Ltd. remain in contact with the University but the firm's founding academics continued on as directors in the firm, in addition to continuing their affiliation with the University. Furthermore, the firm's successes were recognised, supported and promoted by governing bodies through both awards and funding. The collaboration and alignment of the three resources of business, academia and government for the goal of sustainable economic success represents the triple helix of innovation. In recent decades Universities are becoming increasingly involved in the formation of firms resulting from academic research, and this has cemented its role in the triple helix of innovation alongside industry and government (Etzkowitz, 2003). In the case of Renishaw Diagnostics Ltd. the supports of the triple helix relationship allowed the firm to develop and grow its R&D without the immediate pressure of returning a profit. Renishaw Diagnostics Ltd. was almost four years in existence before its first major product was launched, thus this firm needed this type of environment for it to become a success. Ultimately, although the firm's economic success was not immediate, the entire premise of the triple helix is to create long-term, sustainable economic success, something the Renishaw Diagnostics Ltd. looks set to achieve.

Case Questions

1. How has the triple helix influenced and shaped the development of Reinshaw Diagnostics?
2. Outline how the EU's Innovation Union strategy could benefit Reinshaw Diagnostic?
3. Discuss how convergent technology space opportunities can impact on Reinshaw Diagnostics?

Case Study References

Etzkowitz, H. (2003) "Innovation in Innovation: The Triple Helix of University-Industry-Government Relations", *Social Science Information*, 42(3), 293–337.

Innovation UK website, Accessed online on 13 March 2013 at http://www.innovationuk.org/news/innovation-uk-vol4–1/0147-iti-scotland.html.

"News and Views" (2009) *International Wound Journal*, 6(4), 250–257. Published online 26 August 2009. Accessed online on 12 March at http://onlinelibrary.wiley.com/store/10.1111/j.1742–81X.2009.00617.x/asset/j.1742–481X.2009.00617.x.pdf?v=1&t=he71ylyi&s=c47ca11fa164028bfd5be27f3f1bc3a863fd0586.

Newsweaver website, Accessed online on 11 March 2013 at http://archive.newsweaver.com/lifesciences/newsweaver.co.uk/lifesciences/e_article00100654364e4.html?x=b11,0,w.

Renishaw website, 1, Accessed online on 11 March 2013 at http://www.renishaw.com/en/renishaw-invests-in-d3-technologies-limited – 8041.

Renishaw website, 2, Accessed online on 12 March 2013 at http://www.renishaw.com/en/scottish-business-award-for-spectroscopy-expert – 9265.

Renishaw website, 3, Accessed online on 12 March 2013 at http://www.renishaw.com/en/10571.aspx.

Renishaw website, 4, Accessed online on 12 March 2013 at http://www.renishawdiag-nostics.com/en/ground-breaking-molecular-diagnostics-business-appoints-new-ceo – 12539.

Renishaw website, 5, Accessed online on 13 March 2013 at http://www.renishawdiag-nostics.com/en/renishaw-diagnostics-enables-customised-multiplex-assays-for-pre-cious-research-samples – 14576.

Renishaw website, 6, Accessed online on 13 March 2013 at http://www.renishawdi-agnostics.com/en/renishaw-diagnostics-signs-exclusive-licence-agreement-for-serrs-beacons-with-the-university-of-strathclyde – 14981.

Scotsman website, Accessed online on 11 March 2013 at http://www.scotsman.com/business/industry/strathclyde-university-in-163–5m-spin-out-deal-1-908461.

1.8 REVISION QUESTIONS

1. Discuss how innovation and entrepreneurship policy impacts on technology entrepreneurs.
2. Outline the triple helix model and discuss the roles of the key actors in this model.
3. From section 1.4.2 discuss the commonalities and differences in innovation and entrepreneurship policies between the different countries and trading blocks.
4. From your assessment of the EU Innovation Scoreboard, what are the implications for technology entrepreneurs?
5. Discuss how future trends will impact on technology entrepreneurs and new venture formations.

1.9 FURTHER READING AND RESOURCES

- For detailed EU data on investments in innovation a good source is Eurostat PocketBook published annually on Science, Technology and Innovation in Europe.
- Excellent data, reports and perspective available on the Global Entrepren-eurship Monitor website (see http://www.gemconsortium.org/).
- For an excellent overview of the future of knowledge work see Harvard Business Review January–February 2013.
- See Loet Leydesdorff's book on the Knowledge Based Economy, which outlined the different dimensions of the knowledge-based economy.
- For discussion of entrepreneurial universities, see paper by Maribel Guerrero, David Urbano, James Cunningham and Damien Organ (2013) "Entrepreneurial Universities in Two European Regions: A Case Study Comparison", *Journal of Technology Transfer* (forthcoming).

1.10 NOTE

1. Appendix I includes the list of indicators used for the Innovation Union Score-board as well as the innovation profile of Sweden.

1.11   REFERENCES

Carr, K. (2009) *Powering Ideas: An Innovation Agenda for the 21st Century*, Executive Summary, Commonwealth of Australia.

Crowdsourcing.org (2013) *Crowdfunding*, Accessed 4 April 2013, http://www.crowdsourcing.org/community/crowdfunding/7.

Cunningham, J (2008) "Management 2.0: Challenges and Implications", in *Irish Management 2.0: New Managerial Priorities for a Changing Economy*, James Cunningham and Denis Harrington (eds), Dublin: Blackhall Publishing, 43–69.

Dahlstrand, A.L. and Stevenson, L. (2007) *Linking Innovation and Entrepreneurship Policy, Innovative Policy Research for Economic Growth*, Swedish Foundation for Small Business Research.

Etzkowitz, H. (2002) *MIT and the Rise of Entrepreneurial Science*. London: Routledge.

—— (2003) "Research Groups as 'Quasi Firms': The Invention of the Entrepreneurial University", *Research Policy*, 32, 109–21.

Etzkowitz, H. and Leydesdorff, L. (eds) (1997) *Universities in the Global Economy: A Triple Helix of University-Industry-Government Relations*. London: Cassell Academic.

European Comission (2010) Communication from the Commission to the European Parliament, the Council, the European Economic and Social Committee and the Committee of the Region European 2020 Flagship Initiative Innovation Union SEC(2010) 116, COM (2010) 546 final, Brussels, 6 October 2010.

European Comission (2013) Innovation Union Scoreboard, Beligium, http://ec.europa.eu/enterprise/policies/innovation/files/ius-2013_en.pdf.

http://ec.europa.eu/enterprise/policies/innovation/files/ius-2013_en.pdf

Giblin, M. and Ryan, P. (2012) "Tight Clusters or Loose Networks? The Critical Role of Inward Foreign Direct Investment in Cluster Creation", *Regional Studies*, 46(2): 245–258, [online], DOI: 10.1080/00343404.2010.497137, October 2010.

Global Entrepreneurship Model (2011) 2011 High Impact Entrepreneurship Global Report, Centre for High-Impact Entrepreneurship at Endeavor.

Global Entrepeneurship Monitor (2012) Global Report, http://www.gemconsortium.org/docs/download/2645.

Global Entrepreneurship Model (2013) 2013 Global Report.

Godin, B. (2006) "The Linear Model of Innovation: The Historical Construction of an Analytical Framework", *Science, Technology, and Human Values*, 31(6), November 2006: 639–667.

Kreamer, A. (2012) *The Rise of Coworking Office Spaces*, HBR Blog. Accessed on 4 April 2013, http://blogs.hbr.org/cs/2012/09/the_rise_of_co-working-office.html.

Leydesdorff, L. (2000) "The Triple Helix: An Evolutionary Model of Innovations", *Research Policy, Elsevier*, 29(2), February: 243–255.

Lundström, A., Almerud, M. and Stevenson, L. (2008) Entrepreneurship and Innovation Policies: Analysing measures in European countries, Innovative Policy Research for Economic Growth, Swedish Foundation for Small Business Research.

Mittelstadt, A. and Cerri, F. (2009) *Fostering Entrepreneurship for Innovation*, Organisation for Economic Co-operation and Development, Paris.

MOTIE (2011) *Industry Policies, Ministry of Trade, Industry & Energy.* Accessed 1 April 2013, http://www.mke.go.kr/language/eng/policy/Ipolicies.jsp.

Mowery, D.C., Nelson, R.R., Sampat, B.N. and Ziedonis, A.A. (2004) *Ivory Tower and Industrial Innovation. University-Industry Technology Transfer Before and After the Bayh-Dole Act.* Stanford University Press: Palo Alto, CA.

Obama, B. (2013) *Remarks by the President on the BRAIN Initiative and American Innovation*, 2 April 2013. Accessed on 4 April 2013, http://www.whitehouse.gov/the-press-office/2013/04/02/remarks-president-brain-initiative-and-american-innovation

Park, H.W. and Leydesdorff, L. (2010) "Longitudinal Trends in Networks of University-Industry-Government Relations in South Korea: The Role of Programmatic Incentives", *Research Policy*, 39(5): 640–649.

Piekarski, A.E.T. and Torkomian, A.L.V. (2005) *How R&D Public Financing Incites the Academy-Industry Cooperation: An Assessment of the Effects of a Public Policy in Brazil.* In: Triple Helix 5.

Science Programme, (2011) *Investing in Innovation Pays Off, Science Progress.* Accessed 1 April 2013, http://www.doingbusiness.org/data/exploretopics/entrepreneurship#sub-menu-item-link.

Subotzky, G. (1999) "Alternatives to the Entrepreneurial University: New Modes of Knowledge Production in Community Service Programs. Higher Education", 38(4): 401–440.

White House (2013) *Strategy for American Innovation: Executive Summary*, White House. Accessed 1 April 2013, http://www.whitehouse.gov/innovation/strategy/executive-summary.

World Bank (2013) *Entrepreneurship: Why it matters?* The World Bank Group. Accessed 1 April 2013, http://www.doingbusiness.org/data/exploretopics/entrepreneurship/why%20it%20matters.

1.12 GLOSSARY OF TERMS

American Strategy for Innovation: US national strategy policy for innovation.

Co-working Incubation: Incubation locations for young sectors.

Crowdfunding: Mechanism to seek start-up funding.

Global Entrepreneurship Monitor: Established in 1999 and now is the world's largest assessment of entrepreneurial activities.

High-growth Enterprises: Privately own firms that have a high-growth orientation.

Indicators measures: These are specific measure of innovation and entrepreneurship activities that can be used for comparison purposes.

Innovation Union Scorecard: Annual member state comparative assessment of EU innovation capacities.

Triple Helix: A paradigm that explains the relationship between universities, industry and government.

Universities: Public or privately own organisations that have three missions – teaching, research and commercialisation.

Innovation Union Strategy: Launched by the EU in 2010, which outlined the strategy for the EU in relation to innovation.

APPENDIX 1.1   EUROPEAN UNION (2013) INNOVATION UNION SCOREBOARD INDICATOR

Main type/innovation dimension /indicator	Data source	Years covered
ENABLERS		
Human resources		
1.1.1 New doctorate graduates (ISCED 6) per 1000 population aged 25–34)	Eurostat	2006–2010
1.1.2 Percentage population aged 30–34 having completed tertlary education	Eurostat	2007–2011
1.1.3 Percentage youth aged 20–24 having attained at least upper Secondary level education	Eurostat	2007–2011
Open, excellent and attractive research systems		
1.2.1 International scientific co-piblications per million population	Science-Metrix(Scopus)	2007–2011
1.2.2 Scientific publications among the top 10% most cited piblications worldwide as % of total scientific publications of the country	Science-Metrix (Scopus)	2004–2008
1.2.3 Non-EU doctorate students[1] as a % of all doctorate students	Eurostat	2006–2010
Finance and support		
1.3.1 R&D expenditure in the public sector as % of GDP	Eurostat	2007–2011
1.3.2 Venture Capital Investment as % of GDP	Eurostat	2007–2011
FIRM ACTIVITIES		
Firm investments		
2.1.1 R&D expenditure in the business sector as % of GDP	Eurostat	2007–2010
2.1.2 Non-R&D Innovation expenditures as % of turnover	Eurostat	2006,2008, 2010
Linkages and entrepreneurship		
2.2.1 SMEs innovating in-house as % of SEMs	Eurostat	2006,2008, 2010
2.2.2 Innovative SMEs collaborating with others as % of SMEs	Eurostat	2006,2008, 2010
2.2.3 Public-private co-publications per million population	CWTS (Thomson Reuters)	2007, 2011
Intellectual assets		
2.3.1 PCT patents applications per billion GDP (In PPSE)	Eurostat	2005, 2009
2.3.2 PCT patent applications in societel Chalenge per billion GDP (In PPSE) (environment-related technologies; health)	OECD/Eurostat	2005;2009
2.3.3 Community trademarks per billion GDP (In PPSE)	OHIM[2]/Eurostat	2007, 2011
2.3.4 Community designs per billion GDP (In PPSE)	OHIM/Eurostat	2007, 2011
OUTPUTS		
Innovators		
3.1.1 SMEs introducing product or process innovations as % of SMEs	Eurostat	2006, 2008, 2010
3.1.2 SMEs Introducing marketing or organisational innovations as % of SMEs	Eurostat	2006, 2008, 2010
3.1.3 High-growth innovative firms	N/A	N/A
Economic effects		
3.2.1 Employment in Knowledge-intensive activities (manufacturing and services) as % of total employment	Eurostat	2007, 2010
3.2.2 Contribution of medium and high-tech product exports to the trade balance	UN	2007, 2011
3.2.3 Knowledge-intensive services exports as % total service exports	UN/Eurostat	2006, 2010
3.2.4 Sales of new to market and new to firm Innovations as % of turnover	Eurostat	2006, 2008, 2010
3.2.5 License and patent revenues from abroad as % of GDP	Eurostat	2007, 2011

Source: European Union (2013) *Innovation Union Scoreboard 2013*, © European Union 2013.

APPENDIX 1.2 SWEDEN INNOVATION UNION SCOREBOARD INDICATIONS

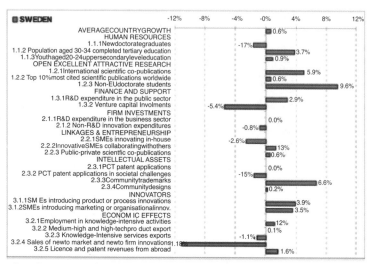

Annual average growth per indicator and average country growth

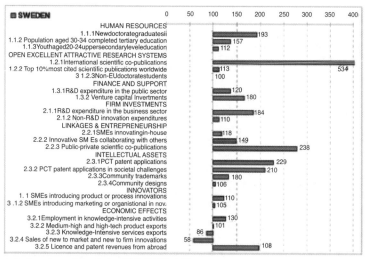

Indicator values relative to the EU27 (EU27=100)

Source: European Union (2013) *Innovation Union Scoreboard 2013*, © European Union 2013.

Chapter 2
RESEARCH AND TECHNOLOGY TRANSFER FROM UNIVERSITIES TO BUSINESS

2.1 LEARNING OBJECTIVES

In this chapter we consider how universities are embracing research commercialisation or what is termed more broadly as "third mission activities". We begin by exploring the theoretical debates on their mission activities, then outline some key technology transfer mechanisms relevant to technology entrepreneurs. These include patents, licensing and company formation – start-ups and spin-offs. We conclude the chapter by examining the stimulants and inhibitors to technology transfer.

After reading this chapter, you will be able to:

1. Understand the different theoretical perspectives on third-mission activities
2. Describe the technology transfer process and some specific mechanism for technology transfer – patents, licensing and company formation (start-ups and spin-outs)
3. Outline the stimulants and barriers to technology transfer

2.2 CHAPTER STRUCTURE

The core elements of this chapter are as follows:

- Introduction
- Third-Mission Activities
  - Linear Model of Technology Transfer
  - Non-linear Model of Technology Transfer
  - TTOs and Technology Entrepreneurs
- Technology Transfer and Mechanisms
- Technology Transfer Process
- Some Specific Mechanisms for Technology Transfer

- Stimulants and Barriers to Technology Transfer
  - Macro-level Factors
  - Micro-level Factors
- Inhibitors to Commercialisation
- Chapter Summary
- Case Study – Allergy Standards Ltd: The Journey from University Incubation
- Revision Questions
- Further Reading and Resources
- References
- Glossary of Terms

2.3   INTRODUCTION

Universities play a significant role in the development, support and shaping of technology entrepreneurship. Third-level institutions are powerful drivers for the technological and economic development of industrial branches and regions as Markman et al. (2005) note: "we found universities increasingly viewing themselves as catalysts of new venture formation and regional development". However, from their study of UK and US technology transfer offices (TTOs), Chapple et al. (2004) note "the strong regional effects lead us to suggest that in some regions, due to lower R&D and economic activity, universities will be less efficient in the commercialisation of technology". Technology entrepreneurs are key actors both in the creation of new knowledge and its exploitation within and outside university boundaries. Those nations with strong research systems and the capacity to leverage the commercial opportunities of their research system through effective technology transfer activities, particularly from universities to industry, will be best placed to prosper both economically and socially.

2.4   THIRD-MISSION ACTIVITIES

Third-level institutions continue to be seen as drivers of knowledge that impact the economy and society through technology and knowledge transfer. Policy-makers desire to see more research and technology from third-level institutions become more easily available to support economic development, firms, jobs and entrepreneurship. This is in keeping with an open innovation model. US universities and their research systems through the passing of the Bayh-Dole Act in 1980 have been at the forefront internationally in the development of third-mission activities in public and private universities. This development has been a significant driver in the broadening out of university missions beyond teaching and research and the establishment of new organisational structures to support technology transfer. As a result many universities set up Technology Transfer Offices to protect IP and also to support innovation and entrepreneurship across campus and in the wider region.

Table 2.1 Government and corporation approaches to technology transfer

Government	Firm
Technical reports	Direct investment
Technology releases	Joint ventures
Conference, workshops, meetings	Personnel exchange
Personnel exchange	Documentation
Collaborations	Licensing
Industry visits	
Licensing and patents	

Source: Based on Kremic (2003).

TTOs have an important role in shaping a university's relationship with its region and more broadly its society. The activities of TTOs can be wide ranging, as Fraiman (2002) suggests, and can include: student internships, jointly sponsored symposia, joint research projects, guest speakers, executive development (e.g., MBAs), roundtables, joint curricula development, outreach programmes, alumni associations/bodies and research commercialisation workshops. The primary motivation for technology transfer varies by actor. Kremic (2003) states that the primary motivation for government is legal whereas the firm's is profit. Moreover Kremic also argues that the approaches and methods that are adopted by governments and firms to achieve technology transfer differ (see Table 2.1). Governments need to communicate or "broadcast" whereas companies take a more controlled approach to technology transfer. In essence, Siegel et al. (2007) summarise the technology transfer objectives as firms/entrepreneurs seek profit, while TTOs seek to protect and generate revenue for IP, and academic scientists seek to share and disseminate their new knowledge.

Much has been written on technology transfer with significant empirical evidence that is delving deeper into different aspects of university-industry research commercialisation. Technology entrepreneurs are products of university research commercialisation. Typical commercialisation routes for technology entrepreneurs are company formations (spin-outs and spin-ins) and licensing. Irrespective of the commercialisation routes, TTOs are under increasing pressure by what Siegel et al. (2007) describe as "a key strategic choice regarding commercialization of IP: whether to emphasize licensing or spin-offs".

In their comprehensive review Harmon et al. (1997) classified the literature on technology transfer into two groups, namely a rational decision-making perspective and a relationship perspective regarding technology transfer and commercialisation.

2.4.1 Linear Model of Technology Transfer

The studies of this group assume a rational decision-making point of view and regard technology transfer as a process that can, and indeed should, be planned. In these models, inventors and future users of the technology function independently, without coordinating their efforts, until the first negotiations regarding a specific technology when the two parties find one another through a formal search process that is usually mediated by a transfer agent. The majority of these studies focus on the process of technology transfer from the research centre to industry and thus the major goal of these studies is to identify the most efficient methods of administering and facilitating the technology transfer process and organisational forms that facilitate this transfer. This linear model of the innovation process is based on factors such as basic research, applied research, prototype development, market research, product development, marketing and selling.

This linear model has had a significant influence on the organisation of public supports for innovation. Interventions are made at different and specific stages by strengthening public infrastructure and providing incentives to the private sector, which is then expected to transform technology, patents and systems into new products and processes. So, for example, in Ireland, Enterprise Ireland has created an innovation voucher scheme designed to support the initial interaction between firms and academics to further develop new ideas that may result in a process, product, service or network innovation (see Chapter 12).

2.4.2 Non-linear Model of Technology Transfer

The second major group of studies reviewed and categorised by Harmon et al. (1997) takes a different perspective on the technology transfer process, emphasising the relationship aspect of it. This group of studies is primarily made up of non-linear models that emphasise multi-directional linkages, interdependency between hard technology and softer issues of people management and information flows (Mitra and Formica, 1997). A number of perspectives are found in this group of studies.

The modern view of research commercialisation and technology transfer tends to be grouped within the latter. Increasingly there is an awareness of the multitude of factors that can have an impact on the technology process or failure of research to progress on this route (Bozeman, 2000; Friedman and Silberman, 2003a; Scott et al., 2001; Siegel et al., 2003a).

According to Howells and MacKinlay (1999), effective use of technology transfer within a university is based on a number of activities that run in parallel and include:

- Effective monitoring of research and inventive activity that is being generated by the university;
- Accurate identification and selection of research inventions that are seen as valuable and worth protecting in terms of generation of future income;
- Comprehensive technology auditing to pick up non-disclosure of intellectual property being generated by academics and owned by the university;
- Flexibility in decision-making as different technologies and circumstances favour different routes to commercialisation and timing;

- Take-up and negotiation of the selected research and inventions with the research team for the protection and defence of the research involving the establishment of appropriate incentive and exploitation schemes;
- Selection and establishment of the appropriate legal IPR defence mechanisms for research and inventions;
- Appropriate decision-making regarding the long-term IPR exploitation and development route of research and inventions.

Incentives, particularly how royalties from licences are distributed, can enhance technology transfer, where the inventor is allocated an higher percentage of royalty income; this means the technology transfer process is more efficient (see Link and Siegel, 2005). Furthermore, the organisation structure of TTOs and how they engages with different stakeholders does matter in facilitating and enabling research commercialisation (Cunningham et al., 2014). For technology entrepreneurs, being able to effectively and efficiently go through a technology transfer process can be an integral part of the new venture process.

Case Box 2.1   Some TTO Mission Statements

KU Leuven

KU Leuven Research & Development (LRD) is the technology transfer office (TTO) of the KU Leuven Association. Since 1972 a multidisciplinary team of experts [has guided] researchers in their interaction with industry and society and the valorisation of their research results. LRD is a separate entity within the university that aims to promote and support the transfer of knowledge and technology between the university on the one hand, and industry and society on the other hand. In order to do this, LRD offers professional advice about legal, technical as well as business-related issues.[1]

MIT Technology Licensing Office

Our mission is to foster commercial investment in the development of inventions and discoveries flowing from the research at the Massachusetts Institute of Technology and Lincoln Laboratory. We do this through licensing of the intellectual property resulting from our research.[2]

University of Cambridge

Cambridge Enterprise exists to help University of Cambridge inventors, innovators and entrepreneurs make their ideas and concepts more commercially successful for the benefit of society, the UK economy, the inventors and the University.[3]

2.4.3   TTOs and Technology Entrepreneurs

Technology entrepreneurs that are based in a university environment or looking to capitalise on research from university research groups will have to deal with technology transfer offices. TTOs not only serve to protect the IP of the university but also seek the best uses for the research. In essence, as described by Siegel et al. (2003b), "the role taken by most TTOs is to facilitate technological diffusion through the licensing to industry of inventions or intellectual property resulting from university research". However there are a diversity of models and channels for transferring knowledge and technology from the research labs to technology entrepreneurs. Mechanisms through which technology transfer take place include:

- University research sponsored by companies;
- Academic consulting;
- Licensing of university-owned intellectual property to existing companies;
- University support for start-up companies in the form of loans, grants and equity ownership;
- "Mega agreements" between individual companies and universities that cover a range of interactions;
- Research centres and other government-supported efforts to encourage university-industry collaboration; and
- Industry consortia to support university research.

Technology transfer offices can therefore transfer university IP to markets in many different ways. The most common of these tend to be collaborating with businesses on research projects and agreeing at the outset ownership rights on any IP created and making deals with companies to use IPs already developed in university research.

2.5 TECHNOLOGY TRANSFER AND MECHANISMS

There are myriad of definitions about what constitutes a technology transfer (Bozeman, 2000). Technology transfer refers to the process whereby invention or intellectual property from academic research is licensed or conveyed through use rights to a for-profit entity and eventually commercialised (Friedman and Silberman, 2003a, p. 18). Technology entrepreneurs participate in a technology transfer process through different mechanisms depending on the opportunity they are seeking to exploit. To give a sense of the scale of technology transfer, the Association of University Technology Managers (AUTM) has highlighted the economic impact of successful technology transfer on the US economy since 1993. A survey carried out by the AUTM of 157 universities in 2011 showed the generation of more than $1.8 billion in licensing revenue, over 12,000 patent filings and 617 company formations. This illustrates the economic impact and scale of university technology transfer in the United States since the Bayh-Dole Act (1980). Bradley et al. (2013) sum up the progress since passage of the Bayh-Dole Act by stating that "universities have increasingly been engaged in technology transfer. Commercialisation of university-discovered technologies is a driver of economic growth and universities have played a major role in bringing innovative ideas and inventions to market. Technology transfer activities, which were once practiced mainly by such elite universities as MIT, Stanford University, and the University of California system, are now nationwide. Technology transfer can potentially generate revenues for universities, create research connections between academia and industry, and enhance regional economic growth and development".

2.5.1 University-Industry Technology Transfer Process

The technology transfer process from university to industry has some common elements. Each university may include some local variations, but the key stages are common to all technology transfer processes. The sequencing of events in terms of university technology transfer usually begins with a scientific discovery. The scientist then files an invention disclosure with the TTO. Once formally disclosed the TTO simultaneously evaluates the commercial potential of the technology and decides whether to patent the invention, as well as deciding the geographical extent of the patent protection. Such a decision to begin filing a patent is dependent on the resource available to the TTO and the real market potential of the technology. Once the patent is awarded, the TTO will market the technology and in many cases the researcher is involved as they may have developed networks of potential licensees. The final stage involves the negotiation of the licensing agreement, including royalty rates, exclusive and non-exclusive rights and fields of use.

Some technology entrepreneurs may take such licences and begin to build prototypes using complimentary intellectual property. This is further exploited by undertaking market and business-model validation (see Chapters 6 and 7 for further discussions). The typical sequencing of technology development includes:

- Basic research patent;
- Proof of concept/invention;
- Early-stage technology development business-model validation;
- Product development innovation: new firm or program; and
- Production/marketing viable business.

Technology transfer can become complex with more parties involved in the development of the technology, subsequent negotiations and market validation. For technology entrepreneurs, this is a complex, often time-consuming, costly and potentially frustrating process. Nevertheless, Friedman and Silberman (2003a) argue: "University research is a source of significant innovation – generating knowledge, which diffuses to adjacent firms and entrepreneurs". The next section examines commercialisation routes in the context of technology transfer in research and third-level institutions.

2.5.2 Some Specific Mechanisms for Technology Transfer in Third-level Institutions

2.5.2.1 Patents

There is a trend towards an increasing number of patents deposited by higher education institutions. The Bayh-Dole Act in 1980 enabled universities and public research laboratories to patent their own inventions. This trend has spread to European and Asian countries, and governments and industries see the quantity of patents as a proxy indicator of university-industry linkages. The extent of the growth in patenting activities by universities is evidenced by the fact that in the United States, for example, in absolute numbers, the magnitude of patenting by the universities has increased more quickly than the overall trend of general patenting from the 1980s to 1999 (Graff et al., 2001), while in the late 1990s, Henderson et al. (1998) reported the number of patents assigned to universities per research dollar spent at university had more than tripled. In 2011, 5.9 per cent of patent applications to the US Patent office came from universities and higher education institutions with the University of California filing 227 patent; MIT, 179; and University of Texas, 127. Within universities and public research laboratories, the patents are an indication of the number of invention disclosures submitted to the TTO. In 2010, an AUTM survey reported 20,642 invention disclosures from 307 universities and research organisations that participated in the survey, while in Australia the rate of invention disclosures grew from 1,498 in 2009 to 1,705 in 2011 (see Commonwealth of Australia, 2012, p. 14). The persistent challenge for TTOs is selecting the technologies that it will protect by patenting and how best to use these technologies once patents have been granted. Graff et al. (2001) suggest some conditions that can influence the probability that a TTO will patent a technology, such as, if the technology is patentable, is there a clear cost benefit case or when there is an opportunity for a buyer to patent collaboratively. In cases where the TTO does not choose to patent the technology, there may be provisions in place giving the researcher the right to pursue patent protection independent of the TTO. This may result in the researcher or the research team using this to start-up their own business.

2.5.2.2 Licensing

When university research leads to technological innovations, one route to commercialisation is to license the technology to other firms rather than trying to use the technology in a direct way. In essence, licenses are permissions granted by the owner of a piece of intellectual property to another party for the use of the invention. Licenses can be granted on an exclusive basis to a single licensee, thus guaranteeing a strong degree of market exclusivity. So, for example, a drug compound would be licensed exclusively to a company for their use only. Licenses can also be granted non-exclusively to many parties. An example of this is where a software company licenses its technology to multiple parties in the same marketplace or across geographical territories. Figure 2.1 illustrates the technology stages for licensing.

Figure 2.1 Licensing technology stages
Source: Based on G.D. Markman et al. (2005).

Generally, negotiating licensing agreements with universities can be challenging as universities seek to ensure that their IP is protected and to maximise the revenue and the potential application and use of the technology. For research that has been funded through publicly funded research, TTOs can be bound by public good considerations. Such considerations influence the licensing strategy adopted by the university. In addition, universities may negotiation strategic clauses that allow them to refuse licenses to any patented products developed by a licensee.

An AUTM survey in 2010 reported 4,284 licenses executed; 1,078 options executed; with 398 executed licenses containing equity and 38,528 active licenses and options. Frequently cited universities, such as MIT in the United States, Oxford, Cambridge in the UK, and KU Leuven in Belgium, have flexible and supportive arrangements in place to support the licensing of technology. Such an approach has seen a growth in licensing activities. For most universities, they will only earn a modest return from licensing revenues, in the region of 10 per cent of their research expenditures from IP commercialisation, with only a small percentage of universities with high-revenue streams, which in some instances was accounted from royalties from one or two patents, such as Warfin for the University of Wisconsin. Moreover, inventor royalty arrangements can vary between institutions, and Lach and Schankerman (2004), based on data from 102 US universities, note: " … higher inventors' royalty shares are associated with higher licensing income at the university, controlling for other factors. … monetary incentives from inventions have real effects in the university sector."

2.5.2.3 *Company Formation (Start-ups and Spin-offs)*

Start-ups and spin-offs are the focus of many technology entrepreneurs and are another form of the technology transfer that is reported by universities and public research organisations. Company formations have direct impacts on an economy in terms of job creation, securing of funding, etc. Start-ups and spin-offs are often used interchangeably, but Graff et al. (2001) provide some clarity. A spin-off is a company that includes among its founding members a person affiliated with the university, while a start-up firm is one that is not founded by a staff member of the university but is developing technology originating at the university (e.g., licensed technology). Over the last two decades, universities, with the support of alumni, state-supported agencies and other stakeholders, have developed incubation units to support both start-ups and spin-offs or have been involved in the creation of science parks to support company formations as well as more established businesses.

There are several factors that influence the rate of company formations from a university environment. O'Shea et al. (2008) notes that there are four main determinants of university spin-off, including: "the attributes and the personality characteristics of academic entrepreneurs; resource endowments and capabilities of the university; university structures and policies facilitating commercialisation; environmental factors influencing academic entrepreneurship". Other related factors include university policies with respect to royalties, venture funds, the commercial orientation of the university and research eminence (see Di Gregorio and Shane, 2003). Observability and tacitness of knowledge in use, the age of the field, tendency of the market towards segmentation and the effectiveness of patents were found to be important factors in a study by Shane (2003) to determine whether new inventions will lead to company formation.

In 2010, an AUTM survey found that there were 651 start-up companies formed, 498 of which had their primary place of business in the licensing institutions' home state, and there were over 3,657 start-ups still operating by the end of 2010. UK data from the HE BCI Survey over an eight-year period beginning in 2003 shows a steady growth of spin-off companies and their longevity after three years (see Table 2.2). Australian data (see Commonwealth of Australia, 2012) reveals that start-up companies with institutional equity rose from 69 in 2000 to 200 in 2007 and declined to 167 in 2011.

For universities to encourage company formations, Howells and MacKinlay (1999) recommend that universities, with clear guidelines, be proactive in providing information, and if the university owns the IP that protects the innovation or technology that forms the basis for the company, then it needs to jointly discuss and decide at the outset with the researchers or prospective entrepreneurs whether setting up a company is the best option. They also suggest that researchers remain in part-time positions with the university, provide advice to researchers in regard to business set up and management, as well as help set up business plans to ensure survival and growth. Rothaermel et al. (2007) identified key themes that enable company formation: IP; networking activities with external stakeholders by spin-off companies; resources, particularly human capital; and the university system and how it effectively supports technology transfer and particularly company formation. For technology entrepreneurs, these are factors and issues to consider in terms of company formation. Having access to effective supports, well-connected networks and a university system that really encourages technology entrepreneurship are critical environmental factors for technology entrepreneurs.

Table 2.2 UK HE BCI survey 2012

Outputs from UK HEIs	2003–2004	2006–2007	2010–2011
Patent applications	1,308	1,913	2,256
Patents granted	463	647	757
Formal spin-offs established	167	226	268
Formal spin-offs still active after three years	688	844	999

Source: Adapted from HEFCE (2012). Accessed 29 January 2012.

Case Box 2.2   Imperial Innovations

Founded in 1986, Imperial Innovations' initial focus was on IP protection and implementation. By 1997, it began a wholly owned subsidiary of Imperial College and, in 2006, was listed on the Alternative Investment Market on the London Stock Exchange. The focus today is on health care, energy, engineering and the environment. Since 2006, Imperial Innovations has raised £370 million, spent £120 million in spin-outs, formed 142 spin-outs, filed 555 patents and they receive on average 360 invention disclosure per annum.[4] Imperial Innovations provides a range of supports to scientists and researchers to assess the commercial potential of their research and ideas, and for inventors that have research that has market potential, they offer different technology transfer mechanisms to protect and utilise IP.

2.6   STIMULANTS AND BARRIERS TO TECHNOLOGY TRANSFER

There are macro- and micro-level factors that stimulate technology transfer and create the environment that encourages the development of technology entrepreneurs. Many universities have taken deliberate steps to embrace third-mission activities by creating Vice Chancellor positions in Innovation, Research and Industry Engagement. Different titles are used to describe this position, but such roles are part of the top management team of universities. Universities have experimented with new structures and developed cross-thematic research topics to encourage greater interactions among different research groups. Many universities offer commercialisation programmes for aspiring technology entrepreneurs designed to validate their inventions and to provide them with the appropriate skills necessary for company formation or other technology transfer mechanisms. The entrepreneurial university paradigm is being adopted by many universities as a way of responding to the third-mission agenda and to provide students and faculty with an environment that encourages entrepreneurship and innovation. An entrepreneurial university is a natural incubator that, by adopting a coordinated strategy across critical activities (e.g., teaching, research and entrepreneurship), tries to provide an adequate organisational culture in which the university community (e.g., academics, students and staff) can explore, evaluate and implement ideas that could be transformed into social and economic entrepreneurial initiatives (Kirby et al., 2011). Factors that influence technology transfer have been the focus of empirical studies that have focused on the stimulants and barriers to research commercialisation (see Cunningham and Harney, 2006; Cunningham et al., 2014; Harman, 2010). General environmental factors, institutional conditions and the individual characteristics influence technology transfer. Friedman and Silberman (2003a) found that clear university mission statement in relation to technology transfer, a concentration of high technology firms around a university, experience of the TTO and rewards for faculty are factors that influence commercialisation. Harman (2010) in his empirical study found: "By far the most important perceived barrier by technology transfer specialists was lack of funds to support commercialisation activities – both lack of government funding and lack of internal university funding. Next were cultural factors (including the cultural gap between universities and industry, and the lack of entrepreneurial culture among scientists), slow-moving university approval processes and the shortage of relevant skills in research commercialisation offices." Moreover, macro- and micro-level factors influence this transformation for technology entrepreneurs (see Figure 2.2) (Cunningham and Harney, 2006).

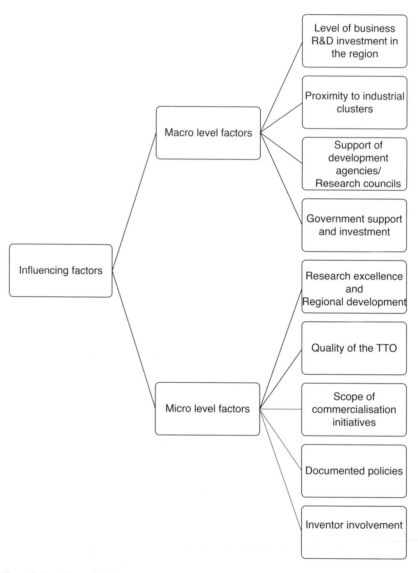

Figure 2.2 Influencing factors: macro and micro factors

2.6.1 Macro-Level Factors

- *The Level of Business Investment in R&D in the Region*: Universities in regions with higher levels of R&D investment are likely to have greater potential and opportunities to develop links with business, exploit university research and creates opportunities for technology entrepreneurship. Regions around universities such as Cambridge, Oxford, Warwick, Grenoble and Louvain have seen a growth in the presence of Multi-National Corporations (MNCs), Small and Medium Enterprises (SMEs) and technology entrepreneurship in their region. For example, the State University of New York (SUNY) has 64 campuses, 24 New York State Small Business Development Centres that supports start-up and existing businesses and over 21,000 research profiles in its SUNY Scholar database; spends over $540 million annually on procurement of products and services; and invests more than $1 billion in research annually through its Research Foundation across the SUNY system. Such an system opens up significant opportunities for technology entrepreneurs.
- *Proximity to Industrial Clusters*: Clusters of economic activity often facilitate strong networking between businesses, universities and local government agencies. Many of these clusters have developed technologically intensive industries where R&D and innovation levels are quite high. As more economic activities are generated, firms begin to make formal and informal connections with universities, public research organisations and knowledge-intensive service providers in the private sector to collaborate with in growing their R&D and new knowledge appropriation capacity. Over time student placement and graduate recruitment into clusters leads to stronger and sustainable linkages. These traditional sources of interaction between universities and enterprises provide a solid foundation for more formalised and strategic linkages. For example, Galway in the West of Ireland has developed a globally competitive industry cluster in medical technologies (see Giblin and Ryan, 2012).
- *Support of Developmental Agencies/Research Councils:* The role and capacity of developmental agencies to support business-university collaboration at a regional level may prove critical in promoting the growth of third-stream activities. Such agencies may have established linkages with businesses in the region and may also be able to provide first-hand expertise, particularly on the more legislative aspects of technology transfer and commercialisation. The Small Business Innovation Research Programme in the United States provides support for technology-orientated firms and entrepreneurs to engage with Federal research on a competitive basis. The Small Business Innovation Research (SBIR) programmes have supported technology entrepreneurship through their various programme to exploit new market opportunities. Another example is the BioInnovate programme in Ireland that is supporting technology entrepreneurs in the medical device sector. This programme is supported by development agencies, such as Enterprise, industry and Irish universities.[5]
- *Government Support and Investment:* Governments can create a supportive context for technology transfer and technology entrepreneurship. In the

United States, President Obama launched the 'Start-up America' initiative "to celebrate, inspire and accelerate high-growth entrepreneurship throughout the nation. This coordinated public/private effort brings together an alliance of the country's most innovative entrepreneurs, corporations, universities, foundations, and other leaders, working in concert with a wide range of federal agencies to dramatically increase the prevalence and success of America's entrepreneurs".[6] In the UK, the government has pursued a strategy of helping UK businesses bring technology to the marketplace through its Technology Assessment Board, using various different mechanisms to support innovative activities in UK businesses.[7] The European Innovation Scorecard from Chapter 1 provides a comparative overview of the level of national government investment in the EU in innovation and entrepreneurship.

2.6.2 Micro-Level Factors

- *Research Excellence & Regional Development:* The quality of scientific excellence provides the basis of technology transfer and opportunities for technology entrepreneurs. There are many measures of university and research excellence such as QS World University Rankings, Higher Times Rankings, and Research Effectiveness Framework in the UK. Such scientific excellence has reputation impacts and does enhance the scope of the university. Moreover, a university's reputation can lead to above average licensing performance (see Sine et al., 2003). University economic impacts can include creation of knowledge, human capital, transfer of know-how, technological innovation, capital investment, regional leadership, infrastructure and regional influence (Goldstein, Maier and Luger, 1995). Universities can have a positive influence over regional development and in turn shape environmental conditions necessary for technology entrepreneurship. In summing up previous studies on economic impacts of universities, Durcker and Goldstein (2007) state: "...the majority of empirical analyses do demonstrate that the impacts of university activities on regional economic development are considerable."
- *Quality of Technology Transfer Office*: Mechanisms for technology transfer will be shaped by the resources, reporting relationships and incentives of technology transfer offices (Bercovitz et al., 2001). Research by Siegel et al. (2003a) notes: "Our empirical results suggest that TTO activity is characterised by constant returns to scale and that environmental and institutional factors explain some of the variation in performance. Productivity may also depend on organizational practices". To improve the effectiveness and ultimately the quality of TTOs, Siegel et al. (2003b) recommend that TTOs focus on organisational and managerial factors. These include "designing flexible university policies on technology transfer, improving staffing practices...encouraging informal relationships and social networks". Institutional research excellence provides the foundation for quality TTOs in terms of performance and productivity. Informal relationships and social networks are effective ways for technology entrepreneurs to gain access to talent and knowledge

that is necessary for their venture or during the company formation process. Figure 2.3 outlines some technology transfer effectiveness criteria developed by Bozeman (2000). In their study of technology transfer efficiency, Anderson et al. (2007) reported no difference in the technology transfer efficiency between US and Canadian universities but differences between US and European universities as well as US and Asian universities.

- *Scope of Commercialisation Initiatives:* TTOs can offer a range of formal and informal initiatives that are designed to engage with potential technology entrepreneurs in marketing and promoting new technologies. These range from hosting showcase events and network meetings around technology areas to hosting entrepreneurs in residence programmes, supporting entrepreneurship and innovation clubs. The scope of activities also includes the scientific fields and the intensity of commercialisation can vary between scientific fields. Siegel et al. (2007) suggest that "university administrators, backed by regional policy makers may also need to make a strategic choice regarding technology field of emphasis".

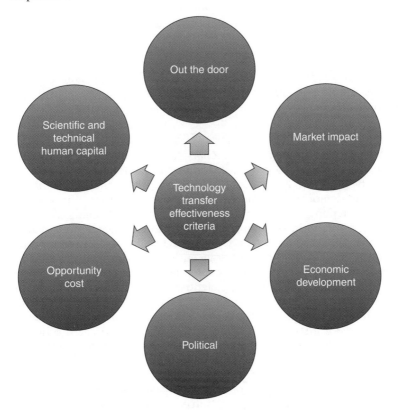

Figure 2.3 Technology transfer effectiveness criteria

Source: Based on Bozeman (2000).

- *Documented Policies:* Clear and well-documented written policies pertaining to most aspects of technology transfer are of real benefit in encouraging commercialisation activities among researchers and in engaging with technology entrepreneurs. Clear policies provide necessary information to potential technology entrepreneurs that are seeking to engage with university TTOs. Lack of clear documentation and policies can create unnecessary tensions and clear policies can be developed in such a way that it does not undermine some degrees of flexibility TTOs need to have in protecting and utilising IP.
- *Inventor Involvement:* The transfer of knowledge from the university to the commercial sector generally requires the active involvement of inventors (Goldfarb and Henrekson, 2003; Meseri and Maital, 2001). In the United States, for example, it has been noted that ideas reach TTOs in primitive states and much of the critical knowledge is often tacit. Jensen and Thursby (2001) found that at least 71 per cent of inventions require further involvement by the academic researcher if they are to be successfully commercialised. Some 48 per cent of the ideas are in proof of concept stage or laboratory scale prototypes (29 per cent) and only 8 per cent are manufacturing feasibility known. A stimulant to successful technology transfer is therefore knowledge and know-how.

2.6.3   Inhibitors to Commercialisation

There are three categories of inhibitors that publicly funded principal investigators/scientists experience – political and environmental, institutional and project based (see Figure 2.4) (Cunningham et al., 2014).

2.6.3.1   *Political and Environmental Factors*

- *Technology transfer policy*: Researchers have to deal with a variety of challenges in relation to project direction and focus, stakeholder demands and IP valuation. For publicly funded researchers, there is an increasing need to demonstrate some technology transfer activities and outcomes in their reporting to their funding agency. This can become an inhibiting factor for them in achieving the appropriate balance between academic publications and an IP-focused approach. Flexible technology transfer policies may mean the technology entrepreneur experiences an efficient technology transfer process in exploiting university IP.
- *Competing stakeholder interests:* Scientists found themselves balancing the competing demands from industry partners and funding agencies, in addition to carrying out the research. Researchers also have to deal with demands of internal stakeholders, particularly if they had other duties such as teaching. The tension comes from having to prioritise these competing demands during the course of the research project.
- *IP Valuation:* The value of IP can impede technology transfer opportunities, but an over-valuation of IP and a conservative managerial approach by a TTO can inhibit the exploitation of technology transfer opportunities that potentially have public, economic or social outcomes. This creates a tension around the independence of IP valuation and whether the TTOs

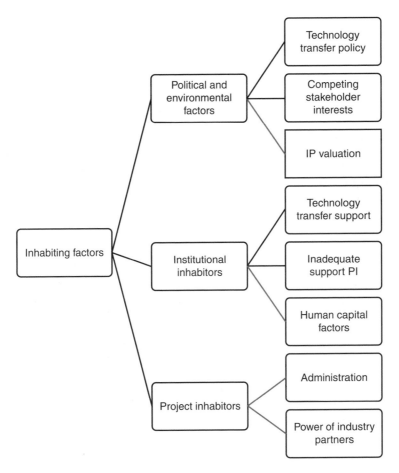

Figure 2.4 Inhibitors to commercialisation

are best placed to carry this out given their primary responsibility of IP protection. IP valuations can have significant influence for technology entrepreneurs during company formation stage.

2.6.3.2 Institutional Inhibitors

- *Technology Transfer Support*: With increasing emphasis by national governments and associated public funding agencies on technology transfer, it is not surprising that scientists experienced limitations in the level of dedicated *technology transfer support* available to them. While scientists recognised the "professionalism" and "dedication" of TTO personnel, some inhibiting factor arose given the lack of expertise in TTOs. Technology transfer inhibiting factors are most acute for researchers who wish to go beyond just protecting the IP and want to commercialise their research through a technology transfer mechanism.

- *Inadequate Support for the Principal Investigator Role*: Researchers who were principal investigators (PIs) were frustrated by the organisational constraints of their institutions, and the experience of the support they received was not "helpful" and was "compliance" based. Publicly funded PIs need some "flexibility" and "proactive" support in delivering on their research objectives. The core source of tension for publicly funded PIs comes when they are encouraged by their institution to seek research funding but after they secure public grants there is inadequate institutional support available. This raises the issue of how institutions should actually support rather than inhibit individual projects and publicly funded PIs. We found that some PIs viewed inadequate PI support as more of a systemic issue to do with the culture of "mentoring" and "nurturing" within the institution.
- *Human Capital Factors*: Recruitment of research officers and career paths for researchers were considered key inhibitors by researchers. The recruitment of research officers was seen as a "crucial task" and one that required significant attention and management. Some researchers found this process "cumbersome" and the time between advertising and filling the post was too long, in some instances up to 18 months. Another key inhibitor was not having a defined career path for researchers, as many researchers experienced high turnover of staff within their teams. This loss of talent and experience could potentially undermine the sustainability of the research effort, and so another challenge for researchers is how best to retain talented people. Some means of retention of researchers included seeking further public fundings or exploring technology transfer mechanisms, particularly start-ups. In reality in the next decade more European researcher will have career paths in industrial settings or as technology entrepreneurs through new venture creation.

2.6.3.3 Project Inhibitors

- *Administration*: The totality of the administration that is required in being a publicly funded researcher is significant and includes personnel issues, technical aspects, project coordination, financial management and collation of information. Researchers experience more of the managerial aspects of the PI role than their research leadership. This creates tension between managing the project from a research leadership perspective – the basis of the award – and research management – project administration.
- *Power of Industry Partners*: The influence that industry has extends from the project conception right through to the project itself, which can be demanding for researchers to deal with. Securing industry partners can be difficult, but maintaining their interest over the duration of the project can be even more so. Furthermore, the mismatch between industry and project timeline can be an inhibiting factor for some researchers, where companies need more immediate outcomes. Moreover, sometimes industrial partners' interest in publicly funded projects can change as key personnel change or as the need of the market changes.

Overall, these inhibitors can have an impact on technology entrepreneurs through technology transfer mechanisms and in their dealing with researchers who research they want to exploit. For technology entrepreneurship to develop and grow between universities and industry, there needs to be flexibility around technology transfer policies and well-developed formal and informal networks that facilitate and enable technology entrepreneurs to access, exploit and leverage new knowledge and resources.

2.7   CHAPTER SUMMARY

Third-mission activities in the form of technology transfer from universities to industry create new opportunities for technology entrepreneurship. Many universities have tailored programmes and supports to encourage entrepreneurship from within their communities and regions. We began by exploring the relationship and linear models of technology transfer. We then focused on technology transfer mechanism and specifically focused on patents, licensing and company formation – start-ups and spin-offs. We concluded the chapter by examining some of the stimulants and barriers to technology transfer from a researcher perspective. In outlining stimulants, we explored some macro- and micro-level factors, and for inhibitors, we presented three categories – political and environmental, institutional and project based.

Case Study 2.1   Allergy Standards Ltd: The Journey From University Incubation

Written by Dr. Grace Walsh, Duesto Business School, Spain.

Trinity Technology and Enterprise Campus is located on an island site in the heart of Dublin, Ireland. Since being purchased by Trinity College in 1999, it has become a knowledge-based company generation and support facility and an integral part of the research function of Trinity College Dublin. One of the internationally successful spin-outs from the university's incubation centre is Allergy Standards Limited (ASL), an international standards and certification body. ASL is "a physician-led global certification company that prepares independent standards for testing a wide range of products to determine their suitability for asthmatics and individuals with associated allergies". The company has developed a series of propriety-testing protocols and suitability specifications for products that when met culminates in the asthma and allergy friendly™ certification mark being awarded. The mark identifies to consumers that the products can be trusted as being rigorously tested to determine suitability for people with asthma and allergies (ASL, a).

The inspiration for founding ASL came to Dr. John McKeon while he was working as a paediatrician in the National Children's Hospital in Tallaght, Dublin. He overheard a nurse telling the mother of a child with asthma about foods that may be asthma-triggers and the mother relaying her confusion about food labelling in the area. "It was then that I saw a need for easy-to-understand asthma and allergy related consumer information", said McKeon (O'Connell, 2010). Dr. McKeon continued to work in Accident and Emergency at the Dublin hospital while exploring the concept of developing a certification programme and went on to found ASL in June 2000. Enterprise Ireland provided the firm with a feasibility grant of €30,000 in 2001, and later in the year, he got a place on the hothouse incubation programme also sponsored by Enterprise Ireland. While participating in the incubator programme, Dr. McKeon was awarded "Lead Entrepreneur Award" by the Irish Prime Minister. The award is a government incentive to help drive the commercialisation of potential business ideas and was based on the quality of the final business plan (ASL, b). These supports encouraged Dr. McKeon to continue with his vision for the company and assured him of the firm's viability. On the funding front, ASL also received €100,000 in seed capital and €300,000 in Business Expansion Scheme (BES) funding (Dromey, 2010). BES is a government initiative, tax-relief incentive scheme that provides tax-relief for investment in certain corporate trades. These initial investments afforded the firm the ability to spend the first three and a half years developing the firm's intellectual property, writing protocols and registering patents (Dromey, 2010).

Another award given to ASL was the Dublin Docklands Innovation Award, the prize aimed at firms based in the Docklands Innovation Park, and it was ASL's strong investment proposal that saw them take the prize in 2003 (ASL, c). On a broader front the initiative is aimed at showcasing the best innovative companies to investors. It also provides early-stage firms with the exposure and networking environment necessary to attract investment. In 2003 ASL also became a finalist for the Equity Network Intertrade Ireland award (ASL, d).

The breathing space afforded by the government supports and initial investments allowed the founders time to develop a comprehensive set of standards and tests. This proved fruitful and ASL's first customer, at the end of 2002, was the Canadian division of the international toy firm Toys "R" Us, securing a deal with Toys "R" Us International a few months later (O'Regan, 2003). This was followed by a major US bedding company, Hollander. In 2005 a partnership agreement with the Asthma and Allergy Foundation in the United States, which backs ASL's certification programme, was signed. A similar agreement was agreed to with the Asthma Society in Canada, a market that accounts for 15 per cent of sales (Dromey, 2010). Further customers include LG, a consumer electronics and appliances conglomerate, which uses ASL's certification on washing machines, and Dyson technology company. Further agreements were secured with Walmart and Target in the United States, which have certified product areas, and a range of asthma-friendly toys for Disney have also been certified by the company (Dromey, 2010).

ASL also began expanding into indoor air testing and circulation, which resulted in a new client pool. In 2009, it was announced that Amway Corporation, a multi-billion dollar global firm, would join their list of customers, and also Forbo Flooring, the largest manufacturer of linoleum in addition to other flooring systems (ASL, e). The same year ASL announced a new strategic partnership with TESTEX, an independent Swiss textile-testing institute with subsidiary companies in Hong Kong and Beijing. This new partnership further strengthens the company's network in the massive Asian market and builds on ASL's existing relationship with manufacturers in China, Japan and South Korea who are keen to have "asthma & allergy friendly" certification on their products sold in Europe and the United States (O'Connell, 2010).

The industry's recognition of the firm's success continued in 2010. ASL was shortlisted for the prestigious Business and Finance Awards for "Enterprise of the Year". The Business and Finance Awards have been recognising excellence in Irish business for almost 40 years, making it the longest running and most coveted business awards programme in Ireland.[8] Opportunities lie ahead for the ASL to roll our more certification programmes across different countries and product lines and to continue the on-going global journey envisioned Dr. Keon.

Case Questions

1. Discuss the macro and micro factors that influence allergy standards.
2. Why is government support and third-level incubation important for allergy standards.
3. Outline some technology transfer strategies that John should consider in growing allergy standards.
4. From your reading of the Allergy Standard Ltd case study, make some recommendations to the founder Dr. John McKeon in relation to how his company could use technology transfer mechanisms from universities to continue to develop his business.

Case Study References

Allergy Standards Limited website, a, accessed online on 30 January 2013 at http://www.allergystandards.com/about-asl.html.

Allergy Standards Limited website, b, accessed online on 30 January 2013 at http://www.allergystandards.com/component/content/article/41.html.

Allergy Standards Limited website, c, accessed online on 30 January 2013 at http://www.allergystandards.com/component/content/article/39.html.

Allergy Standards Limited website, d, accessed online on 30 January 2013 at http://www.allergystandards.com/component/content/article/38.html.

Allergy Standards Limited website, e, accessed online on 30 January 2013 at http://www.allergystandards.com/images/stories/pdfs/Press_Releases_Page/usa_march_2009-st_patricks_day-amway__forbo.pdf.

Business and Finance Awards website. Accessed online on 31 January 2013 at http://www.businessandfinanceawards.ie/awards.html.

Dromey, T. (2010) "'Allergy friendly' certification", *The Irish Examiner*, 11 January 2010. Accessed online on 30 January 2013 at http://www.allergystandards.com/images/stories/pdfs/Press_Coverage/examiner_article.pdf.

Intertrade Ireland website. Accessed online on 31 January 2013 at http://www.intertradeireland.com/newsevents/news/2012/name,14459,en.html.

Irish Revenue website. Accessed online on 30 January 2013 at http://www.revenue.ie/en/tax/it/leaflets/it55.html

O'Connell, C. (2010) "Irish companies provides assurance for asthma and allergy sufferers." Technology Ireland, Jan/Feb 2010. Accessed online on 30 January 2010 at http://www.enterprise-ireland.com/en/Publications/Technology-Ireland/Jan-Feb-2010-Issue.pdf.

O'Regan, E. (2003) "Dublin company patents asthma-friendly brand", *Sunday Business Post*, 16 March 2003. Accessed online on 30 January 2013 at http://www.allergystandards.com/component/content/article/40.html.

Trinity College Dublin website. Accessed online on 30 January 2013 at http://www.tcd.ie/research_innovation/entrepreneurship/campus.php.

2.8 REVISION QUESTIONS

1. Outline the core concepts of the linear and relationship model of technology transfer. What are the implications for technology entrepreneurs?
2. Discuss why third-mission activities are of growing importance and significance to universities and technology entrepreneurs.
3. Describe the basic technology transfer process, and discuss how technology entrepreneurs can exploit it in furthering their technology.
4. Company formations – start-ups and spin-ins – are considered key metrics for universities in supporting entrepreneurship. Discuss how universities can effectively support increased numbers of company formations.
5. Taking a university that you are familiar with, using the identified macro- and micro-level stimulants presented in section 2.6, conduct an analysis. What are you main conclusions and what other stimulant would you include?

2.9 FURTHER READING AND RESOURCES

- A good article to understand the strategic orientation of scientists and conformance in relation to competition for research funding, see Conor O'Kane, James Cunningham, Paul O'Reilly and Vincent Mangematin's "Underpinning Strategic Behaviours and Posture of Principal Investigators in Transition/ Uncertain Environments", Long Range Planning.
- Association of Scientific and Technology Practitioners (ASTP) is a good resource for those interested in university technology transfer data and new developments from technology transfer practitioners in Europe (see http://www.astp.com/).
- Association of University Technology Managers is a good resource for those interested in university technology transfer data and new developments from technology transfer practitioners in North America (see http://www.autm.net/).
- University-Industry Innovation Network is a resource and networking platform fostering the exchange of knowledge and information between universities and industry (see http://www.uiin.org/).
- For academic research on university research commercialisation, search *Journal of Technology Transfer* (see http://link.springer.com/journal/10961).

2.10 NOTES

1. Source: KU Leuven. Accessed online on 2 July 2013 at http://lrd.kuleuven.be/en/mission-statement-knowledge-and-technology-transfer.
2. Source: MIT Technology Licensing Office. Accessed online on the 2 July 2013 at http://web.mit.edu/tlo/www/.
3. Source: Cambridge Enterprises Ltd. Accessed online on the 2 July 2013 at http://www.enterprise.cam.ac.uk/company-information/mission-goals-principles/.

4. Source: Imperial Innovations Innovation Impacts. Accessed online on the 3rd July 2013 at ttp://www.imperialinnovations.co.uk/technology-transfer/innovations-impacts/.
5. http://www.bioinnovate.ie/.
6. http://www.whitehouse.gov/startup-america-fact-sheet.
7. http://www.innovateuk.org/_assets/0511/technology_strategy_board_concept_to_commercialisation.pdf.
8. www.businessandfinanceawards.ie.

2.11 REFERENCES

Anderson, T.R., Daim, R.U and Lavoie, F.F. (2007) "Measuring the Efficiency of University Technology Transfer", *Technovation*, 27: 307–318.

Bercovitz, J., Feldman, M., Feller, I. and Burton, R. (2001) "Organizational Structure as a Determinant of Academic Patent and Licensing Behavior: An Exploratory Study of Duke, Johns Hopkins, and Pennsylvania State Universities", *Journal of Technology Transfer*, 26(1–2): 21–35.

Bozeman, B. (2000) "Technology Transfer and Public Policy: A Review of Research and Theory", *Research Policy*, 29(4–5): 627–655.

Bradley, S.R., Hayter, C.S. and Link, A.N. (2013) "Models and Methods of University Technology Transfer", *Foundations and Trends in Entrepreneurship*, 9(6): 571–650.

Chapple, W., Lockett, A., Siegel, D. and Wright, M. (2004) "Assessing the Relative Performance of UK University Technology Transfer Offices: Parametric and Non Parametric Evidence", Rensselaer Working Papers in Economics, Number 0423.

Conor O'Kane, James Cunningham, Vincent Mangematin and Paul O'Reilly, "Underpinning Strategic Behaviours and Posture of Principal Investigators In Transition/Uncertain Environments, Long Range Planning", Available online 20 September 2013, http://dx.doi.org/10.1016/j.lrp.2013.08.008

Cunningham, J. and Harney, B. (2006) *Strategic Management of Technology Transfer: The New Challenge on Campus.* Oak Tree Press, Cork.

Cunningham, J., O'Reilly, P., O'Kane, C. and Mangematin, V. (2014) "The Inhibiting Factors that Principal Investigators Experience in Leading Publicly Funded Research Projects," *Journal of Technology Transfer*, Forthcoming

Di Gregorio, D. and Shane, S. (2003) "Why Do Some Universities Generate More Start-ups Than Others?" *Research Policy*, 32(2): 209–227.

Durcker, J. and Goldstein, H. (2007) "Assessing the Regional Economic Development Impacts of Universities: A Review of Current Approaches", *International Regional Science Review*, 30(1): 20–46.

Fraiman, N.M. (2002) "Building Relationships Between Universities and Businesses: The Case at Columbia Business School", *Interfaces*, 32(2): 52–55.

Friedman, J. and Silberman, J. (2003a) "University Technology Transfer: Do Incentives, Management, and Location Matter?" *Journal of Technology Transfer*, 28(1): 17.

—— (2003b) "University Technology Transfer: Do Incentives, Management, and Location Matter?" *Journal of Technology Transfer*, 28, 1, 17–30.

Giblin, M. and Ryan, P. (2012) "Tight Clusters or Loose Networks? The Critical Role of Inward Foreign Direct Investment in Cluster Creation", *Regional Studies*, [online], DOI: 10.1080/00343404.2010.497137.

Goldfarb, B. and Henrekson, M. (2003) "Bottom-up versus Top-down Policies towards the Commercialization of University Intellectual Property, *Research Policy*, 32(4): 639–658

Goldstein, H.A., Maier, G. and Luger, M.I. (1995) "The University as an Instruments for Economic and Business Development: US and European Comparisons", in *Emerging Patterns of Social Demand and University Reform: Through a Glass Darkly*, Dill, D.D. and Sporn, D. (eds), Elmsford, NY: Pergamon, 105–133.

Graff, G., Heiman, A., Zilberman, D., Castillo, F. and Parker, D. (2001) *Universities, Technology Transfer, and Industrial R&D.*

Harman, G. (2010) "Australian University Research Commercialisation: Perceptions of Technology Transfer Specialists and Science and Technology Academics", *Journal of Higher Education Policy and Management*, 32(1): 69–83.

Harmon, B., Ardishvili, A., Cardozo, R., Elder, T., Leuthold, J., Parshall, J., Raghian, M. and Smith, M. (1997) "Mapping the university technology transfer process", *Journal of Business Venturing*, 12(6): 423–434.

HEFCE (2012) Accessed 29 January 2012, http://www.hefce.ac.uk/news/newsarchive/2012/ name,73740,en.html.

Henderson, R., Jaffe, A. and Trajtenberg, M. (1998) "Universities as a Source of Commercial Technology: A Detailed Analysis of University Patenting, 1956–1998", *Review of Economics and Statistics*, 80(1): 119–127.

Howells, J. and MacKinlay, C. (1999) "Commercialisation of University Research in Europe", Report to the Expert Panel on the Commercialisation of University Research for Advisory Council on Science and Technology, Ontario, Canada.

Jensen, R. and Thursby, M. (2001) "Proofs and Prototypes For Sale: The Tale of University Licensing", *American Economic Review*, 91(1): 240–259.

Kirby, D.A, Guerrero, M. and Urbano, D. (2011) "The Theoretical and Empirical Side of Entrepreneurial Universities: An Institutional Approach", *Canadian Journal of Administrative Sciences,* 28: 302–316.

Kremic, T. (2003) "Technology Transfer: A Contextual Approach", *Journal of Technology Transfer*, 28, 149–158.

Lach, S. and Schankerman, M. (2004) "Royalty Sharing and Technology Licensing in Universities", *Journal of European Economic Association,* 2(2–3): 252–264.

Lambert, R. (2003) *Lambert Review of Business-University Collaboration: Final Report*. London: HM Treasury.

Link. A.N. and Siegel, D.S. (2005) "Generating Science Based Growth: An Econometric Analysis of the Impact of Organizational Incentives on University Industry Technology Transfer", *European Journal of Finance*, 11: 169–182.

Markman, G.D., Phan, P.H., Balkin, D.B and Gianiodis, P.T. (2005) "Entrepreneurship and University Based Technology Transfer", *Journal of Business Venturing,* 20: 241–263.

Meseri, O. and Maital, S. (2001). "A Survey Analysis of University-Technology Transfer in Israel: Evaluation of Projects and Determinants of Success", *Journal of Technology Transfer*, 26(1): 115–125.

Mitra, J. and Formica, P. (1997) *Innovation and Economic Development.* Dublin: Oak Tree Press.

O'Shea, R.P., Chugh, H. and Allen, T.J. (2008) "Determinants and Consequences of University Spinoff Activity: A Conceptual Framework", *Journal of Technology Transfer*, 33: 653–666.

OECD (2003) *Turning Business Into Science: Patenting and Licensing at Public Research Organisations.* Paris: OECD.

Rothaermel, F.T., Agung, S.D. and Jiang, L. (2007) "University Entrepreneurship: A Taxonomy of Literature", *Industrial and Corporate Change*, 16(4): 691–791.

Scott, A, Steyn, G., Geuna, A., Brusoni, S. and Steinmueller, E. (2001) "The Economic Returns to Basic Research and the Benefits of University–Industry Relationships: A Literature Review and Update of Findings", Report for the Office of Science and Technology by SPRU – Science and Technology Policy Research.

Shane, S. (2003) *A General Theory of Entrepreneurship.* Cheltenham: Edward Elgar.

Siegel, D.S., Veugelers, R. and Wright, M. (2007) "Technology Transfer Offices and Commercialization of University Intellectual Property: Performance and Policy Implications", *Oxford Review of Economic Policy,* 23(4): 640–660.

Siegel, D.S., Waldman, D. and Link, A. (2003a) "Assessing the Impact of Organizational Practices on the Relative Productivity of University Technology Transfer Offices: An Exploratory Study", *Research Policy*, 32: 27–48.

Siegel, D.S., Waldman, D.A., Atwater, L.E. and Link, A.N. (2003b) "Commercial Knowledge Transfers from Universities to Firms: Improving the Effectiveness of University-Industry Collaboration", *Journal of High Technology Management Research*, 14: 111–133.

Sine, W.D., Shane, S. and Di Gregorio, D. (2003) "The Halo Effect and Technology Licensing: The Influence of Institutional Prestige on the Licensing of University Inventions", *Management Science,* 49(4): 478–496.

2.12   GLOSSARY OF TERMS

Company Formation: Start-up and Spin-offs companies from public or private universities.

Inhibitors to Commercialisation: Factors that prevent or limit technology transfer activities.

Licensing: Permission granted by an owner of intellectual property to another party for the use of an invention.

Linear Model: A technology transfer where two parties find one another through a formal section process.

Macro-level factors: External environmental factors that influence technology transfer.

Micro-level factors: Organisational factors that influence technology transfer.

Patents: The legal protection given to an inventor for knowledge novelty.

Project inhibitors: Factors within a funded project that prevent or limit technology transfer activities.

Proof of Concept: Process by which entrepreneurs validate their business idea.

Stimulants and Barriers to Technology Transfer: External, internal and individual conditions that are necessary to or that can migrate against technology transfer.

Technology Transfer: Term used to describe how intellectual property or know-how is transferred from one organisation or individuals to another organisation or individuals.

Technology Transfer Process: Process by which technology is transferred from public or private university or public research laboratory to a third-party organisation.

Technology Transfer Mechanisms: Different ways intellectual property or know-how is transferred from one organisation or individuals to another organisation or individuals including patents, licences and company formations.

Third-Mission Activities: Used to describe the research commercialisation and knowledge transfer activities of public and private universities and public research organisations.

Chapter 3

TECHNOLOGY ENTREPRENEURS AND NEW TECHNOLOGY VENTURES

3.1 LEARNING OBJECTIVES

This chapter explores three areas with respect to technology entrepreneurs and new technology ventures. We begin by exploring the different definitions of entrepreneurship and then examine how technology entrepreneurs are different from other types of entrepreneurship. We then turn our focus to examining the characteristics of technology entrepreneurs. We present the common characteristics of entrepreneurships and technology entrepreneurs to explore the commonalities and differences. We conclude the chapter by outlining the motivations and entrepreneurial intent of entrepreneurs and technology entrepreneurs.

After reading this chapter, you will be able to:

1. Define entrepreneur and technology entrepreneur;
2. Understand the common characteristics of entrepreneurs and technology entrepreneurs;
3. Describe and explain the motivations of technology entrepreneurs; and
4. Understand the psychological characteristics of entrepreneurship.

3.2 CHAPTER STRUCTURE

The core elements of this chapter are as follows:

- Introduction
- Defining the Entrepreneur and Technology Entrepreneurs
- Technology Entrepreneurs' Characteristics
- Motivations and Intentions
- Chapter Summary
- Case Study – Rovio Entertainment: The Angry Birds Creators
- Revision Questions

- Further Reading and Resources
- References
- Glossary of Terms

3.3 INTRODUCTION

Becoming an entrepreneur is now considered a socially acceptable career path in many societies. Economies need entrepreneurs to support economic activity and growth. For those considering the entrepreneurial route, it is a significant move where they have total responsibility over their idea and in bringing it to the market. They also have to deal with fear and uncertainty as to whether their idea will make it in competitive market places. Consideration must be given to the level of risk and the capital they need in order to realise their idea. This can involve investing personal savings, appropriating financial support from family and friends, as well as availing of any state supports to get from idea stage to launching the product or service into a market place. The entrepreneurial process stretches the capabilities of entrepreneurs in terms of skills, decision-making and business acumen. For technology entrepreneurs the danger is having exclusive focus on the product or service without due consideration to whether it addresses a real market problem with customers who would be willing to pay for it. The excitement around the technology can mean that technology entrepreneurs often neglects robust market-validation (see Chapter 7) and do not develop an appropriate business model to sell their product to the key customer (see Chapter 6). In many cases technology entrepreneurs can lack knowledge and skills around strategy, marketing and finance and learn by doing as they bring their ideas through to a viable product or service. The success of any venture can depend on a variety of external factors such as market and economic conditions, reaction of competitors, regulations and other products and services. The success of the venture can also be shaped by the entrepreneur as Baron (2004) notes: "the decision they make, the strategies they develop, the style of leadership they exercise..."

3.4 DEFINING THE ENTREPRENEUR AND TECHNOLOGY ENTREPRENEURS

Is an app developer a technology entrepreneur? Is a web developer using WordPress as a content management system a technology entrepreneur? Is a social media consultant a technology entrepreneur? Is an existing business that moves to selling products online a technology entrepreneurship? Is an academic seeking to spin-out a biotechnology company based on their research a technology entrepreneur? Within the entrepreneurship literature there is a myriad of definitions about entrepreneurship. Richard Cantillon (1979), an Irish-born French economist, has been credited with the first use of the term *entrepreneur*. Beginning with his definition of entrepreneurship, he described them as "the agent who purchases the means of production and combines them into marketable products". In his definition of entrepreneurship, he focused on the individual – the agent – and process – the means – by which what we now term "value" can be created for the customer; that is what Cantillon described as a "marketable product". Let us take Dyson as an example, who created a new design for vacuum cleaners, which used dust bags and the traditional suction system that had not really changed for many decades since Hoover's original products. Dyson designed their vacuum cleaners using a dust bag free system, focusing on improving manoeuvrability using their ball technology and improving the cleaning process for users. As well as the value they created with these innovations, they also designed their vacuum cleaners for homes with pets and their products are certified asthma and allergy friendly. From the initial canister product, they designed a project range including upright, handheld/cordless and groom tools for dogs. All of the products in their own right are addressing real customer problems. The "means" as Cantillon describes involves what Dyson (2013) describes as 550 tests, which involved the following: "Hoses are contorted and stretched. Cleaner heads are slammed into iron table legs. Performance is tested in temperatures as low as -4°F in an environmental chamber. Things haven't changed all that much though. Every 100th bin off the production line is whacked with a hammer just to make sure". Schumpter (1965) simply defined the "entrepreneur as individuals who exploit market opportunity through technical and/or organization innovation".

Other definitions of entrepreneurship emphasise the different aspects of the entrepreneurial experience, the individuals, the opportunities as well as the risks and returns. Drucker (1985) argues that "The entrepreneur, by definition, shifts resources from areas of low productivity and yield to areas of higher productivity and yield. Of course, there is a risk the entrepreneur may not succeed". In this definition Drucker emphasises the return and risk associated with an opportunity. Sometimes entrepreneurs focus on the positive aspects of the opportunity, the ability to shape and influence a market place. They can underestimate the true costs and the length of time it takes to get a product to the market, or the cost of getting product samples to customers may be higher than anticipated. So, for example, an app developer not only has to develop an app that will sell to a large customer base but one that will create repeat customers in terms of other related apps. The developer also has to weigh up the costs of the various routes to the market to connect and sell the app to a large customer base. In essence, they have to weigh up the risks, the cost of capital, time and effort against the rewards that they will attain over a period of time. In many sectors entrepreneurs don't succeed as we have seen in Chapter 1 – in the United States culturally this is seen as a positive rather than a negative.

Kuratko (2014, p. 3) defined entrepreneurs as simply: "individuals who recognize opportunities where others see chaos, contradictions and confusion. They are aggressive catalysts for change within the marketplace". Entrepreneurship is about creating something new and taking a proactive and dynamic approach in persuading individual consumers and market segments of the need for something new. It also requires a degree of risk taking. It may mean giving up income, a stable career path and large organisational support to pursue new venture creation. The ability to act on the idea is a significant step for entrepreneurs to make. In essence, entrepreneurs are able to distinguish a market opportunity and then act to take advantage of it. For technology entrepreneurs, these two issues are important considerations. In terms of pitching ideas, technology entrepreneurs have to consider making it as accessible as possible to specialists and non-specialists stakeholders. The use of appropriate language to describe the overall vision, the actual benefits and also describing the core offering is vitally important. For Vserv.Mobi, an India-based technology company named by Techcircle and one of India's 20 hottest technology start-ups in 2012, they position themselves as a "pioneering global ad network" based on their global team and coverage. They describe themselves as "at the forefront of the Mobile Advertising revolution, in turn being evangelists, thought leaders and pioneers in this space. With premium App inventory on both Feature phone and Smart phone, we offer unparalled reach to a wide demographic" (Vserv Mobi, 2013). To realise this position, they have assembled a management team and have secured venture capital (VC) support from IDG Venture, one of India's top technology VC firms.

The growth in entrepreneurial activity in many economies and regions (see Chapter 1) has been reflected in the rise of journal papers and books on the topic. In 1988, Sexton was one of the first to begin to question the growth of entrepreneurship research in terms of quality and quantity, and by the early 1990s, Gartner (1990), among others, argued for the need to understand the characteristics of entrepreneurship and for the development of a solid theoretical basis for the field. One of the challenges for the field of entrepreneurship has been reaching a common definition. However progress has been made in agreeing on common tenants such as the recognition of the individual and their ability to learn, create, develop value and that the environment stimulates the rate of entrepreneurship (see Bruyat and Julien, 2000). During the 1980s, studies emerged on the attempts to build typologies of characteristics based on venture strategies, as in the case of Hoy and Carland (1983), or on motivations (Dubini, 1989). One of these categorisations has been focused on academic entrepreneurs, which Brennan et al. (2007) define as someone who "engages in related entrepreneurial endeavours, as an adjunct to their academic activities". In essence, within the academic literature as Oviatt and McDougall (2005) note: "The definition of entrepreneurship, however, is a matter of continuing debate and evolution".

So how do technology entrepreneurs differ from other categories of entrepreneurship? Within the entrepreneurship field there has been much debate about entrepreneurial intent, the entrepreneurial process and the supports that entrepreneurs need to move effectively from ideas to actualisation and implementation. While much progress has been made on deepening our understanding of entrepreneurship from an entrepreneurial practice perspective, from the mid-1980s onwards there was growing evidence of what we now term "technology entrepreneurship" and "start-ups". This growth was driven by technology itself and its application across many industry settings, which was facilitated in part by US public investment in technology platform programmes. Another driver was the Bayh-Dole Act 1980 (see Chapter 2) that enabled universities and public research laboratories to commercialise their research. Economic factors and the returns investors were accruing meant that they were seeking even higher returns from taking higher levels of risk. Technology-based firms offered good returns and opportunities for growth but carried higher levels of risk. Gans and Stern (2003) reinforce this growth phenomenon as: "The past two decades have witnessed a dramatic increase in investment in technology entrepreneurship – the founding of small, start-up firms developing inventions and technology with significant potential commercial application. Because of their youth and small size, start-up innovators usually have little experience in the market for which their innovations are most appropriate, and they have at most two or three technologies at the stage of potential market introduction. For these firms, a key management challenge is how to translate promising technologies into a stream of economic returns for their founders, investors and employees. In other words, the main problem is not so much invention but commercialisation".

Reflecting on the changes in entrepreneurship and the technological orientation of start-up businesses, in 2003 *Research Policy* published a special issue on Technology Entrepreneurship edited by Scott Shane and Sankaran Venkataraman, which reflected contributions to conferences they ran on technology entrepreneurs in 2000 and 2001. The focus of the special issue was on the "interface of the study of entrepreneurship and technological innovation". In summarising the papers in the special issue, Shane and Venkataraman (2003) argue that "in contrast to the traditional literature in entrepreneurship, which is person-centric, these papers emphasise the role of technology, technical systems, and institutions in the founding processes of firms. The policies at major research universities have a significant effect on the propensity of entrepreneurs to found firms to exploit university intentions". Furthermore from this special issue some interesting perspectives emerged that highlighted some unique features of technology entrepreneurship, including:

- Context matters in the formation of technology entrepreneurship companies. From Chapter 1, we see that rates of entrepreneurship vary from country to country but that there are locations in the world, such as Silicon Valley in the United States, that have a concentration of technology entrepreneurship and companies that are supported by a vibrant eco-system.
- The entrepreneurial process or "founding process" is ad hoc and emergent, and technology entrepreneurs do not follow traditional prescriptive models of strategy development and business initiation. The process is improvised and non-linear.
- The danger for technology entrepreneurs is that the technology focus that they have may constrain the business. For example, a software company using a content management system for web page development, which is on the decline, potentially limits future growth and makes the company path dependent on a particular technology.
- The development of technology entrepreneurship is linked to technology management, technology systems and knowledge flows as well as complementary assets – marketing, distribution, manufacturing and patent protection. This has meant that many technology entrepreneurs

often begin with developing the technology strategy and then move to business strategy and modelling. By having a clear technology strategy they can interface with business modelling (see Chapter 6) and market research (see Chapter 7) to validate the core offering and the potential opportunity.

Moreover, Evan (1995, p. 11) argues that the basis of a technology firm is centred around the skills of the individual or team, technology and knowledge base they engage with. It is this combination that supports the implementation of entrepreneurial ideas into technology-based products, processes and services. Furthermore within the entrepreneurship literature there has been a focus on new technology-based firms as well as technology entrepreneurship as outlined. While there is no universal definition of new technology-based firms, Bollinger et al. (1983) suggest they are distinguished by small number of founders, being independent from larger firms and "the primary motivation for founding such enterprises should be to exploit a technically innovative idea....it should be the first time this particular application is being used". Jones-Evans (1995) distinguished four typologies of technology-based entrepreneurs as research, research producers, producer technical, user and opportunist. Different explicit policy initiatives have been put in place in Europe to support the technology-based firms and entrepreneurs. These include science parks, increasing the supply of doctoral students, linkages between universities and technology-based firms, direct governments support and support services (Storey and Tether, 1998). Ultimately, the success of the new ventures will depend on multiple factors from external economic conditions to the actions of the entrepreneur. However, new technology-based ventures do achieve higher growth rates that other firm categories (Almus and Nerlinger, 1999).

Case Box 3.1   Irish Support for Research Commercialisation for Third-level Researchers

One of the remits of Enterprise Ireland, one of Ireland's state develop agencies responsible for supporting entrepreneurs, high-growth firms and third-level researchers. In 2006 Enterprise Ireland began the implementation of *Technology Transfer Strengthening Initiative* to support research commercialisation from third-level institutions to Irish-based companies and firms not based in Ireland. This initiative resulted in 316 licences; 86 spin-outs; 1,566 invention disclosure; and 575 patent applications between 2007–2010. Some 32 per cent of licences went to academic spin-out firms. To support on-going research commercialisation from third-level institutions, Enterprise Ireland offers a commercialisation fund for the exploitation of market opportunities with new technologies, which is open to all third-level researchers in science and engineering. Furthermore, Enterprise Ireland runs an *Innovation Voucher* scheme, which provides opportunities for SMEs to work with third-level researchers on business challenges and opportunities. Another scheme to encourage greater commercialisation is that *Innovation Partnership* will afford researchers the opportunity to collaborate with companies with a particular focus new product development.

3.5 TECHNOLOGY ENTREPRENEURS CHARACTERISTICS

Contextual factors influence the rate of entrepreneurship in a region and economy. Social characteristics, socio-economic development and the unregistered economy all have a bearing on entrepreneurship and new venture creation (Reynolds, 1991). Different contextual factors shape the characteristics and categories of entrepreneurs within an economy and society. Social norms, attitudes, perceived feasibility and credibility contribute to entrepreneurial potential (Krueger and Brazeal, 1994). In a study of entrepreneurs in India, Turkey and the United States, Gupta and Fernandez (2009) found that "competent, strong need for achievement, self-reliant, curious, intelligent and logical" attributes were evident in all three countries, but they also found some differences in the attitudes towards entrepreneurs in these countries. However, given the mixture of levels of technological skills and knowledge of technology entrepreneurs in these three countries, they share some common characteristics with other categories of entrepreneurs. There are some distinct common characteristics and personal characteristics of entrepreneurs (see Figure 3.1).

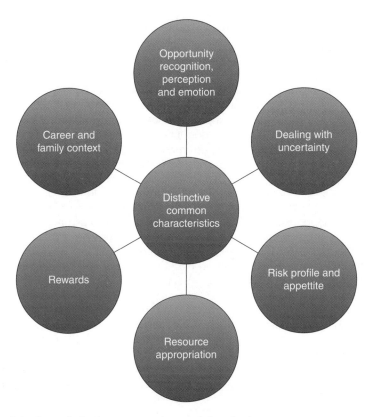

Figure 3.1 Some distinctive common characteristics of entrepreneurs

- *Opportunity Recognition, Perception and Emotions*: A key characteristic of all entrepreneurs is the ability to recognise opportunities for economic returns. This opportunity recognition comes from different experiences, knowledge, and networks or other experiences of entrepreneurs. Education, networks, personal wealth and motivation all have an influence on how entrepreneurs recognise an opportunity and how they convert that recognition into a new business for economic returns. In exploring opportunity recognition of entrepreneurs, Baron (2004) notes that the "entrepreneurs' decisions to found new ventures often stem from their belief that they have identified an opportunity no one else has yet recognized and so can benefit from being first to enter the marketplace". Furthermore Baron (2004) suggests three distinctive features of opportunities, namely – "concept of newness", "being bona fide" and "novelty or uniqueness". Entrepreneurs' perception of an opportunity contributes to opportunity recognition. This perception is developed from picking up signals from the external environment from dealings with different actors in the marketplace – customers, suppliers, competitors and regulators coupled with the entrepreneurs' cognitive and personal characteristics. The cognitive perspective is an area of growing interest among entrepreneurship scholars (see Gregoire et al., 2011). For technology entrepreneurs, Shane (2000) found that they combined knowledge, experiences and problems, and this came before the technology.

  Coupled with entrepreneurial recognition and perception is the entrepreneurial emotion that Cardon et al. (2012) define as: "the affect, emotions, moods, and/or feelings – of individual or a collective – that are antecedent to, concurrent with, and/or a consequence of the entrepreneurial process, meaning the recognition/creation, evaluation, reformulation, and/or the exploitation of a possibility". Moods and feelings play a role in how entrepreneurs cognitively recognise, interpret and evaluate an opportunity. For some entrepreneurs founding a business is a hugely personal and emotion experience where they see the venture as an extension of their family. Such an emotional attachment to a venture may cloud their judgement in making strategic choices about the development and growth of their venture. Opportunity recognition may come from customers' problems where existing companies are not addressing the problems that customers are facing or from a particular technology field or application. For BehavioSec,[1] a university spin-off based in Lapland and founded in 2009, saw an opportunity to develop more sophisticated authentication products based on their research. By 2013 BehavioSec had developed authentication products that enhanced security for enterprise, mobile and web applications. The authentication products are meeting the increasing demands in financial services or other market sectors for additional layers of security to protect enterprise systems and customers. In summary, their product "monitors the environment and interactions such as typing rhythm or mouse patterns, our technology is able to recognize it someone other than the intended user is operating the device. If a security breach is detected additional security measures can be carried out to prevent fraud and stop identity theft". (BehavioSec, 2013, http://www.behaviosec.com/).

- *Resource Appropriation*: During the founding process period and beyond, entrepreneurs of all types have an ability to procure all manner of resources to bring their ideas to fruition and implementation. Soft resource appropriation might include securing professional and mentoring support from existing entrepreneurs in different industry sectors or, where they have a deficit of skills – in marketing, for example – they would procure this from their own networks or based on recommendations. In some instances they may barter their expertise to gain the soft resources that they need during new venture formation stage. Entrepreneurs can be highly effective in securing capital to invest in their business beyond personal resources. However Hogan and Huston (2005) found that equity was the primary source of external finance. They will avail of State supports such as entrepreneurship programmes, grants and investments to support the development of their business. Also entrepreneurs have an ability to secure customers or their interest during the market-validation phase to potentially lock in future sales. In essence, entrepreneurs have the ability to spot opportunities and to procure all the necessary resources from a variety of networks and sources during and beyond the foundation process. The reality for most entrepreneurs during the early stages of foundation is that they don't have resources in place, and they have to be very innovative in the manner in which they secure the necessary resources to survive.
- *Dealing with Uncertainty*: All entrepreneurs, irrespective of type, have to deal with significant levels of uncertainty. From an external environment perspective uncertainties can centre on whether there is a demand for their product or service, will the customers pay market value, or will the product or service deliver on the unique selling points communicated to the customer. More general uncertainities will relate to general economic condition such as consumer spending, interest rates, taxation, etc. Internal uncertainties can present themselves across a range of issues such as funding, cash flow, human resources, operations around securing the expertise to deliver the product or service and reaching required operating standards and procedures. These uncertainties can mean that the entrepreneur may be challenged to put in place operational-level strategies to deal with these uncertainties. Successful entrepreneurs possess the ability to manage effectively such uncertainities.
- *Risk Profile and Appetite*: Starting up a business is a risk. It requires capital from personal funds, family and friends or investors such as state agencies and venture capital funds. During the founding process, the entrepreneur just does not know if the business will be a success or not. Conducting market research, validating business models and the capital structure of the business will help the entrepreneur to deal with the risks associated with the business. Making the idea a reality and actually doing the different activities in setting up a business is when entrepreneurs feel the risk and uncertainty the most. Ward (2004) neatly captures this as: "In addition to being able to generate ideas and recognize good one when they see them, entrepreneurs presumably ought to have high levels of intrinsic motivation, belief enough in their ideas to push them even

in the face of negative feedback, at least some expectation of external rewards, and a capacity to persuade other of their worth".

The risk profile for different industry sectors can vary depending on capital requirements. For example, a software development company may have lower capital requirements than a medical device company that is seeking to develop and take a product through a clinical trial phase compared to the entrepreneur that is setting up a small coffee shop. Entrepreneurs make their own judgement as to the level that they are comfortable with as they go through the founding process. Entrepreneurs have slightly higher risk tolerance but can perceive it as lower. As a venture evolves and survives the "valley of death", the risk profile and appetite of the business and the entrepreneur may change. Entrepreneurs will gauge risk differently through this period. If a business does not survive, the entrepreneur has to make calculations like how much personal capital would be lost as well as the potential avenues of future employment within the same industry. This is an issue addressed in a study by Naire and Pandey (2006) where they found "some evidence that the more economically better-off a family, the greater the chance of its embarking on entrepreneurial ventures and succeeding in them". Stewart and Roth (2001) in their study of risk propensity between entrepreneurs and managers found "that entrepreneurs have a somewhat higher risk propensity than do managers". In summary, the entrepreneur has to cognitively weigh up the capital risk, and, in the event of the business not being successful, the social and capital costs associated with failure.

- *Rewards*: The primary motivation for the majority of entrepreneurs is not financial, but to challenge themselves to see if they can build a business based on an opportunity that they see. Amit et al.'s (2001) study reaffirmed this again and showed that money is not a key motivation in deciding to create a new technology business. Moreover they argue that entrepreneurs don't always choose a career structure that will maximise their personal wealth and argue that "money does not matter to decision to found new ventures, the pattern of results is quite persuasive". If the business is successful the entrepreneur benefits in terms of return on investment for the initial capital investment and a stable income. However, Carter (2011) argues that "the financial rewards for entrepreneurship are multifaceted and include different types and amounts of rewards at different stages of the business life cycle. How the components of rewards collectively contribute to economic well-being and how variance may occur over the course of the business life cycle has yet to be determined". Other rewards can range from providing opportunities for skilled workers to join the company, contributions to providing in kind support or financial support for social initiatives or activities.
- *Career and Family Context*: Career stage and career development can influence the decision to form a new venture. This factor can be shape with respect to career ambitions and goals. In essence this comes down to the ambition and achievement needs of an individual (see section 3.6). Moreover, the economic circumstances of an individual can also influence the decision to pursue an entrepreneurial career. Furthermore, in

Table 3.1 Family system characteristics

Transitions	Resources	Norms, attitudes, values
Marriage	Financial	Norms regarding family member interaction
Divorce	Human	Attitude towards work and family
Childbirth	Social	Instrumental and terminal value
Employment	Physical	
Retirement	Informational	
Death	Time	

Source: Based on Aldrick and Cliff (2003).

Table 3.1, Aldrick and Cliff suggest that family system characteristics have a bearing on all aspect of new venture creations, such as family composition and roles and relationships. In their model of family system characteristics they include resources, norms, attitudes, values, and transitions.

Beyond these common characteristics, there are personal entrepreneurial-based factors that influence the development of technology entrepreneurs within economies. Some of these characteristics are common with other categories of entrepreneurship. In an early empirical study of technology entrepreneurship and technology-based firms on Route 128 in Boston, Sirbu et al. (1976) found common characteristics. Such founder characteristics included entrepreneurial family background; high levels of education (to Master's level), young average age (32), strong technical skills and high achievement needs. With respect to firm characteristics, the firms possessed attributes denoting high levels of technology transfer experience, and a strong focus on human capital and marketing. Based on an empirical study of Swedish and Norwegian technology-based firms Aspelund et al. (2005) found that the newness or radical nature of the technology and the entrepreneurial team are significant predictors of survival.

- *Work Experience*: Previous work experience has bearing on new venture formation in terms of sector, the formation of the management team and the overall ambition of the business venture. For some technology entrepreneurs, previous work experience may have focused exclusively on the technical and operational aspects. Over time, some technology entrepreneurs may have progressed in different company contexts to more middle- or senior-management roles, which expands their skills, knowledge and experiences around the strategic issues of a business. Jones-Evans (1995) found in his study of technology entrepreneurs that "over thirds...hand one type of occupational background" while the other third had other occupational experience. In some cases, technology entrepreneurs may have not had any significant managerial experience. Take UK teenager Nick D'Aloisio, who at 15 years of age created the Summly app that summarises news stories and was bought by Yahoo in March 2013 for a multi-million pound deal.[2] Previous work experience shapes how they manage a new start-up, the types of resources they appropriate for the business and how they cope with challenges, operational, managerial and strategic, in ensuring their business survives the first three years, or what is termed the "valley of death". Moreover, Marvel and Lumpkin (2007) note that for technology entrepreneurs the "breadth in work experience provides access to new information that facilities opportunity recognition.... variation in market experience provides access to different types of information that may be used in the discovery process". Experience matters and does have positive impacts for technology entrepreneurs in terms of new start-ups and the ultimate success of the business. The more experience that technology entrepreneurs have, the more they have to draw on when they are launching their business (Casson, 1995). This is further reinforced by a study of technology ventures by Colombo and Grilli (2005) that concluded: " it is the technical work experience of founders as opposed to their commercial work experience that determines growth. The fact that within the founding team there are synergistic gains from the combination of the complimentary capabilities of founders relating to (i) economic-managerial and scientific-technical education and (ii) technical and commercial industry-specific work experiences". Such experiences can help the technology entrepreneur deal more effectively with uncertainties around the opportunity they are going to exploit with the skills and knowledge that they have acquired.

- *Educational Attainment*: For technology entrepreneurs, an expert knowledge of the technical or technology domain is a must. For many successful technology entrepreneurs this forms a cornerstone for their start-up. This educational attainment might be gained through formal education up to third-level and on-going professional development activities. Others might have gone through formal training and certification programmes run by certified trainers and organisations, in programming languages, for example. In general, there is growing evidence that entrepreneurs, irrespective of category, are more highly educated than other categories of workers. This educational attainment not only provides technology entrepreneurs with expert knowledge but also other skills and access to networks that can support them for a business start-up. For example in a study of Canadian biotech firms, Baum et al. (2001) discovered that founders had Masters or higher qualifications. This educational attainment as well as work experience was further reaffirmed by Colombo et al. (2004) who state: "the human capital of entrepreneurs measured by several indicators of educational attainment and work experience turns out to have a crucial influence on start-up size". Mark Pincus, the co-founder of Zynga, one of the leading online games companies, graduated with a B.Sc. in Economics from Wharton and an MBA from Harvard Business School.
- *Age*: The Global Entrepreneurship Monitor (GEM) provides some insights into the age profile of entrepreneurs. The GEM (2013) results "emphasize that entrepreneurial endeavours can be started at any time in a person's life, although this activity is mostly prevalent among those 25–34 years of age. These individuals are likely to have had some time to develop

their skills and knowledge through higher education and work experience. They may have developed networks and have access to financial resources" (p. 27). For entrepreneurs, issues of risk, personal wealth and capital, levels of personal debt, personal family commitments and circumstances all have a bearing on when they decide to launch a business. The age profile of technology entrepreneurs varies in different sectors. With the advent of technologies and socialisation of new products and services and low barriers to entry, the age profile is lower, whereas in the biotech sector, the technology entrepreneur age profile is older given the nature of the sector and the significant venture investment that is required to enter the industry.

Case Box 3.2   SoundCloud (www.soundcloud.com)

In 2013 SoundCloud were there overall winners of Europioneer, organised by the European Commission. This award celebrates European technology entrepreneurship. Founded in 2008 by Alexander Ljung and Eric Wahlfross, SoundCloud (2013): "allow[s] everyone to discover original music and audio, connect with each other and share their sounds with the world. In addition, sound creators can use the platform to instantly record, upload and share sounds across the internet, as well as receive detailed stats and feedback from the SoundCloud Community". SoundCloud's business model allows for new sounds to be uploaded easily and to enable creators and users to engage effectively and simply. SoundCloud has built a reputation among artists as the site of choice.

3.6   MOTIVATIONS AND INTENTIONS

Technology entrepreneurs share common motivations to other categories of entrepreneurs. These motivations underpin new venture creations of the technology entrepreneurs and complement their entrepreneurial characteristics. For all entrepreneurs, their personal traits are central to their motivations. Stewart et al. (1998) in a major US study of entrepreneurs found: "The profile of the entrepreneur as a driven, creative risk taker is consistent with much of the classic literature concerning the entrepreneur". Many entrepreneurs display what is described as Type-A personalities, whereby they are highly driven, ambitious and competitive. They are driven to achieve goals in as short a time as possible. When a business is in a start-up phase, such a personality enables entrepreneurs to overcome barriers, but as the business grows, different personality traits may be needed as Type-A may undermine long-term prospects or alienate key stakeholders or investors. Some common motivations for entrepreneurs and technology entrepreneurs include:

- *Independence and Control*: One of the strongest motivations of entrepreneurs is that of independence and having their own control to work on their own and shape their own direction. This sense of independence is also borne out of a desire to have control over their venture and their idea. This means they have control over how and when they undertake activities within the venture, what type of employees they hire into the business and how they engage with customers. For men internal locus of control is a prerequisite for starting a new business, but not for women (Hansemark, 2003). Nevertheless, Roberts (1988) found in his study that being "your own boss" is a key motivation for technology entrepreneurs, and he sums this up as "technical entrepreneurs seem to be fulfilling a long felt need (or lead ambition) in starting their companies, reflecting at least several years of prior general contemplation about going into their own businesses. ... reveal primarily a heavy orientation toward independence, being their own boss". The core motivation for technology entrepreneurs is focused on getting the technology and the innovation, as Hogan and Huston (2005) describe: " ... founders of high technology ventures usually need large quantities of start-up capital, the goal of independence may be moderated by the goal of innovation".

With independence comes significant responsibilities for the entrepreneur, wherein the previous contexts they worked in may not have had the broad range of responsibilities that they would have in a new venture. Having no boss as such can be a significant change for entrepreneurs, and they are now solely responsible for the success of the venture. With independence also comes a sense of fear about whether the venture will be successful, will it attract customers and will the business and financial model succeed once launched into the marketplace. Also, with independence comes additional pressures on time. Hyytinen and Ruuskanen (2006) in their study found that entrepreneurs work longer hours over the week than those working in organised employment.

- *Achievement*: For entrepreneurs one of the significant challenges they have to meet is whether the venture survives and grows. Entrepreneurs have high achievement needs and are high achievers. Consequently, they will use their resources, networks and supports to ensure the success of a venture. They view the financial success as a measure of their success, not as an outcome. The motivation for entrepreneurs is to continue to challenge themselves by bringing new ideas to a venture and getting the feedback and engagement with stakeholders. High achievers need feedback and also they have a consistent focus on higher performance. Furthermore, high-achieving entrepreneurs believe with consistent hard work that they have an ability to determine outcomes and success and have a positive disposition. David McClelland (1961) pioneered research into high achievers and achievement. For technology entrepreneurs, Roberts (1988) found in his study that many of them had thought about creating a new venture long before they did so.

Other motivating factors identified by Shane et al. (2003) include self-efficacy, goal setting, drive and egoistic passion.

In understanding the motivation of technology entrepreneurs, some studies have focused on entrepreneurial intent. Entrepreneurial intent is linked to personality traits and the likelihood that an individual would set up a new venture. Shane and Venkataraman (2003) define it as "situations in which new goods, services, raw materials, markets and organizing methods can be introduced through the formation of new means, ends or means-ends relationship". Internal personal motivations can be decisive for technological entrepreneurs in making their decision to start-up a new venture (Autio and Kauranen, 2006), and Wainer and Rubin (1969) found that for technology entrepreneurs "high need for achievement and moderate needs for power are associated with higher company performance". For technical visionaries in large US corporations, internal motivating factors of "desire to see their idea become a reality, and enjoying working 'on-the-edge' and innovating" were found by Hebda et al. (2007). In a study of entrepreneurial intent among engineering students at MIT, Luthje and Franke (2003) found "that the perceived contextual barriers and supports play a significant role for the entrepreneurial behaviour of technical students. These perceptions may be altered by suitable initiatives". They also found that the attitude and personality type of students with high risk taking and strong internal loci of control should be supported and nurtured in becoming technology entrepreneurs. Similarly Chell and Allman (2003) in examining motivation and intentions argue that greater focus should be put on the individual and their development to encourage them to become technology entrepreneurs and suggest that "the whole person and their development: cognitive, behavioural and emotional dimensions" be included. Moreover, the contextual environment also impacts on the motivation of entrepreneurs, particularly public policy initiatives that supports and encourages entrepreneurship. Lafuente and Salas (1989), based on their Spanish study of entrepreneurs and firms, note that "entrepreneurs differ in their personal characteristics and in particular in their aspirations and work expectations, suggesting a necessity for public policies that are responsive to such differences and which provide the most adequate stimulus to each entrepreneurial type". In a Finnish study, Autio and Renko (1998) found the intention and motivation of the creation of new technology firms were "partially motivated by the commercialisation of results of research undertaken by a university or research institution".

3.7 CHAPTER SUMMARY

We began the chapter by examining the definition of entrepreneurship and technology entrepreneurs. We discovered that what distinguished technology entrepreneurs is the technology/technical systems involved and the ad hoc nature of the new venture creation process. We then turned our focus to technology entrepreneurs' characteristics and found that they have many common characteristics to other categories of entrepreneurs. We examined characteristics, such as opportunity recognition, dealing with uncertainty, risk profile and appetite, resource appropriation and rewards, as well as work experience, educational attainment and age. Our next focus was on motivation and intentions, where we outlined some key motivations of independence and control, achievement, as well as examining entrepreneurial intent.

Case study 3.1 Rovio Entertainment: The Angry Birds Creators

Written by Dr. Grace Walsh, Duesto Business School, Spain.

Released in December 2009 by Rovio Entertainment Inc., Angry Birds is a game that requires the user to project belligerent cannonball-shaped birds at catatonic green pigs living in fragile houses on an island in the Pacific, who have stolen the birds' eggs. Through use of a slingshot, the goal is to collapse the glass and wood houses on the pigs' sometimes helmeted heads, in an effort to bring about their demise (Mauro, 2011). On the surface this sounds like an absurd game that requires little strategy and technique, however, despite of, or perhaps because of this, it has gone on to enjoy the biggest mobile application success the world has seen so far (Holthe, Eriken and Abdymomunov, 2011).

Rovio Entertainment Inc. started its life in Finland in 2003 as Relude. It began when three students from Helsinki University of Technology (currently Aalto University School of Science), Niklas Hed, Jarno Väkeväinen and Kim Dikert, participated in a mobile game development competition and won by creating a game called *King of the Cabbage World*. On winning the competition and through words of encouragement from the competition organiser Peter Vesterbacka, the trio set up their own company, and so Relude was born. As for *King of the Cabbage World,* this was sold on to Sumea Studios, was renamed *Mole War* and became the first commercial multiplayer real-time mobile game in the world (Vlad, 2011).

The future looked bright for the fledgling game developers, and in January 2005, it received its first round of investment from a business angel and changed its name to Rovio ("bonfire" in Finnish) Mobile (Cheshire, 2011). Prior to the development of Angry Birds, the boutique company created 51 games over 6 years, but none of them were hits, and the firm was faced with the real threat of bankruptcy (Soh, 2012). In 2007, Niklas Hed, one of the co-founders began reducing its employee, and by 2009, Rovio had shrunk from a peak of 50 employees to 12. In March 2009 when senior game designer Jaakko Iisalo first pitched the idea of Angry Birds, the team were immediately drawn to the characters and subsequently designed the game around the birds (Soh, 2012). Eight months and numerous revisions later, after almost completely abandoning the project, Hed watched as his mother burnt a Christmas turkey, so engrossed in finishing the game. "She doesn't play any games...I realised: this is it" (Cheshire, 2011).

The simplicity and addiction factor of Angry Birds has led to parallels being drawn to the enduringly popular game, Tetris (Holthe Eriken and Abdymomunov, 2011). Celebrity and media endorsements have also contributed to its mainstream popularity with pop star Justin Bieber tweeting about his inability to put the game down, Salman Rushdie admitting he's a fan, and the award-winning comedy show Saturday Night Live spoofed Angry Birds in one of its episodes (Soh, 2012; Cheshire, 2011). On 9 May 2012, Rovio announced that its mobile game sensation had reached its one-billionth download (Pan, 2012).

A key success factor undoubtedly comes from the game's design, with the unpredictable nature of the game meaning you can try the same level multiple times without success and then suddenly you are able to progress to the next level (Holthe Eriken and Abdymomunov, 2011). It is also a game that keeps on giving; the original Angry Birds game launched with 63 levels, and after more than three years since the game launched, Rovio continues to add new stages to the game (Soh, 2012). As of January 2013, there are 420 levels, all of which were given as free updates to players.[3] This unselfish approach to building a fan base has resulted in Angry Birds remaining in the top 20 games in the App Store with every bundle update serving to ensure the game remains on the customers' phone, and the brand is kept fresh and to the fore of people's minds (Soh, 2012). Rovio continues to capitalise on their brand power. Peter Vesterbacka, the competition organiser who originally encouraged the students to begin the firm, who came on board as the firm's Chief Marketing Officer in May 2010, declared, "We haven't seen ourselves as a games company for a long time... we've now sold over 10 million plush toys... and we also have other products: board games, card games, and we've recently launched our first book" (Vlad, 2011; Dredge, 2011).

The "Angry Birds Bad Piggies" cookbook was announced in early 2011 and in March 2012 the company even ventured into education. Rovio teamed up with National Geographic to release a book on planets, galaxies and the mysteries of the universe as an official companion to the "Angry Birds Space" game. Vesterbacka is very conscious of diversifying the company's product portfolio and hinted at a possibility of a future switch to e-books when he spoke of Rovio's interest in the digital side of publishing. Providing a further insight into the firms future strategic desires Vesterbacka said "we're building the first entertainment brand on the planet with a billion fans... but we're only getting started" (Dredge, 2011). The company changed its name from Rovio Mobile to Rovio Entertainment Ltd. in July 2011.

The game developers' clever use of technology allows the forging of unexpected brand partnerships that combine virtual and physical worlds with the use of the program "Magic Places". Rovio teamed up with US retailer Barnes and Noble to provide special features when gamers visited their stores whilst playing Angry Birds on their devices. This is a highly innovated form of marketing and has the potential to be further expanded and developed as Vesterbacka noted, "there's a lot that can be done by really creating these kinds of experiences when people are in a particular area". The Chief Marketing Officer also revealed the firm's intentions to move out of its current single mechanic gaming and into other forms, genres and settings (Dredge, 2011).

Rovio also extends much credit for its success to Apple's App Store, as rather than negotiating individually with device manufacturers and network carriers, game developers could access worldwide distribution through a single contact, Apple (Cheshire, 2011). "The key is to offer it for free and reach volume. You need to get the game out to the masses", says Vesterbacka (Holthe Eriken and Abdymomunov, 2011). In addition to nurturing the success of Angry Birds, Rovio is also spinning off new franchises with the release of Bad Piggies, a game focused solely on the pig characters from the original game, which three hours after its release was top of the charts on Apple's App Store (Dredge, 2012a).

The future of Rovio looks promising with the firm's own executives comparing them to early Disney. In December 2012, Rovio announced plans for a 3D Angry Birds movie with a planned release date of summer 2016. Rovio has decided to keep the movie's finance, production and distribution in-house, potentially making it available on smartphones and tablets following its cinematic debut (Dredge, 2012b). The firm has also been working on a series of Angry Birds animated shorts, with 80 animators working at its Helsinki headquarters (Dredge, 2012a). Of the future the firm's executive vice president Andrew Stalbow has said, "We're trying to make some very important decisions and some strategic bets on partners we can really grow with over the next five years...you look at how Hello Kitty has evolved, or Super Mario...It's about trying to have an impact on pop culture" (Dredge, 2012a). Angry Birds previous linkages to McDonalds Happy Meals and the Star Wars franchise has cemented and solidified its position in current popular culture, and it looks set to remain there for the foreseeable future.

Case Questions

1. Using the technology entrepreneurship definitions in Chapter 3, apply and discuss.
2. Is Rovio Entertainment a technology-based company? Outline your rationale.
3. What are the factors that have made Rovio Entertainment an international success? Discuss how Rovio Entertainment can protect and grow?

Case Study References

Angry Birds Wikia website. Accessed online on 29 January 2013 at http://angrybirds. wikia.com/wiki/Angry_Birds.

Cheshire, T. (2011) "In Depth: How Rovio Made Angry Birds a Winner (and What's Next)", *Wired.com*, 7 March 2011. Accessed online on 29 January 2013 at http:// www.wired.co.uk/magazine/archive/2011/04/features/how-rovio-made-angry-birds-a-winner?page=all.

Dredge, S. (2011) "Angry Birds Flying beyond Smartphones to Target the Developing World", *The Guardian Newspaper*, 26 October 2011. Accessed online on 29 January 2013 at http://www.guardian.co.uk/technology/appsblog/2011/oct/26/angry-birds-feature-phones-nokia.

Dredge, S. (2012a) "Angry Birds Games Have 200m Monthly Active Players", *The Guardian Newspaper*, 10 October 2012. Accessed online on 29 January 2013 at http://www.guardian.co.uk/technology/appsblog/2012/oct/10/angry-birds-200m-monthly-users.

Dredge, S. (2012b) "Angry Birds Movie Confirmed...for Summer 2016", *The Guardian Newspaper*, 11 December 2012. Accessed online on 29 January 2013 at http://www.guardian.co.uk/technology/appsblog/2012/dec/11/angry-birds-movie-john-cohen.

Holthe Eriken, E. and Abdymomunov, A. (2011) "Angry Birds Will Be Bigger Than Mickey Mouse and Mario. Is There a Success Formula for Apps?" *MIT Entrepreneurship Review*, 18 February 2011. Accessed online on 29 January 2013 at http://miter.mit.edu/articleangry-birds-will-be-bigger-mickey-mouse-and-mario-there-success-formula-apps/.

Mauro, C.L. (2011) "Why Angry Birds Is So Successful and Popular: A Cognitive Teardown of the User Experience", *Mauronewmedia.com*, 6 February 2011. Accessed online on 29 January 2013 at http://www.mauronewmedia.com/blog/why-angry-birds-is-so-successful-a-cognitive-teardown-of-the-user-experience/.

Pan, J. (2012) "Rovio Rejoices Over Billionth Angry Birds Download", *Mashable.com*, 9 May 2012. Accessed online on 29 January 2013 at http://mashable.com/2012/05/09/angry-birds-1-billion-downloads/.

Soh, H. (2012) "Angry Birds Case Study: A Look into the Game's History, Success and Influence", *Popconversation.com*, March 2012. Accessed online on 29 January 2013 at http://www.popconversation.com/2012/03/popstudy-angry-birds.html.

Vlad. M. (2011) "Interview: Rovio's Peter Vesterbacka on the History of the Company", *Criticalgamer.com*, 11 July 2011. Accessed online on 29 January 2013 at http:// www.criticalgamer.co.uk/2011/07/11/interview-rovio's-peter-vesterbacka-on-the-history-of-the-company/.

Xavier, S. R., Kelley, D., Kew, J., Herrington, M. and Vorderwülbecke, A. (2013), *GEM Global Report* 2012.

3.8 REVISION QUESTIONS

1. Outline the main aspects of a definition of entrepreneurship. Discuss how they differ from definitions of technology entrepreneurs.
2. Discuss why context matters more for technology entrepreneurs and their new venture.
3. Outline and discuss the main characteristics of technology entrepreneurs.
4. Taking a technology entrepreneur that you are familiar with, apply their main characteristics. Discuss the implications of your analysis?
5. Discuss how entrepreneurial intent influences technology entrepreneurs.
6. Describe the motivations of technology entrepreneurs and the consequences for the new venture creation.

3.9 FURTHER READING AND RESOURCES

- A seminal article for understanding the motivation of entrepreneurs is Wainer and Rubin (1969) published in the *Journal of Applied Psychology*.
- For a deeper understanding of achievement, read David McClelland's book on *The Achieving Society* published in 1961.
- For an understanding of entrepreneurship from a sociological perspective, read Reynolds's 1991 article in *Entrepreneurship Theory and Practice*.
- For an interesting history of technology and Silicon Valley, read *Technology, Entrepreneurs and Silicon Valley* authored by Carol Whiteley and John McLaughlin and published by the Institute for the History of Technology in 2002.

3.10 NOTES

1. http://www.behaviosec.com.
2. http://www.bbc.co.uk/news/technology-21924243.
3. www.angrybirds.wikia.com.

3.11 REFERENCES

Aldrich, H.E. and Cliff, J.E. (2003) "The Pervasive Effects of Family on Entrepreneurship: Toward a Family Embeddedness Perspective", *Journal of Business Venturing*, 18: 573–596.

Almus, M. and Nerlinger, E.A. (1999) "Growth of New Technology Based Firms: Which Factors Matter?" *Small Business Economics*, 13: 141–154.

Amit, R., MacCrimmon, K.R., Zietsma, C. and Oesch, J. (2001) "Does Money Matter? Wealth Attainment as the Motive for Initiating Growth Oriented Technology Ventures", *Journal of Business Venturing*, 16: 119–143.

Aspelund, A., Berg-Utby, T. and Skjevdal, R. (2005) "Initial Resources' Influence on New Venture Survival: A Longitudinal Study of New Technology-based Firms", *Technovation*, 25: 1337–1347.

Autio, E. and Kauranen, I (2006) "Technologist-Entrepreneurs versus Non Entrepreneurial Eechnologists: Analysis of Motivational Triggering Factors. *Entrepreneurship and Regional Development*, 6(4): 315–328.

Autio, E. and Renko, H.Y. (1998) "New, Technology-based Firms in Small Open Economies –An Analysis Based on the Finnish Experience", *Research Policy*, 26: 973–987.

Baron, R.A. (2004) "The Cognitive Perspective: A Valuable Tool of Answering Entrepreneurship's Basic 'Why' Questions", *Journal of Business Venturing*, 19: 221–239.

Baum, J.R., Locke, E.A. and Smith, K.G. (2001) "A Multidimensional Model of Venture Growth", *Academy of Management Journal*, 44(2): 292–303.

Bollinger, L., Hope, K. and Utterback, J.M. (1983) "A Review of Literature and Hypotheses on New Technology-based Firms", *Research Policy*, 12: 1–14.

Brennan, M., McGovern, P. and McGowan, P. (2007) "Academic Entrepreneurship on the Island of Ireland: Re-Orientating Academia Within the Knowledge Economy", *The Irish Journal of Management*, 1: 51–57.

Bruyat, C. and Julien, P. (2000) "Defining the Field of Research in Entrepreneurship", *Journal of Business Venturing*, 16: 165–180.

Cantillon, R. (1979) Essai sur la Nature du Commerce en Général, In Takumi Tsuda (ed.), *Essai sur la Nature du Commerce en general*. Tokyo: Kinokuniya Book Store Co.

Cardon, M. SD., Shepherd, D. and Wiklund, J. (2012) "Exploring the Heart: Entrepreneurial Emotion Is a Hot Topic", *Entrepreneurship Theory and Practice*, 36(January): 1–9.

Carter, S. (2011) "The Rewards of Entrepreneurship: Exploring the Incomes, Wealth, and Economic Well-being of Entrepreneurial Households", *Entrepreneurship Theory and Practice*, 35(1): 39–55.

Casson, M. (1995) *Entrepreneurship and Business Culture*. Bookfield, CT: Edward Elgar.

Chell, E. and Allman, K. (2003) "Mapping the Motivation and Intentions of Technology Oriented Entrepreneurs", *R&D Management*, 33(2): 117–133.

Colombo, M.G., Delmastro, M. and Grilli, L. (2004) "Entrepreneurs' Human Capital and the Start-up Size of New Technology-based Firms", *International Journal of Industrial Organization*, 22: 1183–1211.

Colombo, M.G. and Grilli, L. (2005) "Founders' Human Capital and the Growth of New Technology-based Firms: A Competence-based View", *Research Policy*, 34: 795–816.

Drucker, P.F. (1985) *Innovation and Entrepreneurship.* New York: Collins Business.

Dubini, P. (1989) "The Influence of Motivations and Environment on Business Start-ups Some Hints for Public Policies", *Journal of Business Venturing*, 4(1): 11–26.

Dyson (2013) *The Hammer Test.* Accessed online on 26 February 2013 at http://content.dyson.com/insidedyson/default.asp#thehammer.

Evans, D.J. (1995) "A Typology of Technology-based Entrepreneurs: A Model Based on Previous Occupational Background", *International Journal of Entrepreneurial Behaviour and Research*, 1(1): 26–47.

Gans, J. and Stern, S. (2003) "The Product Market and the Market for 'Ideas': Commercialization Strategies for Technology Entrepreneurs", *Research Policy*, February, 32(2): 333–350.

Gartner, W.B. (1990) "What Are We Talking About When We Talk About Entrepreneurship?" *Journal of Business Venturing*, 5(1): 15–28.

Gregoire, D.A., Corbette, A.C. and McMullen, J.S. (2011) "The Cognitive Perspective in Entrepreneurship: An Agenda for Future Research", *Journal of Management Studies*, 48(6): 1443–1477.

Gupta, V. and Fernandez, C. (2009) "Cross Cultural Similarities and Differences in Characteristics Attributed to Entrepreneurs: A Three-nation Study", *Journal of Leadership and Organizational Studies*, 15(3): 304–318.

Hansemark, O.C. (2003) "Need for Achievement, Locus of Control and the Prediction of Business Start-ups: A Longitudinal Study", *Journal of Economic Psychology*, 24: 301–319.

Hebda, J.M., Vojak, B.A, Griffin, A. and Price, R.L. (2007) "Motivating Technical Visionaries in Large American Companies", *IEEE Transactions on Engineering Management*, 54(3): 433–444.

Hogan, T. and Hutson, E. (2005) "Capital Structure in New Technology-based Firms: Evidence from the Irish Software Sector", *Global Finance Journal*, 15: 369–387.

Hoy, F. and Carland J.W. (1983) "Differentiating between Entrepreneurs and Small Business Owners in New Venture Formation", Frontiers of Entrepreneurship Research, Babson Centre for Entrepreneurial Studies, Wellesley, MA, 157–166.

Hyytinen, A. and Ruuskanen, O.P. (2006) "What Makes an Entrepreneur? Evidence from Time US Survey", The Research Institute of the Finnish Economy, Discussion Paper, 1029.

Jones-Evans, D. (1995) "A Typology of Technology Based Entrepreneurs: A Model Based on Previous Occupational Background", *International Journal of Entrepreneurial Behaviour and Research*, 1(1): 26–47.

Krueger, N.F. and Brazeal, D.V. (1994) "Entrepreneurial Potential and Potential Entrepreneurs", *Entrepreneurship Theory and Practice*, Spring, 91–104.

Kuratko, D. (2014) *Introduction to Entrepreneurship*. Canada: South Western Cengage Learning.

Lafuente, A. and Salas, V. (1989) "Types of Entrepreneurs and Firms: The Case of New Spanish Firms", *Strategic Management Journal*, 10: 17–30.

Luthje, C. and Franke, N. (2003) "The 'Making' of an Entrepreneur: Testing a Model of Entrepreneurial Intent among Engineering Students at MIT", *R&D Management*, 33(2): 135–147.

Marvel, M. and Lumpkin, G.T. (2007) "Technology Entrepreneurs' Human Capital and Its Effects on Innovation Radicalness", *Entrepreneurship Theory & Practice*, 31(6): 807–828.

McClelland, D.C. (1961) *The Achieving Society*. New York: D. Van Nostrand Company, Inc.

Naire, K.R.G. and Pandey, A. (2006) "Characteristics of Entrepreneurs: An Empirical Analysis", *Journal of Entrepreneurship*, 15(10): 47–61.

Oviatt, B. and McDougall, P.P. (2005) "Defining International Entrepreneurship and Modeling the Speed of Internationalization", *Entrepreneurship Theory and Practice*, September, 537–553.

Reynolds, P.D. (1991) "Sociology and Entrepreneurship: Concepts and Contributions", *Entrepreneurship Theory and Practice*, Winter, 47–70.

Roberts, E.B. (1988) "The Personality and Motivations of Technology Entrepreneurs", MIT Sloan School of Management, Working Paper, 2078–2088.

Schumpeter J.A. (1965) "Economic Theory and Entrepreneurial History", in Aitken H.G. (ed.), *Explorations in Enterprise*. Cambridge, MA: Harvard University Press.

Sexton, D. (1988) "The Field of Entrepreneurship: Is It Growing or Just Getting Bigger?" *Journal of Small Business Management*, 26(1): 4–8.

Shane, S. and Venkataraman, S. (2003) "Guest Editors' Introduction to the Special Issue on Technological Entrepreneurship", *Research Policy*, 32(2): 181–184.

Shane, S., Locke, E.A. and Collins, C.J. (2003) "Entrepreneurial motivation", *Human Resource Management Review*, 13: 257–279.

Shane. S. (2000) "Prior Knowledge and the Discovery of Entrepreneurial Opportunities", *Organization Science*, 11(4): 448–469.

SoundCloud (2013) *Press Information and Resources*. Accessed online on 4 July 2013 at Soundcloud.com/press.

Stewart, W.H., Watson, W.E. and Carland, J.C. (1998) "A Proclivity for Entrepreneurship: A Comparison of Entrepreneurs, Small Business Owners, and Corporate Managers", *Journal of Business Venturing*, 14: 189–214.

Stewart, W.H. and Roth, P.L. (2001) "Risk Propensity Differences between Entrepreneurs and Managers: A Meta Analytic Review", *Journal of Applied Psychology*, 86(1): 145–153.

Storey, D.J. and Tether, B.S. (1998) "Public Policy Measures to Support New Technology-based Firms in the European Union", *Research Policy*, 26: 1037–1057.

Timmons, J., Smollen, L. and Dingee, A. (1985) *New Venture Creation*. Homewood, IL: Irwin.

Vserv Mobi (2013) *We Love the Mobile Ecosystem*. Accessed online on 26 February 2013 at http;//vserv.mobu/about.html.

Wainer, H.A. and Rubin, I.M. (1969) "Motivation of Research and Development Entrepreneurs: Determinants of Company Success", *Journal of Applied Psychology*, 53(3): 178–184.

Ward, T.B. (2004) "Cognition, Creativity, and Entrepreneurship", *Journal of Business Venturing*, 19: 173–188.

Wiklund, J., Davidsson, P., Audretsch, D.B. and Karlsson, C. (2011) "The Future of Entrepreneurship Research", *Entrepreneurship Theory and Practice*, 35(1): 1–9.

3.12   GLOSSARY OF TERMS

Characteristics: Factors that influence the entrepreneurs and new venture formation.

Educational attainment: Level of formal education achieved.

Entrepreneur: An individual who starts their own venture to exploit a market opportunity.

Motivations: Personal factors that influence individual in becoming an entrepreneur.

Opportunity Recognition: Cognition and process by which entrepreneurs conceptualise market opportunities.

Rewards: The financial and personal returns accruing to an entrepreneur when a new venture succeeds.

Risk Profile and Appetite: How entrepreneurs cope under the risks involved in starting up a business and how much risk an entrepreneur is willing to take on.

Resource appropriation: How entrepreneurs gather resources, financial, human capital and other supports during the new venture formation and beyond.

Technology Entrepreneur: an individual who starts their own venture to exploit a market opportunity with an innovative or new technology.

PART II

CREATING, PROTECTING AND MANAGING TECHNOLOGY AND INNOVATION

II.1 INTRODUCTION

Innovation is at the heart technology entrepreneurship. In fact, Schumpeter (1942) argued that the role of the entrepreneur is to bring innovations into the economy. As discussed in-depth in the previous chapters, technological innovation needs to be seen as an interactive phenomenon, where universities, companies and governments play their part (triple helix).

While the previous chapters focused on the "innovation system", outlining the roles, functions and relationships of various actors and activities, the following chapters will take a closer look at the actual processes of technology innovation in practice. This means zooming in on researching, developing, protecting and commercialising inventions. Innovation is more than invention; it is the whole process, from idea to successful implementation, whether in a market (e.g., new products and services), in organisations (e.g., new production and distribution methods or novel ways of organising), or in wider parts of society (e.g., new infrastructures such as broadband or transport systems).

II.2 DOING INNOVATION IN PRACTICE

Everyone who has been involved in – or studied – innovation processes in practice knows that innovation rarely happens in very linear and structured ways. The number of uncertainties involved means that technology innovation is more like a discovery process, where solutions, numerous unexpected events and effects have to be improvised along the way. Hence, there are three aspects that we want to highlight: First, innovation processes are *messy*. While we highly recommend what Honig (2004) calls "contingent planning", that is planning as you go, while continuously taking the situation and how the process evolves into account, we do not think that it is possible to make the ultimate long-term plan and then just execute from it. Innovation processes are simply too messy and uncertain. Second, innovation processes are *iterative*. Rather than following linear stages from start to end, the process is likely to take the innovators through several cycles of developing, testing and learning. This tends also to create tensions between innovators and decision-makers, as it may sometimes be hard to defend and argue for the continuation of a project in light of several changes of direction from the original idea and plan. Third, innovation processes are *networked*. From Stevenson's (1983) definition we learn that entrepreneurship is "the pursuit of opportunity without regard to resources currently controlled". In practice this means that resources, such as knowledge, technology, production facilities, distribution, money, etc. have to be mobilised in personal and organisational networks. Triple helix relationships, as well as personal acquaintances and business partners have to be actively engaged as part of realising the innovation. Network interaction creates interaction effects, meaning that it is impossible to anticipate the responses and outputs from related actors, hence increasing the uncertainty of innovation. While network interaction is crucial for succeeding with innovation, it does also present challenges in terms of collaboration and competition. Sometimes entrepreneurs avoid interaction to stay in control of the process.

II.3 A MATTER OF PERSPECTIVE

It is important to recognise innovation processes as messy, iterative, and networked in both the study and practice of technology innovation. We have therefore sought to present theories and models of innovation in Part II. This part both introduces the reader to basic concepts and classifications of innovation, and that reflects how innovation tends to happen in practice.

For practitioners, there has been a shift in recent years towards more iterative methodologies and tools for doing innovation and entrepreneurial work; tools that support messy, iterative and networked processes. This "iterative turn" in innovation and entrepreneurship practice made business plans less important. A range of new methods and tools is available, such as business modelling (where Osterwalder's canvases are well-known tools (see Chapter 6 for more)), the Lean Start-up approach (Ries, 2011) with effective tools for user-oriented development of products and customer value, the customer development approach (Blank, 2005) and the effectuation approach (Sarasvathyand Dew, 2005) with its realistic principles for how entrepreneurs succeed in developing new businesses and markets.

In Part II of the book, we will provide a systematic understanding of how intellectual property (IP) affects knowledge-to-cash processes. We will encourage a critical awareness of contemporary challenges facing engineers and scientists in bringing products of scientific research into industrial application. In addition, we will explore the practical intellectual property issues of relevance during the technological innovation process – from the idea stage throughout the product development process and launch of the new value proposition into the marketplace. Inventions are not only to become successful *products* but also often they will need to become part of *new organizations* – whether a new company or a new product department in an established company – in order to be successfully brought into use in markets and organisations.

II.4   THE THREE CHAPTERS OF PART II

Chapter 4 introduces the core issues and central ways of understanding innovations and innovation processes. The variety and complexity of innovation will become clear, as well as some of the main challenges related to managing innovation. Insights into the concepts and classifications of innovation and innovation platforms are presented. Next, methods to organise and manage innovation processes, from the idea development stage to prototyping of the innovation lifecycle, are presented. Some key challenges for organising and managing innovation processes are identified along with some suggestions for overcoming them. Finally, Chapter 4 addresses the technology diffusion process of moving innovations through commercialisation into widespread use. The end-of-chapter case study, Salma, tells the story of a biotechnical innovation research project in the food industry from the product development stage through marketing of the product. It illustrates the typical non-linear path of innovation processes, and how dead-ends may spur new ideas that eventually lead to success in the market.

Chapter 5 presents fundamental and critical issues behind intellectual property faced by technology entrepreneurs. While many are familiar with some of the basic concepts behind intellectual property, e.g., patents, copyrights or trademarks, for the first-time entrepreneur, managing intellectual property can take on the aura of a full-blown crusade. Assessing intellectual property, its value and whether or not it is important to a start-up can seem like a minefield. This chapter unravels some of the conundrums and mysteries associated with the unique cross-disciplinary skills at the interface of business, law and technology required to manage IP. The chapter covers four main themes: first, it explores how scientists, engineers and technological researchers think and act in creating and capturing IP. It then highlights the legal issues in protecting IP and provides a comparison of legal perspectives in the different geographical territories, namely the United States, Europe and Asia. It then provides an investor's and entrepreneur's perspective in evaluating IP and how it can be used to create value. It also takes a looks at the commercialisation process and how technology entrepreneurs marshal resources in exploiting IP, either licensing it or transforming it into a successful new venture, which is covered in more depth in Chapter 8. The chapter concludes with an end case outlining the challenges presented in the realm of nanotechnology.

Chapter 6 emphasises the development of business concepts and business models for testing and learning how to create a profitable match between customer values, production factors, and income factors.

Business model innovation has become an important way to get ahead of competitors in today's globalising and increasingly connected world. The final chapter of this section includes the business plan as an important outcome of business model development, followed by most current metrics for measuring business growth. Chapter 6 invites the reader to work on the commercialisation of the invention and the organising of the venture: How can the invention create value for users and revenues for the venture? How should it be produced and brought to market, with what activities and resources? Business modelling is put to the centre in this chapter instead of the business plan (as in most traditional entrepreneurship textbooks). This change signals the preference for business modelling and other iterative and learning-oriented tools that are better suited to assist entrepreneurs in the early stages of a start-up. We would also like to highlight that a well-developed business model is beneficial for building a high-growth venture (which will be discussed from different angles in Part 4).

First, we seek to explain that opportunities need to be developed into *business concepts* consisting of products/services and what value they will create in the market (value proposition). Second, we argue that the iterative development of a viable *business model* helps configure the available resources in order to create unique customer value (value proposition) and how the company will capture economic and other value from this. In other words, how to organise the business in order to meet the customers' needs and make money. Third, the importance of the business plan and the components of business plans are outlined. Finally, we explain how to develop metrics for measuring growth and business model performance.

The end-of-chapter case study in this chapter is Spotify Inc. The Swedish music-streaming service has taken a strong position in many countries with a potentially disruptive service, showing that people are willing to pay for user-friendly and socially oriented online services.

II.5 REFERENCES

Blank, S.G. (2005) *The Four Steps to the Epiphany: Successful Strategies for Products That Win*, 2nd edition, Cafepress.com.

Honig, B. (2004) "Entrepreneurship Education: Toward a Model of Contingency-based Business Planning", *Academy of Management Learning and Education*, 9(1): 258–273.

Ries, E. (2011) *The Lean Startup: How Today's Entrepreneurs Use Continuous Innovation to Create Radically Successful Businesses*. New York: Crown Publishing Group.

Sarasvathy, S.D. and Dew, N. (2005) "New Market Creation through Transformation", *Journal of Evolutionary Economics*, 15: 533–565.

Schumpeter, J. (1942) *Capitalism, Socialism, and Democracy*. New York: Harper and Row.

Stevenson, H.H. (1983) "A Perspective on Entrepreneurship", working paper, Harvard Business School, Cambridge, MA.

Chapter 4

INNOVATION AND DIFFUSION OF TECHNOLOGY IN PRODUCTS AND SERVICES

4.1   LEARNING OBJECTIVES

In this chapter, core issues and central ways of understanding innovations and innovation processes are introduced. The variety and complexity of innovation will become clear, as well as some of the main challenges related to managing innovation. First, an overview of the concepts and classifications of innovation and innovation platforms is provided. Next, methods to organise and manage innovation processes, from the idea development stage to prototyping of the innovation lifecycle, are presented. We also share common challenges and suggestions for overcoming them. Last, the diffusion process of moving innovations through commercialisation into widespread use is reviewed.

After reading this chapter, you will be able to:

1. Define innovation and classify different kinds of innovations;
2. Identify different sources of innovations;
3. Understand some of the complexities of managing processes with high levels of uncertainty; and
4. Outline the various stages of the innovation life cycle and their particular challenges

4.2   CHAPTER STRUCTURE

The core elements of this chapter are as follows:

- Introduction
- Defining Innovation
- Classifying Innovations
  - Product versus process innovations
  - Infrastructure and platform innovations
  - Incremental versus radical innovations
  - Disruptive innovations
  - Open innovation

- Sources of Innovation
- The Technology Innovation Life Cycle
- Diffusion of Innovations
  - Diffusion of Innovation and Adopter Categories
  - The Roger's Diffusion of Innovation Paradigm
  - Moore's Technology Adoption Life Cycle
  - Diffusion in Practice
- Managing Innovation
  - The Management of Uncertainty
  - Managing (in) Networks
  - Managing Iteration
  - The Contrary Forces of Innovation
  - Innovation Investments
- Chapter Summary
- Case Study – Salma: Novel Technology and Branding in a Traditional Market
- Revision Questions
- Further Reading and Resources
- References
- Glossary of Terms

4.3 INTRODUCTION

This chapter will define innovation, review different types and classi-fications of innovations, and identify some of the key characteristics of each type. Further, discussion includes from where innovative ideas come and the technology innovation life cycle to put the innovation into practice. Sometimes ideas emerge from local settings such as cross-professional teams, creative individuals, or boundary-spanning activities. Other times ideas are sourced via increasingly global networks, and concepts such as "open innovation" help us grasp how ideas and patents may be sourced via Internet communities, knowledge databases, business networks, and even via businesses creating global markets for Intellectual Property (IP).

4.4 DEFINING INNOVATION

Innovation can be defined in many ways. The bottom line is that *innova-tion* (an idea, practice or object) is more than just the invention of some-thing new; it is about the whole process from the inception of an idea through developing and testing to successfully putting the innovation in use – whether commercially in a market or as part of improving a business. Scholars studying the management of innovation tend to use open defini-tions such as anything "new to the involved actors" (Van de Ven et al., 1999) or something that changes the practice of which it is a part (Mørk et al., 2010). Other times one may talk about innovation being something new to the industry, to the region, or – ultimately – to the world (Garcia and Calantone, 2002).

However, innovation is different than invention. "Invention is the first occurrence of an idea for a new product or process, while innovation is the first attempt to carry it out into practice" (Fagerberg, 2005, p. 4). Frequently, there is a delay of years, if not decades, before an invention has the potential to become an innovation (Rogers, 1995). The time-gap from invention to innovation to common usage and acceptance is bridged by the entrepreneur.

Although innovative ideas may be easy to comprehend, the role of the entrepreneur is to achieve "successful economic implementation" (Fagerberg, 2002: 11). The *entrepreneur* is a passionate visionary who has the responsibilities of combining the factors necessary to successfully lead innovations to market. The entrepreneur pursues business opportunities that can change the market and is considered "an innovative economic agent" (Wadhwani, 2010). This concept directly connects the success of an innovation with entrepreneurship as it is the entrepreneur's responsibility to guide the innovation.

However, the role of the entrepreneur differs from the business manager within the firm. Business managers provide results by imitating existing methods, while entrepreneurs overcome obstacles – including the resistance to change – to bring their vision to fruition (Schumpeter, 1928: 380). New innovations are difficult to develop and implement, so the collaborative effort of a well-rounded team will be essential to long-term success. This will be discussed in further detail in Chapter 10.

Schumpeter (1942) found that entrepreneurs had the role of introducing new products, services and even production methods to the economy. While established companies are concerned with incremental improvements of their on-going activities, new entrants (innovators) coming with new technologies and new ideas can have the effect of "creative destruction" in the economy. *Creative destruction* is when innovative solutions are introduced by entrepreneurs, undermining the current practice in the economy, and thereby moving existing products, production methods and even companies out of business. Paradoxically, this is both what brings growth to the economy, e.g., by opening up new markets, and at the same time destroys the position and profits of established dominant companies.

Entrepreneurs may be part of undermining the traditional ways of doing things and hence trigger large-scale industry and market changes. In this way, Schumpeter believed entrepreneurial practices of supporting innovation served as the catalyst for building the economy. The frequency or infrequency of ideas and successful innovations explained the ups and downs of economic waves and the cyclical nature of economic development.

The remainder of this chapter will discuss the elements of innovation management that are essential for entrepreneurial success. For technology innovation and the purposes of this book, we will focus on the innovation process in the context of new technology-based products or services that are introduced to and implemented in user settings, such as commercialisation.

4.5 CLASSIFYING INNOVATIONS

4.5.1 Product versus Process Innovations

A *product innovation* is the introduction of a good or service that is new or significantly improved with respect to its characteristics or intended uses. This includes significant improvements in technical specifications, components and materials, incorporated software, user friendliness or other functional characteristics. Product innovations can utilise new knowledge or technologies or can be based on new uses or combinations of existing knowledge or technologies (OECD, 2005). An example of a product innovation is the development of electrical vehicles (EV), like Tesla, and hybrid electric vehicles (HEV), like Toyota Prius, where elements of traditional cars (e.g., wheels, steering wheel, break systems, etc.) are combined with new power sources (electric motors) and control systems (e.g., electronic control of efficient use and recharging of battery power).

A *process innovation* is the implementation of a new or significantly improved production or delivery method. This includes significant changes in techniques, equipment and/or software. Process innovations are typically intended to decrease unit costs of production or delivery, to increase quality or to produce or deliver new or significantly improved products or services (OECD, 2005). End users may not always be aware of process innovation, as the tangible product itself may not be altered significantly; however, process innovation might still have led to improved methods of production for that product. The scaling up of the production of EVs and HEVs has required intensive process innovation, particularly related to the production of batteries and the software-based control systems of the power trains. The continuous innovation of production methods for semiconductor chips paved the way for making smaller and smaller computers.

Yet another example is the continuous technical innovation efforts that enabled IKEA to keep the price low and constant on their Lack tables for decades. From manufacturing these tables in solid wood in the 1970s, the production has gradually been completely transformed through a number of process innovations. While the Lack tables look externally similar over the years, the production technologies and the material composition of the table was altered constantly to maintain a steady price point. Currently, they are produced with a cost-effective pulp and advanced printing technology to simulate the wood finish (Baraldi and Waluszewski, 2005).

In many cases, *technology-based service innovations* can provide more efficient processes through the use of technology in cases where the service was previously delivered without technology. An example is software-as-a-service (SaaS) for media monitoring or project management.

Most *product innovations* occur at the beginning of the product life cycle (PLC), as designers analyse possible issues and make changes – consequently innovating – before they agree on design standards. As opposed to this,

Table 4.1   Product versus process innovation classification matrix

Type of innovation	Definition	Examples	Product life cycle attributes
Product innovation	The introduction of a good or service that is new or significantly improved with respect to its characteristics or intended uses	Electrical vehicles (EV), such as Tesla; tablet computers, such as the Apple iPad; Online services, such as Dropbox and Skype	Typically occurs at the beginning of the PLC before design standards are set
Process innovation	The implementation of a new or significantly improved production or delivery method	Use of 3D modelling for product development; Innovative production methods for semiconductor chips for computers; Dell's production and delivery of mass customised computers; Improving production processes and software control systems for EV batteries; IKEA Lack table material composition improvements to maintain a low and steady price point for decades	Typically occurs after design standards are set to improve quality, effectiveness or efficiency

process innovations usually intensify once the design standard has been established and the development team searches for improvements in quality, efficiency, or effectiveness throughout the production process. In reality, product and process innovation are closely linked to one another. Many product innovations are based on process innovations and vice versa.

4.5.2   Infrastructure and Platform Innovations

In addition to product and process innovation, there are two somewhat related additional types of innovation that are highly relevant to technology entrepreneurs. First, *infrastructure innovations* (Van de Ven et al., 1999) are wider technical systems that enable or improve communication, such as transport systems, energy grids, and financial systems. The realisation of infrastructure innovations most often depends on joint efforts by a number of actors; often involving science and business as well as politics. Van de Ven et al. (1999) refer to successful infrastructure innovators as a number of different actors that "run in packs". The common investments will in the longer run provide joint resources for improved action, often

Table 4.2   Infrastructure versus platform innovation classification matrix

Type of Innovation	Definition	Example	Common attributes
Infrastructure innovation	Wider technical systems that enable or improve usability	Transport systems, energy grids, the Internet and financial systems	Typically requires joint efforts and investments from a variety of actors
Platform innovation	Novel technological solutions that serve as a platform for the distribution of services with the aim of attracting large numbers of users through complementary and competing services	Apple App Store; Google Play; Amazon's Webstore; Spotify	Opening up new technologies to larger user groups

Source: Based on Van de Ven et al. (1999).

even enlarging the market opportunities for all. The Internet is obviously a large-scale example of what could be called an infrastructure innovation.

Second, there are *platform innovations*. These are novel technological solutions that serve as a platform for distribution of services. The aim is usually for the innovators to create an "ecology" of complementary and competing services that may attract large numbers of users. Hence, an innovative actor can get "help" to speed up and expand product and/or service innovation and thereby further develop the market, or the use, for the new technology. This may also be seen as part of the "open innovation" trend (Chesbrough, 2006). Apple App Store and Google Play are examples of platform innovations where innovative companies created platforms for thousands of new and established businesses to distribute services, such as games and other applications. Amazon.com provides their Webstore as a distribution platform for other businesses to establish trust while reaching a larger customer base. Amazon.com offers their server space and payment systems to external businesses, which is a powerful example of how service and process innovations for Amazon's own business developed further into platform innovations. It is also interesting to see how the music-streaming service, Spotify, is providing editorial and service content by opening their application for "apps". This has enabled Spotify to offer their users concert tickets, music reviews, lyrics, playlists and recommendations from both entrepreneurs and major players in the press and the music industry (see Chapter 6 "Spotify" long case).

4.5.3   Incremental versus Radical Innovations

Another classification of innovation relates more to the degree of novelty – whether the innovation concerns smaller improvements or a relatively high number of new elements thus creating a bigger divide between the innovation and established products.

Incremental innovations are evolutionary in nature; they consist of smaller improvements in product, processes or organisational activities introduced over time. They are often based on extensions of existing products, processes or organisational activities. As these innovations typically come about in response to specific and articulated customer needs, they occur in demand-side markets (Shanklin and Ryans, 1984) and tend to be based on what we call "market pull" (as opposed to "technology push"). Most firms engage daily in incremental innovation, although some firms are more conscious and strategic about the benefits of empowering their employees to engage in incremental innovation and improvement work. In many instances, as illustrated in the previous IKEA Lack table example, we can see how a series of incremental innovations over time add up to significant change in companies.

> *Market Pull* is a term commonly used when users or market forces drive changes within an innovation. The opposite is called *technology push*, which is when the firm pushes new technologies without the request from the market or users (Shanklin and Ryans, 1984).

Incremental innovation is more appealing for many firms than radical innovation because it involves lower risks and a lower degree of change in the processes that the organisation is already successfully conducting. However, there are also fewer increases in returns associated with incremental innovation; moreover, if firms become too inward-looking and only pursue incremental change, they run the risk of not discovering new and disruptive trends in their environment before it is too late.

As opposed to incremental innovation, *radical* or *breakthrough* innovations involve bigger changes, may be more disruptive and require more network relationships to change. In other words, radical innovations tend to trigger more friction with established counterparts, as well as confrontations between the new and the old (Hoholm and Olsen, 2012). But, while a radical innovation in this way implies higher levels of risks, it also carries the potential of higher returns if successful. Radical innovations are revolutionary in nature; they break the accepted norm, bringing about new and superior advantages as compared to the old technology. As customer needs are often unknown, breakthrough innovations often occur in supply-side markets (Shanklin and Ryans, 1984), meaning that the "technology push" governs the process.

Generally, the more radical the innovation, the higher the risk, while potentially also bringing higher rewards. Often radical technologies emerge from research laboratories. These can operate within publicly funded research institutions (i.e., universities) or as part of larger companies, which have their own research laboratories. Companies and public research bodies patent their discoveries and later can pursue the commercialisation themselves or license the technology to others who apply it in the creation of new products, services or processes.

Table 4.3 Incremental versus radical innovation classification matrix

Type of Innovation	Definition	Example	Common attributes
Incremental innovation	Evolutionary in nature; consists of smaller improvements in products, processes or organisational activities introduced over time; often based on extensions of existing products, processes or organisational activities	Kodak's continuous improvement of traditional film for the camera industry; Continuous development of traditional surgery	Lower risk; tend to come from market pull[a]
Radical innovation	Revolutionary in nature; break the accepted norm, bringing about new and superior advantages as compared to the old technology	Development of digital imaging; Development of minimally invasive surgery (laparoscopy), using advanced imaging, sensor and robot technologies, etc.	Higher risk; tend to be driven by technology push[a]

[a]Shanklin and Ryans, 1984

Radical and incremental are relative terms; we can say that a radical innovation contains a relatively high number of novel elements and combinations. Most technology innovations are not entirely new. They are in fact modifications of the existing body of technologies, evolving from current technologies, or combining several existing technologies. In other words, technological change, to a significant extent, is based on the cumulative effects of small incremental innovations. The classification of the innovation as incremental or radical is relative to degrees on a continuum.

4.5.4 Disruptive Innovations

An innovation which brings about significant upheaval within an industry with major implications for all the major stakeholders is known as *disruptive* (e.g., digital technology has dramatically changed many industries). However, to be disruptive, an innovation does not necessarily have to be radical in the sense of containing radically new breakthrough technologies. The distinction is whether the technology "fits in" or challenges the established system.

Clayton M. Christensen (1997) has pioneered our understanding of *disruptive innovation*. He identified how new technologies, like the internet, enabled a range of inventions that implied radical breaks with the established market. Key characteristics of disruptive innovation are that they are often simpler and are lower quality on some parameters, but – importantly – they are also more user-friendly and cheaper than the established alternatives or incumbent technologies. Typically, although not necessarily, disruptive innovations emerge from "below" – from entrepreneurs finding their niche in the "shadow" of the high-quality and high-priced alternatives of established firms – before growing into the mainstream and threatening the existing market.

Key Characteristics of Disruptive Innovations (Christensen, 1997):

1. Solution is simpler and lower quality
2. Solution is more user-friendly
3. Solution is cheaper

For established firms, Christensen (1997) states the three main challenges from disruptive innovation are, first, that such technologies seem so immature and of such low quality that they are not perceived as a threat to the company or their market position. This is normally a very favourable situation for entrepreneurs with emerging technologies. Second, when disruptive technologies mature more and gain a significant volume of users, they may sometimes be too late for the established firms to catch up with the latest entrepreneurial ventures already populating the new field. Third, a change from an established to a disruptive technology will for many established firms mean extremely high costs as they have invested heavily in the present techno-economic system, which may be rendered of less use to the company. Such expensive changes, as well as the fear of contributing to the cannibalisation of the established firm's own products in the marketplace, typically lead to conservative attitudes toward potentially disruptive emerging technologies among many firms.

Main Challenges Disruptive Innovations create for Established Firms (Christensen 1997):

1. Newer technologies are not viewed as a threat due to the market position of the firm and the immaturity and low quality of the product
2. Late reaction to the innovative technology may be unrecoverable
3. Path dependency to established technologies makes transitioning to newer technologies costly

---

A classic example is the mp3 file format, which enabled users to share their music without the help of record companies, distributors and retail stores. This technology spread without any help from traditional distributors of music, either through pirate consumers or through more or less legal websites. It was an information and communication technology (ICT) company that gained the market. Apple, by setting up iTunes as a web store for mp3 files, was the first to demonstrate how to earn money from this disruptive technology. Note the quality of an mp3 is far lower to the compact disc format. Combined with the ease of copying, this made the music industry overlook the mp3 threat, which the industry later tried to fight with all means available. Today, the big and once-powerful record companies still shiver from this industrial earthquake. Another example is how cloud-based services, such as Google Apps and Google Drive, are gradually pushing aside the established software solutions packaged with computers. This has put significant pressure on the dominant players, such as Microsoft, in the established market.

In complex industrial systems, sometimes even relatively incremental innovations may bring about disruption. One small example is the attempt to replace traditional surgery with the implementation of a microwave technology for the treatment of enlarged prostates in Swedish hospitals (Wagrell and Waluszewski, 2009). This turned out to challenge the established system in several dimensions: The professional hierarchy was challenged by the innovation, as medical doctors in this field are trained in surgery, and hence many resisted the new method. Every problematic aspect with the new procedure would be used to undermine the legitimacy of the innovation. The reimbursement system and the purchasing function in Swedish hospitals were based on having only one main treatment procedure for each disease, and as the microwave treatment could only be used for some of the patients, it was difficult to fit it into the economic and organisational structure. In sum, this meant that many hospitals did not adopt the innovation – even several of those having participated in the development process.

4.5.5 Open Innovation

Open innovation (Chesbrough, 2006) has become a very popular issue in the last decade. It is putting the tension between openness and protection of knowledge and intellectual property to the fore. It is based on the acknowledgement that the best competence and the best ideas often are found outside the company needing it. Hence, companies that are able to utilise and mobilise knowledge, ideas and resources from other companies and actors will be more innovative. In today's digital knowledge and information society, knowledge has become extremely more available globally. One of the problems related to open innovation is the "not invented here" syndrome. In many companies, people will try to resist innovative ideas coming from the outside because they are unfamiliar, or use something coming from a different setting.

The leadership skills needed to handle open innovation is a strategic understanding of IPR. Companies that are really good at this do not just open up their processes to anyone. They are also very conscious about what processes and knowledge they are willing to open up and what they need to keep secret or protected within the company. There is sometimes a delicate balance between openness and protection. Entrepreneurial leaders thus need negotiation skills and the ability to create win-win situations, because no one will be interested in the long-term collaboration if not co-creating solutions that may benefit both parties. It is also good for a leader to have a multi-disciplinary perspective, to understand people with different professional and industrial backgrounds and to move and translate between different perspectives. Engineers, sales and marketing people, designers and end users all communicate and understand the world differently.

4.5.6 Overview of Classifying Innovations

In general, an organisation will usually be involved in a mixture of the different types of innovation. It is very likely, for instance, that while engaging in product innovation, an organisation will also go through process innovation in an attempt to improve a possible prototype. As the entrepreneurial company matures, we recommend the successful practice of having a well-balanced portfolio of lower risk, short-term projects focusing on incremental innovations, as well as longer term, high-risk projects, focusing on breakthrough technology. Incremental innovation could bring in quick returns, needed for daily activities and the survival of the business, while radical innovations take a more long-term view, with the possibility of more significant positive results in the future. Successful innovators often manage various projects, at different stages in their life cycle so that the company is always involved in new projects before other projects are completed; this ensures continuity, while instilling an organisational culture where innovation is on the daily agenda.

In Chapter 6, we explore additional innovation categories: *organizational innovation* and *business model innovation*. These innovative ways of organising and developing a business are frequently paired with innovative technologies. Further study of these innovation categories will enhance your entrepreneurial tool set.

4.6 SOURCES OF INNOVATION

There are many sources of innovation, from both within and outside the organisation. Ideas can be generated on the basis of some technical insight of an individual or a group of individuals; innovation can also occur following the identification of previous problems or possible future issues. Creative thinking is considered a core competency in new ventures and having creative, inventive employees and teams is a great source of innovation.

Entrepreneurs, as well as creative people within established organisations, are usually able to see novel linkages in the wealth of information gathered from all these various sources (Casson et al., 2006). Once an opportunity is recognised, the idea is evaluated and tested. If successful and in line with the organisation's goals and available resources, it then enters a development process, based on an envisioned new product, service or process. Gathering a wealth of information from varied sources and developing further information creates a good environment for innovation.

However, most of the time the roots of innovation can be traced back to real problems or issues in the market. An essential source of innovation within organisations is the voice of the market: listening and understanding customers' needs and expectations; networking with other players in the market or in a company's own supply chain; collaborating openly with research bodies, etc. Ideas can also be stimulated by specific organisational goals or by external environmental factors (i.e., opportunities).

While a simplistic classification would be to divide innovations into technology-driven (push) or market driven (pull), in reality most innovations occur due to a combination of these major factors. Trott (2008) suggested an interactive model of innovation, where innovation occurs as a result of the interaction between the marketplace, scientific research and the organisation's capabilities. Innovation happens on the borderline and companies must provide those at the boundaries with enough freedom (in both time and resources) to be able to generate and pursue innovative ideas. A successful innovation occurs when a need and a means to resolving that need are simultaneously recognised. However, not all new ideas become successful innovations. Research shows that roughly only 1 in 3,000 raw innovative ideas results in a commercially successful product or service (Stevens and Burley, 2003).

Case Box 4.1   Micro-particles: The case of Conpart[1]

Conpart is a technology company specialising in materials for the international electronics industry. The business is based on a unique and patented process for manufacturing of extremely precise and mono-sized micrometer-sized polymer particles. There are numerous different application areas in electronics where Conpart´s particle technology can be used. By applying nano-layers of different metals on the particle surface, the particles can be made electrically conductive making them suitable as micro-connectors for assembly of micro-components in electronics. One important market is conductive adhesives, where such particles can be filled into epoxy resins to make different types of conductive adhesives, which is commonly used in modern electronics manufacturing. There are several other fields of use for conductive and non-conductive polymer-based particles in the electronics industry.

Micro-particles have been used in electronics for decades, but almost all technology development and volume manufacturing have taken place in Asia, with Japan, Korea and Taiwan having the most important companies. Hence, as for many other Norwegian technology companies, Conpart needed to address an international market from the start. With very limited finances and resources, but with a strong technology basis and world-leading competence in its field, Conpart targeted big companies with a leading position in their respective field. The focus was on areas where the technology could give long lasting technical advantages for the customers either by improved reliability or quality for their products, or by reducing their manufacturing cost with improved manufacturing processes. Just two years after the foundation, Conpart signed a contract with a major Japanese company, and after a three-year joint development project, it got the first supply agreement.

This strategy has been a model for Conpart in order to establish new projects and business. The development time is relatively long and costly for such products, and the development projects require high competence, strong technology and hence good funding. Conpart has successfully established many collaborative projects with the industry, supported by either Norwegian governmental funding, like the research council, or EU-funding. Through these development projects, Conpart generates new applications and markets for its polymer particles, and the plan is to become a world-leading supplier of these highly specialised materials to the electronics industry.

The outcome of innovation initiatives should be closely monitored and assessed with companies gaining valuable insights from each experience whether the experience was a failure or a success. According to O'Sullivan and Dooley (2009), innovation management should be based on a specific methodology or a set of steps that must be implemented; organisations should either adopt or develop their own methodology around managing innovation, which usually encompasses the following steps:

1. Understand requirements and define goals – understand the requirements of the organisation's stakeholders, define state-of-the-art and best practice in other organisations and define goals based on these considerations. This step is usually executed at the beginning of each planning period.
2. Engage users and model processes – engage various users and providers in problem identification and idea generation; then create models in order to help users understand how the innovative value proposition works and how it differs from the current offer. This step is executed several times throughout the period of the plan.
3. Create actions and empower teams – ideas are converted into initiatives and projects with their associated teams. This step occurs often as new actions are defined.
4. Develop migration plan – this is a dynamic plan, which changes according to the progress achieved in reaching (and changing) goals, and as various actions are implemented. It is usually part of a knowledge management system within the firm. This step is very frequent, it should be reviewed once a week, as goals, actions and teams change.
5. Implement actions and monitor results – this consists of the implementation and monitoring of goals, actions and teams over time and its results. Monitoring what is happening should provide feedback to the first steps, as results are used to redefine goals. Step five occurs daily as the performance outputs of each organisational effort is monitored.

The trends regarding the increasing speed and globalisation of innovation have led to a number of new perspectives on how to keep up or, preferably, be at the forefront of innovation. An important movement in the field of innovation management is towards observing and/or involving the *users* in the process. In the field of user-driven (or sometimes "customer driven") innovation (Von Hippel, 2006), methods and tools are being developed to get beyond the scarce information about users' needs that can be gotten from market/consumer surveys and focus groups. The problem is that in the face of more or less radical inventions, the user is often not able to articulate his/her own need, nor to predict his/her own consumer behaviour in the future. Instead sometimes companies seek to observe the user in his/her own "natural environment" to unveil their frustrations, daily routines and relations to other technologies. Other times, companies develop "toolkits" along with their inventions to enable "lead users" (highly skilled and highly interested users) to develop and adapt the product to their own user patterns and context. Design innovation methods have recently been introduced to technical and service innovation settings (Jevnaker, 2005; Verganti, 2009), since designers have a long tradition of identifying users' needs.

At the end of this phase, at least one idea should be formulated. The following section will provide further information on the Technology Innovation Life Cycle, which will guide the innovation to implementation.

4.7 THE TECHNOLOGY INNOVATION LIFE CYCLE

There are several systematic steps within the innovation process: idea generation (or problem analysis), idea evaluation, project planning, product development, testing and launching the product into the marketplace. These steps are not usually linear but rather overlap each other. The entrepreneur needs to iterate several cycles of the innovation lifecycle before succeeding in developing both a product and a market. There are mainly three stages in the technology innovation lifecycle:

1. Diagnose. The aim of this stage is to identify and evaluate new ideas for products and processes, usually done through a comprehensive analysis of environmental and internal factors that will impact the potential success of innovative ideas. Next, ideas are screened and evaluated, as innovators try to assess the feasibility and possible rate of success of each project. A Strengths, Weaknesses, Opportunities and Threats (SWOT) analysis should be conducted in order to identify possible opportunities and threats in the marketplace, including working with customers in the process of identifying what is important to them. Examples of best practice should also be identified. This external scanning should be paired with an internal assessment, which would help decide on which strengths to exploit and weaknesses to address (SWOT analysis tool is covered in Chapter 7).
2. Develop. After identifying the most promising avenues, move on to the development stage, whereby the idea is transformed through planning and developing into a viable product or process. Ideas are developed further in response to the result of the initial analysis, and propositions should be analysed and ranked according to their importance and potential. Resources should be devoted to the most promising initiatives, and prototypes should be developed and tested with users. Objectives should be developed as the understanding of the product and its use evolves (see Chapter 7).
3. Deploy. This phase consists of planning the migration and roll-out. Roll-out is the process of introducing the new product to the market or employing the new or improved process in particular areas of the business. The new technology should be continuously monitored and assessed in terms of meeting the initial objectives; support systems should be in place and on-going training should be provided to all those affected by the change brought about in the organisation through the innovation. Continuous learning from current experiences would help in future decisions, and objectives should therefore be revised often (Marketing of Technology is covered in Chapter 9).

The stages in the innovation process are all interrelated and each individual decision at every stage will influence all the other stages. These stages also show the different contexts within which the innovation needs to "fit in" or find alliances; the development setting, the production setting and the user setting. While the initial stages (also termed the "fuzzy front end") in the innovation process allows for higher level of uncertainty and encourages creativity, the remaining stages of the process do not tolerate the same level of uncertainty, where more structure and solid business decisions are required.

Technology innovation is most successfully implemented when conducted as a continuous process, which is viewed as part of the daily activities of the organisation. However, the scope of the resources available must be considered when going through the technology innovation life cycle. New ideas that will add value to the innovation cannot be continually added but must be held back for inclusion in later phases after the innovation demonstrates initial success.

4.8 DIFFUSION OF INNOVATIONS

This section explains *innovation/market dynamics*. The *theory of diffusion* (Tarde, 1903; Rogers, 1995) reveals the "S-curve" of how innovations reach different segments of users and how this impacts the development and the economic returns. Rogers's theory on the diffusion of innovation has been adapted for the high technology context by Geoffrey Moore. Before we explain diffusion theory, we will elaborate a bit on why people may resist adopting/buying technological innovations.

4.8.1 Diffusion of Innovation and Adopter Categories

Diffusion is the process by which an innovation is communicated through certain channels over time among the members of a social system. Social studies conducted in the area of innovation have found that the rate of adoption for an innovation is highly dependent on the social system it occurs in; the social system constitutes a boundary within which an innovation diffuses. It affects the process of diffusion in two ways:

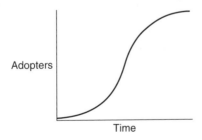

Figure 4.1 S-shaped curve
Source: Tarde, 1903.

- through the norms establishing behaviour patterns; and
- through opinion leadership (the degree to which an individual is able to influence informally other individuals' attitudes or overt behaviour).

Originating in the research conducted by Gabriel Tarde in 1903, the *S-shaped curve* (shown in Figure 4.1) is the most widely used diagram in describing how people adopt new innovations. According to the speed of the diffusion, the slope of the S-curve might be steeper (for rapidly diffused innovations) or more gradual (for innovations that take longer to become accepted in the market).

Forty years later, a study conducted by Ryan and Gross (1943) analysing the spread of hybrid seed corn among Iowa farmers, led to the identification of different adopter categories. By researching the speed at which different groups in the market adopted an innovation after its introduction on the market, this study acknowledged the existence of five adopter categories: innovators, early adopters, early majority, late majority and laggards.

Five Adopter Categories (Ryan and Gross, 1943):

1. Innovators
2. Early Adopters
3. Early Majority
4. Late Majority
5. Laggards

4.8.2 The Roger's Diffusion of Innovation Paradigm

The most widely acknowledged author in the study of diffusion is Everett M. Rogers. His book, *Diffusion of Innovations* (1995), is highly influential in the established paradigm of the diffusion of innovation. Rogers put forward four theories of diffusion: the individual innovativeness theory; the theory of perceived attributes; the rate of adoption theory; and the innovation decision process theory.

The individual innovativeness theory states that the rate of adoption depends on the degree of innovativeness of an individual or other unit (e.g., group or organisation). *Innovativeness* is the degree to which an individual or other unit of adoption is earlier in adopting new ideas than other members of a social system. Individuals are divided into five categories on the basis on their innovativeness (see Figure 4.2).

Rogers (1995) further defines the five adoption categories as part of this theory.

1. **Innovators** (on average 2.5% of adopters) are venturesome, interested in new and risky ideas, able to understand and apply complex technical knowledge and able to cope with a high degree of uncertainty about an innovation at the time of adoption. Innovators are also usually engaged in more cosmopolite social relationships, in control of substantial financial resources and eager to communicate with other innovators. Even though innovators might not always be accepted within their own

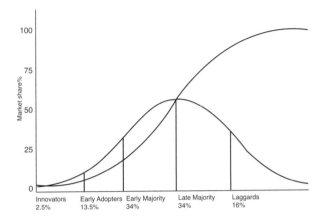

Figure 4.2   Five categories of innovators

Source: Based on Rogers, E. (1995) *Diffusion of Innovations*. London, New York: Free Press.

social network, they play an important role in the diffusion process, by launching the new idea in the system.

2. **Early adopters** (13.5%) are a more respected and integrated part of the local social system than are innovators, with developed interpersonal networks. This adopter category, more than any other, has the greatest degree of opinion leadership in most systems. Early adopters provide advice and information about the innovation and they serve as a role-model for many other members of a social system. They adopt innovations based on seemingly well-judged decisions. Early adopters are instrumental in getting an innovation to the point of critical mass, which occurs when enough individuals have adopted an innovation that is being further adopted by other individuals, and thereby becomes self-sustaining.

3. **Early majority** (34%) adopt new ideas just before the average member of a system. They do not like to take the high-risk associated with "being the first," but they want to benefit of the advantages of new discoveries. The early majority interact frequently with their peers and often hold positions of opinion leadership in a system. This group may deliberate for some time before completely adopting a new idea, but they seldom lead.

4. **Late majority** (34%) adopt new ideas just after the average member of a system. This group is more sceptical towards anything new that would imply a change on their behalf. They are more traditional and do not adopt until most others in their system have done so. Sometimes the pressure of peers is necessary to motivate adoption.

5. **Laggards** (16%) are the most traditional group and hence most suspicious of innovations. The point of reference for the laggard is the past. Decisions are often made in terms of what has been done previously. Their resources are often limited and they need certainty that a new idea will not fail before they can adopt. Because of all, these they possess no opinion leadership.

Second, *the theory of perceived attributes* states that there are five attributes or characteristics of the innovation that determine its rate of adoption and success:

1. **Relative advantage** is the degree to which an innovation is perceived by users as better than the idea it supersedes. This is based on perception and may be measured in economic terms, but social prestige, convenience and satisfaction are also important factors. In simple terms, the greater the perceived relative advantage of an innovation, the more rapid its rate of adoption will be.
2. **Compatibility** is the degree to which an innovation is perceived as being consistent with the existing values, past experiences and needs of potential adopters. This may speed up adoption.
3. **Complexity** is the degree to which an innovation is perceived as difficult to understand and use. More complicated innovations will be adopted more slowly, as they require the adopter to develop new skills and understandings.
4. **Trialability** is the degree to which an innovation may be experimented with on a limited basis. New ideas that can be tried and have visible results will generally be adopted more quickly than innovations that cannot. A higher degree of trialability reduces uncertainty for the individual who is considering it for adoption.
5. **Observability** is the degree to which the results and benefits of an innovation are visible to others. The easier the attributes can be observed, imagined or described to potential customers, the more likely they are to adopt it.

Third, *the rate of adoption theory* states that an innovation goes through a period of slow, gradual growth before a period of speedy and significant growth. The point is that as users gradually spread their recommendations of the product, one may see exponential growth until the market is saturated. In this case, the rate of adoption is measured as the number of members of a social system who adopt the innovation in a given time period. The rate of adoption is influenced by the five perceived categories of adoption of an innovation, as introduced above.

Finally, *the innovation decision process theory* states that that diffusion is the mental process through which an individual (or other decision-making unit) passes through five distinct stages, from first knowledge of an innovation to the confirmation decision to adopt the innovation. The five stages are:

1. **Knowledge** – a person becomes aware of the innovation and has some idea of how it functions
2. **Persuasion** – a person forms a favourable or unfavourable attitude toward the innovation
3. **Decision** – a person engages in activities that lead to the decision to adopt or reject the innovation
4. **Implementation** – a person puts the innovation into use
5. **Confirmation** – a person evaluates the results of the innovation

In terms of communication channels, research shows that while mass media channels are more effective in creating knowledge of innovations, interpersonal channels carry more weight in the later stages of the mental process of adopting an innovation. Interpersonal channels are more effective in forming and changing attitudes, as well as influencing the decision to adopt or reject a new idea. In other words, most individuals evaluate an innovation, not on the basis of expert advice, but through the subjective evaluations of near-peers who have adopted the innovation.

Rogers's theory of diffusion has been very important in explaining how innovations find users and how mass markets are shaped. However, in relation to technology innovation, Moore (2002) found that some of the transitions between adopter categories were more problematic than Rogers' theory suggested. This is what we now turn to.

4.8.3 Moore's Technology Adoption Life Cycle

Rogers' theory on the diffusion of innovation was adapted for the high technology context by Geoffrey Moore (2002). In the Technology Adoption Life Cycle (TALC), the groups are still characterised by different responses to the new technology, yet there is a major difference in the cycle of market penetration: it is not a continuum. In this distinction, Moore pinpoints the important problem of moving from one adopter group to another, because their interests, needs and resources may be very different. Hence, an innovation's ability to reach one group does not necessarily mean that it is interesting to other groups.

For disruptive technologies, Moore (2002) proposes a variation of the original life cycle, suggesting that there is a gap or chasm between the early adopters' group (the visionaries) and the early majority group (the pragmatists or starting point of the mainstream market) (see Figure 4.3).

Also, Moore updated the labels for the five adopter categories. The Early Market consists of the first two groups: Technology Enthusiasts and the Visionaries.

Innovators are **Technology Enthusiasts** who having technology as a central interest in their lives. Techies are always looking for state-of-the-art technology and are intrigued with the advancement of technology in general. However, as opposed to the Innovators group in the classical theory of the diffusion of innovations, the Technology Enthusiasts do not typically have the money to fund further development.

Techies are not numerous in any market, but they provide good testing ground for a new technology, and they are extremely important in reaching to the Visionaries group. According to Moore (2002), Technology Enthusiasts fulfil the role of gatekeepers to the next group. In other words, a technology-based product has to impress the Technology Enthusiasts in order to get the attention of the Visionaries (Moore, 2002).

Visionaries, or Early Adopters, are industry revolutionaries looking for breakthrough applications. They have the qualities necessary to envision and understand discontinuous innovations for the potential

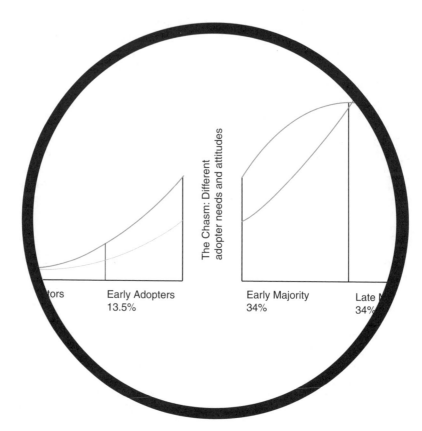

Figure 4.3 Discontinuous technology adoption

Source: Based on Moore (2002), *The Revised Technology Adoption Life Cycle.*

advantage it might provide, yet they need the endorsement of the Technology Enthusiasts.

Visionaries can easily match the potential of a new idea with strategic opportunities. They are very important because they have the ability to fund development, as well as positively communicate and persuade within their own organisation and also within an industry. The Visionaries are essential to opening the high technology segment for a specific technology (Moore, 2002).

The Early Majority are called **Pragmatists** by Moore (2002). They are a group that value practicality more than the innovation aspect. They will not venture into buying new products unless they can have the reassurance of established and credible references. They are risk averse and price sensitive. They usually favour products and brands that are established as market leaders, which provide reassurance. Because they represent a substantial segment in the market, they are essential in achieving critical mass – substantial profits and growth.

Table 4.4 Five innovation adoption categories (based on Moore (2002))

Market phase	Adoption group	Key characteristics	Challenges
EARLY MARKET	**Technology enthusiasts** (Innovators)	Technology is a central interest Always looking for state-of-the-art technology and are intrigued with the advancement of technology in general Do not typically have the money to fund further development Provide good testing ground for a new technology	Not numerous in any market Gatekeepers to the Visionaries group Technology-based products must impress them in order to get the attention of the Visionaries
	Visionaries (Early adopters)	Industry revolutionaries looking for breakthrough applications Possess the qualities necessary to envision and understand discontinuous innovations for the potential advantage it might provide Can easily match the potential of a new idea with strategic opportunities Can fund development Communicates and persuades within their own organisation and within an industry	Requires the endorsement of the Technology Enthusiasts Essential to opening the high technology segment for a specific technology
THE CHASM			
MAINSTREAM MARKET	**Pragmatists** (Early majority)	Values practicality more than the innovation aspect Risk averse and price sensitive Will not venture into buying new products unless reassured by established and credible references, preferably by market leaders Want a completely functional product and are only willing to accept incremental improvements	Biggest challenge: making the transition between Visionaries and Pragmatists, what Moore refers to as *the chasm* Represents a substantial segment in the market and are essential in achieving critical mass Cross the chasm only by switching from a marketing strategy focusing on functionality to one that can present the innovation as the new industry standard, which is necessary for the Pragmatists
	Conservatives (Late majority)	Not comfortable with handling novelty Usually wait until the technology becomes the accepted standard before purchasing it Averse to high prices Prefer well-known companies and expect significant support during and after the purchase	One-third of the market, so the size of this segment makes it highly attractive May be successfully targeted once the product reaches the maturity stage
	Sceptics (Laggards)	Not interested in new technology in any form, be it for economic or personal reasons Might even oppose technological developments	No challenges, as Sceptics are not pursued by technology-driven companies

The biggest challenge is making the transition between the Visionaries and the Pragmatists, as these two groups have very different attitudes and hence buying behaviour towards innovative, technology-based products. This is what Moore refers to as **the chasm**. He suggests that companies can cross the chasm only by switching from a marketing strategy focusing on functionality (to which the Visionaries are responsive) to one that can present the innovation as the new industry standard, which is necessary for the Pragmatists (Moore, 2002). Unlike the Early Market's willingness to accept prototypes, Pragmatics want a complete functional product (i.e., the main product plus additional hardware or software, installation, training and further support services) and are only willing to accept incremental improvements (versus disruptive innovations) (Moore, 2002).

The late majority are the **Conservatives**. They differ from the Pragmatists, as they are not as comfortable with handling novelty, so they will usually wait until the technology becomes the accepted standard before purchasing it. Also, they are averse to high prices. Similar to the Pragmatists, the Conservatives prefer well-known companies and expect significant support during and after the purchase. Consisting of about one-third of the market, the size of this segment makes it highly attractive for companies, especially since the Conservatives may be very successfully targeted once the product reaches the maturity stage (Moore, 2002).

The laggards are the **Sceptics**. They are not interested in new technology in any form, be it for economic or personal reasons. They might even oppose technological developments. For these considerations, laggards are not pursued by technology-driven companies (Moore, 2002).

According to Moore (2002), these important differences between the adopter categories imply that the adoption process is not continuous. From a marketing perspective, the variations in target group perspectives requires companies to prepare and address the different categories with different marketing mixes.

4.8.4 Diffusion in Practice

While powerful on a meso-level, and for pinpointing certain challenges of innovation, the diffusion theory comes short of explaining how this challenge plays out in practice in the company and its network. Meanwhile, theories of "translation" and of industrial networks do exactly this by helping us understand the hard work for entrepreneurs and their allies of actually transforming technical (or other) ideas into products or services that are adopted and used by users (Håkansson and Waluszewski, 2007; Pinch and Oudshoorn, 2003; Hoholm, 2011). First, this is partly a game of mobilising and convincing actors to create powerful alliances to support the innovation (see the Contrary Forces Model below). Second, it is partly of producing not only the product, but also its environment. In other words, to get a product into use it will both have to be closely adapted to the established setting, and the established setting will have to be changed too. During this process, the innovators will encounter confrontations and frictions, as well as unintended effects in the established or emerging network. The adaptation process between innovation and users is mutual, and the aim is to produce an interdependent relationship between them.

4.9   MANAGING INNOVATION

Scientific inventions are mainly driven by the passion and curiosity of scientists and technologists (Knorr Cetina, 2001). The same passion that inspires the inventor to search for the solution also drives the entrepreneur. However, many technology entrepreneurs have experienced how the idealism of science and the rigidity of scientific methods are necessarily compromised on the path from invention to commercialised innovation. This evolution is often confusing and frustrating for the entrepreneur. The business of transforming an invention into a commercialised innovation is a highly pragmatic practice of drawing together the often diverse interests and practices of economic actors, as well as consumers and industrial partners, making compromises necessary (Hoholm, 2011). Hence, the encounter between the inventions of techno-science and the tough realities of business often produces the question of what will remain of the initial innovation in the end. Along with the question how will the innovation to be combined with existing business practices in order to find users, it is uncertain how the innovation will take part in changing standard practices. Increasing levels of uncertainty can produce insecurity within the team; therefore, strong leadership and confidence from the entrepreneur are needed to guide the team through times of struggle.

4.9.1   The Management of Uncertainty

The management of innovation always carries a degree of uncertainty. In short, the entrepreneur takes on the responsibility of transforming *uncertainty* of what is not known into manageable risk through analysis of risk levels and applying strategies to overcome challenges. Throughout the innovation process, systematic learning and continuous feedback from the market are needed to reduce uncertainty, although uncertainty can never be removed completely.

McMullen and Shepherd (2006) discuss whether entrepreneurial "opportunity" should be viewed as something being *discovered* (realists) or as something *enacted* and co-created (constructivists) by the actors involved in interpreting knowledge in the situation. Both views emphasise that opportunities are characterised by uncertainty and that this is central to understanding entrepreneurial action. Yet, the realists' uncertainty is mainly about availability and sometimes the interpretation of objective knowledge of existing markets. Constructivists' uncertainty, however, relates to the enactment of perceived opportunity by the involved actors, hence multiplying the sources of uncertainty. Uncertainty, then, comes from the unpredictability of interaction, both between human actors (individuals or groups), and between humans and material elements – "natural", technical and textual. In this view, novel solutions and their use, through markets, have to be co-created in interaction between different involved actors – developers, producers and users (Håkansson and Waluszewski, 2007).

As mentioned in the Incremental versus Radical Innovation section above, the degree of uncertainty in innovation processes are "strongly correlated with the amount of advance" (Kline and Rosenberg, 1986, p. 294), and the risk of failure in innovation processes will increase "with the number of practices and competencies that need to be changed" (Pavitt, 2005, p. 105). Innovation processes are therefore equal to processes of learning, where "overplanning" may distort the process, because the future cannot, by definition, be fully known. Furthermore, the *false summit effect* – or repeatedly finding new mountaintops behind the one that was believed to be the real summit – produces a kind of uncertainty that cannot be planned for in detail. In general, innovators tend "to underestimate the number of tasks that must be solved and hence also the time and costs" (Kline and Rosenberg, 1986, p. 298). In addition to the technical side, then, uncertainty is increased by rising development costs, resistance to radical innovation, financial risks and coupling of technical and economic elements. Hence, economic forces, technical knowledge and consumer demand need to be closely connected during innovation processes.

4.9.2 Managing (in) Networks

Innovation is often a highly networked process, involving many actors, and is rarely the result of one "designer" (Håkansson and Ford, 2002, p. 135). Hence, the outcome of an innovation process is never given at the outset; it is the object of controversial and collaborative interactions often over long periods of time. Within business networks, numerous combinations are possible, enabling innovation only as long as it is "designed appropriately and seen to be positive by those who support its needs" (135). Moreover, new relationships with new counterparts are both necessary and difficult to put in place because of the existing structure that has to be taken into account. This means that innovation has a better basis for success if current investments, technologies and resources are included in the development process, and are combined with the new solution. "The more the new solution can be embedded into the existing structure, the larger the economic advantage for both the supply and user sides" (Waluszewski, 2004, p. 147). At the same time, it is important that a place for the innovation is created, which often demands the "interactors" to break with parts of the existing structure (147).

4.9.3 Managing Iteration

Kline and Rosenberg (1986) claimed that economists, who predominantly focus on market forces, did not understand the technical transformation process, which is perceived to be in a black box. Meanwhile, technologists often failed to take the "external forces of the marketplace" into consideration, because their focus is honed to the development of the innovation. Innovation, from this perspective, is a complex and uncertain process, and

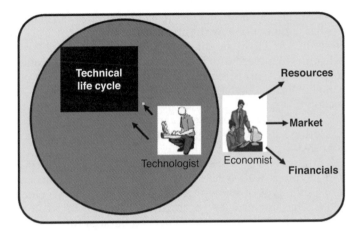

Figure 4.4 Visual interpretation of Kline and Rosenberg's (1986) opposing perspectives of technologist and economist during innovation development

an "exercise in the management and reduction of uncertainty" (276). In other words, it is as if the technologist and economist are standing back-to-back, with the technologists looking into the black box and the economist looking away. However, both perspectives must be interlaced to develop successful innovations.

Hence, several authors have suggested that iterative and systematic learning methods are needed to manage innovation and entrepreneurship processes. One such example is Eric Ries's "Lean Startup" model (2011). It aims to speed up learning through repeated cycles of: *building* prototypes, or "minimum viable products"; *measuring* through tests and measurements among users (see "Growth Metrics" in Chapter 6); and *learning* by making minor adjustments or major shifts, "pivots", in the product/service, its delivery to users or the income model.

Sarasvathy and Dew (2005) found that successful serial entrepreneurs typically started out, not with market analysis, but with asking themselves three crucial questions: Who am I (what are my interests and passions)? What have I got (competence, resources)? And who do I know (network)? Sarasvathy and Dew call this "the bird in hand principle", starting out with one's own unique set of resources and relationships. From this, the entrepreneur continues with "effectuation", i.e., improvisation and systematic testing of alternative offers to users and markets. This is contrasted with "causation", which represents the more static planning approach (systematic analysis and planning before action), typically used by managers in established businesses.

4.9.4   The Contrary Forces of Innovation

With the above mentioned uncertainties from interaction and potential resistances from the establishment (frictions and confrontations), we see how innovation management both in entrepreneurial ventures and in established companies has to do not only with the quality of the technology or product but also with the strength of the entrepreneur's arguments and ability to build alliances. In order to succeed with innovation, there is a need to acquire power via *coalition building*. This is accomplished through "selling" the project to various stakeholders in different ways during the process (see also Chapter 8 for the section on "pitching"). In the *Contrary Forces Model* (Hoholm, 2011), innovation is outlined as a dual process in terms of (1) mobilising resources and (2) exploring knowledge (developing the innovation). Mobilisation and exploration are the contrary forces in this model.

First, during processes of *mobilisation*, network actors are recruited and committed to things with which they are initially unfamiliar: an idea, a prospect or a prototype of something that may or may not become feasible and useable. The aim may be to convince partners, to secure funding and to get enough resources (competence, technology, distribution, etc.). Paradoxically, to enable mobilisation for such uncertain projects, a degree of certainty has to be presumed in the vision and story told by the entrepreneur (in a pitch, in a business plan, etc.).

Second, during processes of *knowledge exploration*, the aim is to explore the innovation's potential. Propositions about reality, whether the technology or the market, are formulated and tested in practice. By actually exploring and learning about the technology and the product, as well as exploring and learning about the market potential in practice, the entrepreneur gains knowledge of what can possibly be realised and of the challenges that must be overcome to get there. The second paradox is that this process of generating knowledge (to realise the innovation, find solutions and clear answers) tends to generate the opposite: more complexity and risk, more choices to be made and more problems to be solved.

Sometimes it appears almost like the innovation process is at war with itself. Whereas mobilisation is directed towards aligning interests and reducing risks, exploration is directed towards formulating and testing propositions about reality (i.e., will the technology work, will users be interested, etc.). While mobilisation seeks to converge and simplify the idea, exploration frequently leads to divergence of the innovation. Entrepreneurs thus have to produce two different kinds of knowledge: first, a chain of arguments suited for convincing, mobilising, and maintaining network partners and their resources, and second, they need to produce testable propositions about reality (e.g., of how to make the technology work and what users have interest in such a product).

Finally, the *interaction* between mobilisation and exploration processes often leads to controversies and compromises that may set the project off in new directions. This typically happens when the project has run out of money or time, and the entrepreneur has to go back to the different stakeholders. Preliminary results are presented, and new plans have to be negotiated, because the project has moved in different directions than anticipated initially. In these interactions, it is common to change the direction of the project, sometimes by doing smaller adjustments, and other times by making a pivot (Ries, 2011).

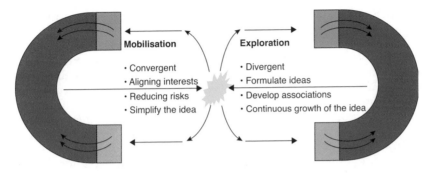

Figure 4.5   Visual interpretation of Hoholm's (2011) Contrary Forces Model

Lock-in, or *path dependency*, is when a technology decision strongly influences (or forces) future choices due to the original choice. Typical technology lock-ins are the result of resource constraints.

Innovation processes are propositional at their core. The original idea is a proposition about the potential that stems from a new combination of elements. This idea needs some resources to get started, and then the idea needs to be explored in practice – testing whether and how the proposition may hold. This will normally happen by breaking the original idea into a series of new and smaller propositions. As the innovation is opened up and investigated, it is revealed as a more or less complex set of problems, all having many different solutions *in potentia*. However, in order to enrol allies, it is necessary to make the idea and concept converge on a number of aspects (simplify the innovation), and this will often create a choice and therefore a "lock-in" for the subsequent process – at least for a period of time.

To build the innovation into commercial relations is likely to destabilise the innovation and produce new phases of development, mobilisation and exploration. Hence, finding or creating *use* for the innovation means that it will need many changes and adjustments. When partially stabilised innovations (and their internal propositions about users) are tested with potential users, new propositions and adaptations of the established will arise and thus lead to new development phases and new selection processes. In order to minimise such challenges, thereby reducing development costs, businesses are often forced into radical simplification of the innovation, stripping it of many of the novel elements, and to closely adapt to what already exists.

4.9.5   Innovation Investments

Innovation management is the process of managing innovation within as well as across organisations, and this includes managing people, ideas, information, initiatives and projects and all other aspects pertaining to innovation so that extra efficiency can be successfully added to a firm's activities and extra value can be added to the firm's value proposition for its customers.

In order to be successful, innovative organisations must invest (what is usually a percentage of their turnover) in innovation. Firms differ in terms of investment value, as well as in the objectives they want to achieve in the returns of their investments. Where some firms invest in innovation with the objective to expand into new markets, or to increase the quality of existing products, others may pursue an improvement of their manufacturing processes or lowering the environmental impact of their operations.

Investments towards innovation are not guaranteed certain returns; firms must always factor in high-risk factors when budgeting for innovation. Empirical data shows that research investments often do not meet the initial organisational goals. These high failure rates can have significant consequences on the organisation, not only in terms of financial loss (as many investments are not recuperated and do not result in any other organisational benefits) but failure can also negatively impact the morale of the workforce. In turn, this can lead to an organisational culture, which rejects attempts at innovation from the very beginning. This is why companies must accept failure as an integral part of the innovation process. Having policies and procedures in place will help in carefully assessing and screening ideas and give those involved the possibility to eliminate projects that are potential failures from the earlier stages in the process. Previous experience and encouraging open questioning of ideas can provide great insights in identifying possible causes of failure.

Organisations must strive to identify the threats before failure occurs. The major internal causes are either associated with the cultural infrastructure (e.g., poor leadership, poor communication, poor organisation, etc.) or with the innovation process itself (e.g., poor definition of goal, poor alignment of actions to goals, poor monitoring of results etc.) (O'Sullivan, 2002).

4.10 CHAPTER SUMMARY

This chapter introduced different types of innovations and discussed how to classify innovations including key characteristics of each. Sources of innovation and a review of the technology innovation life cycle provided a framework in which to structure innovation projects. The chapter concluded with the diffusion of innovations theory, the theory's relationship to Geoffrey Moore's (2002) idea of "the chasm", and managing innovation through uncertainty and contrary forces.

Throughout these sections, the reader learned about the translation of innovations – to explain the hard work of actually getting innovations into use by entrepreneurs and their allies. The key concepts were presented, such as user-driven innovation, open innovation (Chesbrough, 2006), disruptive innovation (Christensen, 1997) and network innovation.

Related to the management of innovation processes, we presented the product life cycle and its implications for innovation in practice, in addition to reviewing how innovation processes emerge in practice and how to manage such complex, uncertain and contingent processes. Innovation is based on activities with high uncertainty, often involving a high number of actors in developing, producing and finding use for the new product or service. Entrepreneurial ventures need to focus their resources towards the core issues of the process and sometimes make tough choices of what to do and what to leave. Incremental innovations, i.e., innovations that are relatively similar to previous products and services, and that fit well into the established system, are more often successful than radical innovations. However, often the economic value of succeeding with radical innovation may be higher.

As the company grows and matures, the matter becomes one of maintaining the entrepreneurial spirit. To drive continuous innovation in the established company includes the challenging task of balancing *exploration* of new opportunities and *exploitation* of what is already developed (March, 1991). The *Ambidextrous* organisation has developed strategies and culture for doing both of these simultaneously (O'Reilly and Tushman, 2004). In many firms, this requires them to differentiate these activities into separate departments or groups, as the creative and expansive process of exploring may be experienced as very disturbing to the process of exploiting (or economising) on established products and services – which may include rationalisation of production and distribution, incremental improvements and market development. Ries (2011) suggests that entrepreneurship should be organised as a distinct function in established organisations (often called "intrapreneurship" or "corporate entrepreneurship" in such settings). This can be done, for example, by establishing "experimental testbeds", where novel concepts can be explored and which might evolve into commercial departments or new ventures (Concept testing and research techniques are covered in Chapter 7).

Case Study 4.1 Salma: Novel Technology and Branding in a Traditional Market

Adapted from Hoholm and Håkansson (2012) and Hoholm (2011).

This chapter outlined how innovation to a large extent is about testing new combinations. In this case study, the innovators planned to use high-quality, farmed salmon as an input into salmon salami (Salma Cured), but the product instead became a special, high-quality fillet (Salma Fresh). The case study includes two industrial actors forming a new venture called "Salmon Brands": Bremnes Seashore, a family-owned fish farm, and Tine SA, Norway's largest dairy producer.

Bremnes Seashore developed and patented novel technologies for slaughtering salmon, together with researchers from the Norwegian University of Life Sciences. These were new slaughtering and processing technologies for farmed salmon, which reduced the stress levels of the fish and enabled pre-rigor[1] processing of the fish to an extent that no competitors could achieve. In addition to the advantage of time – getting fresher fish out to the customers – the raw material proved to have some new and very interesting characteristics regarding colour, texture and taste. This new way of slaughtering the salmon gave a significant rise in the quality of the raw material. Nevertheless, to their disappointment, Bremnes Seashore failed to get a better price from their customers, because the major distributors in the fish industry were not interested in paying a higher price for this premium raw material.

Tine, on the other hand, had been trying to combine agricultural and biomarine resources in different projects for several years, such as in a project that combined using milk proteins and fermentation cultures to cure fish. A creative researcher at the Institute of Marine Research (IMR) had the idea of making "salami" out of fish. He then convinced Tine and the Norwegian Food Research Institute (FRI) to join him in a research project. Later, he sold the patent to Tine, acknowledging that Tine's market position had more power to push this product into the market. In the first instance, Tine had a hard time stabilising the salmon salami technologically and commercialising it.

These two, partly failed, innovation projects – Bremnes Seashore fish slaughtering and Tine's fish salami – then became the basis for an interesting cooperation between Tine and Bremnes Seashore, which eventually lead to a great success.

Tine developed the brand "Salma" to sell their salmon salami (Salma Cured). Afterwards, the marketing director went on an international marketing tour to solicit customers for the product. Existing business relations, food fairs and new contacts were visited in the United States, France, Singapore, Brussels, Moscow, etc. While visiting Hong Kong, the team met representatives from FoodCorp,[2] a multinational restaurant corporation. It was seen as the "ultimate customer" for Salma Cured at this stage, representing everything Tine hoped for: restaurant chains (relatively easy logistics), world-wide distribution and associations with acknowledged brands. The Research and Development Director at FoodCorp suggested that it could be tested in their Japanese restaurants as their "monthly special" campaign later the same year, with TV commercials and special offers in the restaurants. This would have meant massive attention to Salma Cured in a huge market. After altering some of the processing on request from FoodCorp, the results were positive. Unfortunately, in the meantime, FoodCorp had dropped the contact. The customer had, for unknown reasons, lost interest, and the attempt to mobilise the desired customer had brought about both a great deal of work and a failure. Then, an agreement was signed between with an agent in the German market for test sales of Salma Cured in German hypermarkets. The marketing emphasised its similarity with meat products, while still choosing to locate the product together with smoked salmon and other cured seafood products in the shelves. However, the sales of the "Lax Salami" did not go particularly well, and after adjusting packaging and marketing a couple of times, the campaign was put on hold.

At the same time, a joint venture was formed between Bremnes Seashore and Tine, intending to combine the high-quality salmon technology from Bremnes with the salami technology and marketing competence of Tine. At this point, Salma had still not found its final shape with regard to what customers wanted to buy. Its fate was fully in the hands of the customers (industrial actors) and their customers (consumers). After the failed attempts at selling the product, Salmon Brands chose to take the salami back to the laboratory and the marketing department to develop new versions of the product. At this point, an idea that had been considered for a while gained strength. The idea of marketing the fresh salmon loins instead of curing them eventually got strong support. As opposed to the international marketing of the salami version, the marketing of "Salma Fresh" started domestically, in a familiar setting where Tine already had relations, recognition and a strong market position with several other brands and products (dairy and easy-meal products). Neatly cut premium loins without skin and bones were packaged in transparent foil and with the same minimalist Salma design and brand concept. A gourmet supermarket immediately became interested and agreed to a test campaign. After having the product out in test stores for a couple of weeks, they found the consumer response to be very good. Because the supermarket was associated with a large retail chain, NorgesGruppen,[3] – a long-time customer of Tine's dairy products – access to nation-wide distribution opened up. Distribution of Salma Fresh was gradually rolled out in Norwegian and German supermarkets, as well as a number of high-quality restaurants. Finally, after years of researching, developing and marketing, Salma became a success story. Salma Fresh did not contain the radical product innovation (salmon salami) as part of the product; instead, it included a highly innovative processing technology as the basis for a high-end brand that was loved by gourmet chefs and foodies.

For the original salmon salami (Salma Cured) product, Salmon Brands tried to find matching distribution partners all over the world and tested the response for different versions of their product idea. Initially, it failed in every attempt, because a consumer product has to fit into an assortment of the retailers or of other consumer oriented companies. Each product has to find a logical place. This is the interesting aspect with the final version of the product (Salma Fresh) in this case study, because there were few, high-quality, specialty fish products in the market. The new Salma Fresh filled a gap in the fish product category, and the commercialisation became so much easier especially when Tine could use its old relationships to bring the product to consumers. Salmon Brands' highly successful commercialisation of high-end salmon products based on the patented, novel processing technologies illustrates how new technology may trigger the work of expanding market categories, as well as the struggles to get market access by convincing distributors and end users to adopt a new product.

Case Questions

1. What were the key strengths to Salmon Brands' approach to getting the salmon salami (Salma Cured) to market? What are some weaknesses to Salmon Brands' approach?
2. Discuss the five phases of the user adoption bell curve. What stage did Salma Cured likely reach and why? What stage did Salma Fresh likely reach and why?
3. Identify possible causes for the immediate success of Salma Fresh. Compare to Salma Cured.
4. Could Salma Fresh have been developed and brought to users without developing Salma Cured first?

Case Notes

1. Pre-rigor processing means processing the fish before it becomes "death stiff" (rigor mortis), thereby, getting very fresh filets of extraordinary high-quality. Rigor occurs just a few hours after slaughter, and it is not possible to take away skin and bones industrially during this phase. Therefore, all fish to be processed are stored for around three days before processing according to the common procedure. This storing can also be done on a trailer on its way to Denmark or France, hence there seems to be less advantage in post-rigor processing in Norway. Bremnes's new method, based on cooling down the fish, extended the time window for pre-rigor processing.
2. Not its real name.
3. "NorgesGruppen is Norway's largest trading enterprise. The group's core business is grocery retailing and wholesaling. Through its [retail] chains, the group holds a market share of 39.2 per cent of the grocery market....A total of 1,919 grocery stores and 790 kiosks are affiliated to NorgesGruppen". (downloaded on 12 May 2009 from http://www.norgesgruppen.no/norgesgruppen/norgesgruppen/english/).

4.11 REVISION QUESTIONS

1. Using the concepts and typologies in this chapter, how would you classify your invention?
2. How can you best improve your knowledge of the users' needs?
3. Where would your product (and its "group of products") be placed on the diffusion S-curve, and (if placed early on the curve) how can it be brought to the next level?
4. Who are the critical actors (partners, users, institutions, etc.) to bring on board in your loyal network to increase the chances of commercialisation/bringing the innovation into use?

4.12 FURTHER READING AND RESOURCES

Chesbrough, H (2006) *Open Innovation: The New Imperative for Creating and Profiting from Technology*. Cambridge, MA: Harvard Business School Press.

Christensen, C.M. (1997) *The Innovator's Dilemma: The Revolutionary Book that Will Change the Way You Do Business*. New York: Harper Business,.

Hoholm, T. (2011) *The Contrary Forces of Innovation: An Ethnography of Innovation in the Food Industry*. London: Palgrave Macmillan,

Moore, G. (2002) *Crossing the Chasm: Marketing and Selling High-tech Products to Mainstream Customer*. New York: Harper Business Essentials.

Van de Ven, A.H., Polley D.E., Garud, R. and Venkataraman, S. (1999) *The Innovation Journey*. Oxford: Oxford University Press.

4.13 NOTE

1. Case written by Tom Ove Grønlund, CEO, Conpart.

4.14 REFERENCES

Baraldi, E. and Waluszewski, A. (2005) "Information Technology at IKEA: An 'Open Sesame' Solution or Just Another Type of Factory?" *Journal of Business Research*, 58: 1251–1260.

Barringer, B.R. and Ireland, D. (2007) *Entrepreneurship: Successfully Launching New Ventures*. New York: Prentice Hall.

Bright, J.R. (1969) "Some Management Lessons from Technological Innovation Research", *Long Range Planning*, 2: 36–41.

Casson, M., Yeung, B., Basu, A. and Wadeson, N. (eds) (2006) *The Oxford Handbook of Entrepreneurship*. Oxford: Oxford University Press.

Chesbrough, H. (2006) *Open Innovation: The New Imperative for Creating and Profiting from Technology*. Cambridge, MA: Harvard Business School Press.

Christensen, C.M. (1997) *The Innovator's Dilemma: The Revolutionary Book that Will Change the Way You Do Business*. New York: Harper Business.

Cooper, R.G. (2001) *Winning at New Products – Accelerating the Process from Idea to Launch*. New York: Perseus Publishing.

Drucker, P.F. (2002) "The Discipline of Innovation", *Harvard Business Review,* Harvard Business School Publication Corp, Cambridge, MA.

Fagerberg, J. (2002) *A Layman's Guide to Evolutionary Economics,* TIK Working paper no. 17, Centre for technology, innovation and culture, Oslo. http://folk.uio.no/janf/downloadable_papers.html

Fagerberg, J. (2005) "Innovation. A Guide to the Literature", in J. Fagerberg, D.C., Mowery and R.R. Nelson (eds), *The Oxford handbook of Innovation.* Oxford: Oxford University Press.

Garcia, R. and Calantone, R. (2002) "A Critical Look at Technological Innovation Typology and Innovativeness Terminology: A Literature Review", *Journal of Product Innovation Management,* 19: 110–132.

Håkansson, H. and Ford, D. (2002) "How Should Companies Interact?" *Journal of Business Research,* 55: 133–39.

Håkansson, H. and Waluszewski, A. (2007) *Knowledge and Innovation in Business and Industry: The Importance of Using Others.* Oxford: Routledge.

Hoholm, T. (2011) *The Contrary Forces of Innovation: An Ethnography of Innovation in the Food Industry.* London: Palgrave Macmillan.

Hoholm, T. and Håkansson, H. (2012) "Interaction to Bridge Network Gaps: The Problem of Specialization and Innovation in Fish Technology", *IMP Journal,* 6(3): 254–266.

Hoholm, T. and Olsen, P.I. (2012) "The Contrary Forces of Innovation: A Conceptual Model for Studying Networked Innovation Processes", *Industrial Marketing Management,* 41(2): 344–356.

Jevnaker, B.H. (2005) "Vita Activa: On Relationships Between Design(ers) and Business", *Design Issues,* 21(3): 25–48.

Kalanje, C.M. (Consultant, SMEs Division, World Intellectual Property Organization) (2005) *Role of Intellectual Property in Innovation and New Product Development,* Accessed online on 9 July 2013 at <http://www.wipo.int/sme/en/documents/ip_innovation_development.htm>.

Kline, S.J. and Rosenberg, N. (1986) "An Overview of Innovation", in R. Landau and N. Rosenberg (eds), *The Positive Sum Strategy: Harnessing Technology for Economic Growth.* Washington, DC: National Academies Press.

Knorr Cetina, K. (2001) "Objectual Practice", in T. R. Schatzki, K. K. Cetina and E. von Savigny (eds), *The Practice Turn in Contemporary Theory.* London: Routledge.

Levitt, T. (1967) "Innovative Imitation", *McKinsey Quarterly,* 4: 35–45.

Lundvall, B.A. (1992) *Towards a Theory of Innovation and Interactive Learning.* London: Pinter Publishers.

March, J. (1991) "Exploration and Exploitation in Organizational Learning", *Organizational Science* (March), 2(1): 71–87.

McMullen, J.S. and Shepherd, D.A. (2006) "Entrepreneurial Action and the Role of Uncertainty in the Theory of the Entrepreneur", *Academy of Management Review,* 31, 1.

Moore, G. (2002) *Crossing the Chasm: Marketing and Selling High-tech Products to Mainstream Customers.* New York: Harper Business Essentials.

Murray, F. (2008) *Managing Innovation & Entrepreneurship: Lecture Notes.* Cambridge, MA: MIT Sloan School of Management.

Mørk, B.E., Hoholm, T., Ellingsen, G., Edwin, B. and Aanestad, M. (2010) "Challenging Expertise on Power Relations within and across Communities of Practice in Medical Innovation", *Management Learning*, 41(5), 575–592.

O'Reilly, C.A., III and Tushman, M.L. (2004) "The Ambidextrous Organization", *Harvard Business Review*, April, Harvard Business School Publishing, Cambridge, MA.

O'Sullivan, D. (2002) "Framework for Managing Development in the Networked Organisations", *Journal of Computers in Industry*, 47: 77–88.

O'Sullivan, D. and Dooley, L. (2009) *Applying Innovation*. Thousand Oaks, CA: Sage Publications.

OECD (2005) *The Measurement of Scientific and Technological Activities Oslo Manual: Guidelines for Collecting and Interpreting Innovation Data*, 3rd edition. Luxembourg: OECD.

Pavitt, K. (2005) "Innovation process", in J. Fagerberg, D.C. Mowery and R.R. Nelson (eds), *The Oxford Handbook of Innovation*. Oxford: Oxford University Press.

Pinch, T. and Oudshoorn, N. (2005) *How Users Matter: The Co-construction of Users and Technology*. Cambridge: MIT Press.

Ries, E. (2011) *The Lean Startup: How Today's Entrepreneurs Use Continuous Innovation to Create Radically Successful Businesses*. New York: Crown Publishing Group.

Rogers, E. (1995) *Diffusion of Innovations*, 4th edition. New York: The Free Press.

Ryan, B. and Gross, N. (1943) "The Diffusion of Hybrid Seed Corn in Tow Iowa Communities", *Rural Sociology*, 8(1): 15–24.

Sarasvathy, S.D. and Dew, N. (2005) "New Market Creation through Transformation", *Journal of Evolutionary Economics*, 15: 533–565.

Schumpeter, J. (1928) "The Instability of Capitalism", *The Economic Journal*, 38: 361–386.

Schumpeter, J. (1942) *Capitalism, Socialism, and Democracy*. New York: Harper and Row.

Shanklin, W.L. and Ryans, J.K. (1984) "Organizing for High-tech Marketing", *Harvard Business Review*, 62: 164–71.

Stevens, G.A. and Burley, J. (2003) "Piloting the Rocket of Radical Innovation", *Research Technology Management*, 46: 16–25.

Tarde, G. de (1903) *The Laws of Imitation*. New York: Holt and Company.

Trott, P. (2008) *Innovation Management and New Product Development*, 3rd edition. New York: Prentice Hall.

Van de Ven, A.H., Polley D.E., Garud, R. and Venkataraman, S. (1999) *The Innovation Journey*. Oxford: Oxford University Press.

Verganti, R. (2009) *Design Driven Innovation: Changing the Rules of Competition by Radically Innovating What Things Mean*. Cambridge: Harvard University Press.

Von Hippel, E. (2006) *Democratizing Innovation*. Cambridge, MA: MIT Press.

Wadhwani, R.D. (2010) "Historical Reasoning and the Development of Entrepreneurship Theory", in H. Landstrom and F. Lohrke (eds), *Historical Foun-

dations of Entrepreneurship Research. Cheltenham, England: Edward Elgar Publishing.

Wagrell, S. and Waluszewski, A. (2009) "The Innovation Process and Its Organisational Setting – Fit it or Misfit?" *IMP Journal*, 3(2): 57–85.

Waluszewski, A. (2004) "A Competing or Co-operating Cluster or Seven Decades of Combinatory Resources? What's Behind a Prospering Biotech Valley?" *Scandinavian Journal of Management*, 20: 125–150.

4.15   GLOSSARY OF TERMS

Breakthrough innovation: See *radical innovation*.

Coalition Building: The practice of building alliances based on the strength of the entrepreneur's arguments in combination with a well-developed product or technology.

Contrary Forces Model: (Hoholm, 2011) – A dual process in terms of mobilising resources and exploring knowledge (developing the innovation).

Creative Destruction: When innovative solutions are introduced by entrepreneurs, which undermine the current practice in the economy and thereby moves other products, production methods and even companies out of business. Paradoxically, this is both what brings growth to the economy and at the same time destroys the position and profits of established dominant companies.

Customer-Driven Innovations: See *user-driven innovations* below.

Disruptive Innovations: Radical innovations that bring about significant implications for all the major stakeholders in an industry (Christensen, 1997).

Entrepreneur: A passionate visionary who has the responsibilities of combining the factors necessary to successfully lead innovations to market.

False Summit Effect: Repeatedly finding new mountaintops behind the one that was believed to be the real summit.

Incremental Innovations: Evolutionary in nature and consist of smaller improvements in product, processes or organisational activities introduced over time.

Infrastructure Innovations: Wider technical systems that enable or improve communication, such as transport systems, energy grids, and financial systems (Van de Ven et al., 1999).

Innovation: The whole process from the inception of an idea, through developing and testing, to successfully putting the innovation in use – whether commercially in a market or as part of improving a business.

Innovativeness: The degree to which an individual or other unit of adoption is relatively earlier in adopting new ideas than other members of a social system.

Invention: The first documentation of a new process or product.

Open Innovation: The acknowledgement that the best competence and the best ideas often are found outside the company needing it. Sharing protected ideas is encouraged to generate new innovations (Chesbrough, 2006).

Platform Innovations: Novel technological solutions that serve as a platform for distribution of services with the aim of attracting large numbers of users through complementary and competing services.

Process Innovation: The implementation of a new or significantly improved production or delivery method.

Product innovation: The introduction of a good or service that is new or significantly improved with respect to its characteristics or intended uses.

Radical Innovations or Breakthrough Innovations: Innovations involving bigger changes, more disruption, and more network relationships to change.

Technology-based Service Innovations: Innovations that provide more efficient processes via technology that had previously been delivered without technology.

Uncertainty: The perception when the entrepreneur takes on the responsibility of transforming uncertainty of what is not known into manageable risk through analysis of risk levels and applying strategies to overcome challenges.

Users: The people who use the product, process or technology.

User-driven Innovations or Customer-driven Innovations: Observing users to better understand the needs that they are typically unable to articulate in market/consumer surveys and focus groups.

Chapter 5

MANAGING INTELLECTUAL PROPERTY FOR NEW VENTURE DEVELOPMENT

5.1 LEARNING OBJECTIVES

After reading this chapter, you should be able to:

1. understand what is intellectual property and its significance to technology start-ups;
2. to understand the processes for identifying and capturing, legally protecting and commercially exploiting intellectual property;
3. to integrate an IP strategy into a business plan and follow guiding principles for the management of intellectual property; and
4. to appreciate the importance of validating new technologies and how intellectual property can be valued.

5.2 CHAPTER STRUCTURE

The core elements of this chapter are as follows:

- Introduction: What is Intellectual Property?
- Identifying and Capturing Intellectual Property
- Intellectual Property Rights
- Choosing the Appropriate Protection for Your Intellectual Property
- Protecting Intellectual Property
- Developing an IP Strategy
- Searching Patents and Other IP Information
- Enforcin IP Rights and Dealing with Infringement
- Chapter Summary
- Case Study – Nanotechnology
- Revision Questions
- References
- Glossary of Terms and Useful Sources

5.3 INTRODUCTION: WHAT IS INTELLECTUAL PROPERTY?

New products and designs resulting from innovation driven by entrepreneurs and SMEs often have short life cycles, appearing and disappearing regularly in the marketplace. These innovations usually require significant investment of time and money. In recognition of this investment, entrepreneurs can protect, what is referred to as, their intellectual property (IP). Protecting their IP can deter others from benefiting from their hard work, thereby facilitating their best possible return on their investment. Acquiring and maintaining intellectual property rights helps to deter potential infringers, which is particularly important during the process of turning news ideas into business assets with market value.[1]

Examples of IP might include:

Electronic circuits	Computation techniques	Some software
Product prototypes	Business methods	Diagnostic techniques
Manufacturing Processes	Literary creations	Unique names
Documented ideas	Publications and presentations	Artistic expressions

Like physical assets, such as products, IP can generate revenue and, therefore, has value in the marketplace. Commercialisation of IP is one the ways in which the outputs of scientific research in a laboratory are scaled into new technologies for industrial application or into new products for the marketplace. While documents relating to IP can seem legalistic and complex, the spirit of intent of the IP concept is to encourage the principle that as IP is developed it should be used for greatest public benefit. Proponents of IP argue that its commercialisation is often the most efficient means of promoting its widest possible dissemination and use as it incentivises entrepreneurs and investors through the provision of legal protection that allows them to share in rewards. Many technology start-ups may have intellectual property worth protecting through a basket of the different types of intellectual property rights (Enterprise Ireland, 2006), including:

- patents for inventions (new technologies with potential for industrial application);
- designs for product (appearance, contours, colours, shape, texture);
- trademarks for brand identity of goods and services; and
- copyright for material (literary, artistic, music, films, sound, multimedia).

Even for those who may choose not to protect their IP, they still need to be aware of the potential to infringe on the intellectual property rights of others, which could lead to the loss of valuable business and incurring costs of expensive litigation. In the same way as entrepreneurs should by mindful of tax and employment laws, they should also be acutely aware of intellectual property laws and how they might impact their business.

A popular myth often portrayed is that is very difficult for a start-up with its limited resources to enforce against infringements on its IP, particularly against much bigger players or, worse still, against infringements in legal jurisdictions where IP protection is not strong. Why then might capturing and protecting intellectual property be important for a technology start-up bearing in mind that IP can be expensive to protect and maintain? The answer lies in that intellectual property can provide an important source of competitive advantage, however temporary, by erecting barriers to entry. Potential investors, for example, will often seek to evaluate any intellectual property underpinning a new start-up before making a decision to invest. IP, in whatever form, will often signal to an investor that the entrepreneur has some underlying and deep-rooted know-how that may be difficult to copy.

While entrepreneurs and SMEs who recognise the value of their IP and invest in protecting and exploiting that IP as part of their business strategy can gain competitive advantage from it; the opposite also holds. Failure to protect IP can lead to undesirable outcomes and increase risk for any potential investor in a new business start-up.

Ignoring intellectual property inherent in a new business opens the possibility of competitors profiting from the entrepreneur's technological innovations and business ideas. The threat of lawsuit may be sufficient to deter infringers and thereby improve an entrepreneur's negotiating position. Conversely, failure to protect IP can weaken an entrepreneur's negotiating position, may make it more difficult for them to attract investors and could lose them opportunities to forge partnerships and gain traction for their business idea.

5.4   IDENTIFYING AND CAPTURING INTELLECTUAL PROPERTY

Until the 1990s a business's assets were typically classified as physical (land, buildings, equipment, raw material, inventory) and financial (cash deposits, trade credit). Yet, this approach does not explain why or how the market value of a business often differs significantly from the book value. In the United States, for example, almost 40 per cent of a company's market value is not displayed on its balance sheet. This difference can be accounted for by the existence of intangible assets, derived from human intellect: knowledge, know-how, creativity, inventiveness, relationships, processes and systems.

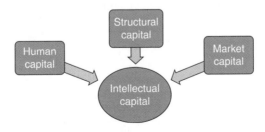

Figure 5.1   Constituents of intellectual capital
Source: Based on Abhijit Talukdar (2008).

- Human Capital refers to the bank of skills, talent and know-how of employees that are used to execute the everyday tasks of a business.
- Structural Capital refers to the provision of critical knowledge infrastructure, such as information systems, applications, databases, processes, to support a business.
- Market Capital refers the set of external relationships of a business with its suppliers, partners and customers that enables it to procure and sell goods and services in an effortless manner as a going concern.

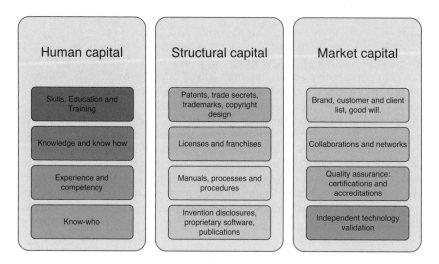

Figure 5.2 Auditing your intellectual capital

Source: Adapted from European Commission (2003) *Intellectual Property: Good Practice Guide*, p. 6.

It is important, therefore, for entrepreneurs to identify intellectual assets that are critical to the expected performance of a new business. A simple starting point is to conduct an IP Audit. This could be as a simple as making a list of intangible assets using the checklist above.

Consultancy firms deploy a range of methodologies that can assist with auditing intellectual assets. Some of these assets may be protected legally by intellectual property rights, which are now among the most critical assets of many of the world's largest technology companies.

5.5 INTELLECTUAL PROPERTY RIGHTS

5.5.1 Patents

Patents relate to inventions producing a technical result, e.g., new technologies, improved products or processes or new techniques. A patent grants the holder the right to exclude others from making, using, selling or offering for sale or importing the invention, in exchange for full disclosure of that invention (NUI Maynooth, 2011). To all intents and purposes, it is a legal form of temporary monopoly intended to promote innovation and provide incentives for investment in new technologies. An inventor does not need a patent to commercially exploit an invention, but, without a patent, the inventor would not be able to prevent others from copying that invention. A patent is a form of intellectual property that can be bought, sold or licensed. The patent claims represent the legal definition of the protected invention. Patentable technology must satisfy three criteria:

- Novelty
- Non-Obviousness (Inventive Step)
- Utility (Applicability)

A patent application may fail the "novelty" criteria if an identical invention has already been disclosed or details of the invention were disclosed in public where people could see how it could work. Disclosure of an invention prior to filing a patent application can destroy its novelty and prevent a patent being obtained. All patents require an inventive step: the "non-obviousness" criteria imply that the solution offered by the invention is not obvious to someone with average knowledge of the technical field. Finally, for a patent application to be successful, the invention must be have an "industrial application", implying that it cannot be purely theoretical and that it must be possible to apply the invention for practical purposes. Not all inventions qualify for a patent. Inventions cannot be contrary to public order and morality. Under the European Patent Convention, for example, a patent cannot be obtained for:

- a discovery, a scientific theory or mathematical method;
- an artistic creation;
- presentation of information;
- methods of medical treatment (as opposed to medical products);
- plant or animal varieties;
- schemes, rules or methods for performing mental acts, playing games, doing business or computer programs.

In some countries, short-term patents can be granted. This option is particularly useful where the inventor or entrepreneur may find that a 20-year patent is unnecessary and often suits less technologically complex inventions. A short-term patent can be granted without prior examination of the patentability criteria with respect to novelty, and usefulness and can be, consequently, faster to obtain and cheaper to maintain.

Case Box 5.1 Apple v. Samsung Patent War[2]

Perhaps, this is exemplified best in the Apple versus Samsung patent-infringement lawsuits. In the spring of 2011, Apple began litigating against Samsung for several patent and trademarks infringements. By July 2012, the two companies were still embroiled in over 50 lawsuits around the globe, with billions of dollars in damages claimed between them.

While Apple won a ruling with damages of over $1 billion in the United States, Samsung won rulings in South Korea, Japan and the UK. The high-stakes significance has been played out in battle for market share between the Apple's iPhone 5 and Samsung Galaxy S Note II.

From a legal perspective, assigning inventorship requires an intensive analysis. In the United States, patents are awarded to those who are "first to file". Inventorship requires two steps in US law: conception and reduction-to-practice.

Conception has a well-defined meaning in patent law: it is the formation, in the mind of the inventor, of a definite and permanent idea of the complete and operative invention, as it is to be applied in practice. In other words, the idea must be described in such detail that any person of ordinary skill in that field would be able to put the idea into practice from the details described.

Reduction-to-Practice, the second requirement for inventorship, refers to the physical making of the invention and the demonstrating that it works. Under these requirements, a technician who performs experiments under instruction, but does not design or modify, cannot be the inventor, regardless of the amount of hard work contributed. The laboratory technician is considered to be the inventor's "pair of hands" in carrying out the reduction-to-practice. Similarly, the supervisor of an experiment or project is not an inventor unless he or she makes a creative contribution to the invention, for example, by designing experiments or by suggesting materials or processes that end up as part of the invention. Where two parties file patent applications for the same invention the party that shows an earlier date of conception and earlier reduction-to-practice is usually assigned inventorship.

Inventorship claims must be corroborated by evidence from either relevant documentation or the testimony of non-inventors. The applicant's status amongst peers in the research field or past accomplishments cannot be taken into account. It is critical, therefore, that scientists and technologists maintain careful records of their ideas, documented progress of their research and research results in laboratory notebooks (dated and witnessed) as evidence of conception and reduction-to-practice to ensure the correct naming of the inventors.

Figure 5.3 Conception and reduction-to-practice

5.5.2   Designs

Designs relate to the look and feel or aesthetics of a product, part of whole, including shape, size, configuration, layout, colours, lines and contours, texture and ornamentation, not dictated by functional considerations.

Case Box 5.2   Example of Registered Design

In 2009, the European Trademark Office published five sequences of registered designs under 001185821–0001 to 0005 for Apple's Magic Mouse with Apple's Andre Bartley as the designer.[3]

In legal terms, a design means the appearance of part or the whole product. It can comprise 2D features, such as patterns, lines or colour, and/ or 3D features, such as shape, texture or surface. Any feature that relates to the appearance of the product and not its function can be registered as a design. Registered designs are typically granted a duration of 5 to 25 years and usually require periodic renewal fees. Registration requires that the design:

- cannot be the same as, and should be clearly distinguishable from, other designs in the public domain; and
- must not have been disclosed in advance of filing the application.

Some countries provide a short-term copyright for industrial designs. In these cases, while registration is not required and protection kicks-in, the duration of protection is much shorter. Good practice, however, suggests that it is always best to register the design to benefit from stronger protection.

5.5.3   Trademarks (TM)

Trademarks are primarily related to brand identity. A trademark is a mark (generally a word or symbol) used to distinguish the goods or services of one particular business from those of its competitors. Properly promoted and protected, trademarks can become the single most valuable asset of a business as they help to make deep connections in the minds of their customers between their products and the overall business.

Any sign that can be represented graphically can be registered as a trademark, including slogans, catch-phrases and combinations of words, letters and numerals. Trademarks may also comprise symbols, shapes, drawings, 3D surfaces and, in some cases, audio. The key prerequisites for registering a trademark are (European Commission, 2003c):

- it must be distinctive enough to allow customers to immediately associate the product to a particular business;
- it must not be misleading to the extent that it could deceive the public as to the true nature of the product, such as geographical origin or quality;

- it cannot describe the product in any way or a common descriptive term;
- it must conform to public order and morality, and;
- it cannot be categorised by exclusions in law, e.g., photographs, names or drawings of places or people.

Infringement can occur if a mark is deemed to cause confusion among consumers. In determining whether confusion is likely, courts typically investigate the similarity between the two marks; the similarity of the products that the respective marks represent; similarity in target markets; the level of public awareness of the mark, the number and nature of similar marks on similar products and whether or not buyers feel confused by the competing marks.

Do not confuse the registration of an Internet domain name, company name or business names with registration of a trademark. Their requirements are entirely different. In common law countries, the right to a trademark can be acquired through usage, making registration unnecessary. However, it is always wise to register your trademark.

In some cases, companies can associate their products with membership of an association to indicate various benefits, such as: compliance to quality standards and geographical origin.

5.5.4 Copyright

Copyright refers to the right to reproduce one's own original work. Copyright usually relates to musical, artistic or literary or dramatic works, such as books, magazines and academic papers, working documents, drawings, maps, photographs, films, crafts, sound recordings, etc. In fact, the definition of artistic can be quite wide. Copyright allows the creators of original works to control their subsequent use. Unlike a patent it is not a form of monopoly as the copyright principle recognises that two people could possibly create identical items, however unlikely, completely independently without copying. In such circumstances, there is no infringement so both people would be entitled to hold copyright for their respective work. There is no requirement to register a copyright as it is bestowed automatically on the creator, so long as his or her work was original. The copyright principles offer a range of economic rights (UK Intellectual Property Office, 2011) that are often granted to performing artists, broadcasters, musicians, entitling them to control use of their creations in a number of ways, including making copies, selling copies to the public, performing in public, etc. Without copyright protection, it would be very easy for others to exploit works without paying the creator.

Case Box 5.3   Napster

In 1999, a young Shawn Fanning developed a combined search engine, chat room and MP3 file-sharing application that evolved into Napster, a very popular music-trading program. One of the most high-profile cases of copyright infringement in the technology world occurred in when the Recording Industry Association of America (RIAA), the trade association that represents the vast majority of creators, manufacturers and distributors of sound recordings in the United States, filed a lawsuit against Napster, who, by its own admission, made millions of MP3 music files available on the Internet. RIAA argued that it amounted to piracy. Rock band, Metallica, also sued Napster and several universities claiming that they violated their copyrights by facilitating students' access to Napster and illegally trading Metallica music using university servers.

5.5.5   Trade Secrets and Know-How

Perhaps, some of the most valuable intellectual property comes in the form of trade secrets or know-how. Know-how relates to practice and knowledge acquired through experience. Trade secret laws protect proprietary information of commercial value including, for example, formulas, patterns, physical devices, procedures and other compilations of information (Uniform Trade Secrets Act, USA)

- that provide the owner of with a competitive advantage in the marketplace, and
- that prevent the public or competitors from learning about it other than through improper acquisition or theft.

Unlike other types of IP, such as copyrights, trademarks, and patents, trade secrets are not registered: the information simply has to be kept confidential. Once a trade secret is disclosed to the public, legal protection ends. Simply deeming information a trade secret will not make it so. A business must prove, through its actions, its desire to keep the information secret. Examples of information that may help entrepreneurs to identify trade secrets include:

• Business methods	• Cost and pricing information	• Ingredients
• Financial forecasts	• Purchasing information	• Devices
• Market research	• Personnel databases	• Experimental methods
• Business plans	• Manuals, procedures, policies	• Manufacturing techniques
• R&D information	• Notebooks and other logs	• Systems
• Key networks and relationships	• Inventions	• Maintenance techniques
• Critical product specifications	• Designs, patterns, drawings	• Computer algorithms
• Critical product specifications	• Maps, formulas	• Customer databases

Some companies go to extraordinary lengths to keep information secret. The Coca-Cola formula, for example, is kept under lock and key in a bank vault that can be opened only by a resolution of Coca-Cola's board of directors. It allows for only two employees to know the formula concurrently. In 2007, two ex-employees of Coca-Cola were sentenced to serve prison sentences for conspiring to steal and sell trade secrets to Pepsi (CNN, 2007).

5.5.6   Handling Confidential Information

Confidential information relates to any business information that companies do not wish to share with any third-party. It is of often particular concern to entrepreneurs in the pre-seed stage. It relates to any information that they may not wish to share. This often presents a challenge when the entrepreneur must strike a balancing act between providing enough information to win to supporters of his or her business idea, such as investors, potential customers and key staff, while not giving too much away that their idea could be appropriated by someone else. A common mechanism to overcome this problem is for entrepreneurs to ask those with whom they share vital information to sign a non-disclosure agreement (NDA). An NDA obliges the receiving party to keep certain information confidential and to protect its unauthorised use (UK Intellectual Property Office).

5.6 CHOOSING THE APPROPRIATE PROTECTION FOR YOUR INTELLECTUAL PROPERTY

Protection is provided in different ways depending on the type of intellectual property right. Some require a formal application, such as for patents or trademarks, whereas others are automatic, such as for copyright or unregistered designs. Any application for an intellectual property right should be done as early as possible. Once granted, annual fees must be paid to maintain the rights. Entrepreneurs and SMEs should, therefore, conduct a cost-benefit analysis of maintaining different intellectual property rights for their business. A temporary monopoly provided by a patent, for example, while expensive, could bring with it critical first-mover advantage that can be maintained long after the patent expires.

5.6.1 Importance of Copyrighting

Given that copyright protection is automatic, it may be an unanticipated source of income as it entitles entrepreneurs and SMEs to demand royalties for the exploitation of their work. Copyright also bestows moral rights that prevent distortion or mutilation of the work. The scope for copyright is quite broad as it includes any literary, artistic or musical works. It is good practice to copyright all sensitive information pertaining to a start-up, including business plans, budgets, product and process specifications.

5.6.2 Importance of Trademarks

If brand identity and associating product with the parent business is critical then trademarks become important. Registering a trademark is not particularly expensive and can become a valuable source of revenue through franchising or licensing. A common strategy is to back-up a patent or registered design with a trademark so that when the patent or registered design expires the trademark maintains the value of the IP through brand recognition and goodwill.

5.6.3 Importance of Industrial Designs

If the visual aspects of a product represent its unique selling point or are critical to its image, then registered designs become important. Registered designs can be a useful marketing tool in differentiating the visual uniqueness of a product from that of its competitors. Registered designs provide stronger protection than copyright as they offer the owner exclusive rights to manufacture or sell any product to which the design has been applied to allow others to use the design by agreement. It gives the owner the right to file lawsuit against those who infringe on the design and to claim damages.

5.6.4   Importance of Patents

Obtaining a patent in large industrialised markets such as United States, Japan or Europe can be costly. However, the potential returns resulting from the monopoly right to a successful invention may be substantial. If an expert can understand an invention by reverse engineering the product in which it is embedded then a trade secret will not provide adequate protection and the invention should be protected by patent. Similarly, if analysis of a product can provide vital clues to new inventions in its manufacturing processes then those inventions should be protected by patent.

5.6.5   Bundling Intellectual Property Rights

It is possible for different intellectual property rights to be applied to the same creation. As previously mentioned, it is common to use trademarks as a mode of protection when patents expire. Similarly, patents combined with trade secrets are often combined to protect critical know-how in a research environment. Consider a new products developed by a technology start-up. The name and logo of the business could be registered as a trademark. The technological invention could be registered as a patent or kept as a trade secret. The aesthetics of the product could be registered as an industrial design and other aspects could be protected by copyright. An effective IP strategy may, therefore, involve a wide range of intellectual property rights to provide layers of protection for a start-up and strengthen its position in the market.

5.6.6   Geographical Coverage

As a rule of thumb, costs of obtaining and maintaining IP rights are proportional to the number of countries in which protection is being sought. A business can choose to seek protection in countries individually or seek protection internationally. Patent attorneys can advise on the different procedures: rules may vary considerably from country to country. Patents are granted on a first-inventor-to-file (FITF) basis in all countries. This includes the USA, which switched from a first to invent system to the FITF system on 16 March 2013 after the enactment of the American Invents Act (AIA). All of this should take account of the expected market coverage for the product or service. It is also important to be mindful of the underlying IP culture in different countries. Western thinking promotes innovation through intellectual property and, more recently, open innovation, as a universal and efficient way to move development forward throughout the world.

However, as intellectual property protection slowly converges towards uniformity across the globe, the degree of protection in different culture still varies significantly. In many parts of the Middle East, intellectual property laws are difficult to enforce (Carrol, 2001). Over the past few decades Americans have complained about Chinese theft of intellectual property, yet, increasingly, the Chinese business community is calling for its legal system to get serious about protecting peoples' ideas (*The Economist*, 2012).

5.7 PROTECTING INTELLECTUAL PROPERTY

Patenting

Normally, the first step in the patenting process is to file a provisional application in the home country. The date of application, commonly referred to as the priority date, has significance later in the patenting process. Through international convention, most countries respect the priority date recorded in another country provided that the application is filed in those countries within 12 months of the original application (WIPO, 2012). The information required for a patent application filing, depending on the invention, can be fairly extensive. The following is a description of what is required in preparing patent applications:

1. Extensive drawings illustrating the invention, including diagrams, tables, flowcharts; whatever best explains the particular invention;
2. Technical description of the invention. Usually this means describing the overall invention first and then explaining the invention in greater detail;
3. All aspects of the invention should be explained. An illustrative explanation of how the invention would be implemented in each of its aspects is important;
4. One or more examples of the implementation of the invention;
5. Advantages of the invention over the prior art, resulting in the need for the invention.

Patent documents are deliberately quite complex and drafting them is usually done by a patent attorney. The contents of the application, including scope and validity of the claims, have a significant bearing on whether or not a patent is granted. Experts working at the national patent office of the home country will assess the patent application against the patentability criteria. A patent search is done to verify the claims of novelty and inventive step. Once satisfied, the national patent office will grant the patent.

European patent applications can be field at the European Patent office (EPO). Applications must be in English, French or German. Once the patent is granted, it can be maintained in all or some of the designated countries. The Patent Cooperation Treaty (PCT) facilitates the process of filing an international patent in over 117 nations (including most industrialised countries). When an inventor is ready to file for patent protection,

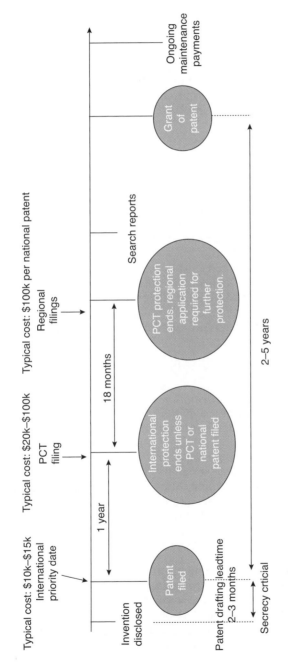

Figure 5.4 Timeline for filing international patents

Source: Based on "Guide to Commercialisation at NUI Maynooth", Rev5 – 01/04/11, figure 2, p.16.

usually in his or her home nation, he or she can also choose to file a PCT application. As the home nation patent office processes the application, an international authority will run a search to determine patentability in other nations on the basis of uniqueness and other characteristics, generating a written report. This system:

- simplifies the process of filing patent applications;
- delays the need to file in other countries buying the inventor time to determine if the patent is worthwhile; and
- allows the inventor time to assess the commercial viability of his/her invention.

5.7.1   Trademark Registration

The symbols™ or ® are commonly used on products to indicate that the mark is registered. If a business proposes to use a trademark then it should be registered as soon as possible to avoid any potential for someone else to register the same or similar mark first. This can be done by filing for trademark registration, with a clear reproduction of the proposed mark, at a national or regional trademark office.

The application should include a list of products and services to which the trademark would apply. The national office then assesses the mark for suitability for registration. If a business relies on significant sales in Europe then it should apply to the *Office of Harmonization for the Internal Market* (OHIM). International trademarks are facilitated by the Madrid System of International Registration.

5.7.2   Design Registration

Applying for a national design registration is usually straightforward. The applicant must be the owner of the design or the employer of the person who created the design. The design submitted in the application must be suitable for reproduction. Multiple designs within the same international design classification may be submitted in the same application. Under the CTM Agreement, European coverage can be provided by OHIM. Under the Madrid Protocol, international applications can be submitted directly to the World Intellectual Property Organisation (WIPO). Usually a registered design is published on registration, but this can be deferred.

5.7.3   Obtaining Copyright Protection

Copyright protection does not require any formal application process. However, some countries do allow for registration of artistic and literary work, which can serve as legal evidence in cases of infringement The normal practice in claiming copyright for a piece of work is to mark the work using the recognised symbol © indicating clearly who the is the copyright owner and dating it. Sometimes, it is necessary to record, with proof, when the copyright was created. This can be done by depositing a copy of the work with, for example, a solicitor or bank and formally recording the time and date of the deposition.

5.8   DEVELOPING AN IP STRATEGY

Developing an effective IP strategy can be particularly relevant to technology entrepreneurs and SMEs. Many business models are focused exclusively on selling or licensing IP and even, where this is not the case, a properly implemented IP strategy could generate significant revenues for a modest cost. However, failure to protect a significant innovation can be incredibly costly to a new business. For a new technology venture business, it is important, therefore, to:

- build awareness first amongst the start-up team and later amongst key employees of the importance of IP;
- always search for any existing solution(s) before starting a new innovation project;
- capture all current and potential IP and use it to add value to its products and create a culture of best practice in its creation and capture;
- maintain confidentiality on new technologies until professional advice is provided;
- conduct competitor analysis to avoid infringement of their IP and to challenge, if appropriate;
- plan and routinely review its entire IP portfolio.

5.8.1   Capturing Intellectual Property

The importance of an IP strategy is largely dependent on the industry sector in which the business operates and its approach to the competition. In some cases, for examples, where it is easy to copy the IP, protection may be absolutely necessary. In other cases, maintaining secrecy and first-mover advantage can be effective. Large companies with the financial muscle often pursue a strategy of acquiring and maintaining a portfolio of patents and other forms of IP. This strategy can be prohibitively expensive for start-ups unless it has significant investment behind it. They key for technology entrepreneurs and SMEs is to focus on one or a small number of flagship patents as a cost-effective way of developing a valuable IP portfolio. It is important, in such circumstances to implement mechanisms for identifying, creating, capturing and protecting IP, where appropriate.

While, it may not seem like it at the time, *the way in which IP is created and captured is very important.* Investors in a business underpinned by IP will always look to ensure that the IP is "clean", i.e., that its creation is fully documented and there are no disputes over who created it or who owns it. A good practice is to use a paper-trail or online system to record your project work. In laboratory environments, for example, R&D work is often recorded daily but if not weekly laboratory notebooks. Best-practice often necessitates each page of notebook to be signed by the researcher and their supervisor and, perhaps, by an independent witness who is not part of the project but has sufficient knowledge to understand the field of work (McManus, 2009).

Laboratory notebooks may serve, for example, as legal documents in evidencing inventive steps and include:

- data to support patent applications;
- a record of procedures undertaken to meet regulatory requirements;
- evidence of background IP provided by partners in collaborative projects;
- verification of inventorship;
- information underpinning know-how relevant to a licensing deal;
- contribute to a company's repository of IP for valuation purposes.

5.8.2   Invention Disclosure Forms

Having a formal process for disclosing inventions is also important. The purpose of the Invention Disclosure Form (IDF) is to record the capture intellectual property so that its legal protection commercial potential can be evaluated. The IDF can enable a business to record the creation of the IP and provide information that would assist it in determining the legal title and any third-party claims to IP rights associated with that creation. The IDF is often used for information sharing with external patent attorneys as the basis of drafting a patent application. Although each invention begins as an idea, the inventor should demonstrate feasibility by reducing the idea to practice with experimental data and/or working prototypes. In general, an invention that is still at an idea stage should be further developed before disclosure. IDFs are typically kept confidential and distribution of copies of an IDF to third parties is prohibited, except where the technical description provided in the IDF is shared with prospective licensees under a confidentiality agreement. When disclosing an invention it is always worth completing a patent search for prior art and a review of scientific publications.

5.8.3   Technology Trends

It is vitally important for technology entrepreneurs to maintain currency of their knowledge within their technical field. In Europe, for example, it is estimated that over €200m per annum is lost working on inventions already patented, which could otherwise have been invested in other projects.[4] It is useful to routinely conduct a thorough search in fields of interest. Independent services, such as technology watch reports, can provide up-to-date assessment of new technologies and emerging trends that provide valuable information in de-risking investment decisions. It is important not to confuse technology watching with industrial espionage, benchmarking or technology foresight. Technology watch services can:

- determine the start-of-the-art in a particular technology sector;
- provide information on new patents in a particular sector;
- highlight technologies available for licensing and provide information on licensing activities;
- highlight new applications and markets for existing technologies; and
- monitor developments in technology platforms.

Entrepreneurs should also monitor developments of their competitors. Competitive intelligence is the ethical gathering and analysis of competitor and market information from open sources.

5.8.4   Intellectual Property Policy

Clear policies and procedures that determine ownership and assignment of rights can help incentivise innovation within a business. In particular, employee contacts and contracts with external partners should spell out clear provisions on IP ownership and how (if) they can share in the economic benefits from commercialisation. A growing international trend is for research institutions, including universities and government owned laboratories, to encourage innovation. This trend can be traced back to the Bayh-Dole Act of 1980, which essentially allowed US universities to own their own inventions and placed responsibility on them to make their IP more widely accessible to its communities. It had the knock-on effect of encouraging universities to establish technology-transfer offices to help researchers commercialise inventions; the number of patents shot up, as did venture funding for innovations developed at academic institutions. Commercialisation is often the most efficient means of promoting the widest possible dissemination and use of this IP. It is appropriate, therefore, for both the institutions and the creators to benefit from its commercial exploitation.

All new ventures should consider a policy on IP. After all, commercialisation of IP requires significant investment and effective protection and management of IP are essential to attracting investment. A potential investor will seek clarity on IP ownership and that the venture's innovation processes will facilitate optimal commercial potential. Most importantly, policy can facilitate implementation of harmonised systems and procedures for all stakeholders in a new venture.

5.9   SEARCHING PATENTS AND OTHER IP INFORMATION

In addition to being an important mechanism for protecting innovation, intellectual property can be an important source of information for technology entrepreneurs. Patent specifications, for example, contain important technical information that might highlight current innovation trends, and they can inform entrepreneurs on pursuing wasteful developments or unnecessary infringements. Trademarks and design registrations can provide important insight into competitor marketing strategies.

5.9.1 Patent Information Sources

Patent information can be gathered from free online databases as well as from paid services. Individual country patent often host their patent databases online. The European Patent Office (EPO) provides an online patent search called http://ep.espacenet.com, which provides information on patents from over 60 different countries. Similarly the US Patent and Trade Mark Office (USPTO) and the Japanese Patent Office provide online text and image databases. Google Patents offers a search engine that indexes patents from the USPTO and, more recently, from the EPO.

Searching is generally conducted using one or more "keywords". However, in the "advanced" searching, users are allowed to specify the search using a number of search parameters, including: *inventor, publication date, patent assignee, patent type, international patent classification, patent number,* etc. From an entrepreneur's perspective, the benefits of patent information can be applied to:

- spotting emerging technology trends and understanding the "state-of-the-art";
- informing on the direction of development efforts;
- eliminating wasteful research efforts due to patents already filed by competitors or dominance by established companies; and
- recognising possible patterns and identifying technology licensing opportunities.

A further method of searching is to search using the International Patent Classification (IPC). Details of the IPC coding system can be found on the WIPO website. There are approximately 70,000 different IPC codes that can facilitate searches in very specific fields of work. A summary is provided below:

A	Human necessities
B	Performing operations and transporting
C	Chemistry and metallurgy
D	Textiles and paper
E	Fixed constructions
F	Mechanical engineering, heating, lighting, blasting
G	Physics
H	Electricity

Commonly used patent search tools are available online, including:

European Patent Office	http://ep.espacenet.com/
British Patent Search Engine	http://www.ipo.gov.uk/types/patent
US Patent Office Search Engine	http://patft.uspto.gov/
International Patent Searching	http://www.wipo.int/pctdb/en/
WIPO IP Digital Library	http://ipdl.wipo.int

There are also a number of commercially available patent databases and private patent search firms. It is important to point out that patent searching can be quite complex due to the huge volumes of existing patent data in multiple languages and, while a do-it-yourself approach is OK for provisional searches, it is best to have this carried out by professionals.

Case Box 5.4   The Fountain Pen

A simple word search on Google Patents for "Fountain Pen" will show details of the patent behind this well-known product. Its patent number **EP 1299249 B1** indicates that it is a European patent. Patents are commonly referenced by the last three digits of the patent number. In this case, we would refer to European Patent 249. Mechanical drawings or schematics are often included to describe the invention visually. The issue date is just below the patent number. The owner's rights and the patent's validity begin on the issue date, in this case 10 March 2004. The title of the patent is "Fountain Pen".

However, the scope of the monopoly sought by a patent is defined by its claims, not its title. Understanding what a claim covers is crucial to assessing infringement and validity hence patent office searches are based on claims. Just beneath the title is a list of the inventors, Francois Jacques and Bernard Pulfer. The applicant may be different to the inventor. Employment contracts often require, for example, that employees must assign their IP rights during their employment to their employer. Note that the actual filing date was exactly one year after the priority date.

5.9.2   Other IP Information Sources

There also databases for other forms of IP, including registered designs and trademarks. The Office of Harmonization in the International Market (OHIM) can provide information on European trademarks and WIPO can provide searching of internationally registered designs.

5.9.3   Protection of Software

Software is copyrightable in almost all PCT countries and copyright has been the traditional method of protection. Copyright protects the precise *expression* of an idea (or algorithm) rather than the idea/algorithm itself (UK Intellectual Property Office, 2011). The major advantage of copyright protection lies in its simplicity. Although copyright protects the "literal expression" of computer programs, it does not protect the "ideas" underlying the computer program, which often have considerable commercial value.

Software is patentable in the US and Japan but less so in Europe. Perhaps, the best known legal precedence comes from *Diamond v. Diehr* (1981) in which it was deemed that a computer algorithm that controlled a physical process could be patented.

EPO Guidelines state that "a computer program claimed by itself or as a record on a carrier is not patentable irrespective of its contents" (Hart et al., 1999). Consequently, there has been a significant increase in patenting by software firms since early 1990s, partly fuelled by the lack of "prior art" and a weakening of the "non-obviousness" test through court decisions (Graham and Mowery, 2010).

Software	Protection Possible?
Idea	✕
Algorithm	✓
Flow Chart	✓
Source Code	✓
Object Code	✓

5.10 ENFORCING IP RIGHTS AND DEALING WITH INFRINGEMENT

Infringement of IP rights allows the owners to sue for damages. Not everyone respects the rights of others and infringers can inflict significant damage through erosion of market share and poor quality imitations ruining brand reputation.

In respect of patents, it is always important to obtain a broad scope and if well drafted it will often be enough to deter potential infringement. It is a good idea, for example, for the inventor to encourage colleagues to try to design around the patent. One way to do this is to study the patent claims and to then try and identify which key features of the invention can be modified.

In respect of design registration and trademarks, as an entrepreneur it is always advisable to seek legal advice on options for redress against others with products that have a very similar appearance to yours or against those who have used, without authorisation, your mark. Otherwise, the value of your business may be diluted or lost.

However, litigation can be very expensive and any venture relying on IP protection should consider IP insurance. It is always wise to assess the cost of legal fees in taking a court action vis-á-vis the chances of winning and the amount of damages that could be reasonably expected from the infringing party. It may also be possible to avoid the courts and negotiate a settlement through arbitration or mediation. Useful information for entrepreneurs and SMEs on IPR enforcement can be found in the IP Disputes resolution section of http://www.wipo.int/sme.

5.11 CHAPTER SUMMARY

The capture, legal protection and commercial exploitation of intellectual property is particularly relevant to any new technology venture.

Whether the venture is developing the technology itself or licensing the technology from outside sources, understanding how intellectual property impacts the business model is a critical factor in the likely success of the venture.

Investors often seek to understand the nature of any IP underpinning a business as a means of ascertaining its uniqueness and the barriers to entry that the IP creates for the competition. Securing full intellectual property rights can be very expensive, however, particularly for start-ups who may not necessarily have the resources. To offset this cost, entrepreneurs can deploy IP strategies to help secure investment. Provisional patents, for example, may be adequate to signal a genuine opportunity to outside investors. In many innovation economies, mechanisms are in place to match-fund collaborations between SMEs and government-research institutions and universities.

The process of capturing IP is something that should be developed as part of the organisational culture from the early stages of a venture's development. Investors will always seek, in conducting due diligence, to ensure that the IP is clean, i.e., that there is documented evidence to support any ownership claims. Any R&D or innovation management functions within the organisation, therefore, need to implement good processes for capturing the creation of any IP. The protection of IP and the pursuit of IP rights is best done with the appropriate legal advice. However, entrepreneurs need to be aware of the various types of intellectual property rights and how they may apply to their business.

Even if the business model is not premised on the creation of any new intellectual property, entrepreneurs need to be aware of any potential infringements.

Case Study 5.1   The Challenge of Nanotechnology

Unlike emerging technologies of the recent past, nanotechnology has far-reaching potential to impact our lives and, according to some, to alter the fabric of society, even the very concept of humanity. Nanotechnology is multi-disciplinary in nature, encompassing scientific fields and industry sectors in chemistry, physics, materials, biotechnology, pharmaceuticals and medicine. Nanotechnology also has the potential to revolutionise how things are manufactured, constructing them atom-by-atom rather than shaping and assembling existing material into a final product.

Examples of Commercial Nanotechnology Applications

- In 2010, Intel announced it would invest $6–8 billion in nanotechnology manufacturing capabilities for future transistor and processor applications.[5]
- Nancore Technologies recently demonstrated a flexible thin-film photovoltaic solar cell using its patented liquid phase deposition (LPD) process.[6]
- Bioni Hygienic is the first antibacterial and antimicrobial wall coating as a substitute for biocides (that leak into the environment). The product was

developed by researchers at the Fraunhofer Institute for Chemical Technology, Germany, in collaboration with Bioni CS GmbH. It works on the basis of nano-particles made out of silver.

What's interesting about nanotechnology is that many regard it as the first research field in over a century where the outputs are being patented extremely early in development. This makes the task of finding relevant prior patents with which to compare new applications very challenging. It is a new field, and most of its patents are for basic inventions with wide applications but not linked directly to specific products. Adapting the patent regime to nanotechnology is proving particularly challenging. Innovations in nanotechnology can be particularly complex due to their multi-disciplinary nature, broad claims and difficulties in fulfilling patentability criteria. IP laws covering products and technology since the Industrial Revolution may not apply to nanotechnology. How do you protect, for example, a molecule-sized device from being illegally copied? Even coming up with a precise definition for nanotechnology has proved problematic. The USPTO classifies nanotechnology patents based on the concept of a nanostructure where at least one physical dimension is of the order 1–100 nm.[7] The EPO's Y01N code defines nanotechnology as "entities with a controlled geometrical size of at least one functional component below 100 nanometers in one or more dimensions susceptible of making physical, chemical or biological effects available, which are intrinsic to that size".[8] One hundred nanometers is about 1,000 times thinner than a human hair.

Recall that for an invention to be patentable, it must be useful (utility), novel (novelty), and non-obvious in light of the prior art. Critical to this is the fact that a patentable invention must have some known application. The current stage of development of nanotechnology still provides for relatively low utility for four main reasons: (1) nanotechnology often spans across disciplines, complicating the application of patent law; (2) many nanotechnology patent claims are potentially "inoperable", such as that as the perpetual motion machine, and patent examiners often are not well versed in what is reality and what is science fiction; (3) the useful of nanotechnology inventions is often uncertain; and (4) much of the research in nanotechnology remains relatively far removed from marketable products (Almeling, 2004).

Perhaps one of the most high-profile emerging cases of the commercialisation of nanotechnology has been the acquisition of Innovalight by DuPont in 2011 (Ganguli and Jabade, 2012). As part of the US Department of Energy Photovoltaic Incubator Programme, Innovalight developed ink that contains silicon nano-particles for boosting absorption of solar energy along with a number of proprietary processing technologies. In 2008, Innovalight initially planned to manufacture solar modules, but it could not raise the $50 million financing to build a small production plant. In 2010, it was awarded a US patent for the manufacture of crystalline wafer solar cells with its proprietary ink. As a result, it switched to being an intellectual property company, adopting a strategy to licence its ink to photovoltaic cell manufacturers to improve solar cell efficiency. Since then, it has grown a huge customer base in China and South-East Asia. Innovalight has adopted a hybrid intellectual property business model, both selling silicon ink powders to its customers as well as collecting royalties under an intellectual property license. This unusual model helps to solve two problems. First, customers feel they are receiving something tangible for their money and, secondly the combination of a sales contract and an IP license provides Innovalight with more legal clout.

Dupont's acquisition of Innovalight highlights an unexpected trend taking place in intellectual property, namely, the interest among Asian manufacturers to commercialise IP generated in the US and Europe. Although US companies often complain about the protection of intellectual rights in China and South-East Asia, Asian conglomerates have become more actively interested in US know-how than their Western counterparts. Innovalight, for example, does not have US customers.

Case Questions

1. Identify the key challenges in protecting intellectual property generated in nanotechnology. Do you think those challenges are being alleviated as more and more applications of nanotechnology are being commercialised?
2. Why do you think Dupont was particularly interested in Innovalight?
3. Investigate the claims of US Patent 7,615,393? Do you believe the claims to be broad enough to provide Innovalight and its customers with a sustainable competitive advantage?

5.12   REVISION QUESTIONS

1. Briefly outline the requirements for a new invention to be patentable. What are two critical steps in the inventorship process?
2. What are the rights bestowed on the owner of intellectual property?
3. What is the difference between a copyright and a patent?
4. What are the advantages of filing a PCT International patent application?
5. Briefly outline the complexities in protecting intellectual property for software. What are the typical IPRs associated with software?

5.13   NOTES

1. For a detailed exploration of intellectual property, please refer to the J.P. McManus text, *Intellectual Property: From Creation to Commercialisation* (2012).
2. Turrentine, 2012.
3. www.patentlyapple.com.
4. Watching and Competitive Intelligence, http://www.europe-innova.eu/c/document_library/get_file?folderId=177014&name=DLFE-13510.pdf.
5. http://www.nanowerk.com/news/newsid=18597.php.
6. http://www.nanowerk.com/news2/newsid=31283.php.
7. Available at http://www.uspto.gov/go/classification/uspc977/defs977.htm (Accessed October 2009).
8. www.epo.org.

5.14   REFERENCES

Almeling, D.S. (2004) "Patenting Nanotechnology: Problems with the Utility Requirement", Stanford Technology Law Review, 4, http://stlr.stanford.edu/STLR/Articles/04_STLR_N1.

Carrol, J. (2001) "Intellectual Property Rights in the Middle East: A Cultural Perspective", *Fordham Intellectual Property, Media and Entertainment Law Journal*, 11(3): 555–600.

CNN (2007) *Two Ex-Coke Workers Sentenced in Pepsi Plot Deal*, http://www.cnn.com/2007/LAW/05/23/coca.cola.sentencing (Accessed 15 October 2013).

Enterprise Ireland (2006) *Legal Guide to Technology Licensing*. Enterprise Ireland and Beauchamps Solicitors.

European Commission (2003) *Intellectual Property: Good Practice Guide,* p.6.

European Commission (2003c) *Intellectual Property: Good Practice Guide*, p. 10.

Ganguli, P. and Jabade, S. (2012) *Nanotechnology Intellectual Property Rights: Research, Design, and Commercialization*. London: CRC Press.

Graham, S. and Mowery, D. (2010) *Intellectual Property Protection in the U.S. Software Industry*. Berkeley, CA: University of California Press.

Hart, R., Homes, P. and Reid, J. (1999) *The Economic Impact of Patentability of Computer Programs: Report to the European Commission*. London: Intellectual Property Institute.

McManus, J. (2009) *Implementing & Managing an Intellectual Property Policy*. Ireland: Enterprise.

NUI Maynooth (2011) *Guide to Commercialisation at NUI Maynooth,* http://commercialisation.nuim.ie/sites/commercialisation.nuim.ie/files/documents/commercialisation%20guide%20rev%201st%20April%202011.pdf (Accessed 15 October 2013).

The Economist (2012) "Intellectual Property in China: Shill Murky", 21 April 2012.

Turrentine, L. (2012) *Galaxy S3 Beats IPhone5 for Best Device 2012*, www.cnet.com.

UK Intellectual Property Office (2011) *Copyright: Essential Reading,* http://www.ipo.gov.uk/c-essential.pdf (Accessed 15 October 2013).

UK Intellectual Property Office (2012) *Designs: How to Protect Your Design,* http://www.ipo.gov.uk/d-basicfacts.pdf (Accessed 15 October 2013).

WIPO (2009) *Making Intellectual Property Work for Business: A Handbook for Chambers of Commerce and Business Associations setting Up Intellectual Property Services*, International Chamber of Commerce and World Intellectual Property Organization.

5.15   GLOSSARY OF TERMS AND USEFUL SOURCES

African Regional Industrial Property Organisation (ARIPO): Established under the Lusaka agreement, ARIPO provides a number of intellectual property protection services for member states. Its main office is located in Zimbabwe. www.aripo.net.

Assignment: Usually refers to the transfer of ownership of an intellectual property right from one person to another.

Patent Claims: As part of the patent application, the claims define the legal scope of the patent. Usually written in technical terms, the claims outline the extent of the protection sought in a patent application.

European Communities Trade Mark Association (ECTA): ECTA was set up to maintain and improve the professional standards and expertise trade mark matters within the European Union and concentrates on key issues common to all members. www.ecta.org.

European Patent Convention (EPC): The EPC came into effect in 1977 facilitating patent rights to be obtained in any one or more of the member states. European applications can be filed with a national patent office or with the European Patent Office.

European Patent Office (EPO): Using a single patent application, the EPO can grant a bundle of national patents from member states. www.epo.org.

Industrial Designs: Refers to the aesthetics or non-functional aspects to a product. The design may comprise 2D features, such as lines, patterns or colour, and 3D features, such as shape or texture.

Infringement: This refers to the use of someone else's intellectual property rights without having the necessary right or licence to do so. The range of prohibited activities differs according to the nature of the right. Patent-infringement consists of the unauthorised making, using, offering for sale or selling of any patented invention. Copyright infringement includes the unauthorised or unlicensed copying of a work subject to copyright.

Intellectual Property: The creations of the mind: inventions; literary and artistic works; and symbols, names and images used in commerce.

International Trade Mark Association (INTA): INTA is a not-for-profit membership association dedicated to the support and advancement of trademarks and related intellectual property as elements of fair and effective commerce. www.inta.org.

Inventive Step: A pre-requisite for the grant of a patent, which requires that the invention, having regard to the state-of-the-art, is inventive and not obvious to a person skilled in the art.

Inventor: An inventor is someone who contributed to the conception and reduction to practice of the invention.

License: A license is a form of contract that gives permission for the use of one party's intellectual property by another party.

Novelty: For an invention to be patented, it requires novelty, i.e., must not be part of current state-of-the-art. The state-of-the-art comprises anything disclosed to the public, e.g., a previous patent, an oral presentation, an academic paper, etc.

Office for Harmonisation in the Internal Market (OHIM): OHIM is the official trade mark and design office of the European Union. It registers the Community trade mark (CTM) and Registered Community Design (RCD), covering the 27 EU countries.

Patentability: Patentability is a measure of a patent application's ability to satisfy the legal Requirements for a patent, including novelty, inventive step and application.

Patent Pending: Patent pending serves notice that an application for a patent has been filed and that legal protection may be forthcoming.

Patent Cooperation Treaty (PCT): PCT is an international treaty in operation since 1978 and is administered by the WIPO. It created a system whereby a single international patent application in one of the contracting states allows for the designation of up to 145 (as at June 2012) other contracting states in which to obtain patent protection.

Prior Art: A technical legal term encompassing anything that has ever existed in the universe before the invention was made. It refers to existing technological data against which a patent application or design can be assessed to determine if it is novel.

Priority: Once an application is filed the applicant can claim priority, 6 months for a trade mark and 12 months for a patent. The filing date of the first application is referred to as the priority date. The initial application would have priority over all subsequent applications made after the priority date. Being first-to-file, therefore, provides competitive advantage.

Provisional Patent Applications: Provisional filings enable Iinventors to establish an early effective filing date in a non-provisional patent application, and allow Inventors to attach the term "Patent Pending" to their Iinventions.

Search Report: Once a patent search is carried out, the search report provides a list of cited published prior that could be used to determine the novelty of a patent application.

State-of-the-Art: It comprises everything previously available to the public by means of description, use or in any other way before the filing of a patent or design application.

Technology-Transfer: Often relevant to academic and industry collaborations, it refers to the movement of technology, either by assignment or licence, from its creators or owner to one or more third parties for their development, commercialisation or use.

United States Patent and Trade Mark Office (USPTO): Locationed in Virginia, the USPTO issues patents and trade marks on behalf of the US Government. www.uspto.gov.

Chapter 6
THE BUSINESS MODEL AND BUSINESS PLAN

6.1 LEARNING OBJECTIVES

This chapter presents business modelling as a tool for developing the business and for systematic learning throughout the venturing process. First, it seeks to explain that opportunities need to be developed into *business concepts* consisting of products/services, and what value they will create in the market (value proposition). Second, it argues that the iterative development of a viable *business model* helps configure the available resources in order to create unique customer value (value proposition) and how the company will capture economic and other value from this. In other words, how to organise the business in order to meet the customers' needs and make money. Third, the importance of the business plan and the components of business plans are outlined. Finally, how to develop metrics for measuring growth and business model performance is explained.

After reading this chapter, you will be able to:

1. Describe, develop and test business models for your business;
2. Understand the structure for writing business plans to attract funding from investors and others; and
3. Develop relevant growth metrics for systematic testing and learning of your business model.

6.2 CHAPTER STRUCTURE

The core elements of this chapter are as follows:

- Introduction
- The Vision
- Creating Value
- Industry-driven Business Models
- Business Modelling for Competitive Advantage
- The Business Plan
- Growth Metrics
- Chapter Summary

- Case Study – Spotify
- Revision Questions
- Further Reading and Resources
- References
- Glossary of Terms

6.3 INTRODUCTION

Many technical entrepreneurs are "in love" with their idea/invention and tend to forget to think about how to build a business around it. It is important to notice that not even the best ideas are likely to sell by themselves. In technology environments, it is common to see business plans with very convincing technology and product descriptions but with little sign of how the idea will create value for customers and owners, adapt to the existing business landscape and capture economic value in order to profit from it. Research shows clearly how companies with similar products within the same industry may have very different abilities to capture economic value from their business models.

6.4 THE VISION

Visionary entrepreneurs typically want to change something in society, to improve the work conditions or the daily life of certain groups of people. The task of the entrepreneur in this respect is to focus and configure the limited resources of the venture in order for them to work as effectively and efficiently towards realising the business opportunity as possible.

The entrepreneur captures the purpose of the business in the business idea and the vision. The *vision* relates to a future state, a situation where critical needs are served better than today. When it comes to the *business idea*, it is more concrete; it relates to how things are now. It is the current state that is in question. It outlines a principled attitude to what should happen in the business. Vision is an important source of business opportunity and often inspiring visions grow out of the desire to resolve frustrations. The vision should be changed as the firm achieves the goals implied in the vision. However, often visions have utopian aspects not likely to change much over time. For example, Nokia's "connecting people" will always be able to lead the company further in their development of products and customer value; it is a universal and utopian ideal where they can always continue working and developing based on the same vision.

6.5 CREATING VALUE

A start-up company creates value in two ways: the *value proposition*, which is a suggestion to customers on how a new product or concept will meet their needs and create value, and the *configuration of value*, which tells how resources and activities need to fit together in order to create and sustain value.

When developing a business concept, the aim is to develop a novel technology or a creative idea of some kind into something assumed to create value for the customer. Stated in another way, a business concept should be based on a "value proposition." A basic definition of a value proposition can be "an offering that helps customers more effectively, reliably, conveniently, or affordably solve an important problem (or satisfy a job-to-be-done) at a given price" (Johnson, 2010, p. 28). "Job to be done" is used as the metaphor for why a customer would hire (buy) your product. Customers are generally not interested in your product per se; they hire it to get something done. In-depth understanding of customers' real everyday challenges and needs are therefore a must for the innovative start-up. Johnson (2010) further recommends start-ups to critically examine how important this problem is for the customer, how satisfied they are with current solutions and how much better your product can solve the customer's problem. The basis for this idea is that economic value is created by satisfying customers' real needs (Kaplan and Norton, 2004).

A company may find it necessary to create several value propositions; one for each customer segment they want to serve (Hamel, 2000). Every value proposition may consist of a bundle of products and services that together helps to solve important problems for targeted customer segments (Osterwalder and Pigneur, 2010). This implies a view of innovation based on deep insight into the targeted customer segments to create *new* value. For *new* customers, entrepreneurs may develop "value innovation" (Kim and Mauborgne, 2005, pp. 12–13). The focus, then, is not so much on competing with other firms, as on opening up "new and uncontested market space" (ibid.), thereby getting far ahead of potential competitors. Kim and Mauborgne argue that such *value innovation* occurs only when companies make sure to both drive value for the customer (differentiation) and drive down cost for the company at the same time. The value proposition is often a key starting point for building the Business Model, which we now turn to (please note that Chapter 9 examines value proposition development).

6.5.1   Value Configurations

Porter (1985) developed the idea of the value chain for analysing value creation and profitability. Input is transformed into products through the value chain, and if the cost of doing this is lower than the resulting value when the product reaches the end consumer, then you have got a profitable value chain. Stabell and Fjeldstad (1998) expanded on this by arguing that the value chain helps to explain some types of businesses, while other businesses are not easy to analyse through this model. What about the service sector and network-based companies? The value chain configuration does not explain what happens or the essence of value creation in those kinds of businesses. Stabell and Fjeldstad therefore added two new models: the value shop and the value network. Value shops deliver value by resolving unique problems for customers. The value network delivers value by facilitating direct and indirect exchange between customers.

6.5.1.1 Value Shop

In a value chain, the value is created by transforming inputs into products. The primary activities, then, are the inbound logistics, the operations, the outbound logistics, the marketing and the service. It is sequential; one thing happens after the other and actions are interdependent. The key cost drivers in a value chain are scale and capacity utilisation. By increasing the scale and utilising the maximum capacity, the firm will decrease the cost of production, which may then lead to higher profits. Value chains are part of interlinked systems, so one may find value chains within value chains, within value chains. Porter (1985) prescribes that a firm will have a competitive advantage in the market if they offer products with the following:

- a higher perceived value to the customers
- lower relative costs than competing firms.

Figure 6.1 describes how economic rents are generated through the components of the competitive triangle.

6.5.1.2 Value shop

In the value shop (Stabell and Fjeldstad, 1998), the value creation logic is about solving customer problems. Some examples are hospitals, management consultancies, or research and development (R&D) departments. The primary activities in a *value shop* are sequential and cyclical; it is about finding problems, acquiring the rights to solve them, choosing between alternative ways of solving them, executing the problem solution, and lastly controlling and evaluating the implemented solution. At this point, many value shops have integrated methods for making new sales, solving more aspects of the existing problem, or using the familiarity with the customer to identify and solve new problems.

Value shops are driving value based on expertise and reputation. Expertise for finding and implementing the best solutions, which then may drive reputation. There are often significant advantages to location, because it is

Figure 6.1 Competitive triangle

Source: Adapted from Hollensen (2011) *Global Marketing*, 5th edition, figure 4.1, p. 105. © Pearson Education Limited 2001, 2011. (Draws information from Porter, *The Competitive Advantage of Nations*.).

advantageous to know the customer. Price is often not emphasised, hence potentially leading to the delivery of wrong solutions with a too high price. Value shops often have limitations or limited advantages of scale. There are, however, ways of changing this game now, for example, through software-as-a-service solutions that allow firms to automate and scale-up activities people previously had to do manually.

6.5.1.3   Value Network

Value networks (Stabell and Fjeldstad, 1998) serve as networking services that link customers who are or wish to be interdependent. Examples of value network are telephone companies, retail banks, insurance companies, postal services and some Internet services like Facebook or Skype. The value creation logic is based on the organisation and facilitation of exchange between people, both direct, as in telephone services, and indirect, as in retail banking.

Mediators act as "club managers" by managing customer contracts to make sure that both customers and the company commit to a mutual set of obligations. The number of users is crucial to the success of value networks, so many different ways of mobilising users have been invented. In addition to increasing the number of customers within the network, the service capacity, the linking opportunity, and the actual use all increase the value of the network.

It will sometimes be possible to charge customers twice, first for their network membership (linking opportunity), and second for their actual use of the services. There are several different revenue models out there. For instance within the "Freemium" model, which is in massive use among online social networking services like Skype, users can sign up for a moderate service for free. However, as soon as professional services or expanded services are required, the user must pay.

Table 6.1   Value configurations

Value configuration	Key characteristics	Examples	Why it is valuable
Value chain	The sequential and interdependent process of transforming inputs into products	Product manufacturers	Increasing scale and maximising capacity leads to decreasing production costs and greater profits
Value shop	Solving customer problems through sequential and cyclical processes	Hospitals; Consulting firms; R&D Centres	Focuses on the customer with dependence on expertise and reputation
Value network	Facilitates an exchange and advantages by linking customers who are or wish to be interconnected	Telephone services; Postal services; Facebook	Successful linkages add value to the other members of the network, which then receives better service

6.6   BUSINESS MODELLING

Many recent studies have shown that the writing of business plans alone is insufficient for dealing with the level of uncertainty that is normally found in a new venture. This insight has led to the development of more iterative tools to support entrepreneurs in their on-going processes of developing a new firm and commercialising innovations. Business modelling is one such tool.

Business modelling has been argued as a "fresh way to consider their options in uncertain, fast-moving and unpredictable environments" (McGrath, 2010, p. 247). Due to fast-changing environments, competitive advantage has become harder to achieve on a long-term basis, hence a continual search for better ways of doing business makes more sense.

This section addresses the role of business modelling for the new venture and outlines the core components of the Business Model (see Figure 6.2). The iterative development of a viable *business model* helps configure the available resources in order to create unique customer value (value proposition) and how the company will capture economic and other value from this. In other words, how to organise the business in order to meet the customers' needs and make money. A business model can be defined as a mode that "allows expressing the business logic of a specific firm. It is a description of the value a company offers to one or several segments of customers and of the architecture of the firm and its network of partners for creating, marketing, and delivering this value and relationship capital, to generate profitable and sustainable revenue streams" (Osterwalder et al., 2005, pp. 17–18). During the last two decades, numerous new business models were tested out, not least because of the emergence of online business opportunities. But also, traditional industries are experimenting with new business models, such as Southwest Airlines' low-cost point-to-point route system.

Business modelling requires entrepreneurs to engage in an active experimentation and active learning rather than the traditional business planning approach. Business modelling provides an outside-in, rather than an inside-out, focus (McGrath, 2010), meaning that customer value is at the core upon which everything rests rather than only the technology and patenting. According to McGrath, business modelling can be divided in two parts: first, the business unit (similar to value proposition), i.e., what customers pay for, and second, the process, or the development of operational advantages. The practice of business modelling stimulates and provides advantages to the entrepreneur through holistic experimentation with the whole company.

An advantage with business modelling is its integration with the entrepreneurial process: the "final" business model is an outcome of an iterative process of developing and testing different business models, often in small scale (low-cost, low risk, make it work, and then scale-up). Teece (2010) suggests that business modelling can be used for creating competitive advantage by "segmenting the market, creating a value proposition for each segment, setting up the apparatus to deliver that value, and then figuring

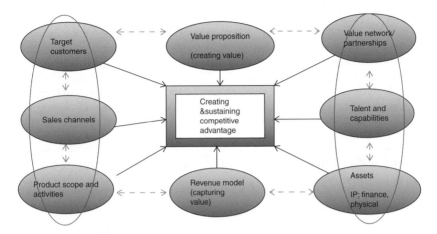

Figure 6.2 Business model dynamics

out 'isolating mechanisms' that can be used to prevent the business model/ strategy from being undermined through imitation by competitors or disintermediation by customers" (p. 180).

Chapter 6 does not cover all of the components in Figure 6.2, but the topics are covered in detail in the relevant chapters throughout the text. It is recommended to use the business model figure as a tool for teams to work out alternative business models for actual business ventures, in workshop settings, or in actual start-up processes. An electronic version apt for copying on large paper sheets (the bigger the better) can be found on the textbook website. Write ideas on sticky notes to easy reshuffle and explore the multitude of possible configurations. Whether using this model, the Osterwalder canvas (see resources below) or one of the many other versions, it is crucial to focus on the three most important issues while working.

1. *The relationships between the components in the model are more important than the content of each of the components.* To make changes in one component is likely to require changes in other components, and this interplay will be unique, yet very important, for each venture, and hence important to explore.
2. *The practice of business modelling is not intended to become another static "form" to fill out.* Figure 6.2 should be used as a dynamic tool to aid exploration and learning in practice. As the start-up firm matures, stabilises their products, and finds customers, the business model can be used for achieving a holistic view of the business, and for more systematic testing.
3. *Use Figure 6.2 to analyse and understand both the opportunities and the limitations for the firm.* Most management models, whether in strategy, marketing or entrepreneurship, tend have a bias towards over-optimism, so use this opportunity to consider strengths and weaknesses. It is not incidental

that successful serial entrepreneurs (Sarasvathy and Dew, 2005) start out analysing their own resources and network. This is where they can find their unique business opportunities, as well as their limitations. Sometimes important resources are inflexible, making certain business model configurations impossible. For example, if having to use expensive high-end technologies and/or highly skilled people for producing a product, then a low-price mass marketing strategy is unlikely to work out in practice (see the Salma case at the end of Chapter 4 for an example of this).

Case Box 6.1   Carbon Recycling International[1]

In the year 2007 K.C. Tran, the CEO of Carbon Recycling International (www. carbonrecycling.is), which had been established a year before, presented an innovative business idea at Seed Forum Iceland, an investor forum in Reykjavik. It was a presentation of a science project that created "energy out of pollution" as a news anchor had described the business idea in the local news. K.C's. argument was compelling: Carbon Recycling International (CRI) captures carbon dioxide from industrial emissions and converts carbon dioxide into Renewable Methanol (RM). RM is a clean fuel that can be blended at different levels with gasoline to meet renewable energy directives. The production process captures carbon dioxide and minimises emissions from energy intensive industries. CRI's methanol is compatible with existing energy and fuel infrastructure.

Financial crisis and political instability in Iceland made it hard for Carbon Recycling International to raise money in Iceland, as the financial system and governmental support for capital intensive projects crumbled. CRI became, however, one of the few innovative ventures that managed to raise international capital in the post-financial crisis of Iceland. The business model is to produce renewable methanol for both domestic consumption and export. The production needs big plants, and CRI has already built one in Reykjanes, which has been used for proof of concept and development of the technology. The plan is to build plants that would require 45 MW of power and cost around €40–50 millions, which are ten times bigger than the current plant in Reykjanes.

The problem for K.C. Tran was how to create credibility for an innovative business idea, which sounded too good to be true. It is the same issue that faces most entrepreneurs. Presenting a vision of a new venture and making that vision credible is one of the hardest tasks facing entrepreneurs. The scientists and founders of CRI focused in the beginning on proofing the technology and applying for patents and creating credibility around the innovation by getting Nobel prize winners on the board of the venture. Furthermore, they hired a CEO who was all business and was able to communicate the business case. Agreements for financing of the first commercial plant in Svartsengi was signed in 2010, as well as a distribution agreement with one of the leading oil distributors in Iceland. Other plant projects are being developed, which shows that Carbon Recycling has come a long way, in one of the worst scenarios, since the presentation of the business idea in 2007.

6.6.1   Creating Value (Value Proposition) and Capturing Value (Revenue Model)

Creating and capturing value are the key characteristics of the centre section of Figure 6.2 (repeated here). The *value proposition* creates customer value by bundling products and services to meet customer needs or solve problems for each customer segment (Osterwalder and Pigneur, 2010). (Note: Chapter 9 addresses how to formulate your venture's value proposition.) The *revenue model*, on the other hand, is crucial for capturing economic value. How to get paid for your products or services is not always a straightforward and simple question. Testing different alternatives may be needed before finding a viable model.

An important part of business modelling is to model how to secure revenue streams for the venture, also called *"value capture"* which in technology ventures often are connected to intellectual property (IP). "Different models of value capture are available where intellectual property rights exist and can be enforced – so designing business models often requires the skill of the intellectual property lawyer as well as that of the entrepreneur" (Teece, 2010, p. 186). The entrepreneur should start out with calculating "how much revenue would be required to throw off enough profit to make an initiative worthwhile" (McGrath, 2010 ,p. 258). Then key metrics (discussed later in this chapter) and key checkpoints can be developed, which then allows the development process to speed up.

Even if the company succeeds in creating great customer value, it is not guaranteeing profitability for the venture. Profitability depends partly on finding how to get paid a decent price for the products and partly on positioning the venture in the value chain in a way that enables it to capture more of the economic value created than the cost of producing the product or service. In some industries, it may be difficult to find such a position, because other established actors may control too much of the remaining value chain. For example, many PC manufacturers struggle with their profitability despite strong brands and high sales volumes, mainly because they depend on supplies from very strong actors like Microsoft and Intel. Apple, on the other hand, has maintained stronger control over their own value chain by developing their own hardware and software; this control, along with premium pricing, has been significantly more profitable that the personal computer business model (Dedrick et al., 2010).

6.6.2 Bringing the Product to the Marketplace (Target Customers, Channels, Scope and Activities)

The left section of Figure 6.2 (repeated below), supports bringing the product to the marketplace. This includes identifying target customers, sales channels (how the product will be distributed, through whom and through number of handling points) and the scope and operational activities of the start-up firm.

The combination of what product or service the company wants to sell, and the market segment it wants to reach, is based on an assumption of value, that its offer will create a certain kind of value for this kind of customer (value proposition). The core questions are: for whom is the company creating value? What are the target groups, and what are the main customer segments? The geographical focus area and through what channels the firm wants to sell the product are also important. The target customers and sales channels components are given rigorous attention in Chapter 9. While product scope and activities are discussed later in this chapter.

6.6.3 Value Networks, Talent and Capabilities and Resourcing

The right section of the model (Figure 6.2, repeated here) identifies value networks, talent and capabilities and resourcing as the final three components of the business model. Human Talent is addressed in Chapter 10; resourcing issues are addressed in Chapter 5 (IP); and finance in Chapter 12. The value network is addressed in detail below.

6.6.4 Value Network and Partnerships

Value is created by the right combination of resources in this bundle of activities so that customers can get the best value or the value that they want. The activities in the value chain cannot be fully or exclusively performed by one organisation, as inputs from other actors in market are needed. This means that each organisation is part of a value system or a value network alongside other organisations. Different activities are performed or facilitated by different members of the value network, because it is the combined effort of all the members that leads to better value creation for them and for the customer.

Case Box 6.2 NextNet AS: Race For The Last Mile[2]

In late 2006, Eirik Grønsund, the founder and CEO of Norwegian wireless communication start-up NextNet, was on the verge of deciding upon a 30 MNOK investment in the 2.6 Ghz wireless spectrum to expand their business nation-wide and unlock new growth in next generation mobile services based on the emerging WiMax standard.

Since 2000, traditional telephone technology had dominated the broadband and wireless communication offerings. But, coming from a software background, the NextNet founders envisioned opportunities in IP-based technology and its potential for value-add services–such as mobile IP telephony–beyond what telecom operators' existing infrastructure were offering.

Having acquired roughly 5,000 customers on the existing, license-free 5 Ghz band, the founders consider whether there would be sufficient long-term adoption of the new technology to justify the investment.

The founders faced a big decision; whether they should proceed with the investment and vision given the uncertainty in technology adoption, or if they should bootstrap and rent access to infrastructure from competitors, focusing on their existing, profitable business at lower margins.

NextNet decided to proceed with the investment. After one week-long auction, bidding against the leading national telecom operators to acquire the license, the founders successfully secured the rights to use the 20 Mhz in the 2.6 GHz spectrum.

In 2008, however, the global economy was in a severe recession. Major software vendors and hardware equipment manufacturers would postpone research and development on the WiMax technology, while telecom operators continued their development on the competing and–the then considered–inferior Long-Term Evolution (LTE) alternative.

As WiMax technology adoption did not catch on quite as hoped for, and competing standards emerged, NextNet was in need for additional funding to invest in the alternative, less mature LTE standard and compete with incumbents.

Raising another round of capital, however, was challenging to the start-up. The founders might lose control of the company's direction and, perhaps, vision. So by January 2010, at 8,000 customers and a profitable business, NextNet founders successfully exited the business to Hafslund's (OSE: HNA) telecom operations.

Looking back, the founders could have followed the safer path, developing lower margin services over the fixed, unlicensed 5 Ghz band. But the big idea and entrepreneurial long-term vision was to build an ecosystem around the future standard provided by the emerging IP-based WiMax technology.

In this process of interaction, there are many different types of relationships depending on the context of the market exchange taking place. For instance, both social and business relationships may be particularly important to new ventures because emerging organisations typically lack established ties (see Figure 6.3 for a typology of network ties). Successfully leveraging and managing relationships is critical for a new venture, which could suffer from the liability of newness or find it difficult to gain credibility within the industry as a nascent venture particularly if in search of seed capital.

Nature of the relationship

		Business relationship	Social relationship
Relationship to the firm	Vertical	– Clients – Suppliers to the firm – Agents and intermediaries – Ancillary suppliers	– Former clients – Other suppliers in the industry – Other operators in ancillary support firms
	Horizontal	– State support agencies and export promotion agencies – University/research institutions – Trade associations – Advisors/consultants – Joint Venture partners	– Competitors – Community organisations – Friends/Family – Acquaintance

Figure 6.3 A typology of social and business relationships in new ventures
Source: Adapted from Evers and O'Gorman, 2011.

The founder may have more close, strong and personal informal ties than business ties at the beginning of a new venture. These ties or relationships can be either horizontal or vertical. Business horizontal relationships include, for example, research institutes and industry associations (Figure 6.3). Vertical business relationships are those the focal firm has with business partners, suppliers, agents and clients. In turn, vertical social ties (sometimes referred to as informal business acquaintances) are those positioned in the supply chain; buyers and suppliers located in the broader business network who have a non-exchange relationship with the focal firm. Horizontal social ties encompass competitors within the industry, as well as family, friends, relatives, social and community organisations (Hoang and Antoncic, 2003). It should also be noted that this is a static representation of network ties; network ties can evolve, and, for example, what starts out as a social relationship may evolve into a client or business partner (a business relationship). The entrepreneur must identify and assess which vertical and horizontal relationships can add value to the new venture's activities by creating an effective value network for the new venture.

6.7 INDUSTRY-DRIVEN BUSINESS MODELS

Dominant business models emerge from the particular constraints of an industry. When those constraints are removed or changed, opportunities for new business models can emerge. Such changes may come out of industrial capacity (like Moore's law for semiconductors), from novel products (like netbooks), from regulation (like environmental policies), from social norms (like with smoking) and from financial constraints (higher gas prices may provide profitability to alternative energy sources). Common to all this is the fact that it is almost impossible to know in advance how this will impact business practice (McGrath, 2010, p. 253). Hence, active experimentation becomes crucial to everyone engaging with business model innovation. In the Internet search area, Infoseek tried to charge their users a subscription fee for their services. Yahoo! instead made the searching free, while selling access to users to advertisers. Google refined this model by creating a better search engine (product/service) and by developing a business model where advertisers got even more valuable information and access to the users (McGrath, 2010, p. 254), while Google found smarter ways of pricing their services (fees related to the popularity of different key words in searches).

Case Box 6.3   Truecaller: The Global Phone Directory[3]

Truecaller is a Swedish Internet firm offering a collaborative global phone directory. The company was founded in 2009 by two engineers to resolve the problem of callers not knowing the origin of incoming phones calls. This had proved a problem in work environments where the employees were not able to screen and prepare for incoming call inquiries. Truecaller provided a dynamic, collaborative phone directory using *crowdsourcing* (i.e., users share and upload their personal phone directories into a common directory) with high-data integrity. The application is available on the web and as an app for iPhone, Android, Blackberry, Symbian and Windows phones.

The revenue model is a freemium model. Initially, Truecaller imported national phone directories available into the system but the amount of data was not sufficient and the quality of data was low. Consequently, a shift was made to a collaborative model where the users are a part of building up the content in the service. Regarding geographical focus, Truecaller commenced by targeting the Nordic markets and then moved on to focus on BRICS countries, particularly India, as well as countries in the Middle East. The company had a global focus from inception. Today, the app has more than 15 million users, and the company is experiencing a high monthly user growth rate. Truecaller works closely with collaborative "ambassadors" on local markets ensuring the spread of the awareness of the app.

6.7.1 Logic Behind Experimentation

The basic logic of business modelling experimentation is to keep the initial investment small, prototype fast, get customer feedback and then be ready for greater investments and vigorous scale-up after the concept is proven in at a small scale. Hence, it is possible to make many experimental tests of value propositions and business models without too high of a risk on any of the value propositions. This is called the "real options" approach (McGrath, 2010, p. 256). Start-up businesses may have a lot of time to experiment because incumbents typically do not show much interest in new business models, which seem to be "designed for customers that an incumbent doesn't serve, at price points they would consider unattractive and builds on resources that they don't have" (McGrath, 2010, p. 257). Such business models just seem totally unattractive to incumbents, at least in an early stage. For example, Kodak's failure to transform into a leader of digital photography cost them enormously. Kodak was very innovative and a digital technology leader from the start but failed to recognise the implications for its business model. Film was so important and profitable to them that it was hard to see how the industry would transform. McGrath (2010) suggests that to discover needs requires entrepreneurs to modify a business model over time. Leaders are advised to engage continuously in three "critical conversations" with:

1. leading technologists (e.g., within the firm);
2. firms competing for the same customer resource (e.g., their time); and
3. current non-consumers that could possibly become consumers in the future (this is often done via anthropological observation).

When developing value propositions (units of business) and a viable business model, firms should adopt a discovery-driven approach rather than a planning approach (to learn as much as possible at the lowest possible cost) (McGrath, 2010, p. 258). Then, entrepreneurs need to formulate and test their assumptions about customer value. Then key metrics and key check-points can be developed, and the development process can speed up.

David Teece (2010) takes a holistic view of business models. He suggests that the "essence of a business model is in defining the manner by which the enterprise delivers value to customers, entices customers to pay for value, and converts those payments to profit. It thus reflects management's hypothesis about what customers want, how they want it, and how the enterprise can organize to best meet those needs, get paid for doing so, and make a profit" (p. 172). He further distinguishes between two basic types of business models: first, the integrated business model where the company bundles innovation and product together and assumes responsibility for the entire value chain; and second, the outsourced business model, such as licensing. For example, Rambus (a manufacturer of semiconductor memory) and Dolby (a noise-reduction technology) are not producing anything them-selves, but they are developing and protecting technologies that others can utilise for a fee. Also, there are hybrid business models that mix these two approaches (Teece, 2010, p. 184).

Several well-known business models can be emphasised here: The "razor-blade" model, used by Rolls Royce, GE, and many more. This refers to how Gillette started selling the main product for shaving, the razor, relatively cheap, while selling the necessary add-ons, the razor-blades, expensively, earning its profits on the add-ons. In sports, equipment producers sponsor top-class athletes to use their products, which again may lead to regular consumers buying the same products. McGrath (2010) is mainly concerned with novel business models containing elements of "free", such as the "free-mium" model used by Flickr, Dropbox, Spotify and many more social ICT services. The freemium model is when a basic version of the product or service is given away for free, and the more advanced version is sold for a monthly subscription (see Case Box 6.1). Also, she refers to "cross-subsidi-zation", which is when the main unit is sold cheaply and necessary add-ons are sold for a relatively high price, like with ink-jet printers and ink or cell phones and usage plans.

6.8 BUSINESS MODELLING FOR COMPETITIVE ADVANTAGE

The business model dynamics, shown in Figure 6.2, depict each of the components upon which the venture needs to be developed and the interconnection between these elements. Drawing on the business model concepts of McGrath (2010), Teece (2010), Hamel (2000), Johnson (2010) and Osterwalder et al. (2005), and in line with the chapter structure of this textbook, we have chosen to represent the business model by the eight factors displayed in Figure 6.2. As mentioned, the most important aspect of such a visual representation of the business model is to show how each factor is dependent on the other factors and that change in one factor is likely to produce new opportunities and/or restrictions for the other factors. This complex interplay between value creation and value capture as well as between resourcing and marketing requires experimentation. As a result, systematic modelling and testing of value propositions and business models is suggested to create and maintain a competitive advantage.

6.8.1 Perspectives on Developing Competitive Advantage

There are two dominant perspectives on how firms create a Competitive Advantage (CA): through the Resource Based View (RBV) of the firm (Barney, 1991) and Dynamic Capabilities View (DCV) of the firm (Teece et al., 1997). Both theories consider firms with a CA to be derived from knowledge inventories, capabilities and unique inimitable resources. The *RBV* suggests that firms in the same industry perform differently because they differ in their resources and capabilities (Wernerfelt, 1984). RBV focuses on more stationary, tangible firm-specific resources. However, the *DCV* implicitly suggests the need to distinguish capabilities from resources and stresses the importance of the dynamic processes of capability building in gaining competitive advantage (Evers et al., 2012).[4] In contrast to the RBV, the dynamic capabilities theory posits that the firm needs to develop new capabilities to identify opportunities and to respond quickly to them (Jarvenpaa and Leidner, 1998).

Dynamic capabilities theory can explain how firms evolve over time through their deployment and acquisition of resources, because firms must continuously renew and reconfigure themselves if they are to survive (Zahra et al., 2006). Helfat et al. (2007, p. 1) defined dynamic capabilities as "the capacity of an organisation to purposely create, extend and modify its resource base" to include knowledge, skills and capabilities, which allow the firm to generate economic rents (Ambrosini et al., 2009). Dynamic capabilities have been defined as "the capacity to renew competencies so as to achieve congruence with the changing business environment" by adapting, integrating and reconfiguring internal and external organisational skills, resources and functional competencies (Teece et al., 1997, p. 515). The DCV considers firms as active generators of competitive resources by which managers "integrate, build, and reconfigure internal and external competencies to address rapidly changing environments" (Teece et al., 1997, p. 516). Dynamic capabilities can create competitive advantage for the venture and suits the context that high-tech firms operate in. It suggests that since marketplaces are dynamic, it is the capabilities of a firm to acquire and deploy resources in a way that matches the changes in its market environment that are significant.

The DCV is further developed in Chapter 11 to understand how new ventures can develop competitive advantages in international markets. Such resources and capabilities can underpin many components of the Business Model (Figure 6.2) and the operational activities of the value chain discussed below.

6.9 THE BUSINESS PLAN

Business plans have been a preferred planning tool for new ventures for decades. It has developed into a shared practice among entrepreneurs, investors, advisors and even big corporations. In fact, the expectation to use a business plan is now so strong that many investors, banks and advisors will not take the entrepreneur seriously before a convincing business plan is presented. However, when investigating what business plans are used for in practice, Honig and Karlsson (2004) found that in most cases business plans are not used much after completion. Some have argued that it is the process of planning that is important. Others have abandoned planning tools all together, recommending instead just to go out and do what one thinks is right. However, this method is partly dependent on the outcome of random luck. It is strongly recommended for entrepreneurs to use more systematic learning processes.

In this book, the business plan is recommended as a tool for documenting the business and making sure every important aspect of the business has been thought through. While value propositions, business models and similar modelling tools are more useful in the early phases, business plans can be written later in the process when moving towards pitching to investors and other key partners.

The template offered in this chapter looks relatively similar to many other templates found in textbooks and on the Internet. This template is a good one for technology entrepreneurs, because it is structured to focus on business, market and financial matters, which are the areas that need to be the most convincing to gain partnerships. Still, as every start-up is unique, it is important also to adapt the business plan and make it represent the actual company in a favourable way. This means that it may be necessary to reshuffle some of the sections, add something, or leave irrelevant sections out.

The business plan serves several purposes. By far the most important one is to provide the basis for pitching and negotiating with investors and institutional support organisations. As long as these actors expect a professional business plan, entrepreneurs need to know how to write them. Second, it may be helpful in clarifying goals and analysing the market for the entrepreneurial team. By working with business modelling first, to explore opportunities and constraints, and understand the relationships between the different parts of the business, the entrepreneur may get a holistic understanding of the product and the business. This insight should then be fed into the business plan. Third, it may be presented for key partners in establishing the business, to convince them that the start-up company is trustworthy and has potential.

The copies of your plan should be controlled, and a distribution record should be kept. This process will allow you to update your distributed plans as needed and help to ensure that your plan is not more widely distributed than you intend. In fact, many plans include ethical disclaimers that limit the ability of individuals distributing or otherwise copying the plan without the consent of the company's owners. Remember too that an appropriate private placement disclaimer should be included if the plan is being used to raise capital.

The main components to be described in the business plan document are outlined in Table 6.2 and briefly described below. (A detailed business

Table 6.2 Summary of components of the business plan

---

1. EXECUTIVE SUMMARY
    1.1 Principals Involved in the Venture
    1.2 The Product/Service
    1.3 Target Market
    1.4 The Business Model
    1.5 Level of Profitability
    1.6 Funding Requirement and Return on Investment
2. OPPORTUNITY ANALYSIS AND MARKET VALIDATION
3. THE VENTURE'S VISION, VALUE PROPOSITION AND BUSINESS MODEL
4. PRODUCT/SERVICE, PRODUCT LIFE CYCLE, IP PROTECTION
5. MARKETING STRATEGY AND SALES PLAN
6. TALENT AND TEAM CAPABILITIES
7. RESOURCING AND OPERATIONAL PLAN
8. FINANCIAL PLAN AND HARVEST
9. CRITICAL RISKS
10. START-UP SCHEDULE
11. APPENDICES

---

plan template with explanations to each section is provided with the online materials for this textbook).

6.9.1 Advice for Writing a Good Business Plan[5]

6.9.1.1 Executive summary

The *executive summary* should emphasise the key issues of the business plan. A critical point that must be communicated in the executive summary is your company's distinctive competence – the factors that will make your business successful in a competitive market.

In total, your executive summary should be less than three pages in length and provide the reader with a succinct overview of your entire business plan. The executive summary should be followed by a brief table of contents designed to assist readers in locating specific sections in the plan. Detailed descriptions of the plan's contents should be avoided in the table of contents.

If your company is new, you could be sending your business plan to potential investors who review hundreds of them each year. More often than not, these individuals do not get past the executive summary of the plans they receive. Your executive summary must therefore give the reader a useful understanding of your business and make the point of most interest to them: "What is in it for the investor?"

6.9.1.2 Opportunity analysis and market validation

The *market analysis* section should reflect your knowledge of your industry, and present highlights and analysis of your market research. Detailed market research studies, however, should be presented as appendices to your plan.

Because your market analysis provides the only basis for your prospective sales and pricing estimates, make sure that this section clearly demonstrates that there is a market need for your product or service, that you as the owner not only understand this need but can meet it and that you can sell at a profit. This section should also include an estimate of your market penetration annually for the next five years.

6.9.1.3 The venture's vision, value proposition and business model

The *company description* section must provide an overview of how all of the elements of your company fit together without going into detail, because most of the subjects will be covered in-depth elsewhere in the plan.

Writing this section is the first real test of your ability to communicate the essence of your business. If this section lacks a clear description of the key concepts of your company, the reader will assume that you have not yet clearly defined the idea in your own mind. Therefore, you must be certain that this section concisely and accurately describes the substance of your new business.

6.9.1.4 Product/service, product life cycle, IP protection

This section should seek to clearly articulate the product and/or service to be offered by the venture. It is good to take the user's perspective when describing the product, to avoid dwelling with technological features without highlighting how the technology creates value with the user. The specific benefits of the product, as well as how the product meets the needs of users. Competitive advantages could be mentioned, particularly if there are elements that are hard to copy for competitors. Then, the business plan should mention the stage of the product's development (idea, prototype, small production runs, etc.) and how it is expected to be scaled up.

Then, the product/service's current position within its life cycle can be described, along with factors that may change the anticipated life cycle.

Last, the company's IP need to be described convincingly, including existing or pending patents (or other filings) and anticipated patents. Key aspects of the product or service that cannot be patented or protected, key aspects that qualify as trade secrets and existing legal agreements with owners' and employees' nondisclosure agreements and non-compete agreements).

The research and development activities are often central for technology ventures. Activities in progress, future activities and milestones and anticipated results of future research and development activities should be outlined, such as new products, new product generations, complementary products or services and replacement products.

If known, research and development activities by others in the same industry could be included, such as direct and indirect competitors, suppliers and customers.

Special attention should be paid to the readers of your business plan as you develop this section. Too much detail will have a negative impact on most external readers of the plan. Avoid turning this section of your business plan into a policies and procedures manual for your employees.

6.9.1.5 Marketing strategy and sales plan

Your objective here is to describe the activities that will allow you to meet the sales and margin levels indicated in your prospective financial statements. Both general and specific information must be included in this part of your plan.

Do not underestimate the importance of presenting a **well-conceived sales strategy**. Without an efficient approach to beating a path to the doors of potential customers, companies with very good products and services often fail. The emphasis in this section should be on your company's unique ability to satisfy the needs of the marketplace. Avoid criticising your competition's products too severely in this section, because the natural tendency of a reader who is not part of your organisation will be to empathise with the unrepresented party – your competition. Concentrate on the positive aspects of your product's ability to meet existing market needs and allow your readers to come to their own conclusions about your competition based on the objective information presented here and in Chapters 7 and 9.

6.9.1.6 Talent and team capabilities

Your management team's talents and skills are some of the few truly unique aspects of your company. If you are going to use your plan to attract investors, this section must emphasise your management's talents and skills and indicate why they are a part of your company's distinctive competence that cannot easily be replicated by your competition.

Remember that individuals invest in people, not ideas. Do not use this section of the plan to negotiate future ownership of the company with potential investors. Simply explain the current ownership. Because your management team is unique, make sure that you stress members' backgrounds and skills, and how they will contribute to the success of your product/service and business. This is especially important to emphasise when you are looking for financing (Chapter 10 addresses this in more detail).

6.9.1.7 Resourcing and operational plan

This section need to build a thorough understanding of how products/services are to be produced, by what procedures, and via what production or service delivery capacity. The use of internal capacity or external contractors to deliver, as well as expected investments in scaling up the capacity is required. Suppliers that can supply critical elements of production should be identified, risks of shortages should be evaluated and existing and anticipated contractual relationships with suppliers should be described.

Because many of the aspects of your new business are still theoretical at this point, special care must be taken to be sure the specifics of your operations do not conflict with the information included in your prospective financial statements. Any inconsistencies between those two areas will result in some unpleasant surprises as your company begins operations. Here again, too much detail can detract from the rest of your plan. Be certain that the level of detail included fits the specific needs of the plan's users.

6.9.1.8 Financial plan and harvest

The *financial data* section contains the financial representation of all the information presented in the other sections. Various prospective scenarios can be included, if appropriate. The financial data section of your business plan is another area where specialised knowledge can be invaluable. If you do not have someone with sufficient financial expertise on your management team, you will probably need to utilise an outside advisor.

Any new or additional funding reflected in your prospective financial statements should be discussed here. Alternative funding scenarios can be presented if appropriate, and corresponding prospective financial statements are presented in subsequent sections of your plan.

Remember, because the rate of return is the investor's most important consideration – and the initial public offering market is sometimes not available – investors will be looking for alternative exit strategies. Therefore, be flexible and creative in developing these opportunities, taking into consideration such recent trends as merger/acquisitions and strategic partnering. Although details can be worked out later, investors need to know that you understand their primary objectives as you develop your overall business strategy (Chapter 12 addresses the financing decisions).

6.9.1.9 Critical risks

In this section, you need to systematically analyse what you find to be critical risks, before outlining how these risks will be (1) minimised (risk prevention), and (2) handled if they materialise. There may be a number of risk factors: internal to the company (e.g., employees taking another job), external (e.g., supplier delivering bad quality), institutional (e.g., new regulations) and financial (e.g., access to venture capital or other).

6.9.1.10 Start-up schedule

Outline the plan for the next steps of the start-up process. In the near future, it could be made relatively detailed about important activities. The long-term aspects of the plan should be more concerned with important milestones and connecting the interdependent activities – how some activities need to be finished to enable other activities. GANTT diagrams and other tools for time planning are often used to aid and visualise the planning.

6.9.1.11 Appendices

Any additional details or confidential information that could be useful to the readers of the business plan but is not appropriate for distribution to everyone receiving the body of the plan can be presented here. Accordingly, appendices and exhibits should be bound separately from the other sections of the plan and provided on an as-needed basis to readers.

In some instances, the thicker the business plan, the less likely a potential investor is to read it thoroughly. However, you do want to be able to demonstrate to potential funding sources that you have done a complete job in preparing your plan and that the comments made within it are well documented. By placing more detailed calculations and plans in the appendices and exhibits, you can keep the size of your business plan palatable to its users and still have the additional information they may require readily available.

6.10 GROWTH METRICS

After starting the business – whether it is in the early development phase or if it has gotten funding – the entrepreneur faces a central question: How do you know if the company is progressing or not? In general, people tend to explain successes with strategies and actions, and failures are blamed on the environment. So, if sales go up, who wants the credit? But what was the real reason for the growth? And will it last? Most entrepreneurs do not have a clue. Hence, the starting point for measuring progress is bad whether progress is made or not. With progress, what factors are important in driving the progress?

McGrath (2010) argues that "key metrics" should measure the sets of activities that are employed to sell the product. In airlines, how full the planes are when they take off is such an essential metric. Dell could build competitive advantage (at least for some time) by getting payments and delivering the product in an unusual way, and this advantage could be accurately evaluated by comparing its operating metrics with its competitors. Key metrics are often "derived from the most critical constraint or rate-limiting step in a particular value chain" (McGrath, 2010, p. 252). Amazon overcame the limitation of floor space for a retail shop by selling online. Food retailers are using advanced tools for analysing the flow and stock of goods, providing increasing negotiation power towards their suppliers.

For iterative methods to make sense, it is of high importance to measure progress in a systematic way rather than just leaving the process to chance. Ries (2011) makes a distinction between "vanity metrics" and real, actionable metrics. Vanity metrics are the kind of metrics you would traditionally find in business plans and well-rehearsed pitches and reports from entrepreneurial teams to their investors. They are designed to make people think the business is successful (Ries, 2011). Vanity metrics typically sum up the total numbers from when the product or service was launched in the market until now. At best the numbers are broken down into annual or even quarterly figures. "Last year we sold 1,000 products, representing a revenue of €50,000," they might say. Or worse, the annual "total market" for this kind of products in our target geographical area is €10,000,000, and if we can have 1 per cent of this, the company will be very profitable, and we aim to achieve this within 3–5 years. In Internet-based businesses, the team might be bragging about a hit rate of 200,000 during the last six months. What all these number have in common is that they do not say anything helpful about how the start-up is performing.

Growth metrics should instead be specifically designed to provide concrete and honest feedback about how the business is progressing. This is best done by (1) defining rigidly what kind of metrics are useful for the particular business in its specific phase; (2) finding reliable ways of testing and measuring progress; and (3) breaking down numbers into smaller and meaningful units: to monthly or perhaps even weekly periods, to very specific and targeted customer segments, distinguishing between first-time and returning customers, by measuring the customers' use of the product, time spent at the website, recommending the product to others, etc. More interesting than knowing the total number of customers is the question: "How many more customers did we get this month compared to last month?"

Many businesses may be able to utilise web-based tools for measuring progress. Google analytics, or the company's own measurement solutions may be used to measure the preferences and behaviour of customers in intelligent ways. It may also be possible to do split-testing, where half of the customers are offered enhanced (or simply different) services and products, hence making it possible to have very concrete feedback related to the higher (or perhaps lower) value of the new/adjusted service. In the Lean Startup framework (the build – test – learn cycle), after having built a "minimum viable product" (e.g., a prototype), the hypothesis of customer value built into the product idea needs to be made as explicit and testable as possible. Then actionable metrics may be designed in a way that is honest and useful while measuring what matters. Often it is about breaking down data into actionable units of information.

Ries suggests several innovation metrics of which four are mentioned here: first is split-testing (A/B experiments, where half of the users get added/changed features, to test whether this creates value to the customers); second is per-customer metrics (data that is happening on a per-customer or per-segment basis. E.g., instead of looking at the total number of page views in a given month, consider looking at the number of page views per new and returning customer); third are funnel metrics and cohort analysis (e.g., consider an e-commerce product that has a couple of key customer life cycle events: registering for the product, signing up for the free trial, using the product and becoming a paying customer. Create a simple report that shows these metrics for subsequent cohorts (groups) over time.); and fourth is keyword metrics (search engine marketing/optimisation (SEM/SEO)). SEM and SEO are great customer acquisition tactics, but they can also reveal important and actionable insights about customers, by treating customers who were acquired with a given keyword as a segment and then tracking their metrics over time.

To sum up the key aspects of creating innovation metrics (Ries, 2011):

1. **Measure what matters.** It's tempting to think that, because some metrics are good, more metrics are better.
2. **Metrics are people.** Great metrics tools allow firms to audit their accuracy by tracing reports back to the individual people who generated their data. This improves accuracy, but more important: it lets firms use the same customers for in-depth qualitative research.
3. **Measure the Macro.** Even when split-testing the impact of a minor change, like a wording or a new button, it's important not to get distracted by intermediate metrics like the click-through rate of the button itself. Customer behaviours that lead to something useful are the

Table 6.3 Growth metrics

- Distribution
  - How many channels? How big is our monthly growth compared to our total user base?
  - What is the cost of our customer acquisition? What is the lifetime value? Are we acquiring customers profitably?
- Engagement
  - Is the number of active users growing? Do customers get what they want/need? What channels work best in finding the right kind of users and engaging them?
  - How many of our customers are using various features? Do we need to change the direction of product development?
- Revenue
  - Is the revenue growing?
  - Conversion rate, from free to paid, or from simple to professional, etc. Is our ability to convert customers to paying customers improving?
  - Churn rate. How well are we retaining our customers?
  - Burn rate. When are we profitable? When do we run out of cash? When do we need to raise money?

Source: Adapted from Tunguz, 2013.

most important, whether purchase, retention for advertising CPM[6] or some other measurable "success" particular to your business model.

In Internet-based companies, Tomasz Tunguz (2013), venture capitalist at RedpointVentures and former product manager at Google, suggests to format and measure growth in the following way. First is the format. From experience with multiple start-ups, he suggests that every board meeting progress report should compare the last month with the previous month, and then calculating the monthly change, a six-month average and finally compare the results with the goal. The six-month average is meant to make up for the volatility of the month-to-month measure. Second is the content, or what should be measured. Here it is absolutely crucial that every start-up makes sure to measure what matters to their specific business and their specific situation/phase. Still, at least for online businesses, some the following metrics may be of high value to evaluate how the start-up process is going. Only pick the most relevant ones for the firm.

6.11   CHAPTER SUMMARY

This chapter described how to expand the business concept from thinking about the idea, technology and product, into thinking about what kind of business to build around your product and value proposition. By using business modelling as an iterative tool during development and early market exploration, your goal should be to organise a venture that will create unique customer value and simultaneously capture a good share of that value, which will lay the foundation for a profitable business. Furthermore, the business plan template was presented along with the elements required to write a good business plan aimed at analysing, planning and convincing key stakeholders about the commercial potential for the venture. This chapter also discussed why and how to write a business plan in the context of research showing that traditional business plans are generally not used by entrepreneurs after having written them. It concluded with tools for measuring progress and how to create actionable metrics – growth metrics.

Case Study 6.1 Spotify

Written by Casey T. Carney, BI Norwegian Business School.

In 2006, two Swedish, serial entrepreneurs – Daniel Ek and Martin Lorentzon – founded Spotify, the European-based, on-demand, music streaming service (Spotify, 2013). The founders recognised the gap in the existing market and developed a service to meet customer needs. Spotify combined the existing business models of online radio and the on-demand features of the iTunes Store. The creation allows listeners to create custom playlists of their favourite songs through Spotify's user interface rather than purchasing individual songs or albums. As a result, the listener is in complete control of the online listening experience, and it is free to use.

To develop Spotify, Ek and Lorentzon considered the resources needed to succeed in such a venture. Historically, the online music format struggled to gain legal rights to the music from the record labels. Spotify collaborated with the record companies, which allowed the service to launch (2008) with a huge library of songs on day one. Its website boasts that 20,000 songs are added daily (Spotify, 2013).

The technical aspects of Spotify were also innovative in that the system was developed to be lightweight; the application has high usability ratings with low buffer times. Much of Spotify's success can be attributed to its understandable user interface and with its more recent seamless integration with Facebook. Deemed "hypersocial" by Salyer (2012), the Spotify experience allows Facebook friends to share playlists and create collaborative playlists, thus expanding artists' outreach and developing a new interactive listening experience. After adding social elements, Spotify balanced the demand for full access social sharing with user settings that allowed the listener to limit or prohibit social media interaction as desired. One of the most recent premium features allows Spotify playlists to be downloaded for listening enjoyment when the user is not directly connected to the Internet. Through these constant upgrades, it is evident that the needs of the customer are considered throughout each iteration of the innovation life cycle.

Originally, Spotify's revenue model consisted of two tiers: *free* – unlimited access to on-demand music supported by advertisements; and *premium* – unlimited, commercial-free music. The only incentive for users to upgrade their service was advert-free listening. The incentives for upselling the premium service were not convincing, so the entrepreneurs added new features and redeveloped their revenue model to increase profitability. Currently, the revenue model consists of three tiers of service: *free* – available only on computers with a limited amount of monthly play time and supported by advertisements; *unlimited* – a small fee (€5) provides unlimited, advertisement-free music on computers; and *premium* – access to commercial-free Spotify on all of your devices, including tablets and phones, at a slightly higher monthly price (€10). With over 24 million total users, the majority of users utilise the free version with 20 to 25 per cent of current listeners opting to purchase advertisement-free access either monthly or annually (Spotify, 2013). Availability to a free solution allows listeners to test out the Spotify service without a cost commitment. However, advertisements produce only about 10 per cent of the firm's revenues (Sandoval, 2012). Meanwhile, the monthly premium subscription price is low for the listener when the cost and effort of purchasing and syncing songs is considered.

During the initial launch, listeners could only gain invitation-only access to the service. This method gained buy-in from "early adopters and influencers" before opening access to all users (Richards, 2013). The holistic social experience of Spotify provided more opportunities for growth into the early majority. The integration with Facebook acted as a recommendation from the early adopters to the early majority; by displaying the listener's preference for the Spotify service and the song the listener was tuned into on Facebook feeds, Spotify reached a much larger social network. Originally available only in European countries, Spotify expanded to Australia, New Zealand, South-East Asia and the United States (Spotify, 2013). Now, anyone in these countries can join without an invitation. In addition to Facebook interactions, Spotify expanded its system to serve as a platform for third parties to develop and launch apps within Spotify, which enhance the overall customer experience. Currently, these imbedded apps share music-related information, such as song lyrics, album reviews and local concerts by listeners' favourite artists (Spotify, 2013). Spotify is developing an ever-growing value network through its usage of social media, creation of a social experience for its listeners, easy usage and high accessibility to songs.

Spotify's respect for legally accessing and compensating artists and record labels slows the company's international expansion while gaining trust from authorities and users, but this approach allows for quicker growth once the legality of the firm is confirmed within a market. Spotify's Terms and Conditions of Use explicitly states, "Spotify respects intellectual property rights and expects you to do the same" (Spotify, 2012). As a result of Spotify's commitment to artists' rights, the heavy metal band Metallica opened their entire catalogue of music to Spotify in December 2012 after over a decade of standing up to music piracy (Huffington Post, 2012). This trusted network encourages more imbedded apps, listeners, services, and musicians to join.

Historically, the music industry is accustomed to a music purchasing business model. The emergence of Apple's iTunes store demonstrated that money could be made with digital music, but this online format continued the purchasing model as it existed in record stores. Unlike the movie and television industries, the paradigm of the music industry has not transitioned to the long-term payment cycle required for a music rental service, such as Spotify's. For example, if a song is purchased on iTunes, the record label and artist receive one payment. While with Spotify, these same recipients are paid based on the percentage an artist is played, and the musicians are gaining a new revenue stream that may last for decades.

Some members of the business community are questioning the sustainability of Spotify's business model. Record labels and artists are paid 70 per cent of Spotify's revenue (Huffington Post, 2012; King, 2012), and Spotify pays artists whether or not the listener pays for the Spotify service. A leak of Spotify's financial situation shows the company to be losing millions of dollars each year, yet the firm continues successfully to solicit investor support (Sandoval, 2012). Spotify pays on a "pro rata" scale with artists receiving a matching percentage of the monthly profits as the percentage of the total plays for their songs within the month (King, 2012). For example, if an artist's songs were played 1 per cent of the monthly song total on Spotify, then the artist or their appropriate management would be paid 1 per cent of the 70 per cent of Spotify's revenue distributed as royalties (King, 2012). This explanation of payment based on Spotify's variable monthly income may explain why some musicians are complaining about poor payment for their music's play time.

Spotify's high-profile success is disrupting the way listeners' consume music. The company's growth has spurred other main players to bring similar services to compete. More time is needed to convince the stakeholders of the long-term impacts the Spotify business model may have on the industry. Meanwhile, Spotify is evolving to continually meet customers' needs and is building their network. Time will tell if the company can maintain its initial growth in the long-term.

Case Questions

1) Discuss the ways that Spotify satisfies customer needs.
2) What aspects of Spotify's business model strengthen its value network? What aspects weaken it?
3) In what ways did Spotify grow as a solution as it completed multiple iterations of the innovation life cycle?
4) Is Spotify's freemium revenue model too risky as the company faces significant threats from other major entrants while the majority of users enjoy the free, advertisement-support service?
5) What aspects of the Spotify solution make listeners' path dependent? Does the Spotify service do enough to ensure loyalty to the solution?
6) Discuss possible modifications to Spotify's revenue model to make the company more profitable while respecting the company's values (i.e., remain a low-cost music provider, pay musicians, maintain on-demand access, etc.).

Case Study References

King, M. (2012) How Does Spotify Pay Artists? Interview with Spotify's D.A. Wallach. *Berklee Music Blogs*, 31 August 2012. Accessed on 8 July 2013 at http://mikeking. berkleemusicblogs.com/2012/09/04/how-does-spotify-pay-artists-interview-with-spotify%E2%80%99s-d-a-wallach/.

Metallica on Spotify: Lars Ulrich and Sean Parker Bury the Hatchet. (2012) *Huffington Post*. 6 December 2012. Accessed on 9 July 2013 at http://www.huffingtonpost.com/2012/12/06/metallica-spotify-lars-ulrich-sean-parker_n_2250977.html.

Richards, K. (2013) What Your Startup Can Learn from Spotify's Success. *Tech Cocktail*. 8 April 2013. Accessed on 8 July 2013 at http://tech.co/what-your-startup-can-learn-from-spotifys-success-2013-04.

Salyer, P. (2012) 5 Ways Spotify Is Pioneering the Hyper-Social Business Model. *Mashable*. 22 March 2012. Accessed on 8 July 2013 at http://mashable.com/2012/03/22/spotify-social-media/.

Sandoval, G. (2012) Is Spotify's Business Model Broken? Financial Numbers for Privately Held Spotify Have Surfaced and the Music Service Appears to Be in a World of Hurt. *CNET*. 5 October 2012. Accessed on 9 July 2013 at http://news.cnet.com/8301-1023_3-57526690-93/is-spotifys-business-model-broken/.

Spotify (2012) *Terms and Conditions of Use*. 17 October 2012. Accessed on 9 July 2013 at https://www.spotify.com/no/legal/end-user-agreement/.

Spotify (2013) *Information Page*. Accessed on 8 July 2013 at http://press.spotify.com/no/information/.

6.12 REVISION QUESTIONS

1. What is a vision, and what difference can it make in a new venture?
2. Can you describe the three value configurations? What are their value and cost drivers?

3. What is a business model, and what is it useful for?
4. What is a business plan? What are the key elements of a well-written business plan?
5. What is the difference between vanity metrics and growth metrics? How should growth be measured?

6.13   FURTHER READING AND RESOURCES

Evers, N., Andersson, S. and Hannibal, M. (2012) "Stakeholders and Marketing Capabilities in International New Ventures: Evidence from Ireland, Sweden and Denmark", *Journal of International Marketing*, 20(4): 46–71.

Johnson, M.W. (2010) *Seizing the White Space: Business Model Innovation for Growth and Renewal*. Cambridge, MA: Harvard Business Press.

Osterwalder, A., Pigneur, Y. and Tucci, C.L. (2005) "Clarifying Business Models: Origins, Present, and Future of the Concept", *Communications of AIS*, 15: 2.

Ries, E. (2011) *The Lean Startup: How Today's Entrepreneurs Use Continuous Innovation to Create Radically Successful Businesses*. New York: Crown Publishing Group.

Stabell, C. and Fjeldstad, Ø. (1998) "Configuring Value for Competitive Advantage: On Chains, Shops, and Networks", *Strategic Management Journal*, 19: 413–437.

Weerawardena, J., Mort, G.S., Liesch, P.W. and Knight, G. (2007) "Conceptualizing Accelerated Internationalization in the Born Global Firm: A Dynamic Capabilities Perspective", *Journal of World Business,* 42(3): 294–306. Business Model Concepts

Hamel, G. (2000) *Leading the Revolution*. Cambridge, MA: Harvard Business School Press.

Johnson, M.W. (2010) *Seizing the White Space: Business Model Innovation for Growth and Renewal*. Cambridge, MA: Harvard Business Press.

McGrath, R.G. (2010) "Business Models: A Discovery Driven Approach", *Long Range Planning*, 43(2–3): 247–261.

Osterwalder, A., Pigneur, Y. and Tucci, C.L. (2005) "Clarifying Business Models: Origins, Present, and Future of the Concept", *Communications of AIS*, 15: 2.

Teece, D.J. (2010) "Business Models, Business Strategy and Innovation", *Long Range Planning*, 42(2–3): 172–194.

6.14   NOTES

1. Written by Eythor Ivar Jonsson, Copenhagen Business School.
2. Case written by Tor Grønsund, Lingo and University of Oslo.
3. Written by Robert Wentrup and Patrik Ström, Centre for International Business Studies, Department of Business Administration, School of Business, Economics and Law, University of Gothenburg, Sweden
4. See Further reading : Evers et al., 2012; Weerawardena et al., 2007
5. The plan is explained in more detail in the provided template (see the textbook website). The template and the description is based on Stein Bjørnstad's (2002) adaptation of Ernst and Young's freely available business plan

template. Numerous others (although most being relatively similar) can be found online, and in textbooks and at financial institutions.
6. Cost per mile, or cost per thousand impressions. Much used expression in advertising industry.

6.15 REFERENCES

Ambrosini, V., Bowman, C. and Collier, N. (2009) "Dynamic Capabilities: An Exploration of How Firms Renew their Resource Base", *British Journal of Management*, 20(1): 9–24.

Barney, J.B. (1991) "Firm Resources and Sustained Competitive Advantage", *Journal of Management*, 17: 99–120.

Bjørnstad, S. (2002) *Business Plan Template*, unpublished teaching materials, Oslo.

Dedrick, J., Kraemer, K.L., and Linden, G. (2010) "Who Profits from Innovation in Global Value Chains? A Study of the iPod and Notebook PCs", *Industrial and Corporate Change*, 19(1): 81–116.

Evers, N., Andersson, S. and Hannibal, M. (2012) "Stakeholders and Marketing Capabilities in International New Ventures: Evidence from Ireland, Sweden and Denmark", *Journal of International Marketing*, 20(4): 46–71.

Evers, N. and O'Gorman, C. (2011) "Improvised Internationalisation in New Ventures: The Role of Prior Knowledge and Networks", *Entrepreneurship and Regional Development,* September 2011, 23(7/8): 549–574.

Ever, N. and O' Gorman. (2011) "Network Intermediaries in the Internationalisation of New Firms in Peripheral Regions", *International Marketing Review*, 28(4): 340–364.

Hamel, G. (2000) *Leading the Revolution*. Cambridge, MA: Harvard Business School Press.

Helfat, C.E., Einkelstein, S., Mitchell, W., Peteraf, M.A., Singh, H., Teece, D. and Winter, S. (2007) *Dynamic Capabilities: Understanding Strategic Change in Organizations*. London: Blackwell.

Hoang, B. and Antoncic, B. (2003) "Network-based Research in Entrepreneurship – A Critical Review", *Journal of Business Venturing*, 18(2): 165–187.

Hollensen, S. (2010) *Marketing Management: A Relationship Approach,* 2nd edn. New York: Financial Times Prentice Hall.

Honig, B. and Karlsson, T. (2004) "Institutional Forces and the Written Business Plan", *Journal of Management*, 30(1): 29–48.

Jarvenpaa, S.L. and Leidner, D.E. (1998) "An Information Company in Mexico: Extending the Resource-based View of the Firm to a Developing Country Context", *Information Systems Research*, 9(4): 342–361.

Johnson, M.W. (2010) *Seizing the White Space: Business Model Innovation for Growth and Renewal*. Cambridge, MA: Harvard Business Press.

Kaplan, R.S. and Norton, D.P. (2004) "The Strategy Map: Guide to Aligning Intangible Resources", *Strategy & Leadership*, 32(5): 10–17.

Kim, W.C. and Mauborgne, R. (2005) *Blue Ocean Strategy: How to Create Uncontested Market Space and Make Competition Irrelevant*. Cambridge, MA: Harvard Business Review Press.

McGrath, R.G. (2010) "Business Models: A Discovery Driven Approach", *Long Range Planning*, 43(2–3): 247–261.

Osterwalder, A. and Pigneur, Y. (2010) *Business Model Generation: A Handbook for Visionaries, Game Changers, and Challengers.* Hoboken, NJ: Wiley.

Osterwalder, A., Pigneur, Y. and Tucci, C.L. (2005) "Clarifying Business Models: Origins, Present, and Future of the Concept", *Communications of AIS*, 15: 2.

Porter, M.E. (1985) *Competitive Advantage: Creating and Sustaining Superior Performance.* New York: Free Press.

Ries, E. (2011) *The Lean Startup: How Today's Entrepreneurs Use Continuous Innovation to Create Radically Successful Businesses.* New York: Crown Publishing Group.

Sarasvathy, S.D. and Dew, N. (2005) "New Market Creation through Transformation", *Journal of Evolutionary Economics*, 15: 533–565.

Stabell, C. and Fjeldstad, Ø. (1998) "Configuring Value for Competitive Advantage: On Chains, Shops, and Networks", *Strategic Management Journal*, 19: 413–437.

Teece, D.J. (2010) "Business Models, Business Strategy and Innovation", *Long Range Planning*, 42(2–3): 172–194.

Teece, D.J. and Pisano, G. (1998) "The Dynamic Capabilities of Forms: An Introduction", in G. Dosi, D.J. Teece and J. Chytry (eds), *Technology, Organization and Competitiveness: Respective on Industrial and Corporate Change.* Oxford: Oxford University Press.

Teece, D.J., Pisano, G. and Shuen, A. (1997) "Dynamic Capabilities and Strategic Management", *Strategic Management Journal*, 18(7): 509–533.

Tunguz, T. (2013) "Your Startup's 10 Most Important Metrics", *Ex Post Facto,* weblog post, 26 March. Accessed on 6 January 2013 at http://tomtunguz.com/your-startups-10-most-important-metrics.

Weerawardena, J., Mort, G.S., Liesch, P.W. and Knight, G. (2007) "Conceptualizing Accelerated Internationalization in the Born Global Firm: A Dynamic Capabilities Perspective", *Journal of World Business,* 42(3): 294–306.

Wernerfelt, B. (1984) "A Resource-based View of the Firm", *Strategic Management Journal,* 5, 171–180.

Zahra, S.A., Sapienza, H.J. and Davidsson, P. (2006) "Entrepreneurs and Dynamic Capabilities: A Review, Model and Research Agenda", *Journal of Management Studies*, 43(4): 917–955.

6.16   GLOSSARY OF TERMS

Business Concept: The idea that can lead to the development of a business.

Business Model: The manner in which a firm will configure its resources to create unique customer value (value proposition) and capture economic and other value; the result of the iterative business modelling process (see *business modelling* below).

Business Modelling: The process of experimenting with the firm's business units and processes to continually search for better ways of doing business with the aim to remain competitive in fast-changing environments.

Business Plan: Questions the current state of business; it outlines a principled attitude to what should happen in the business.

Configuration of Value: Tells how resources and activities need to fit together in order to create and sustain value.

Crowdsourcing: When users are willing to share information with a firm, which the firm can then use to benefit other customers.

Dynamic Capabilities View of the Firm, or DCV: Implicitly suggests the need to distinguish capabilities from resources and stresses the importance of the dynamic processes of capability building in gaining competitive advantage (Evers et al., 2012).

Growth Metrics: Metrics specifically designed to provide concrete and honest feedback about how the business is progressing by (1) defining rigidly what kind of metrics are useful for the particular business in its specific phase, (2) finding reliable ways of testing and measuring progress, and (3) breaking down numbers into smaller and meaningful units (Ries, 2011).

Resource Based View of the Firm, or RBV: Suggests that firms in the same industry perform differently because they differ in their resources and capabilities (Wernerfelt, 1984).

Value capture: The method of making revenue from the value propositions.

Value Chain: Businesses transform inputs to a new product; in most cases, the cost of this transformation is lower than the resulting value when the product reaches the end consumer.

Value Configurations: The manners in which businesses provide value to customers; there are three configurations: *value chain*, *value shop* and *value network*.

Value Innovation: Occurs when companies make sure to both drive value for the customer (differentiation) and drive down cost for the company at the same time.

Value Network: Facilitate direct and indirect exchange between customers.

Value Proposition: A suggestion to customers on how a new product or concept will meet their needs and create value.

Value Shop: Resolves unique problems for customers.

Vision: A future state in which critical needs are served better than today; it is an important source of business opportunity that usually contains utopian aspirations.

Part III

MARKET OPPORTUNITY AND STRATEGY

III.1 INTRODUCTION

According to Baker (2012), "Marketing is the activity that generates revenue, all other activities are costs". The development of successful marketing programs for the commercialisation of new technology represents a challenge for entrepreneurial ventures. The mechanics of developing successful marketing strategies for technological innovations is a complex process from design to implementation (Gliga and Evers, 2011). No matter how innovatively useful or ground breaking the technological invention or innovation, technological superiority is not a guarantee for success with someone to buy it. Put more simply: "No customer means no business". Inventors need to develop their IP into a viable, competitive and marketable offering. Part III is about validating the market for the innovation, identifying the best routes for its commercialisation and developing and sustaining effective marketing strategies to bring innovation to the marketplace.

The importance of marketing remains a core business activity of technology entrepreneurial activities as it is most deeply connected around the customers; if your marketing is not right, then your business will most likely fail. Part III provides an overview of Chapters 7, 8 and 9 and also introduces the core marketing concepts. The three chapters in Part III presents the components of the marketing process, with each step devoted a chapter. Step 1: Market research and market validation processes are presented; Step 2: the commercialisation routes and the importance of sales pitching for initial investor funding are then explored; Step 3: the marketing strategy is designed, formulated and refined for a value proposition; from here operational or tactical marketing decisions are implemented, managed and monitored.

The remainder of Part III introduces the learner to the core principles of marketing. It further addresses some of the misconceptions commonly associated with the role of marketing in the organisation.

III.2   DEFINING MARKETING

With the onset in the last two decades of powerful, emotionally driven and persuasive advertising campaigns, the wave of digital marketing media and the rise in celebrity brand endorsement, many misconceptions have formed about marketing in recent years. Many would confidently state that marketing is purely the art of selling and advertising. On the contrary, marketing encompasses both these activities but involves many other core business activities. Two of the most widely accepted general definitions of Marketing are:

> Marketing is a management process responsible for identifying, antici-pating and satisfying customer requirements profitably. [1]
>
> Marketing is the activity, set of institutions, and processes for creat-ing, communicating, and delivering, and exchanging offerings that have value for customers, clients, partners, and society at large. [2]

Marketing encompasses creating, pricing, distributing and promoting the product. The role of selling is one type of promotional activity and is in its own right a critical one for high-technology offerings. It has been noted that amongst many technology ventures there is an apparent skills deficit in the sales management and personal selling aspects of marketing. Once the product is launched and market needs are identified, the interpersonal and sales know-how of employees to proceed with and close the sale is of paramount importance. The selling process is given special attention in Chapter 9. Further, Chapter 8 addresses start-up stages of the venture when funding is sought. The entrepreneur must have an understanding of how to plan and deliver effectively the sales pitch to attract initial investment to develop the business.

III.3   MARKETING IS ABOUT EXCHANGE RELATIONSHIPS

The *market* is a set of actual and potential buyers of a product or service offered by suppliers (sellers). Marketing is typically a two-way process made of a dyadic relationship between the buyer and seller (and in some cases triadic exchanges; see Figure III.1). A key question the seller must ask them-selves is "Why should a customer buy our product over its competitors or substitute goods?" As discussed in Chapter 6, the sellers develop a value proposition defined as a set of values or it promises to deliver to customers to satisfy their need. The seller develops and delivers its value proposition by using the tools available in the marketing mix (discussed in Chapter 9). The buyer offers payment (value) for the value the seller creates.

Figure III.1 identifies three types of buyer-seller exchanges of technology market offerings. As consumers, we are familiar with *Exchange A* when the process is between seller A and an individual buyer. The seller offers some-thing of value to buyer A – the design, functionality and quality warranty, after-sales customer service and technical support of mobile phone and makes it accessible for purchase to buyer A through retail mobile phone shop or to order and pay online. Buyer A in return pays the price to the seller.

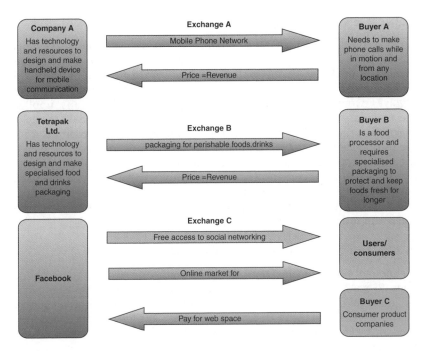

Figure III.1 Types of marketing exchanges

Exchange B deals with the seller B offering something of value to be used by a group of individuals or typically organisations to be used in the manufacturing or support of the production and their business activities so they can deliver to their own buyers. For example, seller B designs and manufactures specialised packing to retain freshness and shelf life for food processors. Seller B may offer packaging, design customised to requirement of buyer B. They negotiate price and organise delivery of product.

For *Exchange C*, we use an example like Facebook's core market offering – a free social media website service designed for personal and social interaction between people. The individual or group users of the service receive an online communication platform to get easy, instantaneous access to friends and social groups around the world. But how does Facebook get revenues for this service? Their customers are advertising companies who pay a price to buy ad space on their website. Hence Facebook's customers are consumer product companies (payer) and the consumer is the user but not necessarily the payer. This three-way exchange relationship is typical for online social media companies where all three needs are socially (Facebook users) and commercially satisfied (Facebook and consumer companies). Facebook acquires advertising revenues; users get free access to social platform; consumer-goods companies have access to Facebook users to promote products. Google has adopted a similar relationship model.

III.3.1   The Marketing Programme (also known as the Marketing Mix)

How do companies satisfy these exchange relationships? Creating exchange relationships take time and effort. Although the formulation and implementation of the *Marketing strategy will be discussed in detail in Chapter 9, we briefly introduce it here.* To put simply, a company's marketing strategy involves two major tasks: 1) identifying target buyers. This means suppliers must validate that a market exists for their technology, decide what buyers to target in that market and ensure the technology can meet their needs; 2) the second step is developing a marketing programme to effectively deliver the value proposition to the target customers. Developing a value proposition means not just creating a superior technology that buyers want that is currently not available on the market. It also means setting the right price and selecting the correct selling and distributing strategies to effectively reach and satisfy needs of target buyers.

III.3.2   Technology Entrepreneurship is about Marketing

Technology entrepreneurs must embrace marketing as a business philosophy to guide the overall business orientation of the venture. Companies are most successful when they match customer need and wants and general market requirements with their value offering. This leads to the creation of superior product and services, as compared to competitor offerings. This is no different for ventures offering products at different levels technological complexity and application portfolios. Further, customers may have a need or problem but may not be aware that innovative solution exists to solve their problem. Equally, the rapid changes in technology and the growing complexity of customer needs means the entrepreneur must be one step ahead of the market. Although customers are ultimately the revenue generators and thus lie at the centre of the marketing process, the ventures also need to recognise the importance of leveraging relationships with stakeholders such as suppliers, state agencies, research institutions, etc. Their technological expertise and an understanding of the market ecosystem can enable them to do this. Therefore, for technology entrepreneurs, we define marketing as:

> A continuous process of proactively creating and exploiting opportunities in the (local and international) marketplace by offering a technology-based value proposition to target customers, through the strategic design, management and implementation of a targeted marketing programme.

III.4   NOTES

1. Chartered Institute of Marketing (UK), 2013. This definition is sourced in the Chartered Institute of Marketing (UK). Source of definition is sourced http://www.cimhk.org.hk/ (Accessed on 16 October 2013).
2. American Marketing Association, approved by Board of Directors in July 2013. This definition is sourced from http://www.marketingpower.com/AboutAMA/Pages/DefinitionofMarketing.aspx (Accessed on 16 October 2013).

Chapter 7
MARKET VALIDATION AND RESEARCH

7.1   LEARNING OBJECTIVES

After reading this chapter, you will be able to:

1. Conduct the market validation process for your idea;
2. Understand and conduct secondary desk research in the validation process and recognise value of private information not in the public domain in gaining first mover advantage;
3. Demonstrate the importance of marketing research in the market validation process and explain key market research concepts;
4. Validate their business concept and identify and employ the required methods for validating it;
5. Undertake and employ the necessary frameworks for carrying out a full market ecosystem analysis for their technology.

7.2   CHAPTER STRUCTURE

The core elements of this chapter are as follows:

- Introduction
- The Market Validation Process
- The Marketing Ecosystem of the New Venture
  - The 5C Framework Analysis (Context, Competitors, Collaborators, Customers, Company)
  - Market Validation Outcome
- Business Concept Testing Tools
- Conducting Marketing Research
- Chapter Summary
- Case Study – Skype
- Revision Questions
- Further Reading and Resources
- References
- Glossary of Terms

7.3 INTRODUCTION

One of the biggest challenges for technology entrepreneurs is validating their value proposition and the market for it. The rapid creation of a new product market space where the firm has some form of positional advantage is critical to those seeking to exploit technology to create or shape markets (Kumar et al., 2000). This chapter presents the key analytical tools for inventors to conduct the Market Validation Process to ensure the product or service is entering a valid and sustainable market. It introduces the learner to the marketing ecosystem and presents the necessary frameworks for carrying out a market ecosystem analysis for new technology. It presents the key processes available for testing their business concept. It further distinguishes between the nature and dynamics of customer and business markets for conducting customer analysis. Finally, it presents the key marketing research techniques needed to carry out the validation process for both consumers and business markets.

7.4 MARKET VALIDATION PROCESS

The market validation process (MVP) for high-tech ventures assesses the market worthiness of ideas that are based around incremental, radical or disruptive innovations. The overarching activity underpinning the MVP is market research, namely gathering and analysing market intelligence. Market research provides the relevant intelligence for developing the right strategy for capitalising on valid market opportunities.

Market Validation in high-tech markets is defined as

> A dynamic and interactive process of integrating the venture's core technology and capabilities with the latent and explicit needs of the customer; with the goals of (1) resolving the customer's "pain-point", (2) creating a superior value proposition for the customer, and (3) generating economic rent. (Miles et al., 2010, p. 4)

Recent research has shown that venture capitalists, business angels, corporate venture capitalists and entrepreneurs state that the process of market validation is a critical antecedent to commercial success and ultimately determines the survival of the venture. Market validation can be a systematic process of estimating demand and potential cash flows of a proposed new market offering. The value proposition (introduced in Chapter 6) can be developed in close consultation with prospective customers to determine market acceptance, to estimate demand, to refine product or service attributes and to assess the product's value to both the customer and the business.

Simply chatting to a few people in the industry and prospective users is not enough to gather market information to validate the business concept or the market for it. A rigorous and systematic approach to conducting

Figure 7.1 The market validation process

the MVP needs to be adopted. Figure 7.1 identifies the two key processes involved in validating your market, supported by marketing research.

1) Marketing Ecosystem Analysis
2) Business Concept Testing

The two core MV activities: (1) marketing ecosystem analysis and (2) business concept testing are not mutually exclusive, and can be conducted simultaneously. As shown in Figure 7.1, an understanding of market research methods is necessary for collecting and analysing market intelligence to perform the two key activities. Before we examine market research methods, we first look at its two core components of the MVP, beginning with the marketing ecosystem.

7.5   THE MARKETING ECOSYSTEM OF THE NEW VENTURE

The market validation process involves a comprehensive examination and analysis of the external environment the venture plans to operate in, and the venture's own resources and capabilities. The marketing ecosystem describes the complex internal and external environment, made up of all the elements and forces that can influence and affect a company's ability to develop and implement its market strategy successfully and sustain long-term relationships with its target customers. Figure 7.2 depicts the components of the marketing ecosystem and their interplay.

The market ecosystem analysis is conducted at macro, meso and micro levels all interacting with each other. The 5C framework is chosen as the main analytical tool to conduct the analysis of the marketing ecosystem in which the venture plans to operate in. As shown in Figure 7.2, the 5Cs are: the Company, its Customers, its Competitors, its Collaborators and the macro and meso-context of the venture. The *Company* (micro-level) represents the internal situation of the venture itself; the other four Cs cover aspects of the external situation. Through data gathering processes, the

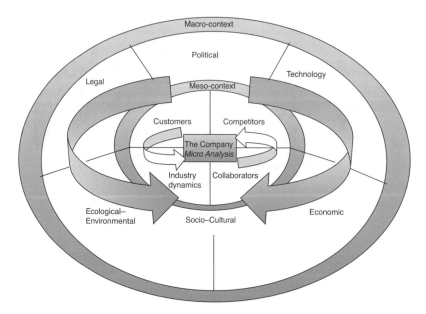

Figure 7.2 The marketing ecosystem

marketing ecosystem of the venture is analysed under each component in the 5C framework. As shown in Figure 7.2, the *Context* in which the venture plans to operate in is examined both at the macro and meso-level – each level examining different forces.

This process is also known as "environmental scanning" and it requires the company to engage in a rigorous and comprehensive data and intelligence gathering exercise to carefully monitor and analyse the marketing ecosystem. This is necessary for both the market validation process and also the strategic market planning process so entrepreneurs can identify opportunities, as well as possible threats, and adapt the elements and activities of their venture accordingly (Aguilar, 1967). That is why marketing is often seen as an interface, a linking mechanism between the organisation and the elements in its ecosystem. Environmental scanning is not a once off activity, and continuous monitoring of trends and developments in a venture's market ecosystem is critical for the growth, development and survival of any organisation irrespective of age or size.

The marketing ecosystem analysis is applicable to marketing decisions to inform whether there is a valid market for the invention and whether the business can sustain and grow under the environmental context it enters into. Each component and level of analysis is described below using the 5C tool and supported by Figure 7.3.

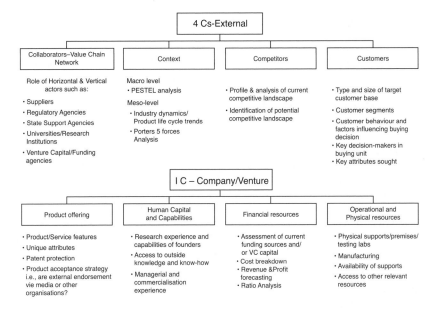

Figure 7.3 5C framework for analysing the ventures market ecosystem

7.5.1   The 5C Framework Analysis

Figure 7.3 presents the factors underpinning each of the five Cs.[1] A number of analytical frameworks and tool template guides are used with the 5C framework to examine each of the Cs as shown in Figure 7.3. For example, the PESTEL analysis and Porter's Five Forces can provide deeper analytical insight into the "Context". For the customer analysis, we present a detailed template guide of questions for conducting market and customer profile analysis. The aim is to present the learner with established tools and guide templates and for them to go and conduct their own validation exercise. Each of the 5Cs are dealt with below.

CONTEXT: For a comprehensive analysis of "Context", we examine it at two levels: macro and meso.

Macro-Context: To conduct a macro-context analysis, the PESTEL analytical tool is used to examine the venture's marketing ecosystem. The PESTEL framework involves examining the macro-environmental components or the larger forces that affect the whole business environment of the venture. The PESTEL acronym stands for: P – political and legal, E – economic, S – socio-cultural, T – technological, E – environmental, L – legal. Even though companies cannot control the environmental forces at the macro level, by collecting and analysing data on their operating environment, they can take a proactive approach and be more aware and responsive to the possible forthcoming opportunities and threats. Furthermore, by having a very good understanding of the environmental forces surrounding them, companies can better meet existing customers' needs and wants, as well as anticipate future trends and be a step ahead of the competition.

Meso-Context: The meso-level analysis involves studying the specific context in which the new venture operates in. The meso-context analysis involves gathering information for conducting an (1) industry analysis and (2) a structured market analysis.

1) Industry Analysis

An industry analysis is used to identify, profile and analyse industry and sector structure, developments and dynamics. An established tool in analysing an organisation's industry context is Michael Porter's Five Forces model (1980). The Five Forces model helps inform the venture if the industry sector they are entering into is attractive. Attractiveness in this context refers to the overall industry profitability and competitive intensity with the sector. Assessing the attractiveness of profitability for the venture can be determined by assessing each of the five forces notably: (1) New Entrants to the industry (2) suppliers (3) buyers (4) competition and (5) substitute offerings.[2]

2) Structured Market Analysis

Similarly, contextual analysis requires a preliminary market analysis. A first look at the market involves conducting secondary research to gauge actual market size in terms of value, number of customers (if possible), their location, the growth patterns and projections as well as identifying the market drivers, developments and trends amongst buyers in the market. The structured market analysis gives a good indication of market growth potential and sustainability.

The market analysis also requires an understanding of the two main types of markets: consumer markets and organisational markets. Although detailed profiles of target customer are examined in the Customer component of the 5C framework, an understanding of market types is required at this level of market analysis. Some entrepreneurs may purely serve and target one type of market with their innovation, while others may target both. Consumer and business markets are very different in terms of the nature of the intended consumer and how the customer uses the product (the intended use of the product) and ultimately require different marketing strategies. Even though the products might be identical, a fundamentally different marketing approach is needed for each (Hutt and Speh, 2007).

Consumer markets consist of individuals and households that buy goods and services for personal, family or household consumption.

Organisational markets consist of profit and non-profit organisations that buy goods and services for incorporation (e.g., ingredient materials), for use and consumption (e.g., office supplies and other equipment) or for resale. Organisational markets include:

- Commercial enterprises: producers (manufacturing products or delivering services) or resellers (distributors, wholesalers and retailers buying goods and services to resell at a profit).

- Government agencies: they can buy goods and services at different levels: state, county, local in order to be able to deliver their services to the public (e.g., health, education, transport, security, etc.).
- Institutions: non-profit or charitable, educational, community and other non-business institutions.

Some companies cater exclusively to either consumer or organisational markets; however other firms market to both. Table 7.1 provides overview of broad characteristics distinguishes generally between types of markets.[3]

Table 7.1 Market types: consumer markets and organisational markets

	Consumer markets	**Organisational markets**
Purchase orientation	Individual/ family requirements	Organisational requirements
Type of buyer	Individuals or households	Commercial enterprises Government agencies Institutions
Intended use of product/service	Finished product for personal, family or household consumption	Products for further production, incorporation, operations usage or resale
Product/service type	Typically standardised	Can vary from standardised to customised solutions
Size of purchase	Typically small transactions	Typically large
Decision-making	Short and often simple, involving one or a small number of people	Long and complex, involving many decision-makers in the buying organisation
Risks	Low for most purchases	High to moderate. Purchasing is critical if strategic buy for buying organisation
Channel of distribution	Long – often involving many intermediaries	Short depending serving domestic or international markets- often direct, agents, distributors

Meso-level analysis also extends to **Competitors, Collaborators and Customers**.

COMPETITORS: Profiling of competitors in your product market space is a critically important part of the market intelligence gathering process. Companies must constantly monitor what competitors are currently doing and plan to do and try to anticipate their future actions and responses. One approach of doing this is to identify and benchmark your innovation against the top three competitors. To identify products and key benefits, and examine how they position their products in the market and to which customer segments. A competitive analysis tool guide (see online material) is a useful exercise that allows entrepreneurs to compare their product and venture with two or three of their most important competitors. A comparative analysis of competitors benchmarked against the entrepreneur's innovation can be an output of this exercise to summarise succinctly the key data into a presentation-like format in the business plan.

Key questions include:

- Who are our major competitors? What are their characteristics (size, growth, profitability, strategies, and target customer markets)?
- What are our prospective or current competitors' key strengths and weaknesses?
- What are our competitors' key marketing capabilities in terms of products, distribution, promotion, and pricing?
- What response can we expect from our competitors if environmental conditions change or if we change our marketing strategy?
- Is this competitive set likely to change in the future? If so, how? Who are our new competitors likely to be?

COLLABORATORS: Collaborators is a generic term incorporating the group of individuals or organisations collaborating with or having an interest in the new venture, conceptualised as the *value network*. The value network surrounding an organisation is comprised of stakeholders and organisations that have an effect on the outcome of the new venture's commercialisation, innovation and future business activities. As shown in Figure 7.3, collaborators can be vertical actors, such as suppliers, and also horizontal actors, such as strategic partners and regulatory agencies. For example, suppliers are those firms and individuals that provide the resources needed by the company to produce goods and service. Vertical intermediaries, such as resellers and distributors, and in some cases horizontal intermediaries, such as state enterprise agencies or export support agencies, can help the company to promote, sell and distribute its goods to final buyers. Both suppliers and intermediaries are a very important part in the company's value delivery system.

The inventor must identify and assess which vertical and horizontal relationships can add value to the new venture's activities. These can be formal or informal and need to be recognised and managed into long-term sustainable relationships to create an effective value network for the new venture. Such exchanges between the new venture and various stakeholders can be in the form of economic transactions but can also include exchanges of knowledge, physical, human or financial resources, support in regulatory compliance, business mentoring and support, building networks and company reputation and referrals. Leveraging and managing the value network is critical for the new venture that would tend to suffer from liability of "newness" and gaining credibility within the industry as a nascent venture particularly if in search of seed capital. Chapter 6 examined the role of network actors and relationships of the new venture.

CUSTOMERS: The analysis of Customers is one of most critical components of the 5C framework and ultimately the MVP. It is in most cases the most challenging C in terms of intelligence gathering and data analysis. If the data is not available via secondary research, then primary data collection is necessary to determine if market validation exists to proceed with full commercialisation. The customer analysis section of the business plan is a more detailed level of market analysis than described above. It involves gathering as much information on target customer group or groups that the venture believes is able to outcompete other suppliers already serving that target with different value propositions. The customer analysis must show the needs of the customer and then links the two together by identifying how the company's services or products can satisfy the needs of the customer better than its competitors.

Conducting a customer analysis requires gathering information and trying to answer some of the following questions:

- Who is my target market/s? What groups of customers are most likely to buy my product?
- What is size and growth pattern of my target market?
- What need does my innovation serve?
- How can I improve my innovation to better serve their needs?
- What is the motivation of my target customers for buying my product?
- What factors influence their purchase behaviour?

COMPANY: The micro-level analysis involves looking inwardly at the new venture – the company – in terms of assessing its resources, experience, product or/and service capabilities and financial situation to develop the venture forward. Figure 7.4 provides some of the key factors to examine when conducting the company analysis to profile the company in terms of key strengths going into the market and the possible weaknesses it needs to address. The key factors are grouped into product offering and resources and capabilities to support the development of the new venture such as operational, financial and human. An internal assessment is necessary for the new venture to identify key strengths to commercialise and grow the company and key weaknesses that innovator must manage effectively to exploit opportunities for their invention. Online material provides an internal analysis tool.

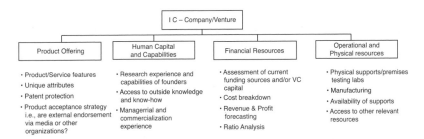

Figure 7.4   Assessing resources of the new venture

7.5.2   Market Validation Outcome

The 5C framework is a useful and comprehensive analytical tool for conducting a comprehensive analysis of the company and its market ecosystem in its entirety. Gathering information sources through secondary desk research (discussed later in this chapter under "Market Research Methods") is the starting point of the 5C analysis. A key output of this analysis is to determine if a market can be validated for the venture's innovation, but it also provides insights into the nature and the dynamics of the environment that the venture plans to operate in and if it is financially lucrative to do so long-term.

A *SWOT Analysis* – involves identifying the strengths, weaknesses, opportunities and threats of an organisation. It is one of the key outputs of the marketing ecosystem analysis. The output of the internal company analysis should highlight the strengths and weaknesses of the new venture. For a new venture starting out there may be more weaknesses than strengths, particularly in terms of finance and managerial experience to bring the innovation onto the market. However, in many cases if the technology is superior to what is on the market already and there is a valid and sustainable market, investors tend to address such weaknesses through seed or venture capital and recruiting an experienced person to bring the company forward.

A SWOT analysis will also condense the market ecosystem analysis into a listing of the most relevant threats and opportunities, helping to assess how well the firm is equipped to deal with them (see online material for SWOT template and example). The SWOT analysis is used in the strategic market planning of the new venture.

7.6   BUSINESS CONCEPT TESTING TOOLS

Understanding the marketplace and identifying customers' needs, wants and requests is the starting point of any successful marketing strategy (Kotler et al., 2008). However, when managing incremental and breakthrough innovation this process is challenging, as it implies "moving on a continuum which ranges from responding to a known need with an improved solution to creating an evolving solution to un uncertain need" (Friar and Balachandra, 1999, p. 42). A technology cannot generate revenue if it has no perceived utility to the customer. Forecasting market demand for the proposed technology is especially difficult. If investment capital is redirected to a commercial activity with no utility for the buyer, failure of the venture is highly probable with significant losses for investors. To mitigate against and to avoid meeting such loss-making consequences, risk assessment techniques can be used to gauge the customer utility of the technology, like concept testing.

Business concept testing is a process used to estimate the potential market demand and attractiveness of a particular idea or concept. Testing techniques rely on customer purchase intent scores, leveraging a wide array of diagnostic information such as product uniqueness, feasibility, desirability, advantages and disadvantages. There are a number of different business concept testing techniques based on the type and level of innovation.[4]

Incremental Innovations: Incremental innovations are evolutionary in nature; smaller improvements introduced over time, based on extensions of existing products. For incremental innovations, the market already exists; specific needs and wants are known and targeted with specific value offerings. As these innovations come about in response to specific and articulated customer needs, they occur in demand-side markets (Shanklin and Ryans, 1984) and are based on market pull. There may be opportunities for the inventor to develop a new technology and position it to replace an old one, by being better, faster or cheaper.

Radical and Disruptive Innovations: By contrast, disruptive innovations do not simply replace an existing technology but might in fact generate multiple new applications addressing new segments and new markets. Breakthrough or radical innovations are revolutionary in nature; they break the accepted norm, bringing about new and superior advantages as compared to the old technology. As customer needs are often unknown, breakthrough innovations occur in supply-side markets (Shanklin and Ryans, 1984), meaning that the technology push governs the process.

At the initial stages of product development, market research methods support data collection processes for business concept testing and provide preliminary insight into market reaction for the invention. For incremental innovations, customers' needs and wants are, or can be, known. In contrast, for more radical innovative products the needs and wants of potential customers are harder to pin down and clearly define, as customers themselves find it difficult to articulate them. Inventors have to assess future markets and demand for products that don't yet exist for customers who don't know about them (Friar and Balachandra, 1999). They have to work with concepts such as future, unknown/unarticulated or latent needs and can involves probe-and-learn processes. Figure 7.5 identifies business testing processes for incremental to radical innovations supported by the type of data collection.[5]

Concept Testing: Concept testing is a process that involves asking prospective customers to evaluate a/some concept/s that the technology

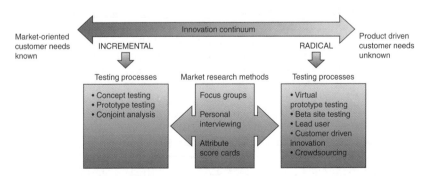

Figure 7.5 Business concept testing process

may offer to the market in order to determine if the concept has market potential and should be pursued further. It is a useful approach to getting a reaction on how prospective customers may evaluate the technology in relation to what is already available on the market. It also allows the entrepreneur to assess the anticipated response of customers to the new product before a prototype design and launch. Data is collected to test the business concept and typically involves the use of qualitative methods such as focus groups and personal interviews from a sample of prospective target users.

For example, a product concept or early prototype may be presented to a focus group (covered under Marketing Research in next section), facilitated by a moderator in order to monitor and record opinions and reaction. As people are motivated to communicate in focus groups, an experienced moderator can infer the meaning of their qualitative opinions, judgments and statements on the issues that they express. Using focus groups, it is possible to get feedback on how well the concept for the product actually performs. The data collected helps to identify the strengths of the product, as perceived by the members of the focus group. At the same time, group members also identify aspects of the concept that are not particularly appealing, or that they believe could be improved upon and thus enhance the desirability of the product. Technologies targeting consumer markets are more suited to the focus group approach.

Personal Interviewing is another form of collecting data on business concepts and mainly suitable for entrepreneurs wishing to target organisational customers such as companies and public- and private-sector institutions.

For both these types of testing, potential customers are asked to rate concepts on various dimensions such as interest, perceived benefits, perceived value, etc. Concept testing allows the entrepreneur to develop, modify or change the concept for their technology and ideally develop a concept based on that data obtained, thus increasing the likeliness of being accepted by the market. This process further allows them to proceed to the next step for building a prototype and to continue with the full market validation process and market ecosystem analysis discussed in the previous section.

As concept testing only focuses on the technology concept and the attributes it may offer, it does not assess how the concept is evaluated in relation to other concepts that may be built around the new technology or in relation to existing products already on the market. To overcome limitations and acquire deeper comparative insight into customer preferences, two other research techniques are available: conjoint analysis is discussed below.

Conjoint Analysis: Conjoint analysis is concerned with understanding how people make choices between products or services. The common aim of conjoint analysis is to test the attractiveness of the various concepts in relation to each other. This method tries to capture what really drives customers to buy one product over another and the key question is: "What do customers really value relative to competitors' products?" The theory behind this type of research is that buyer choice involve compromises and trade-offs among attributes, as the ideal is rarely attainable. If entrepreneurs can find out how people make selections between a limited number of products, based on the relative importance they place on different attributes, they would be able to design better perceived products.

Great care has to be taken in selecting the attributes presented to respondents, as customer choices between poorly defined attributes and levels would render the results meaningless. Identifying attributes is possible after secondary market data is collected and from informal knowledge of industry. When attributes are identified they are presented to prospective users, ideally with a focus group or personal interview setting. Here, respondents are asked to score product profiles according to their preference for preferred combinations of attributes. They will rate the product based on a variety of metrics to evaluate the role of each feature or attribute they are asked to score. Conjoint testing is often based upon purchase intent scores leveraging a wide array of diagnostic information such as product uniqueness, feasibility, desirability, advantages and disadvantages. Sometimes prospective users will be asked to evaluate several different product/service propositions alongside each other to see which one generates the best feedback. From these scores, analysis derives utility scores for each attribute. Attributes that score highest amongst users will reduce the risk for entrepreneur and investors. Conjoint analysis evaluates the relative value of attributes considered jointly, which is a better, more realistic measure than when considered in isolation.

Through understanding the utility values of different attributes, companies can calculate how their product/service compares to that of their competitors, and most importantly, how they can best optimise the value proposition for the customer. For example, according to the importance they place on various attributes and their combination, this method can statistically predict the optimal combination of price and product attributes.

Conjoint analysis is suited for incremental innovations in terms of:

- Identifying market segments for which specific product concepts have greater value;
- Defining a new product for an already existing market;
- Improving an existing product;
- Acquiring ideas for new product functionality bundling;
- Forecasting sales of alternative products, including possible cannibalisation or substitution effects.

As the above techniques are mainly applicable to incremental innovations and can be used individually or combined, the entrepreneur must ensure that their concept is developed based on some meaningful alternative than what is already out there and that their customers are willing to switch and pay for their product over what competitors have on offer. Let's take the example in Case Box 7.1 of how Android phones followed the iPhone, the leader in the smartphone market.

Case Box 7.1   Androids: An Alternative to a Market Leader in Smartphones

In 2007, Apple Mac launched the iPhone as a radical innovation based on superior technology, which made mobile communication more sophisticated and fun.
However, despite their cool technology and design and first mover advantage into
the smartphone market, the subsequent entry a year later of the Android phones
into the market was successful. Why? Androids capitalised on the limitations of
the iPhone. Android phones offered a wider phone choice and price points and
open-source apps.

   Differentiation by focusing on what the market leader couldn't offer were how
Androids competed and captured growing share of the smartphone market. They
developed a significant meaningful alternative offering an incremental innovation to the iPhone. Differences must be meaningful if building business concepts
around incremental innovation, with marginal improvements rarely succeeding
in displacing a market technological leader.

Business Concept Testing for Radical Innovations: In the case of radical
or disruptive technology, customers' needs are harder to define, as customers
themselves might be unaware of these latent or potential needs. Such innovations have no sales history as a product category hence the validation
process will be more rigorous as the product idea aims to create a new market,
which had not previously existed. Because of these challenges, marketers are
employing novel research methods that attempt to gain customer insights
regarding their innovative value propositions. Although the same principles
for concept testing techniques as used for incremental innovations can still
be used for radical inventions (see Figure 7.5), inventors still need to employ
more advanced analytical techniques to provide harder evidence for their
concept and create a market for them rather than throwing the dice. The
techniques shown in Figure 7.5 are discussed below.

Real and Virtual Prototype Testing: Probably the most common and effective
form of testing is prototype testing and also applies to incremental innovations (see Figure 7.4). Real prototyping involves testing a model of the product
or service on the market, so that customers' reactions to it can be observed
and evaluated. The business concept discussed above is converted into an
actual prototype model and presented to a sample of target users. In recent
years, technology has enabled companies to use virtual prototype testing,
also referred to as minimum viable product testing. It is cheaper and easier
to modify, and it is also more suitable in some cases as the "product" itself is
virtual such as a service. (See Case Box 7.2). The process helps crystallise the
necessary core product benefits and is a good way of market testing as it also
demonstrates the tangibility and functionality of the business concept.

Case Box 7.2   Virtual Prototype Testing of Dropbox

*One of the techniques used to validate the concept for Dropbox was so powerful – and
so simple.*

   Drew Houston is the CEO, founder and inventor of Dropbox, one of the most
successful high-tech ventures in file hosting applications (i.e., cloud storage, file

synchronisation and software). The Dropbox application allows users to create a folder on their computer. Anything they drag into that folder is uploaded automatically to the Dropbox service and then instantly replicated across all their selected computers and mobile devices.

When developing the concept, the challenge for Drew was that it was impossible to demonstrate the working software in a prototype form. The product required that they overcome significant technical hurdles; it also had an online service component that required high reliability and availability. To avoid the risk of waking up after years of development with a product nobody wanted, Drew did something unexpectedly easy: he made a virtual representation of the concept in the form of a video. The feedback he received was excellently received and confirmed a workable prototype to further commercialise. Drew recounted, "It drove hundreds of thousands of people to the website. Our beta waiting list went from 5,000 people to 75,000 people literally overnight. It totally blew us away."[6]

Beta-Site Testing: Beta-site testing is a form of prototype testing but occurs towards the final stages of testing. It can involve sending the product out to an external group of users or *beta test sites* to test product or offering the product for a free trial download over the Internet. When the idea has been assessed through the concept, and possibly prototype testing stages, in beta testing, the first prototype version of the product is given to a group of selected users (typically companies) that would be prospective customers of the product. They then provide the inventor with valuable feedback, identifying and evaluating the prototype before it is considered market ready. Identifying the right users and gaining access to beta sites can be however a challenge, hence establishing and managing good relationship is critically important through the new product development process.

In the case of Dropbox (see Case Box 7.2), Dropbox followed up the virtual testing with beta testing. When Dropbox concept received positive feedback after virtual testing, over 1,000 users then logged on to volunteer as beta users. As illustrated by our Dropbox example, beta testing can be preceded by real or virtual prototype testing before it is beta tested on a selected group of external users. Although Dropbox targeted both consumer and business markets, beta testing is a more common approach in markets where the customer will be an organisation or a company and not the end consumer.

Lead User Testing: Similar to beta testing, lead user research is the next more advanced step in the process of business concept testing. The idea behind the lead user theory is that often it is the users themselves (a particular category of users) who develop new products (Eric Von Hippel, 1988).

Lead Users are typically industry users such as companies or other organisations that are well ahead of market trends and have needs that go far beyond those of the average user. Their expertise and experience might provide valuable insights into the future trends that would in time be characteristic of the whole market (or of significant segments in the market) (Von Hippel et al., 1999). Lead users differ from "early adopters" (already discussed in Chapter 6) who are people that are among the first to purchase an existing product. Lead users of a novel or enhanced product, process or service face needs that will be general in the marketplace, but it is months or years before the bulk of that marketplace encounters them. Lead users may not be satisfied with what is being currently offered on the market and may search for a solution or try to develop their own solutions (Herstatt and Von Hippel, 1992). The lead user can have significant influence on the direction and pace of market adoption and is typically a product leader in a sector. From a marketing perspective, what this means is that companies might be able to forecast market opportunities by conducting research on a specific group in the market: the lead users.

Moore's adopter categories have been the starting point for the lead user process, developed by Von Hippel (1988). Four main steps are identified in the lead user market research process (Von Hippel et al., 1999):

1. Identify an important market or technical trend
2. Identify and question lead users
3. Analyse lead user data and develop novel products
4. Adapt and project lead user data on the general market of interest

There are many challenges in the lead user process, starting with the identification of the lead users and ending with the proper application of the findings into the larger market. However, if properly conducted, lead user testing can tap into valuable information on emerging and latent needs. The lead user process can crystallise previous business testing efforts in the latter stages of product development and market launch.[7]

Customer-driven Innovation: Customer-driven innovation is based on the idea that there is more to be gained from an open innovation process, whereby companies connect with customers in an attempt to better identify, create and deliver value. In this type of research the customer takes on an active role; the process points towards multiple and shifting loci of innovation, as firms outsource innovation to others, both firms and customers (Nambisan and Sawhney, 2007). Customer-driven innovations are based on the idea that supplier and consumer can work together and co-create value (Vargo and Lusch, 2004), in an interactive process of learning together (Ballantyne, 2004). Co-developing relationships can diminish the uncertainty risks coming from the lack of information for both seller and buyer. By working together, the sellers can better define market needs, as the buyers impart important tacit information; in turn, the buyers learn first-hand about the capabilities of the new technology, lessening the anxiety of adopting the innovation. Value is thus co-created and the customer becomes an important resource or better said, an integral part of the value proposition. Many firms find it hard to accept customer-driven innovation however, as the "usual" innovators might disregard customers' ideas and generally ignore any initiative not generated internally.

One type of customer-driven innovation that is growing in popularity is *crowdsourcing*. Crowdsourcing is collecting primary market intelligence (usually in qualitative form) on new ideas, products or services targeted at consumer markets and it can also provide insight into branding and the marketing communication strategy (discussed in Chapter 9). Crowdsourcing is a process of identifying a task or group of tasks and inviting, usually online, a group of people or "crowd" outside the company to carry out this task for a fee or prize (Whitla, 2009). It can be done online or offline. (See Case Box 7.3) The invite may be open to anyone or restricted to those qualified to undertake the task or address the problem. Also considered a platform for open innovation, crowdsourcing can be used to assess an idea for a business opportunity.

Case Box 7.3 Nokia's Crowdsourcing Platform

Nokia Labs usually invite customers to test pre-commercialised apps. By crowd-sourcing customer feedback and testing to a user community, they can test market their new applications and get ideas for further development. As "graduated" apps are released in their final versions, the ones that don't make it are archived for future reference. Nokia's crowdsourcing platform includes a discussion board and a user-experience survey.

The principle of crowdsourcing is that more heads are better than one. By canvassing a large crowd of people for ideas, skills or participation, the quality of content and idea generation will be superior. Many technology-based companies are using this approach to test responses to radical ideas or invite the crowd to give feedback on how they can improve the idea or give a solution to a problem. A company called Marblar was recently launched to bring scientific discoveries back from the dead.[8]

7.7 CONDUCTING MARKETING RESEARCH

This section presents market research methods underpinning the above MVP processes. Marketing research is the systematic and objective identification, collection, analysis and dissemination to inform entrepreneur's decision-making in relation to marketing their business and products. Gathering and analysing market intelligence through the market research process is a crucial step in examining the validation of the business concept and the market for it. If further market research is needed to profile the target market(s) and help formulate a well-designed and actionable marketing strategy for bringing innovation into the marketplace. Drawing upon the American Marketing Association's (AMA) definition, marketing research involves the following activities:

1. *Identification*: Identification involves defining the research objective and specifies and determines the information that is needed to address it.
2. *Manages and Implements the Data Collection Process*: Data is then collected through a variety of means and sources. Initially secondary research, and if necessary should secondary research not satisfy research objective then primary data collection is conducted.
3. *Analysis*: Data/results/findings are analysed, interpreted, and inferences are drawn.
4. *Communicate, Disseminate and Respond/Act on/to Research Findings*: The findings, implications and recommendations are provided in a

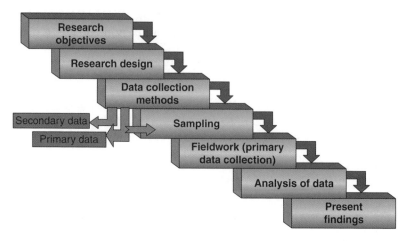

Figure 7.6   The marketing research process

format that makes the data actionable, applicable to the research objectives and directly useful as an input into decision-making.

These four activities are mapped out in Figure 7.6, as a step-by-step model of seven stages, necessary to conduct a marketing research project. Each stage is explained below.[9]

7.7.1   Stage 1: Formulating the Research Objective

The first step, clearly defining the problem at hand and the specific objectives to be met, is extremely important. The purpose of the study, why it is being undertaken and what it needs to achieve have to be clearly determined. For formulating research objective the entrepreneurs needs to ask the following questions:

- What is the purpose of the study?
- What is the decision to be made?
- What information is needed?
- How will the information be used?
- What is to be measured?
- Is there a need for marketing research?

Equally, in the early stages of new venture creation, technology entrepreneurs would be expected to engage in comprehensive marketing research to convince that there is a valid market when presenting to investors in their sales pitch for initial-round funding (see Chapter 8). Typical marketing research objectives of the venture would be:

- Opportunity Identification and Preliminary Market Insight
  - Testing and Validation of the business concepts
- Understand the Marketing Ecosystem in Terms of:

- Competitor information and industry analysis
- Identifying the collaborators and key stakeholders in the industry
- Identify changes and trends within the industry context in the macro- and micro-environment
- Customer Analysis
  - Gauge market size and gain insight into potential market segments
  - To identify and understand customers' needs and wants
  - To identify and analyse target market(s) and the most valuable customers (especially in B2B markets)
  - To see how the actual buying process occurs and to identify the major influencing factors
  - To see how customers interact with the product (the actual use – what they like and dislike)
  - To see how customers rate/compare and contrast their offering against competitors products

7.7.1.1 Formulation of the Marketing Strategy

- To identify the best way to deliver product and/or services to customers
- Benchmark against – develop market value of product to see what customers would perceive as a fair price, within particular market conditions
- To identify and assess the most effective and efficient way to communicate and develop sales strategy with the customers as well as build promotional strategy
- To use customer feedback in the new product development process
- To track customer loyalty and retention and to identify the best ways to build long-term customer relationship and increase customer equity.

All of the above indicate that conducting research is a continuous process; it reduces risks and can increase the viability of the new venture. Young and mature, big and small companies need to proactively listen and align their products and marketing strategies their target markets and ecosystems. Good marketing research leads to better marketing decisions.

7.7.2 Stage 2: Research Design

There are basically three types of research, each fit for different research objectives.

- Exploratory research is used in order to gather preliminary information; it aims to explore the issues around the problem at hand because very little is known about it. Exploratory research usually generates "soft" data; it helps in defining the research problem more clearly and suggests a further course of action within the research plan.
- Descriptive research is used to describe facts and things about the market. It is employed when much is already known about the market and companies want to describe or quantify certain aspects in more detail, such as a thorough

description of customers' geographical spread (single variable) or the relationship between price and quality (association between variables). Descriptive research is very structured and formal and generates "hard" data.

- Causal research in used when testing cause-and-effect relationships between two or more variables. This is specific measurement of dependent and independent variables for specific marketing problem and is rarely used as a research approach for market validation (Domegan and Fleming, 2007).

7.7.3 Stage 3: Data Collection Methods

When the research objective is identified and depending on the nature of the knowledge gap, data can be collected from both secondary and primary sources. When deciding on data collection methods and instruments, the first major question to be answered is whether this information is readily available. Because conducting primary research (i.e., information from actual source such as personal interviews) can be costly, researchers should always make sure they exhaust all sources of secondary data before embarking on a project of collecting primary data.

Secondary Data Collection: The first activity to begin any desk research with is identifying and assessing secondary data already available: data from internal sources (ie. internal product documentation/records) and data from external sources such as published materials, computerised databases, or from syndicated services (see below for secondary data sources). Secondary data gathered and published by government agencies, trade publications, independent research firms and universities provide a valuable and inexpensive (as compared with the high costs of conducting primary research) start to build a knowledge base on a particular market. The Internet especially can provide access to thousands of web pages holding a wealth of information (Figure 7.7). Secondary data is usually easily available and relatively inexpensive to obtain.

However, when relying on secondary sources to address their research question, researchers need to consider, the validity and reliability of the information. Secondary data needs to be assessed in terms of relevancy, validity of source, accuracy and timeliness.[10] Questions to consider are:

- Who collected it?
- Is it from a credible source?
- Why was it collected?
- What methods were used to collect data?
- Is it up to date?
- Is it unbiased and objective data

Primary Data Collection: Primary data can come in two formats: Qualitative and quantitative, each one determined by data collection method. Quantitative data is anything that can be expressed as a number, or quantified; it may be represented by ordinal, interval or ratio scales and lends itself to most statistical manipulation. Quantitative data focuses more on *what people/organizations do*. As opposed to this, qualitative data cannot be

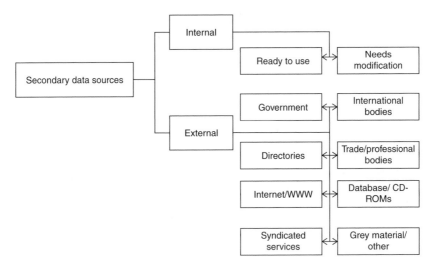

Figure 7.7   Classification of secondary data sources

expressed as a number, as it focuses on people's opinions, with no intention of statistical classifications. Qualitative data is based on *why and how people/ organizations behave* under certain conditions; it is more open to interpretation and helps marketers understand the meaning of actions. Both types of data are valid types of measurement and are sometimes used within the same research project to complement each other.

Qualitative Research Methods: Focus groups involve bringing together a group of 8 to 12 participants who are led by a moderator in a discussion focused on a particular topic or research question, with the objective to understand what people think or feel about an issue or object. A focus group can be representative of people who share some common characteristics, including their expectations for a specific type of product. A focus group is an interview conducted by a trained moderator among a small group of respondents in a non-structured and natural manner. In-depth interviews are another data collection method. This method is especially useful when attempting to understand complicated issues, such as complex decision-making patterns, possibly embarrassing topics or when inquiring about confidential personal data. The in-depth interview is conducted on a one-on-one basis, and the interviewer tries to uncover the respondent's underlying motivations, beliefs, attitudes and feelings on a topic. Great insights can be uncovered. Interviews are also used when the group of customers are business users and hence require a more personal setting for gathering market intelligence. Personal interviewing can be done through face-to-face, telephone or Skype. As compared to interviews, surveys are limited in given opinion on concept to some degree as it is mainly a voting exercise used to ask would they use product or not.

Quantitative Data Methods: The survey is still the most common market research approach as it has the ability to gather a wealth of data. It consists of asking people questions about products and brands, about their knowledge, attitudes, preferences and buying behaviour. The data collection instrument associated with surveys is the questionnaire (Domegan and Fleming, 2007). This can take different forms, according to the type of information that is needed. With a survey, the researcher has to decide on a contact method, be it telephone, personal or online distribution.

7.7.4 Stage 4: Sampling

When methods are selected, a sample or segment of respondents need to be selected from which to collect the data. A sample is a segment of the population selected for research. Sampling implies identifying who has the needed information. Whether a focus group, personal interviewing or survey is used for data collection, a sample of respondents needs to be selected representing or profiling characteristics similar to the target market for the innovation. The sample should be representative so that the researcher can make accurate estimates of the thoughts and behaviours of the larger population (Kotler et al., 2008).

In terms of qualitative methods, the sample is small (i.e., number of focus groups used and/or interviewees) and non-probability methods can be used to select participants. Non-probability methods are not based on statistical probability and are hence more subjective in nature. Even though the sampling error cannot be measured, and results cannot be generalised, non-probability samples can still provide very useful market and customer insights. Non-probability samples are chosen, based on the researcher's judgement, issues of access to population, cost and time constraints (Domegan and Fleming, 2007).

In terms of quantitative methods, such as surveys, the sample size (how many people should be surveyed) and the sampling method (how should people in the sample be chosen) are important decisions. When probability sampling methods are used, the researcher uses statistics and objectivity in selecting who to talk to, ensuring that each population's member has a known chance of being included in the sample. The results can thus be generalised to the wider population of interest.

7.7.5 Stage 5: Fieldwork

Fieldwork consists of collecting all relevant data and information through one or more of the methods described above. Data can be collected by one or more researchers and it involves selection, training and management of the research staff. When planning, organising and conducting the fieldwork, it is essential to remember that the quality of the data gathering process will impact the data analysis and ultimately the accuracy and relevance of the research findings: the better the process, the better the data.

7.7.6 Stage 6: Data Analysis

Data gathered through secondary and primary data collection methods has to be transformed in information in order to be useful in the decision-making process within an organisation. The process starts with data preparation and it includes editing, coding and reduction. According to the type of data (quantitative or qualitative), different analytical methods will be used. For qualitative data the analysis consists of identifying patterns, themes and relations between the elements in the data. No statistical tests are conducted for qualitative data, and analysis may include creating word lists, checking frequency of occurrence, identifying categories, etc. Quantitative data lends itself to statistical analysis; simple and cross-tabulations, frequency distributors, central tendency and dispersion measures, regression, factor analysis, multi-dimensional scaling, etc. are all used to classify and summarise the data.

7.7.7 Stage 7: Present the Findings and the Research Results

The final market research report should start by reiterating the initial marketing research objectives. It should contain a detailed outline of the findings, as well as possible weaknesses of the research (in terms of how reliable and valid the data is). In the final part the report should incorporate feasible recommendations based on the newly acquired information. The report is usually appended to the business plan and key findings on market validation are summarised in the plan itself under the "Marketing" section of the business plan.

Market research activities can be a laborious task, costly and time-draining process, and yet sometimes some market opportunities are ready to be exploited. In new ventures and small established firms, which do not have the resources to conduct a large-scale project, marketing research, can take simpler forms, always starting with a detailed review of secondary data and continuing with simple observations, small-scale surveys, with convenient samples, personal interview meetings with existing or potential customers and industry operators, etc.

7.8 CHAPTER SUMMARY

The chapter presents the importance of market validation for the technology venture and outlines the necessary processes to ensure a rigorous and systematic approach is taken. The two key processes that underpin MVP are: 1) market ecosystem analysis and 2) business concept testing. For market ecosystem analysis, the 5C framework is used to conduct the analysis. For business concept testing, the analytical tools are used to explore and validate their business concepts of their invention and presents research techniques specific for validating market opportunity for the business concept for both end consumers and business customers. Understanding of market research methods is necessary for collecting and analysing market intelligence to perform the two key steps in market validation process. Market research is key in understanding customers and validating a target market. Obtaining and using information on the market is an important tool in not only identifying market opportunities for technology-based products yet ensuring the product is entering a valid and sustainable market for revenue generation. The final part of the chapter discusses the importance of and identifies the market research methods for gathering market intelligence and data to conduct the MVP.

Case Study 7.1   Skype

Written by Gabriela Gliga, NUI Galway.

"Skype is the archetypal Internet phenomenon: a breakthrough technology combining with enormously powerful network effects to revolutionize a gigantic industry." Mr. Marc Andreessen, CoFounder of Andreessen Horowitz.

Skype Technologies is the manufacturer and developer of Skype software, one of Europe's greatest start-up success stories, a company that has changed the way people communicate. Skype offers a software-based communications platform, a high-quality and easy-to-use tool for both consumers and businesses. Skype can be used on phone, computer or TV to communicate, collaborate and share experiences globally through voice, video and text conversations. The software also allows users to make low-cost calls to landlines and mobile telephone lines.

The telecommunications industry has undergone tremendous changes in the last two decades, through the explosive growth of the Internet. VoIP (Voice over Internet Protocol) was the name for the new technologies that allowed the delivery of voice communications over an Internet network. The lower cost VoIP technology was threatening to replace the traditional fixed-line telephony and companies pursuing this avenue included AOL's AIM, MSN Messenger, and Yahoo! Messenger.

In 2004, the industry was buzzing again, this time about a new company called Skype. The new-comers managed to disrupt not only the traditional business model of landline telephone services, but also the model of other VoIP service providers. Skype took advantage of increased broadband access and P2P (peer-to-peer) networking trends to become the rising star in telecommunications. The P2P technology allowed for a new approach to networking, as the division into clients and servers, which was the traditional architecture used by most other VoIP services, could be replaced by a decentralised paradigm, where each node could act as both, suppliers (senders), and consumers (receivers). By using P2P networks, Skype eliminated the need for a central server, as users employ (simultaneously supply and consume) their own computers' resources.

Skype was founded in 2003 and headquartered in Luxembourg by Niklas Zennström and Janus Friis, who have previously created the world's largest peer-to-peer file sharing service, KaZaA. In 2004, only one year after its inception, Skype had already recorded impressive growth, with more than 9 million registered users and more than 20 million downloads for its software.

Skype's growth has of course attracted investor attention. Skype was acquired by eBay Inc. for US $2.6 billion in September 2005. eBay was hoping that the VoIP service would help its auction participants to communicate. The company also believed that Skype would afford cross-marketing opportunities by providing access to a vast pool of users. In 2008, Skype Technologies generated revenues of $551 million, and the registered users totalled 405 million, a 47 per cent increase from 2007.

However, eBay's plans for Skype did not fully materialise, and in November 2009, eBay Inc. has successfully completed the sale of its Skype communications unit in a deal valuing the business at US $2.75 billion. The buyer was an investor group led by Silver Lake, which also included the Canada Pension Plan Investment

Board and Andreessen Horowitz. The deal was also accompanied by a lawsuit from Skype's founders (Joltid Ltd.), who claimed they still owned the P2P technology that was Skype's basic platform. The investor group settled the Joltid litigation and acquired all Skype technology in exchange for equity in the company. Joltid Ltd. ended up with about 14 per cent equity in Skype and have subsequently joined the investors' group, now owning around 70 per cent of Skype, with eBay retaining the remaining 30 per cent.

This deal was perceived as bringing value to both eBay and Skype. eBay got significant cash up front while still retaining a minority stake in Skype and could now focus on their core business and capabilities for the auction site and PayPal. For Skype, the deal provided the opportunity to accelerate the growth of its business by leveraging the deep technological and company development expertise that resided within the investor group, who had a track record of taking technology companies to the next level. As of 2010, Skype was available in 27 languages and became the leading VoIP service provider with 660 million world-wide users, an average of over 100 million active each month. "Skype me" has replaced the phrase "call me" in many conversations, which was something that the Skype creators envisioned in its beginnings.

In October 2011, Skype was acquired by Microsoft Corporation for US$8.5 billion, a deal that got mixed reviews from analysts, particularly in relation with the price of the acquisition. Skype CEO, Tony Bates, is now the president of the Skype Division of Microsoft. While the Skype division continues to offer its current products, Microsoft also plans to integrate Skype across an array of its products. Microsoft and Skype's current common mission is to transform real-time communications for consumers and enterprise customers and to become the communications platform of choice around the world.

Skype's success is attributed to its very simple business model. Initially Skype offered PC-to-PC calling, and this basic service was offered for free at a time when most companies charged for a similar value proposition. Furthermore, Skype was very simple to download and use and offered good quality in audio and video. Later on, the free calling, video conferencing, text messaging and file sharing has been extended with supplementary services. For a low fee, SkypeOut allowed users to place calls from computers to regular telephones. Prices were very competitive with rates as low as 2 cent per minute and somewhat higher for countries where the telecommunication industry had not been liberalised and the interconnection fees were still high. In some markets, SkypeIn was also offered, allowing users to receive calls on their computer (on a regular phone number) from phone users.

Additionally, in 2007 in order to compete against phone companies who offered unlimited local calling for a flat monthly fee, Skype also introduced monthly subscriptions with unlimited calls. And in 2010, Skype launched monthly premium subscriptions, supporting group video calls and group screen sharing at a low cost of US$3.49 per month, bringing additional revenues to the company. Further revenue generators include advertising and e-commerce features, where Skype has partnered with hardware companies. The Skype shop provides headsets and microphones, desktops, home phones, webcams, mobiles, tablets, gaming, apps and gift cards.

Skype is also capitalising on the realities of today's borderless business world and the ever-growing international e-commerce marketplace. Skype illustrates "the death of distance", as it offers a way to communicate in real-time with business partners and customers. Being able to bring the entire ecosystem of workers, partners and customers together to get things done is positively impacting on both business relationships and customer service. In fact, Skype has afforded a new channel of distribution for various service providers, in a variety of sectors, such as education, consultancy, health, fitness, etc. The Skype blogs offer numerous stories of how entrepreneurial individuals are using Skype to create extra value in their business and beyond.

Skype's revenue model is based on the unique and premium features on offer. This is possible as the marginal cost per customer is very low. Skype's marketing costs are also very low. Skype basically promoted itself. The viral promotion strategy for Skype was very effective as it was based on word-of-mouth or "word-of-mouse": individuals recommending the application to their circle of friend. Skype's early adopters, who readily embraced the application, included people who spent considerable amounts of time on a computer, were already using services such as instant messaging and wanted to use the Internet to communicate with other people.

Furthermore TV broadcasters were specifically targeted as key opinion leaders and they were encouraged to integrate Skype into programming. One great success was to become a regular on the influential *The Oprah Winfrey Show* whose host began to include regular Skype video calls in the programme, and in May 2009 an entire show was dedicated to Skype and its significance.

Yet, not everything is quite picture perfect. Skype has had its share of issues, such as the crash of 2007, leaving over 220 million users, some of them small businesses with no communication channels for a day, while Skype executives gave only vague explanations regarding the cause of the problem. Other concerns include Skype and now Microsoft's continued ability to protect their intellectual property rights and to deal with economic and regulatory uncertainties. For example, the regulation of VoIP varies by country, as some nations still own telecommunication carriers and they rely on the income they produce. VoIP services have also been under the radar in terms of security aspects, such as monitoring calls and wiretapping. Furthermore the incumbents in the telecommunication markets are pushing for regulation of the VoIP services, since the latter are not restricted by the traditional telephony regulation and hence do not pay the fees that the traditional providers are subject to. And things are not slowing down in the market. Skype's competition is not only the giants like Yahoo!, MSN and AOL. A plethora of smaller, newer and older (than Skype) companies make competition more intensive and aggressive every day. Names like Jajah, Lycos, Viber, Tango, Phone Power, Lingo, Phone.com, Vonage, 8x8 are but a few in the great pool of competitors for Skype.

Furthermore, Skype has high expectations to meet, as the anticipated continuation of its growth and its potential longer term value has been valued at US$8.5 billion. "Skype and Microsoft have big dreams", reads the Skype homepage. The biggest acquisition in Microsoft's history must still be merged into the giant's vast product portfolio and once this is achieved, it must deliver superior customer value. eBay's CEO Meg Whitman took a gamble with Skype's, which never really paid off. Can Skype pay off for Microsoft?

Case Questions

1. Given the global nature of Skype's operations, which changes in the macro-context are likely to pose the greatest threats to its expansion, as part of the Microsoft Corporation in the coming years?
2. Outline the factors in Skype's meso-context, which have had an impact on the company during its life span.
3. In your opinion, what are the advantages of Skype's early entry into the VoIP market?
4. With its generic value proposition, does Skype still need to address the consumer and organisational markets differently?

5. How could Skype benefit from customer-driven innovation? Can you identify a crowd-sourcing opportunity for Skype?

Case Study References

http://about.skype.com/press/corporate/.

http://about.skype.com/2009/09/ebay_inc_signs_definitive_agre.html.

Lasica, J.D. (2004) "The Engadget Interview: Niklas Zennström", *Engadget*, November 8. Accessed on 1 March 2013 at http://www.engadget.com/2004/11/08/the-engadget-interview-niklas-zennstrom/.

Lee, D. (2011) "How Skype Connected", *BBC*, 10 May. Accessed on 16 February 2013 at http://www.bbc.co.uk/news/technology-13350425.

Lindsay, A. (2009) "Skype Settles Lawsuit with Founders", *Compare Business Products*, November 6. Accessed on 15 February 2013 at http://www.comparebusinessproducts.com/blog/entryid/88/skype-settles-lawsuit-with-founders.aspx.

McCarthy, C. (2009) "eBay sets Skype loose at $2.75 billion valuation", *CNET News*, November 19. Accessed on 1 March 2013 at http://news.cnet.com/8301-1023_3-10402053-93.html.

"Microsoft to acquire Skype", 10 May 2011, *Skype website*. Accessed on 10 March 2013 at http://about.skype.com/press/2011/05/microsoft_to_acquire_skype.html#more.

Roth, D. (2004) "Catch Us If you Can", *CNN Money*, February 9. Accessed on 20 February 2013 at http://money.cnn.com/magazines/fortune/fortune_archive/2004/02/09/360106/index.htm.

Schollmeier, R. (2002) *A Definition of Peer-to-Peer Networking for the Classification of Peer-to-Peer Architectures and Applications*, Proceedings of the First International Conference on Peer-to-Peer Computing, IEEE, http://www.computer.org/csdl/proceedings/p2p/2001/1503/00/15030101.pdf

Stone, B. (2007) "Error in Skype's Software Shuts Down Phone Service", *NY Times*, August 17. Accessed on 13 February 2013 at http://www.nytimes.com/2007/08/17/business/17ebay.html?_r=1&oref=slogin.

Waters, R., Bradshaw, T. and Palmer, M. (2011) "Microsoft in $8.5bn Skype gamble", *Financial Times*, May 10. Accessed on 14 February 2013 at http://www.ft.com/intl/cms/s/2/9461dbb4-7ab8-11e0-8762-00144feabdc0.html#axzz2OC1FBPuYcheck.

"We've settled with Joltid", 2009, *Skype blogs*, November 6. Accessed on 8 February 2013 at http://blogs.skype.com/2009/11/06/joltid-settlement/#fbid=ddG5kofwz5k.

Wingfield, N. (2012) "$8.5 Billion Deal for Calling Service Presents a Puzzle", *NY Times*, May 28. Accessed on 10 March 2013 at http://www.nytimes.com/2012/05/29/technology/microsoft-at-work-on-meshing-its-products-with-skype.html?_r=2&pagewanted=all&.

7.9 REVISION QUESTIONS

1. Identify and explain the key processes involved in market validation processes.
2. Conduct a marketing ecosystem analysis for your technology venture using the 5C Framework. (Please refer to online material for template guide.)
3. Identify and explain the steps in the marketing research process.
4. Distinguish between the methods and data sources when conducting secondary and primary market research.

7.10 FURTHER READING AND RESOURCES

Baines, P. and Chansarkar, B. (2002) *Introducing Marketing Research*. Chichester: John Wiley and Sons.
Domegan, C. and Fleming, D. (2007) *Marketing Research In Ireland*. Dublin: Gill and Macmillan.
Gliga, G. and Evers, N. (2010) "Marketing Challenges for High Tech SMEs", *Innovation Marketing*, 3(6): 104–112.
Malhotra, N.K. (2010) *Marketing Research: An Applied Orientation*. New York: Pearson Education.
Mohr, J., Sengupta, S. and Slater, S. (2010) *Marketing of High-Technology Products and Innovations: International Edition*. Upper Saddle River, N.J.: Prentice Hall.
Porter, M.E. (1979) "How Competitive Forces Shape Strategy", *Harvard Business Review*, 57(2): 137–145.
Vargo, S.L. and Lusch, R.F. (2004) "Evolving to a New Dominant Logic for Marketing", *Journal of Marketing*, 68: 1–17.
Whitla, P. (2009) "Crowdsourcing and Its Application in Marketing Activities", *Contemporary Management Research*, 5: 15–28.

7.11 NOTES

1. *Source*: 5C Framework Analysis, http://www.netmba.com/marketing/situation/.
2. For further reading of Porter's Five Forces Model of Industry Analysis, see Porter's (1979), and the subsequent book that develops these ideas further: Porter (1980).
3. Hutt and Speh (2013). Business marketing management provides an excellent insight into B2B marketing strategies.
4. See also Chapter 4.
5. Further reading on research for incremental and breakthrough innovations, see Gliga and Evers (2010).
6. http://techcrunch.com/2011/10/19/dropbox-minimal-viable-product/.
7. Further reading, see Von Hippel (1988) and Von Hippel et al. (1999).
8. See http://www.marblar.com/; see also http://www.technologyreview.com/news/429171/can-crowdsourcing-bring-unused-patents-back-from/.
9. Further detailed reading on marketing research, see Malhotra (2010).
10. For further reading on "Criteria for Evaluating Secondary Data" see chapter 4 of Malhotra, K. (2010). *Market Research Methods: An Applied Orientation* (6th edn), UK: Pearson.

7.12 REFERENCES

Aguilar, F.J. (1967) *Scanning The Business Environment*. New York: Macmillan.
Baker, M.J. (2012) "What Is Marketing?", *Principles of Marketing: Guidelines For Effective Practice*, The Marketing and Management Collection, Henry Stewart Talks Ltd., London. Accessed on 20 May 2012 at http://Hstalks.Com/Go.
Ballantyne, D. (2004) "Dialogue and Its Role in the Development of Relationship Specific Knowledge", *Journal of Business & Industrial Marketing*, 19: 114–123.

Domegan, C. and Fleming, D. (2007) *Marketing Research in Ireland*. Dublin: Gill and Macmillan.

Friar, J.H. and Balachandra, R. (1999) "Spotting the Customer for Emerging Technologies", *Research Technology Management*, 42: 37–43.

Gliga, G. and Evers, N. (2010) "Marketing Challenges for High Tech SMEs", *Innovative Marketing*, 3: 104–112.

Herstatt, C. and Von Hippel, E. (1992) "From Experience: Developing New Product Concepts via the Lead User Method: A Case Study in a 'Low-tech' Field", *Journal of Product Innovation Management*, 9: 213–221.

Hutt, M.D. and Speh., T.W. (2007) *Business Marketing Management: B2B*. Westford, MA: Thomson South West.

Kotler, P., Armstrong, G., Wong, V. and Saunders, J. (2008) *Principles of Marketing*. Harlow: Financial Times Prentice Hall.

Kumar, N., Scheer, L. and Kotler, P. (2000) "From Market Driven to Market Driving", *European Management Journal*, 18: 129–142.

Malhotra, N.K. (2010) *Marketing Research: An Applied Orientation*. 6th edn. Upper Saddle River, N.J.: Pearson Education.

Miles, M.P., Little, V., Brookes, R. and Morrish, S.C. (2010) *Market Validation in the Context of New High-Tech Ventures*. Accessed on 14 October 2013 at, http://anzmac2010.org/proceedings/pdf/anzmac10Final00087.pdf.

Nambisan, S. and Sawhney, M. (2007) "A Buyer's Guide to the Innovation Bazaar", *Harvard Business Review*, 85: 109–118.

Porter, M.E. (1979) "How Competitive Forces Shape Strategy", *Harvard Business Review*, 57: 137–145.

—— (1980) *Competitive Strategy : Techniques For Analyzing Industries and Competitors*. New York: Free Press; London : Collier Macmillan.

Shanklin, W. L. and Ryans, J. K. (1984) "Organizing for High-tech Marketing", *Harvard Business Review*, 62 (November–December): 164–171.

Vargo, S. L. and Lusch, R.F. (2004) "Evolving to a New Dominant Logic for Marketing", *Journal of Marketing*, 68: 1–17.

Von Hippel, E. (1988) *The Sources of Innovation*. New York, Oxford: Oxford University Press.

Von Hippel, E., Thomke, S. and Sonnack, M. (1999) "Creating Breakthroughs at 3M", *Harvard Business Review*, 77: 47–57.

Whitla, P. (2009) "Crowdsourcing and Its Application in Marketing Activities", *Contemporary Management Research*, 5: 15–28. 5C Framework Analysis. Accessed on 02 July 2013 at http://www.netmba.com/marketing/situation/ (no date).

7.13   GLOSSARY OF TERMS

Business Concept Testing: A process to estimate the potential of a new idea or concept in the market.

Causal Research: A type of research used to explore the effect that one variable has on another.

Competitive Analysis: Identifying who your competitors are. It allows an organisation to benchmark themselves against their competitors, while also identifying their own strengths and weaknesses.

Conjoint Analysis: Understanding how consumers make decisions between one product or service and another.

Crowdsourcing: The process of getting a group together, oftentimes online, in order to complete a task or set of tasks. In return for completing the task, the group are often paid a fee or given a prize.

Data Analysis: Preparing the data and then studying in order to identify common patterns and themes.

Descriptive Research: A type of research used when there is already a significant amount of information known about the problem/market.

Environmental Scanning: Carefully monitoring, analysing and forecasting the marketing ecosystem.

Exploratory Research: A type of research used when there is little known about the issue surrounding the problem.

Incremental Innovations: Small improvements in a product or service that happen over a period of time. They often involve extensions or improvements to an existing product.

Industry Analysis: Assesses the profitability of an industry through identifying, profiling and analysing the industry and sector structure, developments and dynamics.

Market Ecosystem: The internal and external environment of an organisation. The marketing ecosystem looks outside of the firm rather than focusing solely on what is occurring within the firm. A market ecosystem analysis takes place at the macro, meso and micro levels.

Market Validation: The process of estimating demand and cash flows of a potential new venture.

Primary Data: Data collected by the researcher himself/herself. Primary data may be collected either qualitatively or quantitatively.

Prototype Testing: An organisation testing a model if their product in the market in order to observe customers reactions to it and to identify any issues with it prior to going to market.

Qualitative Data: Concerned with the qualities of people/organisations. Qualitative data gains a deeper insight into why people/organisations behave a certain way. Quantitative research methods include surveys and questionnaires.

Quantitative Data: Anything that can be quantified. It focuses on what people/ organisations do. Qualitative research m ethods include focus groups and in-depth interviews.

Radical and Disruptive Innovations: Revolutionary innovations that often create new applications, new segments and new markets.

Sampling: Selecting a subset of individuals within a population to research. From this sample, inferences can be made about the whole population.

Secondary Data: Data collected by someone other than the user. It includes materials published by others in books, articles and online.

Value Network: Comprises the connections an organisation has surrounding it. Such connections may include stakeholders, such as suppliers and distributors.

Value Proposition: The total benefits that an organisation promises a customer they will receive when they purchase a particular product.

Chapter 8

ROUTES TO COMMERCIALISATION AND PITCHING

8.1 LEARNING OBJECTIVES

After reading this chapter, you will be able to:

1. Have a clear understanding of the different routes to commercialisation – and the merits and pitfalls associated with each;
2. Appreciate the importance of "pitching" your idea or new business;
3. Understand the key decision-making criteria of investors to whom you pitch; and
4. Know how to best "paint a picture" of your idea or new business, which gives you the best chance of securing funding.

8.2 CHAPTER STRUCTURE

The core elements of this chapter are as follows:

- Introduction
- Commercialisation
  - The *why?* of commercialisation – reasons for commercialising IP
  - The *which?* of commercialisation – geographical markets and customer segments
  - The *when?* of commercialisation – timing
  - The *how?* of commercialisation – routes to commercialisation
  - The *who?* of commercialisation – promoters
- Pitching
  - The seven steps to a successful pitch
- Chapter Summary
- Case Study – Celtic Catalysts Ltd.
- Revision Questions
- Further Reading and Resources
- References
- Glossary of Terms

8.3   INTRODUCTION

This chapter outlines the different options available for commercialising IP. It then explores the idea of pitching for investment in order to raise the requisite funds for commercialising a given technology. Commercialising IP is a multi-stage process outlined in Figure 8.1 below.

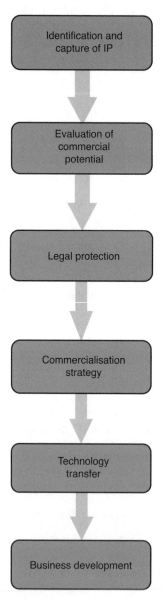

Figure 8.1   IP commercialisation process

Table 8.1 Principle considerations in intellectual property decisions

* although invention should be separated from application, technological development should not be undertaken in isolation from market requirements;
* IP creation and protection should be balanced by a strong focus of resources on commercialisation;
* Successful exploitation of IP requires competent people who can manage at the interface of business and technology;
* if the inventor or entrepreneur is not in a position to exploit fully then there are several other methods that can be used;
* the inventor can assign or license the IP to a new start-up company (and become a shareholder) or to manufacture and market products covered by the IP;
* the entrepreneur can form collaborative agreements with existing companies;
* the IP rights can be licensed to an existing company that has the expertise and capacity to exploit the IP;
* the owner can sell the IP directly without any further involvement in its commercial exploitation.

Any decision to protect intellectual property is usually made on the basis that it has some value in the marketplace. Whether a patent, a design or any other form of IP, protecting and exploiting it represents and investment from which the entrepreneur expects to make a return. Costs of protecting IP can be significant, so it is not something that can be taken lightly.

In many cases, the inventor may not have the resources or experience to exploit a patent fully, in which case assigning or licensing the IP to a business partner should be considered to exploit the invention to its full potential.

Converting the commercial potential of IP into real rewards is primarily the role of the technology entrepreneur. The rewards are largely dictated by the approach taken to its commercialisation and this should be premised on a number of fundamental principles outlined in Table 8.1.

The chapter addresses, therefore, two crucial areas of commercialisation of innovation: first, decisions relating to how best to commercialise IP and second, planning the initial pitch to attract the investment needed to develop the commercial idea further. In most cases, innovative technological ideas require further technical development (and hence funding) to successfully commercialise them in the marketplace. IP and patenting issues have already been addressed in Chapter 5 and are also dealt with comprehensively elsewhere (e.g., McManus 2012).

8.4 COMMERCIALISATION

In examining the topic of commercialisation of intellectual property we will consider *five* fundamental questions, namely:

* *Why* would an individual or organisation consider commercialising IP?
* *Which* geographical market(s) and customer segments should be addressed?
* *When* should they commercialise their IP?

- *How* should they commercialise their IP?
- *Who* should lead the commercialisation effort?

8.4.1 The *Why?* of Commercialisation – Reasons for Commercialising IP

When considering commercialising intellectual property it is important to first consider (a) the context in which the commercialisation of the IP is sought as well as (b) the underlying motivations for seeking to commercialise the IP.

For example, IP that was developed by an academic researcher within a university may end up on a very different commercialisation pathway than IP which has been developed by an individual or team within a company setting. Moreover, an idea or prototype, which forms the basis of intellectual property owned by an individual outside of either of the formal industrial or academic settings, may require yet another approach. Of course the potential commercial application of the IP will also greatly influence the choice of commercialisation pathway with, for example, a technology that has application in the biotechnology industry perhaps following a very different route to market than IP developed in the software industry.

At the same time, the motivation of the inventor/owner of the IP may be very different depending upon context and circumstance. For example, the imperative for companies to commercialise is inevitably driven by a desire to increase shareholder value. It is therefore likely that the requisite commercialisation infrastructure (e.g., operations staff, equipment, finance, sales team, etc.) will already be in place and thus the commercialisation pathway will most likely be defined largely by the models already in operation (or variants thereof) within that company.

For IP developed within an academic setting, the motivation to commercialise may be somewhat different. At an institutional level, given the broader remit of most universities in the areas of teaching and research, there may be a desire to demonstrate to funding bodies that the research being carried out has a real commercial (and hence societal) benefit. While seeking to realise some monetary return on the IP itself, often the institution may view the wider impacts as having an equal or greater level of importance than just purely the revenues directly generated.

For the individual researcher within the academic institution there is often an understandable tension that exists regarding commercialisation. This centres around the fact that tenure or promotion metrics within the institution are often linked to teaching and the publication of peer-reviewed journal articles based upon their research. Thus commercialisation of IP can often be seen by such academics as a distraction from the traditional research and teaching activities against which their performance will be judged. Thus, in institutions where commercialisation/innovation is not used as a metric against which tenure/promotion is assessed, this conflict can serve as a major impediment to the commercialisation of IP. This is particularly highlighted when one considers that in many instances the IP itself is inextricably linked with the know-how of the inventor and hence their availability and willingness to involve themselves in its commercialisation. Notwithstanding the above perceived drawbacks to an individual academic seeking to commercialise his/her IP, there does exist considerable potential for enhanced reputation and personal wealth as well as kudos and promotion within those institutions who meaningfully value commercialisation activities.

For an individual outside of the formal industrial or academic settings the motivation to commercialise IP is likely to be driven mainly by a desire to increase personal wealth. Of course as mentioned above, this motivation will likely be common to the abovementioned cases in varying degrees – but perhaps not to the same extent as that which exists with an individual without the supports/constraints of working within a larger organisation.

8.4.2   The *Which* of Commercialisation – Geographical Markets and Customer Segments

Having established a sufficient underlying motivation within an individual or organisation seeking to commercialise IP, an obvious question which follows in cases where the IP may have applications in a number of markets is "which market(s) should be addressed?" This question needs to be considered from both a geographical perspective (i.e., in which countries or regions the market exists) and an industry segmentation perspective (i.e., in which industries or industrial segments the market exists).

The answer to this question will in large part be dictated by the market research that has been undertaken (discussed in Chapter 7) and will not necessarily be as simple as "all of them" or "whichever market is biggest"! Additional critical factors to be considered that impact upon this decision will include (amongst others) the time and resources required to meaningfully address each market, the competitive landscape within each market, the length of the sales cycle within each market, the growth trends within each market, the accessibility and geographical spread of each market and the ability to sustain a competitive position in a particular market using the IP in question.

8.4.3   The *When* of Commercialisation – Timing

In most instances protection of the IP in question will be a pre-requisite before commencing the process of commercialisation. As discussed in Chapter 5, this may be achieved by way of patents, confidentiality agreements, material transfer agreements, retention of key know-how and trade secrets or various combinations thereof. However beyond protection of IP, the decision of when to commercialise can often be nuanced and fraught with difficulty. Again, a number of factors influence this decision.

One such factor, particularly with respect to IP, which forms the basis of a new start-up company, is the availability of funds to see the process through to the point where the IP is generating sufficient revenues.

Similarly with respect to IP developed in a university setting, the availability of grant funds to further develop IP may influence the timing of commercialisation.

The timing of commercialisation also impacts critically on the nature and magnitude of revenue generation. For example, if a technology were to be licensed at an early stage of development, it is likely to generate far less revenue than would be the case if it were to be licensed in a more mature state. An obvious illustration of this is in the area of drug development where drug candidates in Phase I, II and III tend to be licensed for progressively larger sums, which increase in orders of magnitude from early pre-clinical development onwards. However the costs associated with taking candidates through each phase of development also progressively increase by orders of magnitude and thus this example too is illustrative of the abovementioned point about the availability of funds influencing *when* (and as will be in the next section, *how*) to commercialise a given piece of IP.

8.4.4   The *How* of Commercialisation – Routes of Commercialisation

On the assumption that there exists a sound rationale regarding why to commercialise a particular piece of intellectual property, and that a market opportunity has been clearly established, the obvious question that arises is how should the opportunity best be addressed? The various routes available for commercialisation have been extensively explored by others (e.g., Hindel and Yencken 2004). The advantages and disadvantages of licensing IP as well as a comparison with the option of starting a new venture have already been outlined in the Introduction. Again, there is no simple "catch all" answer to this question. A number of options may present themselves and their degree of appropriateness will vary depending upon circumstances.

Factors such as the target market for the IP, the resources available to the team of promoters, the "shelf life" of the IP (i.e., how long the IP is likely to confer a competitive advantage in the marketplace) will all be important factors in deciding upon how to approach the commercialisation conundrum. In a general sense, however, there tend to be *three* main routes for commercialisation (summarised in Table 8.2) and explored in more depth below:

(i) Provision of a service that leverages expertise and/or IP

To remain in business, most individuals and organisations must have an inherent set of differentiating competences and expertises which form the basis of their market offering. In many cases this will be harnessed by them to make products or technologies, which they then sell to the market. However, an alternative means of realising commercial benefit from this expertise and competence is to offer it to the market by means of a service. At an organisation level, for example, many software "solution providers" go to market on the basis of a range of services that provide their customers with improved business performance. Often this will be done solely on the

Table 8.2 Summary of routes to commercialisation

Routes to Commercialisation	Pros	Cons
Service provision	Little or no investment generally required. Leverages experience and know-how. Provides opportunities for insights into other organisations/industries	Can be difficult to protect market position. Can be difficult to scale.
Licensing	Little or no investment generally required once the IP has been created. Opportunities to address multiple markets. Potential to generate revenues relatively quickly.	Often relinquishing control over the revenue generating capabilities of the technology.
Formation of a new venture	Potential to capture maximal value from the developed IP.	Often capital intensive with a requirement to source investment from third parties.

back of the pure expertise and skills of the staff of the solution provider as opposed to being on the basis of any specific piece of patented intellectual property or differentiated technology. In other instances proprietary pieces of software or technology may form the kernel around which a range of services can be built and thus the business generates the vast bulk of its revenues from the ancillary services rather than on the sale or licence of any specific technology. See Case Box 8.1.

Case Box 8.1 Protein Analyze Ltd. Denmark[1]

Founded in 2002, Protein Analyze Ltd[2] provides high quality protein analysis service to support the research, manufacturing and clinical development of natural and recombinant proteins. Protein Analyze Ltd. was a university spin-out from the University of Southern Denmark was created to offer a standardised "off-the-shelf" protein analysis service to public as well as commercial research labs. This service includes 72-hour result guarantee on any request in Europe and Northern America. As a result of the founders' research expertise a number of customised products were developed in close collaboration with key customers.

With offices now in United States as well as the head office in Denmark, the company started out with a small investment using a small lab facility at the University and some second-hand automated lab machines to run the actual tests. In its first three years no commercial developmental work was done but still the spin-out generated good cashflow through its standard services for protein analysis. In 2005 the founders saw *"large untapped potentials in developing the services that we could offer"*. By that time the linkage to the parent University Department had weakened considerably. As a result, the founders *"experienced that the commercial market was the sole point of reference".* Due to this the founders decided to keep ahead of their immediate competitors who had larger bulk capacity than Protein Analyze Ltd.

Optimisation of the standardised analysis procedures aiming at large scale advantages is still the main issue for Protein Analyze. However, as the customer portfolio grew so did the insight on key customers' work processes. This provided a solid basis for developing a number of products tailor made to key customers. This *"return to the roots of the firm – to regain a focus on front line research"* is thought to facilitate a long-term financial security to Protein Analyze.

(ii) Licensing of intellectual property

Licensing agreements do not transfer ownership of IP rights but merely give the party receiving the technology (licensee) permission to use the IP, through a legal agreement, for commercial exploitation. The company or person licensing the technology (licensor) can place limitations and obligations on the licensee. Licensing agreements usually take one of two basic forms: a non-exclusive licence or an exclusive licence. Companies like exclusive licences because they restrict their competitors from gaining access. This creates more risk for the licensor, because the successful commercialisation of the technology depends entirely on one company. Therefore, the licensing terms are usually more restrictive. For example, exclusive licensing agreements often require the payment of minimum royalties and reasonable efforts on the part of the licensee to commercially exploit the inventions, in order to maintain the exclusivity of the licence. Where the licensee fails to meet these requirements, the agreements usually provide for termination, or conversion to a non-exclusive licence. Licences can also be restricted to an application of the technology or to a geographical area.

The decision as to whether to license IP or technology as opposed to

Table 8.3 Advantages and disadvantages of the licensing route

Advantages of licensing	Disadvantages of licensing
Instant and expert resources dedicated to commercialisation.	Lower financial return than inventor-led commercialisation.
Sharing and diversification of risk.	Difficult to find appropriate licensee.
Earlier financial reward.	Losing partial control of the technology.
Less resource intensive for inventor.	Involvement of the inventor is reduced.

Source: Based on DCU, *Commercialisation Handbook: an introductory guide for researchers.*

pursuing another avenue of commercialisation is often dictated in large part by the resources available to the promoters. Thus for example, vast resources are generally required to take a drug molecule through clinical trials and to subsequently market and sell the final product. This makes it extremely difficult for all but the very large drug companies to undertake this full range of activities. Thus, commercialisation of drug products by smaller players generally involves development of the products to early stage clinical trials (e.g., Phase I and Phase II) followed by a subsequent licence to a larger industry player who has the resources available to complete the clinical development and bring the products to market.

The ability of a licensee to bring the product/IP to market and generate significant revenue in a timely manner is also an important consideration when pursing the option of licensing. For example, from the perspective of the time and money required to set up their own infrastructure, it may be deemed more prudent in some instances for promoters to license the IP around their process/technology to an existing product manufacturer rather than seeking to set up their own manufacturing, marketing and sales operations from scratch. Similar considerations also come into play where the IP in question revolves around a technology which forms the basis of a single component of a larger product. An example of this would be proprietary algorithms that underpin a piece of software that serves as the operating system for an electronic device.

In addition, in cases where IP has applications in number of different markets (both geographical and industrial) the promoters may seek to "slice and dice" the IP (i.e., grant use to a licensee in one particular region or for one particular industrial application and simultaneously grant another licence of the same IP to a different licensee in a different region or non-competitive industrial application).

Other considerations around licensing relate to whether or not to grant a licence on an exclusive or non-exclusive basis. Again, a number of factors will impinge on this decision including amongst others, the nature of the technology, the size and nature of the market and the number of potential licensees. However, generally speaking the promoters of the IP could expect to receive a higher royalty rate in an exclusive licence deal than could be achieved in a deal which was done on a non-exclusive basis.

The licensing route can provide valuable cash-flow in the short term for relatively little effort and provide for development of applications of the technology outside a company's core business. The technology being licensed may have a number of applications in industries that do not fit with the owner's expertise. Alternatively, the owner may not have the expertise or resources to exploit all the potential applications of the technology. He or she may wish to license it to a third party to exploit new markets. It may also be more cost-effective for a third party to manufacture the product in a local market than for the owner to distribute it. From the licensee's perspective, licensing a technology can provide an alternative to researching and developing the technology from scratch. It can, therefore, use licensing as a method to bring its products to market much more quickly.

Case Box 8.2 (MASTER): A licensing Success at RRI, Baycrest, University of Toronto[3]

Baycrest is a global leader in cognitive neuroscience and memory research, developing and providing innovations in aging and brain health. Headquartered in Ontario and fully affiliated with the University of Toronto, Baycrest provides a comprehensive system of care for aging patients, while hosting one of the world's top research institutes in this area: the Rotman Research Institute (RRI). Baycrest has successfully managed to leverage its remarkable complementary strengths in innovative care delivery and research by pursuing a unique commercialisation agenda.

For instance, researchers at RRI (Dr. Terry Picton, Dr. Sasha John, Andrew Dimitrijevic and David Purcell) have developed and clinically evaluated a new technology to allow hearing evaluation of people who cannot communicate and cannot "tell" you whether they can hear what you are saying. The technology, the Multiple Auditory Steady-State Response (MASTER), has been developed over more than a decade, and it is now used in hundreds of hospitals across the globe.

The (MASTER) technology monitors brain activity directly and eliminates the need for patients to respond verbally. Equally, as results are automatically evaluated by a computer, there is no need for extensive training for medical personnel and errors are less likely to occur.

Working together with Baycrest, the researchers at RRI have successfully patented, licensed and commercialised the technique through Bio-logic systems, today owned by Natus, a company that markets and sells its products in over 100 other countries. The revenue from the royalties of the licence for the (MASTER) technology is used to cover the costs of the research division at Baycrest.

Baycrest has now launched a commercialisation arm, which aims to introduce a competitive portfolio of aging-oriented products and goods, as well as consulting and development services to the international marketplace. To this end, Baycrest is partnering with over a hundred private and public sector organisations around the world.[4]

(iii) Formation of a new venture

The third main commercialisation option available to intellectual property developers is to create a spin-out or spin-off venture with the IP at the core of the new venture's product/service offering (see Table 8.2). This company will be a stand-alone venture with a completely independent legal identity to its parent organisation. There are numerous reasons why a company might choose to separate itself from the new venture to be spun off. For example, the spin-off of a large diversified business could enhance the total value of the parent shareholder's holdings, because it might be valued at little or nothing as part of the current corporate whole. In spinning off a more desirable unit, management may see a stock market opportunity where pure plays in specific sectors are highly prized by investors. For IP developed in an academic setting, a spin-out venture is often the route of choice for commercialisation.

Table 8.4 Licensing v. start-up

License	Start-up
Single application	Platform technology (multiple applications)
Once-off opportunity	Scalable business model
No management team	Creators have skills to commercialise
Finance difficult to raise	Clear funding mechanism
Strong barriers to entry	Clear route to market
Strong competition	First mover advantage
No desire of creator for business entry	Ip creator has aptitude for entrepreneurship

Regardless of the provenance of the intellectual property on which the new venture is based, in order to ensure its success it will be important to ensure that it is properly capitalised (i.e., funded). The sources of capital can vary in nature and size but, amongst others, often include funding from the parent organisation, institutional venture capital funding and private equity funding. Table 8.4 below highlights some issues to consider when choosing between forming a start-up company and licensing the IP to an existing company.

Creators of IP, such as inventors, may consider forming company for the following reasons:

- The market potential for the opportunity is worth the added risk;
- To participate in maximising the value of the technology;
- To work with an experienced entrepreneur who can lead the company; and
- They have contacts to create a business team and access other resources.

Where a start-up company is desirable, the owner typically licenses or assigns the enabling IP to the company in return for an equity stake in the company at a point where the company is capitalised sufficiently to pursue its business plan. Building a successful new business is very challenging and often requires a skill-set beyond the capabilities of those who created the IP in the first place. The stark reality is that a very large proportion of start-ups fail. Although creating a new company to commercialise technology holds the highest risk (Figure 8.2), it can also lead to the highest potential reward.

The first hurdle to forming a start-up is often the issue of seed funding. The process of creating a new company has more to do with the market opportunity than the quality of the science behind the technology. It often comes as a shock to inventors or first-time entrepreneurs attempting to promote the company that funding is not readily available and even where it is they may be asked to put their hand in their own pockets to fund the business. This is particularly the case for private equity funds. Angels, for example, as private investors, will want to see demonstrated commitment from the entrepreneurs.

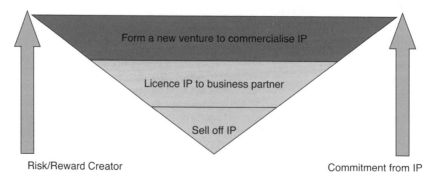

Risk/Reward Creator   Commitment from IP

Figure 8.2   Risk profile of different commercialisation options

8.4.5   The *Who* of Commercialisation – *Promoters*

Finally (and perhaps most importantly) it needs to be decided who should lead the commercialisation effort. In relation to service provision, in the initial stages of commercialisation this is generally led by the technical experts on an individual or team basis. Conversely, with respect to licensing or direct sales, although it may appear strange to some, an intimate knowledge of the technology itself is not necessarily a pre-requisite to this activity. Having this knowledge does not necessarily confer upon the knowledge-holder the ability to extract the maximum commercial benefit from the IP. However, knowledge of the markets in which the IP can be applied, allied to commercial experience and contact base within these markets is generally of far greater importance. This is not to downplay the role of the developer of the IP itself. Rather it is to emphasise that there is a particular set of skills that lends itself to successful commercialisation, which is not always resident within the individual or team responsible for the IP development. Thus the commercialisation effort should be led by an individual or team with a complementary set of technological and commercial skills that can be used to communicate and discuss key technical and commercial issues with potential customers/licensees.

There is often a tension for the inventor or owner of the IP in having to give up some level of control over the IP. No matter which commercialisation path is followed, the original creators of the IP will need to collaborate and communicate with others with different perspectives. For example, potential investors are often less interested in the core technology itself and are focused more on the market opportunity and financial rewards that it can bring. Commercialisation is often collaboration between people with different skill-sets and motives, aligned by common objectives.

Inventors need to be honest with themselves (Croteau and Whitehead, 2005) and others about their ability to commit to the commercialisation of their technology, which can take several years. If inventors are unable to commit to being part of a management team, then a licensing path might be the most appropriate commercialisation route. When creating a start-up, inventors must recognise their limitations and ensure they appoint a well balanced senior management team. Sometimes inventors believe their strengths as researchers can be equally applied to business management, in which case they are often most productive in the role of Chief Technology Officer.

Case Box 8.3   Theta Chemicals: A University Spin-out[5]

THETA, a privately held company, was founded in 2007 to develop and commercialise a novel technology licensed from National University of Ireland, Galway (NUIG) that allows the formulation of a range of soluble metal oxides. Prior to 2007 and within NUI Galway's Chemistry Department, the technology was financially supported by an Enterprise Ireland funded Proof of Concept project, which demonstrated the unique benefits of this novel technology. The TTO at NUI Galway, facilitated and promoted the process of commercialisation to engaging the facilitation of the spin-out.

The technology has a unique mechanism that out-performs anti-pollutant and anti-bacterial self-cleaning products currently on the market. The anti-pollutant coating is 50 per cent more active than the leading competitor product. The anti-bacterial coating remains activated in dark conditions. Application via wet chemistry and flash anneal process's deliver exponential savings in application compared to other methods.

Since, 2011, THETA has developed a platform of products based on this technology, which are now market-ready and commercially available. THETA have a unique development pipeline based on their patented solubilisation technology. THETA have taken this concept and have developed thin film coatings on a nano-scale to deliver functionality to a range of substrates for the steel, glass and ceramic industry sectors. THETA technology benefits industrial users and development partners who are looking for a step change in their coating performance and efficiencies of application.

8.5   PITCHING

8.5.1   The Seven Steps to a Successful Pitch

The ability to "pitch" one's commercial idea is of paramount importance. This has been explored extensively elsewhere (e.g., Clark 2008; Coughter 2012; Steel 2006). An entrepreneur or promoter of an idea or invention is invariably in "pitching" mode. This will include pitching the idea to venture capitalists with a view to securing future investment; or pitching the product/technology to potential customers with a view to making sales or striking a licence deal; or pitching the vision of a technology-based start-up to attract key employees. Specifically however in this chapter, we will focus on the pitch to investors. As illustrated in Figure 8.3, there are *seven* key steps to be considered in this endeavour.

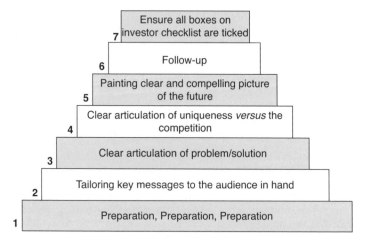

Figure 8.3 The seven steps to making a successful pitch to investors

Step 1: Preparation, preparation, preparation
The need to adequately prepare cannot be overstated. It is the foundation upon which a successful presentation is made. The promoter(s) should have a thorough knowledge of all facts and figures related to the proposed business. This will include all the important headline numbers including market size, projected costs, revenues, staffing levels, etc. as well as key operational and revenue milestones that are anticipated. An ability to communicate in readily understandable terms what is unique and valuable about the technology/IP will also be crucial (see "Technology" and "Working Knowledge" sections below). It will also be important to be able to clearly articulate the business model.

In particular the promoter(s) should focus on two different modes of pitching namely 1) a formal presentation (or "PowerPoint" pitch) in which slides that communicate the key messages are used, and 2) a succinct verbal "elevator" pitch (so-called to reflect the idea that is should be possible to communicate the key messages in the time span of an elevator ride). It is recommended therefore that considerable time be spent preparing both of these pitches and that the promoters avail of feedback from a number of "friendly" audiences and modify the pitches accordingly. Using "friendly" audiences in this way can also provide a useful mechanism to unearth the type of questions that might be asked by investors and present an opportunity to practise answering these questions.

Step 2: Remember your audience
It is important to always bear in mind the audience to whom the promoter is pitching and to anticipate what their background might be and whether or not they are likely to understand much about the technology in question. In many instances the potential investors will understand very little about the detailed nature of the technology itself but may have a much

greater insight of the impact the technology may have on the market once they have an understanding of what the technology does and what the potential benefits may be. With this in mind it is therefore generally a good idea in initial pitches to steer away from intricate details of how a technology works and instead emphasise what the technology does and how it benefits the end user.

Thus it is wise to have prepared a "layered approach" to messaging when communicating with investors. Typically promoters should be able to communicate the value proposition (as discussed in Chapters 6 and 9) of the technology/business to three different audiences as illustrated in Table 8.5 below. This enables the promoters to communicate the key messages in various levels of detail in a succinct manner as and when the occasion and circumstances demand.

Table 8.5 Layered communication of the value proposition

Audience category	Level of detail	Description	Example
General public/ investors	Low	The key concepts and value proposition should be easily understandable to a non-technical audience.	*We supply software to pharmaceutical companies which enables them to bring cancer drugs to market much quicker and cheaper than they could previously.*
Investors/ managerial level in target companies	Medium	The key concepts and value proposition should be detailed enough that someone with a broad understanding of the business area (e.g., an investor or senior manager in a target company) who although not necessarily a technology expert knows enough to understand the value you can bring to their particular company.	*We have developed proprietary algorithms which infer connections in cancer gene networks. This enables rapid target validation and early assessment of toxicity thereby reducing the expense associated with drug candidate attrition.*
Technology savvy individuals (e.g., Researchers, team leaders)	High	The key concepts and value proposition should be pitched at a technical level so as someone who is knowledgeable of the area understands exactly what the technology does and what benefits it confers.	*We have developed algorithms which are capable of inferring network interactions using noisy data and small numbers of perturbation experiments. This enables us to unravel the difference between network wiring in normal and drug resistant cancer cells to search for effective drug combinations killing both drug resistant and naïve cancer cells.*

Step 3: What's the problem? What's the solution?
Generally speaking, it is wise to first communicate that a problem exists in a particular market. This should be articulated in terms of the monetary and/ or social cost of the particular problem in question. Ideally, this should be a very high-level problem statement to which a potential investor can relate and should not be too bogged down with nuanced technical details. This should then be followed up with an explanation (again in non-technical terms) as to how the technology, product or service the company provides will help to solve this problem. It should also be clearly explained why this solution is better than any of the other possible alternatives (see also "Know Your Competition" section below) in this market. This message can also be underlined where possible by reference to a case study, a live product demonstration or video or screenshot or other appropriate means of "making real" the claim of superiority.

Step 4: Know Your Competition
As discussed in Chapter 7 (and also Section 9.6.1), it is important that the promoters know as much information as possible about those companies who can be considered their competitors. This will include their funding history, their key financial data, their customers, their strengths and weaknesses, how they are likely to react to a new entrant in the market, etc. Generally speaking there will be a considerable amount of publicly available material (e.g., website, marketing brochures, etc.) on the competition, which can be helpful to the promoters of new businesses in deciding how to present and shape their key messages. However, with this knowledge in hand, the promoters will need to clearly articulate why their own company's offering is superior to that of the competition.

Step 5: Paint a clear and compelling picture
Ultimately pitching involves telling a story in which a potential investor can believe. In order to make the story as believable as possible it is wise to appeal to the senses of the investor by describing what the company will "look and feel" like at a defined point in time (e.g., five years hence).

Giving a sense of what the company will look and feel like

- **Where will the company be located?**
  e.g., *We will be headquartered in London, with research facilities in Silicon Valley, and sales offices in Frankfurt, New York and Singapore.*
- **What will the staffing level be?**
  e.g., *We expect to have a team of approx. 45 people comprising of a senior management team of 7 people, a sales team of 15 people and approx. 20 people in R&D – the majority of whom will be PhD qualified.*
- **Who will the company list as customers?**
  e.g., *We envisage a customer base consisting of all the major telecoms companies in Europe.*
- **Who will be using the company's technology?**
  e.g., *We project that 1 per cent of all smart phones users will have downloaded our app.*
- **What will the turnover and profitability levels of the company be?**
  e.g., *We project a turnover of €85m in year 5, with a net profit of 30 per cent.*

Of course, statements such as those above will need to be underpinned by a strong business plan with credible assumptions and a viable execution strategy. However on the assumption that these foundations are in place, statements like these can help paint a clear picture to the investor of the potential of the company and give a clear sense of the scale of the opportunity.

Step 6: Follow-up

A single investment pitch very rarely results in an investor writing a cheque on the spot! Usually the pitch will lead to a series of further questions and clarifications for which the investor seeks answers. It is important therefore that these queries are processed as efficiently as possible by the promoters and that they continue to convey the best possible impression of the company and its management. It is also important to take on board the feedback from those investors to whom the promoters have pitched, especially those who have declined to invest. For example, this can offer valuable insights into areas of the business on which the promoters should focus their attention or how they might re-work or tailor key messages.

Step 7: Ticking the boxes on an investor's checklist

Typically speaking, an investor will seek to have a substantial level of comfort regarding key aspects of any investment proposition. These are summarised in table below and explored in more depth in Chapter 12.

Table 8.6   Key items on an investor checklist

(i)	Does the company have a team capable of delivering upon the business plan?
(ii)	Does the company have protectable technology which offers a clear advantage in its target market?
(iii)	Do the company's promoters have an explicit and tacit understanding of their target market?
(iv)	Has the company demonstrated progress and momentum since its foundation?
(v)	Has the company got in-built contingencies and options if things don't work out according to plan?
(vi)	Is there clarity on what money is required and when, to meet the objectives of the business plan?
(vii)	Is there a clear route to the investor exiting the company with a substantial return on investment?

(i) Quality and experience of the team

There is an often quoted maxim within the venture capital community that investors tend to invest in *people first* and *technology second*. Though the ideal of course would be to invest in a business with both a first-class team and a first-class technology, this somewhat whimsical statement does serve to underline the perceived (and actual) importance of the quality of the management team when it comes to driving a business towards success.

Investors will seek reassurance that any money they invest will be managed and used wisely by the management, and they will therefore focus on the experience, skills and track record of the key executives with a view to ensuring that the management team is capable of growing the business and delivering a handsome return on their investment.

Therefore, given the importance of the team, the personality and demeanour of the key executives (particularly that of the CEO) also plays an important role in determining whether or not the investors believe in the capacity of the group individual promoters to be integral parts of a successful team. Building a successful company is not an easy endeavour and therefore the vision, commitment, energy and ambition of the key executives are important to display and will influence whether or not the investors will part with their money. The degree to which the management team communicates and presents in a clear and articulate manner is also important as ultimately these individuals are the public face of the company who will be "pitching" to future customers. The investors, therefore, will seek reassurance that the team are capable. Also key will be whether or not the investors have good personal chemistry with the existing team.

Many businesses, particularly at an early stage in their development have certain skills-gaps in their management team. It is important that these are recognised by the existing promoters and that a plan to fill these gaps in expertise is clearly articulated to the investors. It is not uncommon for investors to make it a pre-requisite for their investment that these skills-gaps are filled or that certain individuals within the management team are replaced.

(ii) Technology

Investors generally like to invest in technologies which (a) confer a clear advantage over other technologies in a given field and (b) there is a clear and defensible position with regard to the associated intellectual property. Thus it will be important to show that the promoters have taken all the necessary steps to protect any IP that is critical to successful operation of the business. Some investors exhibit a preference for investing in so-called "disruptive technologies", i.e., innovative technologies that have the effect of transforming how traditional business and operation methods are undertaken (e.g., email in the age of post office mail). The potential for large returns on such investments can be great – although the risk associated with technology adoption by the market can also be great. Other investors seek technologies that have the potential for deployment across a number of industries thereby reducing the risk of exposure to a downturn in any one particular market.

(iii) Working knowledge of the market

Most investors will take it as read that the core team will deliver on the technological objectives of a business. Instead they tend to be more concerned that the promoters have an in-depth knowledge of the marketplace, understand how their products and services serve that marketplace and know why and how much their customers will pay for the solution that the company is offering. However there is an expectation of having more than just "book knowledge" of the market – i.e., knowing just the raw facts and figures. Rather, there is a huge value placed upon tacit knowledge an individual has of the marketplace. This tacit knowledge will generally have accrued from years of experience of operating within that marketplace and will have imbued the individual with subjective insights and an appreciation of the nuances of the business and its place in the market. While difficult to quantify or articulate, this tacit knowledge will often be deemed a crucial item on an investor's checklist and indeed an investor's own tacit knowledge of the requisite qualities of such individuals will often be called into play when making an assessment.

(iv) Momentum

Being able to show progress over a period of time enables promoters to make a much stronger case to investors than would be possible by just projecting forward from the point in time at which they make their presentation. Therefore, showing the history of the business and how the technology/IP and business has evolved over a period of time gives a valuable set of data points against which the investor can judge. For this reason, it can be advisable for promoters to meet potential investors at an early stage so as they can judge how the technology/business is developing and get a sense that they are being offered a chance to invest in a product/technology/business with momentum.

(v) Margin for error

Even with the best written business plan and great technology and great people, things rarely work out as planned for most businesses. In order to offset the risks of things going wrong and not working out exactly to plan, most investors will seek some in-built risk mitigation. Often this will lead them to invest in businesses in which the core product/technology can generate sales of very high gross margin. Alternatively, they may be willing to invest in companies in which the gross margin is lower but the volume of sales is likely to be high. Other mitigating features may be that the technology has applications in a number of markets thus enabling the company to "hedge their bets" against a downturn in any one market.

(vi) Funding requirements

A concern for many investors is that the company will run out of money before it meets key milestones. Depending on the monetary resources available to the investor, they may or may not have the ability to "follow" their initial investment of money and thus they risk having their shareholding considerably diluted by later stage investors. Thus many investors will weigh up these factors in light of the likely overall funding requirement of the company *versus* the monetary resources they have available to them. Therefore it is advisable for promoters to clearly show the amount and timing of likely future investments and demonstrate that through reaching specific technological and commercial milestones the company will be in a position to secure these later rounds of investment at as high a valuation as possible (i.e., obtaining the money in return for as little shareholding as possible to future investors).

(vii) Exit options and strategies

Two fundamental questions for any investor are: "How much money will I make?" and "How will I get my money out?" A clearly articulated and viable exit strategy should answer these questions. The exit strategy will typically involve one of two scenarios namely (a) listing the company on a stock exchange (called an Initial Public Offering or "IPO") or (b) selling the company to another company in the industry (known as a "trade sale"). The choice of which of these paths the business will take is dependent upon a variety of factors including the industry in which the company operates, the size of the company, the state of the economy at the time of selling. However, an investor will typically judge the opportunity presented to him/her against what other companies in this area have typically achieved in IPOs or trade sales. Typical metrics used for comparison include a "times sales" valuation (i.e., the multiple of a company's annual sales for which it was valued when it sold) or "times profit" valuation, i.e., a multiple of a company's annual profit for which it was valued when it sold). In this way investors can estimate what their shareholding will likely be worth based upon sales/ profit projections provided by the company.

8.6   CHAPTER SUMMARY

The chapter examined two crucial areas of commercialisation of innovation: first, decisions relating to routes for commercialising the IP to generate revenue, and second, planning the initial pitch to attract initial investment to develop the commercial idea further. As the IP and patenting issues had been addressed in Chapter 5, chapter 8 identified the possible commercial options available for commercialising their intellectual property. First, the chapter considered five fundamental questions: *Why* would an individual or organisation consider commercialising IP? *Which* geographical market(s) and customer segments should be addressed? *When* should they commercialise their IP? *How* should they commercialise their IP? *Who* should lead the commercialisation effort? The second part of the chapter identified the seven key steps to a successful pitch for investment in order to raise the requisite funds for commercialising a given technology. The end-of-chapter case study Celtic Catalysts Ltd next takes us through the challenges the founders encountered in commercialising his IP to the actual pitching of the technology to investors.

Case Study 8.1 Celtic Catalysts

Written by Dr. Brian Kelly.

Celtic Catalysts is a specialist supplier of niche chemical products and processes for the pharmaceutical and fine chemicals industry. The company's research and development operation and corporate headquarters are in Dublin, Ireland. The company also has a manufacturing site in the northeast of England, UK where it manufactures large-scale quantities of products using the technologies developed in its research facility in Dublin. The company is a spin-out from University College Dublin and was founded in 2000 with intellectual property developed by the group with Professor Declan Gilheany at its core. Professor Gilheany remains as the company's Chief Technology Officer (CTO) to this day. The decision to commercialise the IP was driven by one of Professor Gilheany's students, Brian Kelly, who identified a commercial opportunity related to the research he was undertaking at the time for his PhD.

The particular IP in question formed the basis for the creation of a potential platform technology that could ultimately render the production of certain pharmaceutical products much cheaper and much more environmentally benign than the production processes being employed by Big Pharma at the time. However at the time of Kelly's identification of the commercial opportunity, the IP was not at a sufficiently mature stage of development to bring directly to market and thus licensing it to a pharmaceutical or fine chemical player was simply not an option. Nor was it feasible for either Gilheany or Kelly to use the IP as the basis of a service that could be offered to industry clients. Having also unsuccessfully sought the possibility of winning grant funding to further develop the IP, Kelly and Gilheany decided to form a new venture called Celtic Catalysts and in-license the sub-optimal IP from University College Dublin.

> At that time, unlike now, the sources of public funding for research were pretty scarce.... so really we had no other option if we wanted to commercialize this IP – we just had to form a company and seek investment to develop the technology fully and bring it to market. (Brian Kelly (Co-founder))
>
> We had the makings of a really good platform technology, but there was no way anyone (other than ourselves) would license it at that stage of its development. (Declan Gilheany (Co-founder))

In these initial meetings with the investment community, it became clear that the initial business model on which Gilheany and Kelly had based the company did not stand up to intensive and rigorous commercial scrutiny. It was also apparent that their lack of commercial track record was a hindrance to their efforts in having their investment proposition being taken seriously or their business model and financial projections being credible.

> The first few occasions pitching to the VCs turned out to be very salutary – although at the time it felt like we were being thrown into the lions' den. However most of the VCs were very helpful and constructive in their assessment of our proposition and made recommendations on how we could improve the overall proposition in such a way as they might be interested in the future. (Declan Gilheany (Co- Founder of Celtic Catalysts))

The feedback received from their initial engagement with the venture capital world, gave the pair a roadmap for what they needed to put in place in order to make their fledgling company an investible proposition to the VC community. Top of the list of requirements was finding someone with experience in the fine chemicals/pharmaceutical industry to lead the company as CEO. The pair were introduced to Brian Elliott – a veteran of Big Pharma having over 20 years senior management experience with Johnson and Johnson and who had subsequent senior management experience with a successful Belgian biotechnology start-up called Tibotec. He agreed to help the company raise its initial amount of seed venture capital (of approximately €750k) and to subsequently act as a part-time CEO of the company. His involvement with the company helped to accelerate the process of securing this first round of venture capital funding. In securing the services of a new CEO, the company was also able to demonstrate a level of momentum and progress when revisiting potential investors who Kelly and Gilheany had met at the beginning of their commercialisation journey.

> Once we had brought Brian [Elliott] on board it certainly helped with the VCs. Neither our vision or our message had really changed all that much – although admittedly by that stage we were much better at articulating things in a much clearer manner than when we started out. However, the crucial thing was that what we were saying carried much more weight once we had someone of his commercial experience there in the room with us, backing us up. (Brian Kelly (Co-founder and Former CEO Celtic Catalysts))

With Elliott as an integral part of the investment proposal, the company secured its first round of investment from a Dublin-based venture capitalist (4th Level Ventures), who Kelly and Gilheany had originally met over a year previously. The funds raised were used to develop the company's core IP to the stage that it was market-ready. The company subsequently raised further funds to accelerate the roll-out of this technology in the marketplace.

Case Questions

1. What were the key factors which eventually led to Celtic Catalysts securing its first significant round of investment?
2. Comment on the main concerns likely to have been articulated by potential investors *prior* to the recruitment of the CEO
3. Comment on the main concerns likely to have been articulated by potential investors *post* the recruitment of the CEO
4. If they were starting again today, what would you have advise the promoters to do differently?

8.7 REVISION QUESTIONS

1. What are the main routes of commercialisation available to the developers of intellectual property?
2. What are the factors which influence the choice of commercialisation route?
3. Describe the key components required for making a successful investor pitch.
4. What are the key factors that influence a potential investor to invest?

8.8   FURTHER READING AND RESOURCES

Katz, J.A. and Green, R.P. (2011) *Entrepreneurial Small Business*. New York: McGraw-Hill Irwin.

8.9   NOTES

1. This case was written by Dr. Martin Hannibal, University of Southern Denmark, (SDU) Odense, Denmark.
2. The author was not permitted to disclose the real name of the company; hence a fictitious name is given.
3. This case was written by Gabriela Gliga, Marketing Discipline, National University of Ireland, Galway.
4. Council of Academic Hospitals of Ontario (2009) *Research Return on Investment: Case Studies from Ontario's Academic Health Science Centres*, http://www.ca-ho-hospitals.com/wp-content/uploads/2012/11/2009-Research-Return-on-Investment-Case-Studies-from-Ontario's-Academic-Health-Science-Centres.pdf; http://www.baycrest.org/about.php; http://research.baycrest.org/rotman; http://www.mastersystem.ca; http://www.natus.com.
5. This case was written by Dr. Neil Ferguson, Commercialisation Executive at Technology Transfer Office, National University of Ireland, Galway.

8.10   REFERENCES

Clark, C. (2008) "The Impact of Entrepreneurs' Oral Pitch Presentation Skills on Business Angels' Initial Screening Investment Sessions", *Venture Capital*, 10(3): 257–279.

Coughter, P. (2012) *The Art of the Pitch: Persuasion and Presentation Skills that Win Business*. New York: Palgrave Macmillan.

Croteau, M. and Whitehead, G. (2005) *Commercialisation Handbook: An Introductory Guide for Researchers*, The Intellectual Property Management Offices of Ontario's Post-Secondary Research Institutions.

DCU (2013) *Commercialisation Handbook: An Introductory Guide* for Researchers, www.dcu.ie/chemistry/asg/commercialisationhandbook.pdf (Accessed 15 October 2013).

Hindle, K. and Yencken, J. (2004) "Public Research Commercialisation, Entrepreneurship and New Technology Based Firms: An Integrated Model", *Technovation*, 24(10): 793–803.

McManus, J. (2012) *Intellectual Property: From Creation to Commercialisation – A Practical Guide for Innovators and Researchers*. Hanford, CA: Oak Tree Press.

Steel, J. (2006) *Perfect Pitch: The Art of Selling Ideas and Winning New Business*. Hoboken, NJ: Wiley and Sons.

8.11   GLOSSARY OF TERMS

Know-How: Closely held knowledge or skills required to do something; usually such knowledge is difficult to communicate by writing down or verbalising

Phase I (Drug Development): A clinical trial on a few persons to determine the safety of a new drug

Phase II (Drug Development): A clinical trial on more persons than in Phase I; intended to evaluate the efficacy of a treatment for the condition it is intended to treat; possible side effects are monitored

Phase III (Drug Development): A larger clinical trial of a treatment or drug that in Phase I and Phase II has been shown to be efficacious with tolerable side effects

Tenure: A permanent contract in a teaching or research post in an academic institution.

Venture Capital: Money invested in a project in which there is a substantial element of risk, typically a new or expanding business.

Chapter 9
THE MARKETING STRATEGY

9.1 LEARNING OBJECTIVES

After reading this chapter, you will be able to:

1. Understand the key steps in market strategy formulation
2. Apply the concepts of *segmentation* and *targeting* to new technologies.
3. Distinguish fully between consumer and organisational customers and appreciate the different market programmes for both types of customers
4. Formulate a value proposition of a new technology.
5. Understand the relationship between the positioning of the value proposition and the marketing programme.
6. Discuss the importance of branding and understand branding strategies available
7. Acquire solid understanding of each of the tools in the marketing programme: product, promotions, pricing and distribution policies for both consumers and organisational markets.
8. Appreciate the stages involved in the sales process for "solution" market offerings
9. Understand and explain the importance of fostering and sustaining customer relationships for conducting a successful marketing strategy.
10. Write up a marketing plan for the venture

9.2 CHAPTER STRUCTURE

The core elements of the chapter are as follows:

- Introduction
- The Marketing Strategy
- Segmentation and Targeting Processes – Stage One
- Developing and Positioning the Value Proposition – Stage Two
- Designing, Activating and Controlling (DAC) the Marketing Programme – Stage Three
- Product and branding decisions
- Promotions and communication decisions
- Distribution decisions

- Pricing decisions
- Marketing Plan
- Chapter Summary
- Case Study – HMS Ltd.
- Revision Questions
- Further Reading and Resources
- References
- Glossary of Terms

9.3 INTRODUCTION

This chapter presents the key analytical tools for inventors to conduct, design, implement and manage effective marketing strategy for a new technology. It addresses the tactical decisions related to using the marketing programme for delivering a value proposition and positioning it correctly in the minds of the target customer. It outlines the different marketing approaches for both consumer and business-to-business marketing markets and the importance of solution-selling processes and relationship building for organisational customers. Finally, this chapter highlights the marketing plan as a key output of the marketing process and activities required to deliver an effective marketing strategy.

9.4 THE MARKETING STRATEGY

The next big challenge for technology entrepreneurs is defining their initial customer base at which to target their value proposition. Although entrepreneurs have at the early stages of product development an idea of the likely use of their product, they must ensure that they identify and understand a market segment in order to successfully penetrate and grow their segments in this market. Having a "gut" sense of probable user and adopting a scattered approach is insufficient. Companies need to know the user profile, values, needs and how to access them amongst the vast landscape of technology users in consumer and industry markets.

As discussed in Chapter 7, organisations operate in very complex environments. While one of the most important goals for any business is to increase profitability, companies must also operate in such a way as to create, manage and sustain relationships with all of their stakeholders. Unless the internal goals of the organisations take into account the conditions in the marketing ecosystem and the requirements of the other stakeholders (see Chapter 7), the tensions of this imbalance will have negative consequences in both the short and long-term.

As shown in Figure 9.1, the marketing strategy involves three stages designed to deliver and implement the value proposition, develop customers and generate revenues.

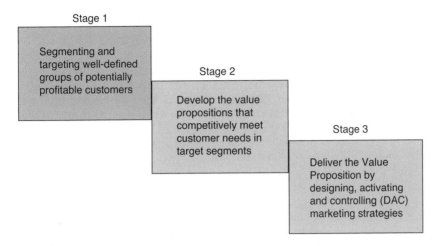

Stage 1

Segmenting and targeting well-defined groups of potentially profitable customers

Stage 2

Develop the value propositions that competitively meet customer needs in target segments

Stage 3

Deliver the Value Proposition by designing, activating and controlling (DAC) marketing strategies

Figure 9.1 Key stages of marketing strategy formulation

9.5 SEGMENTATION AND TARGETING PROCESSES – STAGE ONE

Market segmentation is the division of the market into different and distinct groups (segments) of customers (Smith, 1956). These groups or segments should comprise customers that share similarities and are hence more likely to respond in similar ways to the same marketing stimuli. Segmentation is the first crucial step in marketing, and the key towards satisfying needs profitably. It is often the mix of where-what-who and why (the core benefit or need) that is driving the segmentation. The grouping together of customers with common needs makes it possible to select target customers of interest and set marketing objectives for each of those segments. Once the objectives have been set, strategic marketing programmes can be developed to meet the objectives, using the tactical weapons of the marketing toolbox: product, price, promotion and place.

Entrepreneurs must define and characterise these different and meaningful segments in the market so that they can develop a value proposition and deliver it through the right combination of branding, product offering, price, distribution channels and communications. They should then be in the position to meet the needs and/or wants of a group and hence stimulate action. Segmenting the market effectively, be it consumer or organisational, should lead to the identification of segments or groups of customers, with identifiable differences (segment heterogeneity) and with clear similarities shared by the members of each segment or group (member homogeneity).

There are two key steps to market segmentation:

1. Divide and Profile customers into groups using segmentation variables for:
   - Consumer Markets
   - Organisational Markets

2. Evaluate the attractiveness of the various segments and company strengths to select a target market

Step 1: Divide and profile customer segments
Consumer Markets: For technological offerings aimed at consumer markets, there are various ways in which the market can be segmented. Usually a combination of different criteria is used when defining and dividing the market. The main four criteria used when segmenting consumer markets are illustrated in Figure 9.2.[1]

Organisational or Business Customers: As discussed in Chapter 7, business customers require different marketing strategies than consumers, and hence, segmenting organisational market requires different variables which can add greater complexity to the segmentation process. However, compared to larger consumer markets, organisational market are typically smaller in size and thus may require more targeted, direct sales-orientated strategies. This shall be discussed later in the chapter. There are two groups of interrelated variables used to segment organisational markets or B2B markets as shown in Table 9.1.[2]

A common segmentation strategy unique for B2B high-tech markets is segmenting vertical and horizontal markets. Vertical segments are homogenous segments within a specific sector, while horizontal can be cross-sector requirements with a common market need. For example, HMS Sweden serves many OEMs across different sectors using its network card that connects any device to any network for industrial manufacturing processes. Providers of CRM software platform applications typically opt for the horizontal segmentation approach to target each application for segments in a particular sector.

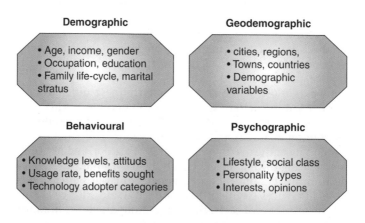

Figure 9.2 Segmentation variables for consumer markets

Note: When combining demographic and geographic variables, marketers get what is known as geo-demographics. This obviously leads to more accurate classifications of groups of buyers in the market. For an example of geo-demographic classification, visit EuroACORN, which is a consumer classification looking at the characteristics of local communities across Europe, available at http://www.caci.co.uk/EuroACORN.aspx.

Table 9.1 Segmenting organisational customers

Segmentation based on organisational characteristics	Segmentation based on buyer characteristics
Size and type of organisation Government bodies Commercial (OEM, User, SME manufacturer) Institutional (University; Hospital)	*Decision-making unit structure*: Numbers and departments in buying unit; location of procurement activities; purchase strategies; policies, procedures; regulations.
Industry/sector type (sic codes) Vertical, Horizontal sectors	*Choice criteria*: Ranking of attributes in order of importance for buying organisation.
Location by geography City, region, country	*Purchase situation of buyer*: New buy; modified rebuy; routine buy

Note: SIC codes stands for Standard Industrial Classification. These codes are a system for classifying industries by a four-digit code.

Case Box 9.1   Surecom NS Ltd: Segmentation Strategy[3]

Surecom NS Ltd
Established in 2005 with offices in Ireland, Greece, the UK and Australia, Surecom Network Solutions (NS) is a leading provider of engineering solutions and services to the telecommunications industry. With a team of highly skilled and trained engineers, Surecom provides a superior single source of managed services in the area of telecommunications engineering, in the highly technical business-to-business space.

Segmentation and Targeting Customers: Surecom focuses on the access network elements of telecommunications, which is at the high end of telecommunications engineering. An access network refers to the series of wires, cables and equipment lying between a consumer/business telephone termination point (the point at which a telephone connection reaches the customer) and the local telephone exchange. The local exchange contains banks of automated switching equipment to direct a call or connection to the consumer. Engineering work is outsourced from the operators and original equipment manufacturers (OEMs) to highly competent and highly qualified companies such as Surecom. Therefore, the segmentation strategy is based on identifying and building relationships with the technical/ services and commercial departments of the network operators and OEMs who are investing in upgrading and optimising telecommunications networks nationally and internationally.

Segment 1: OEMs – Surecom provides network analysis, planning and design services for its customers – from Radio Frequency (RF) and transmission to fixed and core network engineering design in the wireless and fixed-line business. The technologies offered range from the second-generation mobile phone system (GSM), all the way up to the newest, such as technology LTE (4G), Wimax in the RF sphere to Next Generation Network technology in the copper and fibre broadband networks.

Segment 2: Network Operators – Network operators want to focus on delivery of services, customer care and marketing activities to stay competitive. The cost and time involved in managing network build related functions, is increasingly being passed to specialist third parties. Surecom offer a comprehensive network operations and maintenance programme to include emergency fault resolution and trouble ticketing. Surecom's O&M offerings include network monitoring and field maintenance, structural climb-downs and site surveys, technical support and process management.

Segment 3: Managed Service Partners – Surecom offer fully managed network solutions delivered by highly trained professionals with extensive mobile telecoms market. Surecom provides a range of managed services, focused on one primary objective, lowering costs for our customers.

Step 2: Matching the attractiveness of segments to company strengths

Once segments have been identified, deciding which segments to target is the next step. The targeting process involves evaluating each market segment's attractiveness and selecting one or more market segments to enter. Directing the venture's marketing efforts towards a specific target customer group is a more effective and efficient process than adopting a scattered or fragmented approach. A scattered or fragmented approach entails trying to reach many customer groups without segmenting them correctly into proper homogenous clusters. The various groups identified in the segmentation process must be evaluated in terms of their attractiveness and profitability potential. These will have to be matched with the organisation's objectives, value proposition, capabilities skills and resources.

The following criteria can be used to evaluate segments[4]:

1. Measurable: Companies should be able to accurately estimate the size, the purchasing power and the profiles of the customers in a specific segment. Companies should also be able to identify the segments characteristics, its size and growth, thus ensuring stability over time.
2. Profit potential: The market segments should be large enough in order to generate adequate profits for the company targeting them.
3. Distinct: The segments must be conceptually distinguishable and should respond differently to different marketing programs. This means that companies can predict the response of the segments to particular marketing stimuli and market conditions.
4. Matching firm capabilities to segments: Companies should focus on those segments whose needs and wants they can best satisfy through the employment of their internal resources, competencies and capabilities. They have to ensure that they have the resources and skills available to design and deliver effective programs.
5. Defendable: Can the company successfully compete against other companies targeting the same segment? Companies have to consider the level of competition within each segment and assess the barriers and costs of targeting a specific segment. However, even if the company's' technology is superior to its competitors, having an insight into the reactions of competitors is important. Therefore the venture should examine external market conditions and competitors' marketing strategies in segments it wishes to target.

Decisions will then be made about whether each segment will be targeted with a specific marketing mix, or if several segments can be offered the same marketing programme (this is discussed later on in this chapter). Companies do not necessarily have to target multiple segments. Particularly for a new venture, one target segment may validate the launch of innovation into a segment. Another key question which is particular to consumer markets is: "Who is the *buyer*?" vs. "Who is the *user*?". This is relevant when there is a three-way exchange process, as described in the Introduction to Part III. Google Inc. was used as an illustrative example to identify Google customers as advertisers and commercial entities, but consumers are global users of search engines.

Positioning is the process by which marketers strive to design a value proposition, and an image, in the minds of their target market, so that it is perceived as distinct and important when compared to competing brands. However, positioning is based on customers' perceptions, and hence it can only be influenced by marketing activities; a product's position ultimately resides in the minds of customers and consumers. In order to develop a market offering with a strong and sustainable position in the marketplace, entrepreneurs need to have a clear understanding of customers, of the way other brands are positioned and perceived and how their brand can compete effectively against other brands targeting the same segments with other value propositions. This leads us on to developing the value proposition and designing the right marketing programme to deliver it to the target customers.

9.6 DEVELOPING AND POSITIONING THE VALUE PROPOSITION – STAGE TWO

In all kinds of businesses, "the needs of the customer by means of the product and the whole cluster of things associated with creating, delivering, and finally consuming it" (Levitt, 1960, p. 7) must be satisfied. Especially in high-technology venturing, marketing must "invent complete products and drive them to commanding positions in defensible market segments" (Davidow, 1986, p. 13). This was, for example, ultimately the key to Apple's recent success with its iPod technology. Apple did not just produce another MP3 player. It created a whole new way to access music online.

Positioning refers to the place that the firm's product occupies the mind of the consumer relative to competing products on important or determinant attributes (Ries and Trout, 1981). It is a process by which marketers try to create an image, or identity of its market offering in the minds of their target market, relative to its competitors in the same category on critical attributes. Market positioning is closely linked to human perception of a company's products and the company itself. In other words, it relates to how the target customers perceive the venture's value proposition and the venture itself.

Positioning is an important tool in differentiating a product from competing offerings and providing it with a clear identity in the minds of the target market. Table 9.2 identifies the key components to be addressed for formulating a positioning statement that will be placed in the minds of the target customers. Positioning the key attributes encapsulated in the value proposition (introduced in Chapter 6) can positively influence customer perceptions through an effectively designed and actionable marketing programe.[5] Entrepreneurs should establish how they want their products and venture's image positioned. As a first step, they need to identify their value proposition.

Table 9.2   Key components for formulating a positioning statement

For	[Target customers]
Who have	[Compelling reason to buy]
Our product is	[New product category]
That provides	[Key benefit (which solves problem)]
We have	[Key point of differentiation]

Developing the Value Proposition: As discussed in Chapter 6, one of the core components of the business model is the value proposition. Crawford and Matthews (2001) suggest that a company's value proposition should be developed along a range of five key attributes, *Product, price, ease of access, customer service* and *customerexperience/intimacy*. As shown in Table 9.3, a number from 1 to 5 is assigned to each attribute: 5 (dominant), 4 (differentiated), 3 (on par with industry), 2 (below par) and 1 (poor). A company

Table 9.3   Developing the value proposition

Attribute/ Value	Product, Service or Solution	Price/ Value	Access (channels/ distribution)	Customer Service	Customer Experience/ intimacy
Description	Technological performance, Expertise, Features, Quality, Innovation, Functionality, Adaptibility, Style, Design, Durability, Brand.	Competitive, affordable, value for money	Reachability, access, speed, efficiency, Integration, geographic scope	Ordering processes, procurement, flexibility, cross-functional expertise, after sales service Product staf Training	Intimacy; trust, fun, emotional and social benefits, community and environment
Example: Scoring for Apple Mac Range	**5** **Dominant Value**	**3** **Acceptance/ Industry norm**	**3** **Acceptance/ Industry norm**	**3** **Acceptance/ Industry norm**	**4** **Differentiating Value**

Source: Based on Crawford and Matthews (2001).

must not let its standing drop below 3. Thus, a perfect score would be 5,4,3,3,3.

To be dominant or differentiated on more than one attribute is excessive and reduces profitability. For example, as shown in Table 9.3, the Apple Mac Laptop range dominate on product (5) and differentiates on customer experience (4), while its competitor Dell dominates on service and differentiates on price.

These attributes can vary in importance depending on target customer needs. Having a superior technology is not enough; it needs to be delivered as a total marketing offering in order to develop a strongly defined VP for developing a competitive position in the target market; moreover it must be delivered through the marketing programme. It can be simplified as follows: Value = Technology + Expertise[2] + Customer[3].

Hence, all the elements of the marketing programme, not only promotion, can contribute towards the creation of a differentiated value proposition. For example, unique product features, a higher price to symbolise a higher level of quality, place – to signify exclusivity or convenience, etc. See Case Box 9.2 and 9.3 illustrating the Danish global venture Daintel's value proposition.

Case Box 9.2   Daintel: Danish Healthcare IT Company[6]

Daintel is a privately owned Danish Health Care IT Company, founded in 2004 by current CEO Patrick Hulsen. Daintel's main product is Critical Information System (CIS) by Daintel, a complete state-of-the-art and award-winning IT solution software suite developed specifically for intensive care units (ICUs) and anaesthesiological departments.

CIS is a fully integrated system, compatible with existing systems and allowing users access to all relevant patient data. CIS reads values from more than 650 different types of medical devices and monitors and tracks patients throughout the entire clinical workflow. This provides medical staff with a total patient overview: a chronological overview, patient's assessments and treatment plans, pictures and observations, all documented, updated and accessed with just a few clicks.

CIS helps clinicians improving both treatment quality and patient safety. Furthermore the integrated Business Intelligence module provides advanced statistics for both clinicians and managers, supporting the ongoing accumulation of clinical evidence and providing invaluable information to managers, who can optimise capacity utilisation in the ICU.

Since 2010 Daintel has 62 per cent market share for CIS in ICUs in Denmark. Daintel expanded its winning product to anaesthesiological departments in 2012 and is now looking to expand it further to haematological and neonatal departments. Following its phenomenal success in Denmark, Daintel is now expanding the availability of CIS to international markets. In 2012, the company won the first prize for "Best eHealth IT Solution developed by an EU SME", beating 97 eligible European SMEs who participated in the contest. They have also won the "Vaxtfaktor" competition in Denmark, being named the Danish company with the greatest potential for export in 2012.

Case Box 9.3 Daintel's CIS: Value Proposition[7]	
Attribute and Scoring	Description of Attributes offered
Product or service or solution 5 – Dominant Value	• Specialised HealthCare IT systems for hospitals • Delivers the best user experience • Integrated and fully compatible with existing systems • Increases patient safety and quality of care • Provides high-speed, high-capacity treatment pathway for patients with intensive care needs and complex medication
Price/Value 4 – Differentiating Value	• Increases capacity utilisation • Reduces staff cost • Reduces medication cost up to 30% • Repays investment in 12–18 months
Access 3	• Direct to Client – A full implementation of the entire CIS Suite can be accomplished in 3 months from start to finish • Designed to follow the existing workflow and routines in the departments. • Turnkey project implementation model
Customer service/ support 3	• CIS demonstration by Daintel's experienced staff • Website is easy to navigate, providing reach descriptions of the system and a video overview • Daintel offers a CIS training and video training is embedded in the different CIS modules. • Clinical staff need only 2–3 hours training in order to be fully proficient in the entire CIS Suite.
Customer experience 3	• Customer relationship facilitates individual hospital customisation and ongoing service support

9.6.1 Positioning the Value Proposition in the Minds of Customers

Once the value proposition is formulated, it must positioned in the minds of target customers. Within a positioning strategy, a market offering must be given an identity through these various attributes, or benefits, which together make the product what it is and differentiates it from competing value propositions. As a first step, the value proposition needs to be clearly defined and positioned in the minds of the target customers. There are several steps in the positioning the value proposition illustrated in Figure 9.3.

An important part of the positioning strategy is thus identifying the consumer's perception of a product, versus competing products, on important buying dimensions. This is known as perceptual mapping, and it is an exercise that helps companies to understand consumer preferences as well as important product attributes, assess competing offerings and their own product strengths and weaknesses. It also tracks changes regarding consumer preferences as well as identifying future trends.[8] (See also Chapter 7 on product testing methods, e.g., crowdsourcing, beta site.)

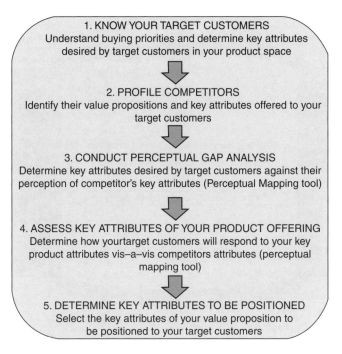

Figure 9.3 Steps in positioning the value proposition

9.7 DESIGNING, ACTIVATING AND CONTROLLING (DAC) THE MARKETING PROGRAMME – STAGE THREE

The elements of the marketing programme are used to develop competitive and targeted marketing strategies in order to deliver the value proposition to the target customer.

Figure 9.4 illustrates the components used to develop a targeted marketing programme to formulate tactical decisions and activities in relation to the 4 Ps – Product, Price, Place (distribution) and Promotions for consumer markets, and SAVE-R – Solutions, Access, Value, Education and – Relationships for B2B markets. For B2B markets, many ventures must embrace a more solution-oriented approach to serving target organisation buyers, given the complexity of the needs. Companies, particularly those with an engineering or a technology focus, find it difficult to move beyond thinking in terms of "technologically superior" products and services and should take a customer-centric perspective based on a solutions mindset throughout the organisation. According to their recent HBR article "Rethinking the 4Ps", Ettenson et al. (2013) suggest traditional 4 Ps irrelevant for business-to-business markets and suggest marketing programmes need to focus on solutions (product), access (place), value (price) and education (promotion). We develop the author's SAVE model and suggest that relationships be added as additional component to B2B marketing programmes. Figure 9.4 illustrates that a SAVE-R approach enables high-tech ventures to develop a marketing programme suited to organisational markets.

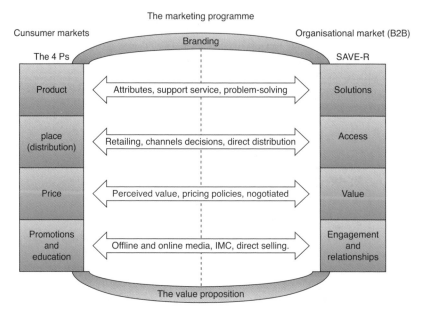

Figure 9.4 Components used to develop a targeted marketing programme

Note: The concept of SAVE[9] has been adapted and added to.

Each of the marketing programmes, whether it be consumer or B2B markets, must be designed to develop the correct value proposition for the target customers. The programme must be designed and managed in order to ensure the optimum combination of all the aspects that make a value proposition attractive for the target market. The decisions for designing the components of the marketing programme will be addressed in subsequent sections of this chapter.

9.8 PRODUCT AND BRANDING DECISIONS

A product is defined as anything that can be offered to a market for attention, acquisition, use or consumption (Kotler et al., 2008). A product can be a physical entity, a service or a combination of both if it fulfils its purpose successfully, that is meeting the needs or wants of customers and thus creating value. A service is any activity or benefit that one party can offer to another, which is essentially intangible and does not result in the ownership of anything. In the context of high-technology ventures, there are two types of core market offerings: a tangibly dominant offering (physical product) and an intangibly (service) dominant offering. Organisational markets consider the product to be more of a "solution" as its integrated combined offering of technologies and services adapted to the industry or organisational user (Ettenson et al., 2013). The term *product* is used to address both the product dominant and service dominant for consumer markets and "solutions" for organisational markets requiring more problem-solving attributes, yet retaining the key decisions to be considered under the product (below). Products must be capable of offering tangible and intangible attributes that individuals, or organisations, regard as necessary, worthwhile or satisfying, to an extent that they are prepared to exchange money, patronage or some other unit of value to acquire it (Brassington and Petit, 2013).

9.8.1   The Services Dominant Logic

In recent years many high-technology ventures have embraced the concept of "Services dominant logic" (Vargo and Lusch, 2004) in defining their products. The new dominant logic of marketing emphasises that customers are not motivated to purchase tangible products as ends in themselves but rather the value the ownership these products/services creates. Hence the service dominant logic focuses on viewing services as an integrated essential part of any good and marketing becomes a process of partnership with customers, seen as co-creators of value (Vargo and Lusch, 2004).

Mohr et al. (2010) suggest that technology can interact with services in various ways and at different degrees. Companies can:

- Augment high-tech products with service. Service revenue can be generated after product purchase, or the company might offer training, repair or maintenance contracts. In order for this strategy to work, the company must ensure that it has sufficiently trained service personnel and that it can balance service proficiency and core competency in product innovation.
- Offer pure high-tech services (e.g., contract research firms, IT consulting). This strategy involves considerations around the creation of a standard platform service (providing efficiency) around which customised solutions (providing customer value) can be offered. The company must also continuously invest in upgrades and training resources.
- Use technology to improve services in traditional products industries (e.g., self-service technologies, make supply chain more efficient).
- Use technology to improve traditional (low-tech) service industries (e.g., automate labour-intensive operations, such as ATMs in the banking industry).

9.8.2   The Product Anatomy

Products and solutions can be thought of as bundles offering different benefits at different levels. There are three basic levels. Each level adds more customer value. The most basic level is the core benefit. This is the actual technology or technology-based service satisfying core functional need. This can be duplicated subject to patent projection. Services cannot be patented. The second level wraps the core benefit with product attributes (unique features, performance, level of quality) and brand name, transforming it into an actual market offering. By offering additional customer services (customised expertise, after-sales service, training, installation, warranty, delivery, credit terms, etc.), the actual product is augmented. Selecting attributes required to augment the product is an important tool to differentiate the product from competing products. A key differentiating device used to underpin the core product attributes, the actual attributes and augmented attributes and build the reputation of the new venture's image and reputation is through effective branding strategies (see Figure 9.6) discussed in the next section.

9.8.3 Branding Decisions

A brand is defined as "a name, term, design, symbol, or any other feature that identifies one seller's good or service as distinct from those of other sellers" (American Marketing Association Dictionary, 2013). A brand also allows a company legal protection for its products. The legal term for brand is *trademark*. A brand may identify one item, a family of items or all items of that seller. If used for the firm as a whole, the preferred term is *trade name* (American Marketing Association, 2010). The purpose of the brand is to convey information to the customer regarding the products or services covered by the brand. Brands, whether they be company names, trademarks, labels, design characteristics, smells, sounds, visual images, etc. are tangible or intangible elements or attributes that are assigned to a set of products or services. To be meaningful, the brand should have some consistency of meaning across the assigned products or services.

A good brand says a lot about the underlying product or service. It can convey information about the product or service itself – price level, quality, features, functions, usability, robustness, design, etc. It can also convey information about the intended customer – young, mature, optimistic, adventurous, serious or perhaps artistic.

Many would argue that customers buy brands, not products. Brands are, for companies, a more important strategic device. Customers use brands to identify not only products, but also, the set of values embedded in those products and a level of quality they can trust. In high-tech markets, in particular, there is an increased level of customer anxiety in high-involvement purchases, and well-known brands can make a customer feel more confident about a purchase. Even though costly, branding strategies must be viewed as long-term investments. Within high-technology environments, the pace of innovation is always increasing, and the product life cycle is getting shorter. As a result, companies do not have a long period of time to build a strong reputation from scratch with each new product set. In this instance, branding should be based on the company's essential attributes, providing a constant and a context to which the customer can refer to with each new innovative value proposition. Each new product can thus be seen as a reflection of the overall company brand and the values it stands for.

9.8.4 Brand Equity

Strong brands are the major enduring asset of any company: they are valuable because they retain old customers (loyalty) and they also attract new ones through the reputation they have established. Brands with strong equity are expected to build and retain loyal customers and protect them against competitors. Brand equity can be measured in terms of its financial value to the company and/or the marketing value of the brand (Lassar, Mittal and Sharma, 1995). From a financial perspective, the brand is an item in the company's financial balance sheet. This financial value of the brand is calculated based on the net value of all the money the brand is expected to generate over its lifetime. Although brands can be the physical assets, it is the sum of goodwill, or reputation, of the brand that determines the financial value of a firm's assets. The marketing perspective of brand equity is based on the brand's image, values and the level of customer attachment and sustained loyalty to the brand.

Furthermore, strong brand equity carries high-brand credibility, enabling the company to launch new products and product lines more easily and to leverage the power of the brand (Kotler et al., 2008).

9.8.5 Branding Strategies

High-tech ventures can opt for one or a combination of the three key branding strategies (or policies) as shown in Figure 9.5. Typically, new ventures brand their product under their corporate name, and, as new technologies emerge from core product, they inherit corporate brand name. Corporate branding (using the company name as the brand) provides identity and stability and can be used with umbrella-branding policy. For example, companies often use this policy including company name, technology platform and then the product (e.g., Microsoft Vista Windows). Similarly, Google have pursued this brand strategy with Google Adwords, Google Maps, Google Chrome, etc. This is also beneficial if the new venture innovation has already been successfully launched and the subsequent launch of new products can piggyback on the reputation of a strong brand as in the case of Google and many well-known branded technologies.

The venture may decide not to associate their company name to brand their products and may choose a new brand to launch a product. The individual policy approach gives each of the product categories a different brand name. This policy is effective if the company does not want to be identified with the branded product, in the event that it fails. The opposite effect occurs with family branding (which is directly associated with company name or branded name given to products). *Corporate ingredient branding* can also be used when the new venture's "ingredient" is integrally related to the performance capabilities of the end product (e.g., Intel inside).[10]

9.9 PROMOTION AND COMMUNICATION DECISIONS

Also known as marketing communications, promotion is about informing, educating and persuading the target audience about the new venture and its technologies. A key decision is communicating the value proposition and the company to the target customer and equally to the stakeholders in the venture's value network (see Chapters 6 and 7 on the value network actors). First, the promotional (communication) tools are described. Offline tools

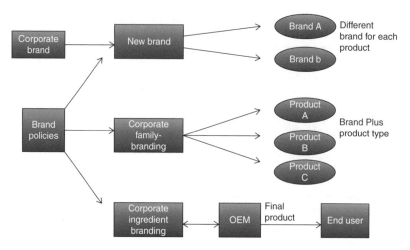

Figure 9.5 Branding strategies

are depicted in Table 9.4. Table 9.5 then presents the more recent web media platforms that have grown significantly in recent years and indeed are still evolving, in order to become more effective and to reach new generations of webophile users. Communication online through new media refers to technology-enabled advertising and promotion tools. New media has gained more importance as communication platform for technology products.

It is becoming more and more challenging as mass markets are more fragmented, and because of technological developments, customers are much better informed and have access to a wealth of data. They are more selective with the marketing communications they choose to pay attention to; they can easily generate positive or negative word-of-mouth about a product or a brand, etc. All of these factors point towards a significant shift in the marketing landscape today, and organisations must find new uses of interactive and engaging media in order to communicate with their customers effectively.

Because of all these fast-paced developments in the new media, and due to its increased popularity, the old media is today faced with serious challenges and therefore, companies must be more creative and entertaining in order to capitalise on it. The Internet empowers customers and provides them with self-service capabilities by obtaining information, comparing prices, finding alternative solutions to specific technical problems, attending online product demonstrations, checking delivery status on orders, etc. From an organisational point of view, the web can also increase efficiency: reaching more prospects at a lower cost through online product demonstrations, seminars or videoconferencing (Hutt and Speh, 2013). The key communication tools are shown in Table 9.4 below.

A key consideration when designing the promotional strategy for the technology is the type of customer market being targeted – consumer and/or organisational market. The difference in marketing communications between consumer and organisational markets is due to the intrinsic characteristics of these markets and the nature of the product (see also Chapter 7). Figure 9.6 identifies the most common tools that can be used within an integrated communications strategy for both consumer and organisational (B2B) markets.

9.9.1 Promotions and Education: Consumer Markets

For technology products in consumer markets, the key goal of promotion is to educate and inform the target audience before more persuasive actions are used. As discussed in Chapter 4, technology users fall into five different categories, and thus, a critical task for new ventures is to inform, educate and persuade target customers to adopt and purchase. Once adopted, the venture is then tasked with promoting their brand through promotional tools that best suit target and prospective users. As consumer markets usually consist of mass markets, where the product is typically standardised,

Table 9.4 Promotional tools – summary description

Advertising Print	Media advertising is any paid form of non-personal presentation and promotion of ideas, goods, or services by an identified sponsor (Kotler et al., 2008) transmitted through a mass medium, such as print, radio, television, billboards, targeted trade journals, etc. (Brassington and Pettitt, 2013). Advertising can reach geographically dispersed segments in the market. It provides for accuracy, consistency (can be repeated many times), and control, and it allows for a lot of creativity. Even though the entire expenditure for the company may be high, the cost per exposure is low, and it enables the seller to repeat the message many times. Advertising also makes brand and companies more trustworthy in the eyes of consumers. On the down side, however, advertising is impersonal, with no real flexibility in terms of specific targeting. Also, measuring results and obtaining relevant feedback is difficult and can be quite costly (conducting research – primary data collection).
Publicity and public relations	Publicity used for building good relations with the company's various publics by obtaining favourable publicity, building up a good corporate image, and handling or heading off unfavourable rumours, stories, and events (Kotler et al., 2008). Public relations is a management function that determines the attitudes and opinions of the organisation's publics, identifies its policies with the interests of its publics, and formulates and executes a programme of action to earn the understanding and goodwill of its publics. PR activities develop goodwill with customers, community, and stakeholders; public relations techniques include the following: innovation/enterprise awards; scientific publications (academic endorsements), press releases and conferences, various events (e.g., social events, charitable events/cause marketing, open days). By making a company/brand name known through news stories, sponsorships, and events makes prospects perceive them as news rather than as an effort to sell, and this provides extra credibility and hence value for the company.

Continued

Table 9.4 Continued

Sales promotions	Sales promotions or trial promotions encourage users to test the product before considering purchasing it or provides other incentives to encourage triability with a view to leading to eventual adoption and purchase. Sales promotions are more focused on product launches and introductions, and are more short term to attract customers' immediate attention. They have less of an impact in creating brand preferences (as compared to advertising and personal selling, for instance). Sales promotions include a variety of tools, including free product trials, monetary offers, sampling to incentivise prospects to test and use.
Personal/ direct selling	Personal/Direct selling is an interpersonal communication tool that involves face-to-face activities undertaken by individuals for the purpose of making sales and building customer relationships in order to inform, persuade or remind an individual or group to take appropriate action.
	Personal selling can be the most effective communication tool for a company, particularly in organisational markets and at certain stages of the buying process. Because it is based on personal interaction, personal selling is extremely efficient in delivering a message, and offers the sales person the opportunity of an individually customised communication with each prospect (fine-tuned targeting). It is also an excellent tool in building relationships with the customers and gathering customer feedback from the market. However personal selling is not always suitable, as it has a relatively poor reach, and it can be very costly. Also, it requires commitment on behalf of the organisation and the sales team.
Trade shows and industry events	Most industries organise annual business shows or exhibitions in order to display new advances and technological developments. This gives them the opportunity to present products and services to interested industry members and to network and establish contact with potential buyers.[a]
Relationship marketing activities	Creating, building and sustaining relationships with customers, as well as actors in the value networks (stakeholders), is critical and requires continuous marketing activity of the venture. Customer relationships need to be created, retained and managed carefully and attentively. This is also the case with industry actors in the value network such as suppliers, agencies, research institutions who are also key stakeholders. The venture must manage such relationships in order to enhance corporate image and credibility, as well for as building knowledge, market information and referrals and networking activities.[b]
Opinion leaders	Opinion leaders have become a key promotional and endorsing influence in both consumer and industry contexts. Key-opinion leaders are crucial in influencing the strategic promotional activities of firms operating in the highly globalised science and medical fields (Evers et al., 2012).

Note: For further reading, see Baines et al. (2011) and Mohr et al. (2010). See Evers et al. (2012). [a]For further reading, see Evers and Knight (2008).[b]See Chapters 6 and 7.

informing and persuading consumers about the product is mainly achieved through the impersonal channels of communication which are suitable. They convey a standard message (often carrying little information) and reach mass, aggregated markets, in a cost efficient way. Major non-person

Table 9.5 Online tools – summary description

Company website	For both markets, the company website is of equal importance. A company's website must be totally integrated with the company's value proposition, marketing communications and all other touch points representing the brand. There are several major factors to consider for a company's website, such as: The website design Search engine optimisation Webmetrics: The website's effectiveness – a website must be evaluated in terms of how many people visit and what their activities on that website are. Web analytics use log files in order to provide a lot of information on a website's activity. Online infomediaries: Subscriptions to business and trade directories and state agencies.
Internet advertising	Internet advertising and promotion include email ads, banner ads, search ads, referrals from another website, video ads and podcasts. The click-through rates on display ads have been decreasing over time; however new technological innovations allow today for behavioural targeting, where the ads being displayed are "targeted" based on previous online behaviour.
Web 2.0 technologies	Web 2.0 tools: social media; Social media includes social networking sites, blogs, podcasting, video sites and virtual worlds. These allow for search ads and embedded advertising.
Web 3.0	Web 3.0 brings a new generation of emerging technologies, such as artificial intelligence allowing computers to utilise the web independently of human intervention.
Viral communications	Viral marketing refers to the use of technology and its tools, such as email, mobile messaging and social media websites, in the spread of compelling marketing offers which is voluntarily passed around by consumers. This includes: Buzz marketing, a term designating word-of-mouth communications, which generate interest and excitement in a company's product Downloadable and interactive podcast and videocasts Virtual environments – still a very new area; companies are still learning how to effectively use marketing in virtual words, such as Second Life, and the niche markets they represent.
Mobile advertising	Mobile advertising refers to SMS or text messages – the mobile phone platform is used as an advertising tool, sending marketing messages to individual phones. Prospects can also get customised texts, based on their location (location-based marketing), through the use of GPS technology.

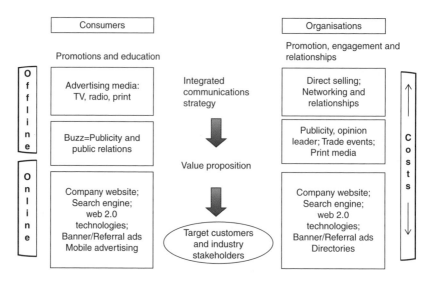

Figure 9.6 Promotions and Communication Tools

media channels include print media, broadcast media, display media, and online media.

9.9.2 Promotions, Engagement and Relationships: Organisational Markets (B2B)

Consumer markets are regularly targeted with mass communications, through impersonal channels, such as advertising and sales promotions. The organisational markets however need a more personal approach. That is the reason why the focus is usually on personal communication such as personal selling, relationship building, trade shows, exhibitions, technical seminars and presentations, etc. (See Figure 9.7). Personal selling is also reinforced by other promotional activities, such as trade shows, sales/trade promotions or catalogues.

As shown in Figure 9.6 above, personal selling and relationship management are the core promotional tools of the B2B context. Organisations usually consist of a few individuals, usually known to one another and customers, who purchase often complex, customised products, with a high risk and high value attached to it. Personal selling involves a two-way, personal communication between salespeople and individual customers (face-to-face, by telephone, through video or web conferences). Through personal selling, companies can demonstrate, explain and test their products in order to inform and engage their target customers. Personal communication channels are effective because they allow for personal addressing and feedback.

Typically in organisational markets, the sales people are the main link between the company and the marketplace; they are the ones who are the key relationship connectors.[11] They present the company to the customers and also take customer requirements and feedback back to the organisation. They also take the company's offer and tailor it to meet the specific demands of individual customers. They play an important and active role in managing the buyer-seller relationship.

Furthermore, the B2B marketing strategy for technological solutions is executed through personal selling, and the seller's image and ability to meet a buyer's needs are conveyed to a large degree by the sales force. Sales people are the ones who absorb much of the uncertainty on both sides, and through negotiations, reduce the conflict in the buyer-seller relationship. The salesperson is thus taking a key role in the customer relationship marketing program of the organisation (Hutt and Speh, 2013). Figure 9.7 captures the solution-orientated selling process that venture can follow.

In terms of advertising media both online and offline, organisational markets have their particularities. The advertising message, for instance, is more factual, focusing on problem-solving capabilities and key attributes valued by organisational customers rather than on the creative or entertaining side as it often happens in consumer markets. They usually include a direct appeal to action by offering product demonstrations and training. The message must also be specifically tailored for more or less technical readers (with different level of technical detail). In terms of delivering the message, the media channels can include trade publications, direct mail, interactive online solutions or a combination of these.

9.9.3 Integrated Marketing Communications

Because everything carries a message to the buyer, an organisation must be careful in managing all marketing communications contacts that may reach the target audience. A company should deliver a clear, consistent message about the company itself, its brands and its products and services. A well-integrated communications programme will ensure that the company's

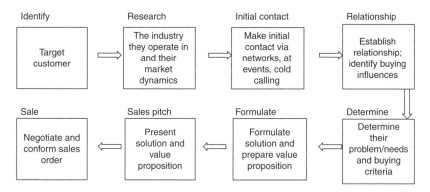

Figure 9.7 Solution-selling process for organisational markets

message is supported and reinforced by all tools employed in its promotional programmes, and all other brand contacts. In order to reap the benefits of reinforcement, companies must carefully analyse, plan, implement and control an integrated marketing programme. Each promotion mix is a vital part of the process that enhances the reputation of the venture and adds value amongst customers but also stakeholders. Hence, all of the promotion mix elements must be efficiently integrated under one strategic umbrella. Relationship marketing is the term used to describe the organisations relationships with its customer, and the wider community that have an interest in the venture's activity, and have commercial interest to the venture itself. An integrated communications (or promotions) programme needs to embrace a wider remit and extend beyond the technology product or solution and thus becomes a core part of the ventures business strategy. The IMC combined relationship marketing management of customer of business relationships in the value network must adhere to an audience-centred activity (Baines et al., 2011).

9.10   DISTRIBUTION DECISIONS

This section addresses issues around the planning of the distribution of the innovation (also referred to as *Place* in the 4Ps programme) for consumer markets and *Access* (in the SAVE-R programme) for organisational markets (Ettenson et al., 2013). Distribution includes all considerations involved in making the venture's technology available for use or consumption by the consumer or organisational user in the right place at the right time and in the right way. A *distribution or marketing channel* is the structure linking a group of individuals, or organisations, through which a product or service is made available to the consumer or industrial user. There are five key issues that the venture must consider in designing this element of the marketing programme.

Box 9.1   Five Key Decisions for Developing the Distribution Strategy

1. Determine the objectives, customer needs, product characteristics, external environment and competitors' distribution systems;
2. Determine the channel structures: direct, indirect, and/or hybrid;
3. Evaluation and selection of channel intermediary/ies;
4. Channel management, control and co-ordination; and
5. Channel performance.

These distribution decisions identified in Box 9.1 are discussed below:[12]

Decision 1   Determine the objectives, customer needs, product characteristics and the external environment

The organisational objectives of the venture and its external market conditions will determine the various channel options available to it and determine its distribution strategy.

Decision 2   Determine the channel structures: direct, indirect, and/or hybrid

The assessment of activities in the above point will determine the type of channel structures and intermediaries used. The three basic channel structures are illustrated in Figure 9.8. Within a *direct channel* of distribution, the goods move directly from the manufacturer to the customer. The main advantage of a direct marketing channel is that the manufacturer is in control and fully responsible for how the customer gets the product and how the entire marketing program is executed. This in turn facilitates the establishment and maintenance of a good relationship with the customers (CRM). A venture can engage in direct distribution by using their own sales force, their company website and/or by engaging in forward integration by owning their own retail outlets (for example, Sony or Apple retail outlets) to directly serve the customer.

In organisational markets, direct channels of distribution are usually the most effective and efficient as the number of customers is small and there is a high degree of interaction between the supplier (the manufacturer or the service provider) and its customers.

Today, most digital goods (e.g. software, information goods such as books and journals, entertainment products such as music or films, and services such as financial or travel) follow an online business model and distribution is therefore digitised. In developed economies broadband technology offers significant economic benefits to the venture, as goods can be distributed electronically direct to customers over the web and/or through e-tailers such as iTunes and Amazon. This enables good coverage and access and, as a result, facilitates intensive distribution as well as making the inventory and fulfilment costs almost insignificant.

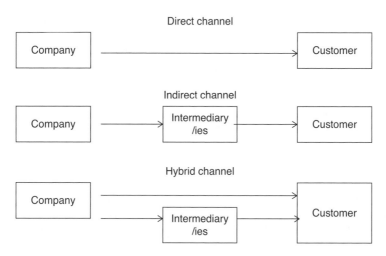

Figure 9.8 Types of channel structures

Within an *indirect channel*, the venture relies on intermediaries in order to transport the goods from production facilities to the customers. Companies prefer to retain as much control as possible; hence careful consideration is required if they choose an indirect channel of distribution. Even though the level of control decreases with the involvement of more channels and intermediaries, their roles and the tasks they perform add value in terms of costs, expertise and customer satisfaction (e.g., provision of after-sales service).

In a *hybrid channel structure*, companies often use a multi-channel distribution system (also known as hybrid or dual-marketing channels), consisting of a combination of direct and indirect channel structures. The main objective of hybrid channels is to increase market coverage. The underlying philosophy behind the marketing concept governs the choice of marketing channels. Hybrid channels are often a "must" as the different variants offer different benefits for different groups of customers. For example, by using both indirect and direct channels to serve international markets, Aerogen Ltd uses a hybrid structure to serve its organisation's customers. Through its direct channel, it serves the original equipment manufacturers (OEMs) and smaller manufacturers with its customised components and uses many distributors for its more stand-alone technology products. Aerogen Ltd (see Chapter 11 for Aerogen case study) sells its technological home device for consumer markets, which it launched in Canada in 2010, to a distributor who sells on to retailers of specialised home-use medical products.

Decision 3   Evaluation and selection of channel intermediaries

Determining one intermediary type over another involves careful assessment of customer needs (i.e. the desired customer service level specific to a particular product/service category and customer-price preferences), as well as organisational objectives and means (costs, desired levels of control and value added by specific channel members). Companies must identify and critically evaluate the alternative channels through which they can reach their target market. Types of intermediaries such as distributors, value added resellers (VARs) and systems integrators (see Figure 9.9) may be used as they can add value to the technology in the manner required by target customers. By joining forces, the different members of a channel of distribution each add value by fulfilling specific roles and tasks. Through this combined effort, they must ensure they deliver the assortment of products wanted by consumers where they want it and when they want it.

Depending on the overall marketing strategy of each individual product, the number of marketing intermediaries can also vary. For fast-moving consumer goods, for example, intensive distribution is suitable, meaning that the product is stocked in as many outlets as possible. However, exclusive distribution is appropriate for luxury goods, as the product must only be stocked with specific dealers associated with a particular element of exclusivity and prestige. In between the above options, there is selective distribution, where specialised intermediaries (more than one, but not all) stock the product.

Decision 4 Channel management, control and co-ordination

A critical task for the venture is to manage and coordinate its channel. Obviously, direct channels are less complex as the venture has full control of the product direct to the customer. However, for indirect channels, intermediaries can take over specific responsibilities.

In consumer markets, indirect channels can be comprised of different types of channel intermediaries, performing specific functions. Wholesalers buy from manufacturers and sell the goods and services to those buying for resale or business use. Retailers sell products or services directly to final consumers.

An effective distribution channel is based on close relationships between all those involved and leads to cost advantages and higher customer satisfaction levels.

However, managing multiple channels of distribution comes with its specific set of issues. A careful assessment of the different costs involved in each option must be carried out, together with a detailed description of tasks to be performed by each member in the channel, as well as possible causes of conflict. Legal issues and pricing margins must be further negotiated with the intermediaries.

Decision 5 Evaluating channel performance

Drawing on indicators identified by Mohr et al. (2010), we identify in Table 9.6 some of the indicators and metrics that can be used for evaluating channel performance, using intermediaries.

9.10.1 Distribution and TALC

In the case of high-tech products, the channels of distribution change as the technology life cycle (TALC) progresses (see Chapter 4), starting with a limited, direct sales approach for the innovators, as the company attempts to break into the market (see Figure 9.9). Once that is achieved, the early adopters become the target market, hence distributors are considered in order to expand the market reach. As the technology is prepared to make the switch towards critical mass and target the considerable larger early majority segment,

Table 9.6 Evaluation of channel performance using intermediaries

Contribution to venture's (supplier) performance
Contribution to venture's (supplier) sales and growth
Contribution of added value in terms of skills and expertise to venture's (supplier)
Compliance with regulatory and technical requirements of venture
Compliance with quality standards of venture
Adaptability to venture's technology and marketing programme
Loyalty and understanding of venture's strategic goals
Overall satisfaction with commercial relationship

Source: Based on Mohr et al. (2010).

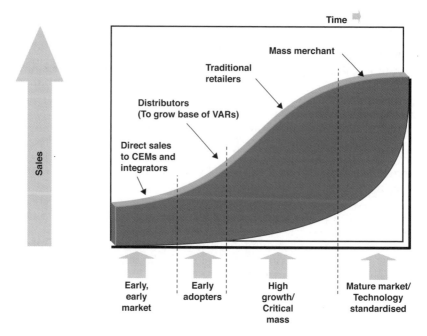

Figure 9.9 Evolution of high-tech channels

Source: Mohr, Jakki, J.; Sengupta, Sanjit; Slater, Stanley, *Marketing of High-Technology Products and Innovations*, 3rd edition, ©2010. Printed and Electronically reproduced by permission of Pearson Education, Inc., Upper Saddle River, New Jersey.

there is a parallel switch in the distribution channels towards the more traditional roads to the market. When the technology enters its maturity stage, and it becomes a standardised product, the distribution strategy addresses the remaining segments of the markets through mass market channels.

However, it should be noted that not all new high-tech products follow this pattern. If a new technology addresses a mass market from the very beginning (by having a wide application for personal use in the home, for example), it will go from the start through retailers (both traditional and online) that stock these types of goods.

9.11 PRICING DECISIONS

Price is the value customers are asked to exchange in return for the benefits that come with the purchase of a product or a service. Even though price is usually thought of in terms of money, there are many other facets of "value" that price incorporates. Pricing or assigning a customer value to the innovation particularly if it is radical, is one of the most challenging decisions for tech entrepreneurs. From an organisational point of view, price is the only tool in the marketing mix that generates revenue (the other 3Ps are all costs). It is often identified as a "challenge": setting the price too high can push customers towards competitor offerings; having a price that is too low might imply that not enough revenues (and ulti-mately profits) are generated. Price is also a communication tool – it delivers certain messages to the customers regarding their perception of value of the product or service. Price is also relevant in the positioning strategy; it communicates something about the product relative to other offerings on the market; it is also a competitive tool used to directly attack competitors' propositions.

The right price has to be primarily defined in terms of customer value. The price (the value they have to give) must seem fair to customers in rela-tion to the value they are getting in return in the marketing exchange. That is the reason why it is extremely important for the marketer to understand price from the customer's point of view. Of course, companies have to also consider the costs they incur in the process of creating and delivering a certain value proposition, as well as other internal and external factors that influence cost structures and hence the final price.

Price is also directly related with the level of demand in a specific market and as a result marketers have to assess price elasticity: how respon-sive demand will be to a change in price. A demand curve, as shown in Figure 9.10, is the graphical representation commonly used to show the relationship between price and demand. Under normal market conditions demand and price are inversely related – that is, the higher the price, the lower the demand; a drop in price would normally generate an increase in demand. In economic terms, this means that the demand is price elastic. If the opposite is true, and a drop in price does not cause an increase in demand, we say that the demand is inelastic.

In high-technology markets, cross-price elasticity of demand is also common, meaning that a change in the price of a product may in fact cause a change in another (complementary) product's sales.

9.11.1 Pricing in High-Tech Markets

Within the specific high-tech context, pricing structures become more complicated because of the rapid pace of change, the short product life cycle, the dependence of compatibility with other technologies and the very high costs of initial and subsequent R&D investments that have to be recuperated. Numerous internal and external factors affects price. The

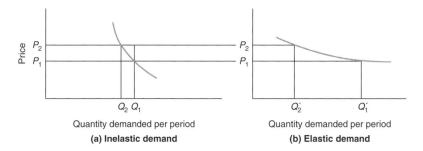

Figure 9.10 Price elasticity

internal factors are mirrored in the firm's own costs, marketing objectives and overall strategy. The external factors are broad environmental factors: the nature of market (the demand patterns), the nature of the competition, the state of the economy, government actions, etc. Furthermore, pricing policies should be considered from the early stages regarding a new product development process. We identify in this section the three main policies for pricing new products. We firstly draw on Mohr et al.'s (2010) three Cs to identify the main considerations when setting the price: Cost, competitors and customers.

1. Costs

Costs can take two forms:

- Fixed costs (or overheads); they do not vary with production or sales level.
- Variable costs; they vary directly with the level of production.

Companies have to cover their costs in order to survive and prosper. Costs in high-tech environments are more complex than in low-tech markets. As mentioned above, there are very high initial investment costs in R&D. This is also known as *unit-one costs*, referring to the fact that the cost of producing the first unit is very high. As production advances, the average costs will gradually fall, due to the accumulated production experience. As production rates grow, the organisation will learn to improve its operation: employees will become more efficient, the production process will improve and become smoother, procuring materials will become less costly as quantity increases and relationships with suppliers are developed. This is called the *experience curve* (or the *learning curve*).

Because of this drop in costs after the high initial investment (unit-one costs), quite often high-technology products are introduced on the market with high prices, which usually lower in time, as companies benefit from the advantages of the learning curve.

Companies' costs, as discussed above, can be thought of as the price floor – companies have to set prices above the floor to cover costs or else they won't be able to survive. In turn, the value customers place on a product can be thought of as the price ceiling – customers will only agree to pay a price in line with their perception of value; if the price is higher than their perception of value, they will not purchase the product or service. This implies that the right price must be found in between the floor and the ceiling, a price that brings in a profit for the company, while at the same time satisfying the value requirements for the target market.

9.11.1.1 Pricing strategy: cost-plus pricing

The simplest pricing method for new products is cost-plus pricing. This consists of adding a standard mark-up to the cost of the product; it is not the most sensible choice when setting prices as it does not even take into consideration the customer's perspective (it takes an inside-out approach, and it is product driven). The alternative is adopting a customer-based approach to pricing discussed below.

2. Competition

Competitors' prices and their reactions to their own pricing must also be considered when setting prices. The company should assess how their product or service compares with competitors' offerings and, most importantly, how the customer perceives the similarities and differences. In other words, benchmarking against competing value propositions has to be undertaken from the customers' perspective, as it is their perception that is the ultimate deciding factor amongst alternatives. Evaluating the competition should broadly extend beyond the borders of the industry, as in technology-based environments substitute products often come from other industries.

Because of the inherent characteristics of high-tech environments, companies also have to evaluate the dependency of their value proposition on other compatible technologies, as well as the existence of other technologies dependent on their own innovation. The establishment of an industry standard and the adjacent complementary products leads to an increase in the value of the entire system, which implies increased returns to the actors involved.

Another consideration in setting prices in high-tech markets is the presence of network externalities (the value of the offering increases the more people use it; e.g., social networking websites).

9.11.1.2   *Pricing strategy: competition-based pricing*

Competition-based pricing (also known as *market penetration pricing*) consists of setting a low initial price, which will attract a large number of buyers quickly and win a large market share. Selling more produce at low prices leads to quantity maximisation.

This approach is appropriate when:

1. The market is highly price sensitive and the demand is price elastic, meaning that a low price produces more market growth.
2. The product appeals to a mass market.
3. Economies of scale can be achieved: the costs of production and distribution are going down as sales volume increases.
4. The competitive threat is high, and the low price must be used as a tool to help keep out the competition.

As technologies mature, products become more commoditised due to a greater number of competitors entering the market. This inevitably leads to price competition.

3. Customers

As the final decision on whether the price is fair or not belongs to the customer, it is very important for the seller to think about price from the buyer's perspective. That is why a very good understanding of what the customer perceives as good value is essential. This takes us back to the marketing concept and the relevance of being customer-oriented in all marketing decisions.

As we have already discussed, the decision on whether or not to buy heavily depends on the customer's perception of value. In assessing the price, customers are looking at the products' benefits. These benefits may be:

- Functional: The design of the products and its ability to fulfil its promised function, e.g., increasing productivity, enhancing an experience, etc. The functional benefits are most attractive to technology enthusiasts.
- Operational: Reliability, ease of use, durability, ability to increase efficiency. In B2B markets, in particular, investing in a new technology would usually be assessed in terms of increasing productivity and efficiency.
- Quality: Quality judgments may be based on more tangible product attributes, such as better material being used, better processes employed or on intangible attributes, such as brand image or corporate reputation.
- Financial: Credit terms, leasing options. In B2B markets, new purchases are regarded as investments, and price is judged as good value when compared to the return on investment.
- Personal: Psychological satisfaction. These benefits are the hardest to describe and assess as they are based on intangible factors, such as self-image and status.

9.11.1.3   Pricing policy: customer value-based pricing

When introducing a new product, customer perception of value remains the main reference point. As we have discussed under the 3C framework, customers' perception of value is very complex, and it is a determinant factor in the buying process.

That is the reason why market-oriented organisations use value-based pricing, taking an outside-in approach and starting with the buyers' perceptions of value (a customer-driven approach). It is therefore obvious that price cannot be considered in isolation. It is an integral part of the marketing mix, in close relationship with the other elements within a marketing programme.

In making their choice customers will weigh the benefits against their own costs. In high-technology markets the customers' costs are higher than in low-tech environments. These costs include not only the price, but also the high levels of risks associated with adopting a new technology; uncertainty, risks of product failure, incompatibility with complementary products, obsolescence, etc. This process is also influenced by the customer's reference price; based on both their own prior experience and competitors' prices. By extracting the costs out of the benefits, customers come to a choice that represents the optimal value for them personally. In order to find out the right price, marketers must understand the different facets involved in these cost/benefit trade-offs the buyer goes through within a purchase decision. At the same time, pricing structures are loosely related with segmentation and targeting. Product benefits are valued differently by different segments in the market, meaning that different pricing strategies are needed when targeting different groups.

Market-skimming pricing is another approach to pricing new innovative products. It consists of setting high initial prices to "skim" revenues from selling to well-targeted segments in the market. Market-skimming is only appropriate when the following market conditions exist:

1. There are enough buyers who want the product and are willing to pay a higher price. This implies the existence of segments of customers who are less price sensitive and a price inelastic demand.
2. The product's quality and image supports its higher price. This is often accompanied by high differentiation.
3. The cost of producing a smaller volume is not detrimental to the revenue stream of the company. Equally, large cost savings are not expected at high volumes.
4. There are no or only a few direct competitors in the market and new entrants are not a threat, meaning that another company will not undercut the high price.

As these are pricing strategies for new products, companies must subsequently analyse the market conditions during the products' life cycle and re-evaluate the pricing strategies in line with the company's own resources, changes in the production process, changes in demand (i.e., the rate of adoption of a new technology), competitive conditions and other environmental factors.

9.12 THE MARKETING PLAN

As discussed above, the new venture's marketing strategy focuses on profiling a target market(s) and developing a value proposition around the technology by designing and implementing a marketing programme to satisfy that target market. When the marketing strategy has been formulated, it must be mapped out in the marketing plan. The marketing plan is a written document outlining and detailing all marketing activities in the marketing programme, including the implementation and control of those activities. Essentially, this plan serves as a written blueprint underpinning a new venture's game plan to achieve its marketing objectives and implement its marketing strategy. The marketing plan:

– Outlines the marketing strategy by specifying the target market and the marketing programme.
– Specifies tasks and responsibilities underpinning each element of the marketing programme (product, price, distribution, communication and sales strategy).
– Assigns responsibilities, required resources and timing for each activity.
– Determines required budgets allocated to marketing programme.
– Ensure sales expectations are realistic.

– Depicts metrics for monitoring of performance and evolving market conditions.

The marketing plan is typically included in the main business plan of the high-tech venture (see the business plan in Chapter 6). A useful marketing template guide, detailing the core components of the marketing plan, is found in the accompanying website.

9.13 CHAPTER SUMMARY

The chapter explains the steps for designing and formulating the market strategy for the technology created by the entrepreneur. It details the type of decisions related to each element of the marketing programme for delivering a value proposition and positioning it correctly in the minds of the target customer. It outlines the different marketing approaches for both consumer and organisational customers and how marketing programmes need to respond to and be implemented according to the type of customer that the value proposition is targeting. The marketing plan maps out the marketing strategy and activities underpinning the design and implementation of the elements of the marketing programme. The marketing plan can be included as a key component of the business plan but also represents a detailed guide for the venture marketing strategy implementation.

Case Study 9.1 HMS Ltd.

Written by Svante Andersson, Halmstad University, Sweden.

HMS (Hassbjer MicroSystems), a high-tech company situated in South-west of Sweden, was founded in 1988 by Nicolas Hassbjer. The company originated from a student project at Halmstad University for measuring paper thickness. Staffan Dahlström, who is the CEO today, was the second person in the company, and he was responsible for the marketing strategies in the company's first international expansion. The founders of the company realised the need to connect devices to different fieldbuses and industrial networks. Hence, the product "Anybus" was developed – a network card that connects any device to any network. The network card is designed for OEM (Original Equipment Manufacturers) and the product is integrated into industrial applications such as PLCs, Drives, Robots, Weighscales, Valves, Controllers, etc.

Already from inception, the company aimed for a global market, and Hitachi from Japan was one of the first large customers. Other important customers are Siemens, Rockwell Automation, Schneider Electric, Toshiba, Sony, Panasonic, ABB.

We got the advice from business counselors to start our internationalization in Denmark. However we thought, Denmark, it's no big market. Japan is much more interesting for our products. (Staffan Dahlström, CEO)

The company's core values are customer commitment, growth and innovation, long-term approach, building relationships and cost awareness.

In 2012, HMS had 240 employees and operations in ten countries: Sweden (Halmstad), Germany (Karlsruhe), United States (Chicago), Japan (Shin-Yokohama), Denmark (Copenhagen), China (Beijing), Italy (Milano), France (Mulhouse), UK (Coventry) and India (Pune). HMS has also distributors in more than 50 countries. In 2011, the revenue was 383.6 million SEK (42.5 million EUR, 59 million USD)

Marketing Strategies

The company started with little planned and systematic marketing research. The company originated from technology development and sales activities towards important key customers. The product was branded Anybus. Sales activities have always been in focus, and today a marketing communication department is supporting the sales activity in the company. Top management points out the importance of sales and customers.

> It is especially important for a technology oriented company as HMS to highlight the importance of customer orientation and sales. (Staffan Dahlstrom, CEO)

In the Anybus area getting large numbers of new customers is extremely important. HMS top management has identified four different phases in the sales process: the hot issue phase, the critical business phase, the win phase and the follow-up phase. A "battle room" is used to discuss how to go through the different phases. A team with responsible sales personnel and the top management team are all involved in the discussion in the "battle room".

> It is important that all members in the top management team are involved in our largest projects. A new large order affects all parts of the company including finance, R&D, HRM and production. (Staffan Dahlstrom, CEO)

Innovation and product development is also pointed out as an important cornerstone in the company's marketing strategies. With more than 30 per cent of the staff involved in R&D, HMS pioneers new technology and customises solutions for specific needs.

> Customers are good at incremental changes but not at radical innovations. We need to create a system to create radical innovations there. HMS is driving the process but still are influenced from the customers. (Jorgen Palmhager, COO)

Segmentation

HMS has two different main segments. These two segments are dealt with in different ways.

• Anybus

The largest segment is Anybus, which represent 70 per cent of the company's turnover. In the Anybus segment close relationships with customers are vital for sales. It takes a long time to sell in the product to a customer, but when the customer has chosen HMS's products, the accumulated sales turnover can be very high over the years. There are several thousand potential customers around the world and the product is either standard or custom made for specific customers. Communication systems are different in different nations and HMS can adapt it for different contexts. Field application engineers in HMS are working in close connection with development engineers at the customers to integrate HMS products inside customer's devices. There are many participants in the buying process, and it is important to influence and have good relationship with actors with different buying roles. Often the alternative to use Anybus is to develop the technology in-house by the customer. Therefore it is important to influence the in-house technician that Anybus is a better solution than their own developed technology, which can take time. Products are priced as a premium product and high quality is more important than low price. However when the products are sold in large volumes, the price per unit will be lower. The customer relationships for the four most important customers are managed by global key account managers.

- Gateway

The *gateway segment* constitutes 30 per cent of the company's turnover but is growing fast. Gateway are sold to electrician companies and there are hundreds of thousand potential customers in the world. It is too costly to have direct relationship with customers in this segment, so these products are sold via distributors. HMS tries to influence the distributors to focus on their products and to sell more by supporting with information materials and trade fair arrangements. HMS personnel is spending whole weeks by distributors to educate them in new products and taking part in customer visits.

Strategies for Developing Stakeholder Relationships

The relationships with the current customers are crucial as they are covering 90 per cent of the turnover. The large customer is very important for HMS, especially in the Anybus segment, and global key account managers are responsible for these. In this segment, nine international sales companies are dealing with the most important markets. Product managers are responsible for developed products, both regarding technology and sales. They develop manuals and educate salespeople. It is important to visit customers to listen to them and to present different sales argument for different actors with different roles in the buying process. For example, in contact with technicians, prototypes and videos are shown to present the technical advantages with the product. For person responsible for economic decisions, calculations are presented that show the value for the customer. There are also international differences in sales argument. In Germany and Japan technical arguments are important, while in the United States, economic and "value for customer" is more important. Distributors are key stakeholders in the Gateway segment. Important for building and maintaining relationships with key customers and distributors is education. HMS is offering education to customers and distributors. HMS has also sponsored a textbook in the industrial network area. This textbook is written of academic key-opinion leaders in the area. For a growing company, as HMS, financing is also vital. HMS strives for fruitful relations with banks, private-equity companies, and since 2007, the company is listed on the stock exchange. HMS also needs personnel to grow; recruitment and HRM are important factors. A good relationship with Halmstad University, with internships and student projects, is fostered to have a source for future employees.

Case Questions

1. How does the offer differ between HMS's different segments?
2. Which distribution channels have HMS in different segments? Discuss why they have chosen different channel strategies.
3. Describe and discuss the buying decision process by HMS customers?
4. Discuss the importance of different relationships for HMS development?

Case Study References

http://usa.um.dk/en/news/newsdisplaypage/?newsid=87a2c1c0–0acf-49d0–9e6c-
4877bf66ad96.

http://www.embarcadero.com/press-releases/daintel-builds-award-winning-ehealth-so-
lution-using-embarcadero-delphi-xe.

http://www.daintel.com.

http://www.itb.dk/Arrangement/Dokumenter/Daintel_præsentation_01062012.pdf.

9.14   REVISION QUESTIONS

1. Define market segmentation and discuss the basis for segmentation methods used in consumer and organisational (business-to-business).
2. Identify some examples of value propositions of established technology companies. Using Table 9.3, develop a value proposition for your own innovation.
3. What special distribution issues must be considered in high-tech markets?
4. What are the main elements of the promotional mix, and what do you understand by the term *integrated marketing communications*?

9.15   FURTHER READING AND RESOURCES

Baines, P., Fill, C. and Page, K. (2011) *Marketing*. New York: Oxford University Press.

Byers, T.H., Dorf, R.C. and. Nelson, A.J. (2011) *Technology Ventures: From Idea to Enterprise*, 3rd edn. New York: McGraw Hill.

Crawford, F. and Mathews, R. (2007). *The Myth of Excellence: Why Great Companies Never Try to Be the Best at Everything*. New York: Crown Business.

Day, G. S. (2000) "Managing Market Relationships", *Journal of the Academy of Marketing Science*, 28: 24–30.

Desai, K.K. and Keller, K.L. (2002) "The Effects of Ingredient Branding Strategies on Host Brand Extendibility", *The Journal of Marketing*, 66(1): 73–93.

Ettenson, R., Conrado, E. and Knowles, J. (2013) "Rethinking the 4Ps", *Harvard Business Review Magazine* (January–February), http://hbr.org/2013/01/rethinking-the-4-ps/ar/1.

Grönroos, C. (1994) "From Marketing Mix to Relationship Marketing: Towards a Paradigm Shift in Marketing", *Management Decision*, 32: 4–20.

Hutt, M.D. and Speh, T.W. (2013) *Business Marketing Management: B2B*. Westford, MA: Thomson South West.

Johnson, M.W. and Marshall, G.W. (2005). *Relationship Selling and Sales Management*. New York: McGraw-Hill/Irwin.

Kotler, P., Armstrong, G., Wong, V. and Saunders, J. (2008) *Principles of Marketing*. Harlow: Financial Times Prentice Hall.

Levitt, T. (1960) "Marketing Myopia", *The Harvard Business Review*, July: 7.

Mohr, J., Sengupta, S. and Slater, S. (2010) *Marketing of High-technology Products and Innovations: International Edition.* Upper Saddle River, NJ: Prentice Hall.

9.16 NOTES

1. See Kotler, P. and Armstrong, G. (2012) *Principles of Marketing,* 14th edn. USA: Prentice Hall.; Baines, P., Fill, C. and Page, K. (2011) *Marketing.* Oxford: Oxford University Press.
2. For further reading, please refer to chapter 4 of Hutt and Speh (2013) and chapter 6 of Baines et al. (2011).
3. Case Written by Dr. Breda Kenny, Cork Institute of Technology, Ireland.
4. For further reading on a useful tool to assess a segment's attractiveness relative to the new venture's strengths, see Day, G.S. (1986) *Analysis for Strategic Market Decisions.* St. Paul, MN: West, p. 204. It shows where the firm could potentially develop a competitive position in that target segment.
5. For further reading, see Ries and Trout (1981).
6. *Sources:* http://usa.um.dk/en/news/newsdisplaypage/?newsid=87a2c1c0–0acf-49d0–9e6c-4877bf66ad96.http://www.embarcadero.com/press-releases/daintel-builds-award-winning-ehealth-solution-using-embarcadero-delphi-xe.http://www.daintel.com.http://www.itb.dk/Arrangement/Dokumenter/Daintel_præsentation_01062012.pdf.
7. Used with kind permission of Daintel Ltd., Denmark.
8. For further reading on perceptual mapping tools, see Mohr et al. (2010) and Baines et al. (2011).
9. Ettenson et al. (2013).
10. For further readings, see Desai and Keller (2002).
11. For further reading in managing relationships, see Day (2000); Johnson and Marshall (2005); Grönroos (1994).
12. For further reading, see Mohr et al. (2010), chapter 8.

9.17 REFERENCES

American Marketing Association Dictionary (2013), http://www.marketingpower.com/_layouts/dictionary.aspx?dLetter=B. Accessed on 16 October 2013.

Baines, P., Fill, C. and Page, K. (2011) *Marketing.* New York: Oxford University Press

Brassington, F. and Pettitt, S. (2013) *Essentials of Marketing,* 3rd edn. Pearson, UK: London.

Byers, T.H., Dorf, R.C. and Nelson, A.J. (2011) *Technology Ventures: From Idea to Enterprise,* 3rd edn. New York: McGraw Hill.

Crawford, F. and Matthews, R. (2001) *The Myth of Excellence: Why Great Companies Never Try to Be the Best at Everything.* New York: Crown Business.

Davidow, W.H. (1986) *Marketing High Technology.* New York: Free Press.

Evers, N. Andersson, S. and M. Hannibal (2012) "Stakeholders and Marketing Capabilities in International New Ventures: Evidence from Ireland, Sweden and Denmark", *Journal of International Marketing,* 20(4): 46–71.

Evers, N. and Knight. J. (2008) "The Role of Trade Shows in Small Firm Internationalisation", *International Marketing Review*, 7: 1182–1198.

Hutt, M.D. and Speh, T.W. (2013) *Business Marketing Management: B2B*. Westford, MA: Thomson South West.

Kotler, P., Armstrong, G., Wong, V. and Saunders, J. (2008) *Principles of Marketing*. Harlow: Financial Times Prentice Hall.

Lassar, W., Mittal, B. and Sharma, A. (1995) "Measuring Customer-based Brand
Equity", *Journal of Consumer Marketing*, 12(4): 11–19.

Mohr, J., Sengupta, S. and Slater, S. (2010) *Marketing of High-Technology Products and Innovations: International Edition*. Upper Saddle River, NJ: Prentice
Hall.

Ries, A. and J. Trout (1981) *Positioning: The Battle for Your Mind*. New York:
McGraw-Hill.

Smith, W.R. (1956) "Product Differentiation and Market Segmentation as Alternative Marketing Strategies", *Journal of Marketing*, 21(1): 3–8.

Vargo, S.L. and Lusch, R.F. (2004) "Evolving to a New Dominant Logic for Marketing", *Journal of Marketing*, 68: 1–17.

9.18   GLOSSARY OF TERMS

Brand: Any feature that identifies one firm's products and services from another
company's product and services. These features may include name, design,
symbols, etc.

Brand Equity: A set of assets and liabilities that are associated with a particular
product or service. Brand equity is based on the brands image, values and the
level of customer loyalty.

Branding Strategies: High-tech ventures can choose from three types of branding
strategies; new brand, corporate family brand or corporate ingredient brand.

Channel Structure: There are three basic channel structures that may be used by
high-tech firms. These are direct channel structures, indirect channel structures and hybrid channel structures.

Competition-Based Pricing: Setting a low initial price in order to attract a large
number of customers initially.

Cost-Plus Pricing: The simplest pricing method for new products. This involves
adding a standard mark-up price to the cost of each product.

Customer Value-Based Pricing: An outside-in approach, starting with the customer's perception of value. This strategy is also influenced by the customer's
reference price.

Direct Channel Structure: The products move directly from the manufacturer to
the customer.

Distribution: The channels linking a group of individuals or organisations through
which a product or service is made available to the consumer.

E-tailer: A business that sells goods and services to consumers over the internet.

Fixed Costs: Costs that do not vary with production or sales levels; they remain
the same.

Horizontal Segments: Cross cutting sectors, which may have similar market
needs.

Hybrid Channel Structure: This consists of a mixture of direct and indirect channel structures.

Indirect Channel Structure: The firm relies on intermediaries to transport the product from the production facility to the customer.

Integrated Marketing Communications: Organisations must ensure that all of the information they communicate with their target market is integrated. Many organisations now communicate with their target markets through a variety of different channels. Organisations must ensure they are sending out the same message to their customers through all of these channels.

Market Segmentation: Dividing the population into homogenous segments of customers. The population may be segmented based on demographic, geo-demographic, behavioural and psychographic variables.

Market-Skimming Pricing: Setting a high initial price for the product/service, selling to the well-targeted segments in the market.

Marketing Strategy: Designed in order to deliver and implement the value proposition, develop customer relationships and generate revenues.

Positioning: A process where the marketers aim to develop a value proposition and an image in the minds of their target market that is distinctive and important when compared with competing brands. Positioning is an important element to differentiate a product from competing products.

Price: The value which the customer are asked to exchange in return for the purchase of a product or service. The price of a product or service must be seen as fair to the customers relative to the value they are receiving in return of the marketing exchange.

Product Anatomy: Consists of three levels: the core benefit, product attributes and the actual or augmented product.

Promotion (also known as Marketing Communications): Informs, educates and persuade the target market about the new venture.

Services Dominant Logic: Emphasises that consumers are not motivated to buy tangible products, as an ends in themselves. Instead, they value the ownership which these products and services create.

Targeting: A process whereby each segments attractiveness is evaluated. Once the potential of each segment is calculated, the firm can select one or more market segment to enter.

Variable Costs: Change depending on the level of production and sales.

Vertical Segments: Homogenous segments within a specific sector.

PART IV

GROWING AND MANAGING THE NEW VENTURE

IV.1 INTRODUCTION

One of the critical resource endowments for high-tech venture growth is technological capability. Firms with technological strength are more easily accepted by the market through differentiated product offerings (Zahra et al., 2006). However, innovation itself is not sufficient to create and sustain competitive advantage to grow and expand the business (Zahra and Bogner, 1999). So far we have discussed the key stages in the technology entrepreneurial process. Part I examined the macro-policy context of technology entrepreneurship and theoretical insights into the study of entrepreneurship. Part II examined issues pertaining to creating and managing the innovation, protecting it and then creating value through business model development. In Part III, we guided the learner on how to validate the market for their technology, choosing a commercialisation route and putting an effective value proposition and marketing strategy in place. Entrepreneurs are now faced with the challenge of determining how to grow their new venture.

The overarching theme of Part IV focuses on growing and managing the venture for sales growth, expansion and financial viability, with specific focus on three core areas: First, new ventures need to integrate and combine their technologies with excellent leadership and management of human talent. Hence, Chapter 10 addresses managing teams, leadership and organisational culture within a business. In high-tech ventures, knowledge is embedded in the intellectual capital created by people. A core task for the entrepreneur is to design and execute effective management of people. This requires entrepreneurs to leverage and manage the intellectual capital embedded in human resources, both inside and outside the organisation, as well as leading and nurturing an organisational mindset and culture towards growth and success. Second, for many high-tech ventures, internationalisation has increasingly become a growth strategy to enable the pursuit of larger markets and exploitation of new innovations to full fruition. Chapter 11 introduces the learner to international entrepreneurship and unravels the complexity of the internationalisation processes for the learner. Third, financial capital plays a critical factor in high-tech venture growth. Financial resourcing and planning is an instrumental resource valued primarily for the access it provides to other key resources required by new ventures (Brush et al., 2001). Chapter 12 examines how financial capital is sourced and managed to grow the business and equally ensure the venture is financially viable and can deliver a profitable return for the founder and investors.

The remainder of Part IV introduces the learner to some key concepts underpinning new venture growth.

IV.1.1 Defining and Understanding Firm Growth

Business-growth is essential for the survival of the venture. Business-growth refers to various measures such as an increase in a firm's total sales and revenue targets per annum, an increase in the production capacity, increase in employment and an increase in production volume. Annual revenue and profitability are the primary growth factors on the minds of most nascent techno-entrepreneurs if they want their business to survive and prosper into the future. Growth can shield the venture from resource deficiencies resulting from the liabilities of newness and smallness (Shelton, 2005). When planning for growth, for example, deciding exactly what to do to achieve your growth targets is a key question. High-tech businesses typically follow high-growth trajectories for harnessing their technologies. A business-growth strategy is how the venture achieves its growth targets; decisions made regarding growth are often impacted by both internal and external factors (discussed at the start of Chapter 10). Some of the key reasons typically limiting growth of the venture are lack of finance, unanticipated market decline, human resource issues and poorly executed management and leadership strategies of the entrepreneur.

IV.1.2 Types of Firm Growth

Many high-tech ventures that are in their early stages may follow two types of growth strategies; a combination of the two strategies is also a possibility. The first strategy, organic growth, refers to growing the venture by developing internal resources such as technologies, human capital, R&D for new product or service development (McCann, 1991). High-tech ventures typically follow organic trajectory paths, as their technology capabilities are internally orientated, hence placing emphasis on improving the firm's innovation ability through internal mechanisms such as management of people, knowledge, marketing and finance. New ventures can develop and manage these resources to grow the venture and ultimately attain growth targets as a result of strong leadership, strategic decision-making and robust and effective management of its resources. In high-tech ventures, knowledge is embedded in the intellectual capital created by people. A core task for the entrepreneur is to design and execute effective management and leveraging of people inside and outside the organisation as well as well as leading and nurturing an organisational mindset and culture towards growth and success. We discuss this in Chapter 10.

The second strategy, inorganic growth, refers to growing the venture through external partnering and is usually an extension of the venture's organic growth path. Inorganic growth strategies can enable the venture to leverage the resources and capabilities of external value partners through licensing technology or through other partnership arrangements, such as financial investors or venture capital firms. For example, with sufficient financial support, new ventures can effectively utilise their existing technological capabilities to continuously improve, upgrade and develop advanced products and processes. Financial capital, whether grown internally or externally, allows high-tech ventures to acquire resources from outside to grow and expand the venture and exploit international markets. As discussed in Chapter 6, partners can also be referred to as the value network and can form part of the business model. Many high-tech ventures can adopt a combined approach of organic and inorganic growth strategies to achieve their growth targets, depending on the capability combinations needed by the venture (Chen et al., 2009).[1] Both strategies require the entrepreneur to put in place a strong management team and a financial resource base that can support such growth and support market expansion.

IV.1.3 New High-Tech Venture Growth Model

Many growth models exist that map new venture growth.[2] Growth can have far reaching ramifications to many other aspects of how a new organisation is run. Drawing on Bruce and Scott's (1987) work, Table P4.1 captures how growth can impact other attributes of a high-tech organisation.[3] Most models have the "Survival" as Stage II. However, high-tech ventures would typically be expected to grow rapidly based on their innovation. If they do not manage to establish "Proof of Principle" with a validated market at Stage 1 (inception) to obtain investment capital, survival is unlikely.

Table IV.1 Four stages of high-tech venture growth

	Stage I Inception	Stage II Growth	Stage III Expansion	Stage IV Maturity
Stage in Firm Life Cycle	Emerging, nascent	Growth, competitors, new entrants	Growth, acquire/ takeover/divest/ IPO	Growth/acquire/ divest/mature/ declining
Challenges	Establishing 'Proof of Principle' for technology Sales pitching, marshalling resource, attracting finance Initial customer	Managing growth, ensuring resources, clarification and filling of roles, identification and prioritisation of ongoing research/ development areas	Financing growth, maintaining control	Expanse control, productivity, niche marketing if industry declining
Top management	Entrepreneur/team, direct supervision	Delegation, coordination	Delegation, decentralised	Watchdog, decentralised

Continued

Table IV.1 Continued

	Stage I inception	Stage II growth	Stage III expansion	Stage IV maturity
Innovation	Market validation completed pre-start stages.	New product development, market research	New product innovation, market research	Innovative operational practice
Market development	Single product; one target group; single channel; provision based upon core know-how/ technology	Extended product range; single market, increase distribution channels	Established Product portfolio; increase customer market segments and channels	Product diversification into new markets and channels
Operational controls	Simple bookkeeping	Accounting systems, control reports; simple performance and growth metrics	Budgeting systems, sales and production reports, delegated management	Formal accounting /control systems. Implementation monitoring, performance measurement
Financial sources	Personal, social ties, government agencies, venture capital, angel investors	Financial institutions, new partners, retaining earnings	Retained profits, new partners, secured long-term debt, venture capital	Retained profits, long term debt, IPO, private equity, merger/ acquisition
Liquidity	Negative	Positive but reinvested[a]	Positive with small dividend	Larger dividend
Capital investments	Patents, equipment	working capital, patents, licenses, premises	Acquisition of complementary technology; new premises, plant.	Operational maintenance; new technologies.

Note: [a] This is dependent on the sector. For example, this is not always the case for ICT ventures.

Source: Based on Scott and Bruce (1987).[a] This is dependent on the sector. For example, this is not always the case for ICT ventures.

IV.2 FURTHER READING

Chen, X., Zou, H. and Wang, D.T. (2009) "How Do New Ventures Grow? Firm Capabilities, Growth Strategies and Performance", *International Journal of Research in Marketing*, 26(4): 294–303.

Churchill, N. and Lewis, V.L. (1983) "The Five Stages of Business Growth", *Harvard Business Review*, 61(3): 30–52.

Gilbert, B.A., McDougall, P.P. and Audretsch, D.B. (2006) "New Venture Growth: A Review and Extension", *Journal of Management*, 32(6): 926–950.

IV.3 NOTES

1. Further reading see Chen et al. (2009) also identify "acquisition" as third growth strategy. See Gilbert et al. (2006) and Chen, X., Zou, H. and Wang, D.T. (2009).

2. See Churchill, N. and Lewis, V.L. (1983). "The Five Stages of Small Business", Growth. *Harvard Business Review*, 61(3): 30–52.
3. See Scott, M. and Bruce, R., (1987), "Five stages of growth in small business", *Long Range Planning*, 20(3): 45–52. This model has been recommended by Dr. Mark DeLessio and Dr. S. Vyakarnam in their paper "Growing the Venture" for Enterprise Tuesday at the Centre for Entrepreneurial Learning, Judge School of Business, Cambridge University.

IV.4 REFERENCES

Brush, C.G., Greene, P.G. and Hart, M.M. (2001) "From Initial Idea to Unique Advantage: The Entrepreneurial Challenge of Constructing a Resource Base", *Academy of Management Executive*, 15(1): 64–78.

Chen, X., Zou, H. and Wang, D.T. (2009) "How Do New Ventures Grow? Firm Capabilities, Growth Strategies and Performance", *International Journal of Research in Marketing*, 26(4): 294–303.

DeLessio, M. and Vyakarnam, S. (2012) "Growing Your Venture". Lecture note prepared for Enterprise Tuesday Centre for Entrepreneurial Learning 2012. University of Cambridge, UK.

McCann, J.E. (1991) "Patterns of Growth, Competitive Technology, and Financial Strategies in Young Ventures", *Journal of Business Venturing*, 6(3): 189–208.

Shelton, L.M. (2005) "Scale Barriers and Growth Opportunities: A Resource-based Model of New Venture Expansion", *Journal of Enterprising Culture*, 13(4): 333–357.

Scott, M. and Bruce, R. (1987) "Five Stages of Growth in Small Business", *Long Range Planning*, 20(3): 45–52.

Zahra, S.A. and Bogner, W.C. (1999) "Technology Strategy and Software New Ventures' Performance: Exploring the Moderating Effect of the Competitive Environment", *Journal of Business Venturing*, 15: 135–173.

Zahra, S.A., Sapienza, H.J. and Davidsson, P. (2006) "Entrepreneurship and Dynamic Capabilities: A Review, Model and Research Agenda", *Journal of Management Studies*, 43(4): 917–955.

Chapter 10

DEVELOPING TEAMS AND BUILDING THE ORGANISATION

10.1 LEARNING OBJECTIVES

In Chapter 5, intellectual capital (IC) was divided into human, structural and market capital, before discussing structural capital – intellectual property (IP) in detail. While important aspects of market capital were explained in the value network section (Chapter 6) and in the marketing chapters (7 and 9), this chapter is concerned with developing *human capital*: the availability of skills, talent and know-how of employees that is required to perform the everyday tasks of the business.

After reading this chapter, you will be able to:

1. Make plans for recruiting and developing entrepreneurial teams;
2. Know how to manage entrepreneurial teams through stages of development and growth;
3. Analyse and build a growth-oriented organisation; and
4. Develop and manage a learning organisation.

10.2 CHAPTER STRUCTURE

The core elements of this chapter are as follows:

- Introduction
- Analysing and Managing for Growth
  - Internal Conditions for Growth
  - External Conditions for Growth
- Building the Team
  - Composing Teams
  - Recruiting/Composing
  - Expectations and Agreements
  - Team Roles
- Leading the Entrepreneurial Organisation
  - Shaping Culture

- Leadership Skills
- Frustrations as Source of Innovation
- Reflective Leadership
- Entrepreneurial Network Organising
  - Network Organisation
  - Why Networks are Superior for Start-ups
- Learning From Success and Failure
  - Rapid Growth
  - Crisis
- Entrepreneurial Learning and Change
- Chapter Summary
- Case Study – Meltwater Ltd.
- Revision Questions
- Further Reading
- Resources
- References
- Glossary of Terms

10.3 INTRODUCTION

Why is it so hard to cope with growth? How can we build a great team? And, how can we learn more from failure? These are some of the overarching questions that we want to discuss in this chapter. The aim with this chapter is to make the entrepreneur sensitive to some of the issues related to human capital. First, those issues that are important to create a good team and a good organisation. Second, to help the entrepreneur avoid some of the pitfalls and main reasons for conflicts and failures seen in practice, many of which stem from the human factors: the development of the organisation and the team. Last, the connection between the principles of organising the team are discussed, which includes balancing the organisation and network on the one hand and the business strategy and planning on the other. The organisation and network are connected to the business strategy and planning by developing execution plans or operational plans that include milestones, goals and how to organise in order to meet those targets. An important aim is to understand what competence is needed – including what people, what partners and how to configure the organisation and its network – to deliver the value proposition to the customers. At the same time, change is inevitable, so the start-up firm needs to be flexible in how it solves issues, organises tasks and achieves its goals.

10.4 ANALYSING AND MANAGING FOR GROWTH

There are common challenges that accompany the development of a firm, including how to build and cope with growth. Entrepreneurial technology ventures have to handle limitations and barriers to growth and find ways to turn a shortage of resources (and sometimes experience) into an advantage for the company. The chapters on marketing and business modelling encourage exploring alternative strategies to growth, where venture capital is but one of several paths. Others include bootstrapping, strategic part-nerships/networking, specialising in a narrow segment, going for novel distribution channels, creating new markets and more. A crucial task for the entrepreneur is to develop and prepare the organisation and the team to handle the significant challenges of growth.

The literature states that high-growth ventures are fewer, but they tend to contribute with more jobs to the economy, higher value creation and often survive longer than companies without high-growth ambitions. However, the development of high-growth ventures is hugely challenging related to the mobilisation of resources (such as capital, knowledge and networks) and access to markets. Start-ups that seek international markets ("born globals") seem to be particularly exposed to these challenges (McDougall and Oviatt, 1991; Gabrielsson et al., 2008).

10.4.1 Internal Conditions for Growth

Internally, the technology entrepreneur may be limited by his ability to understand and interpret market opportunities and information (Casson, 2005; Sarasvathy, 2004; Kor et al., 2007) or by insufficient industry expe-rience. Thus the lack of ability to focus the efforts on the "right" aspects (Siegel et al., 1993) and, moreover, weak connections between strategy, leadership and organisation culture may limit growth (O'Regan et al., 2006). Perhaps the most challenging factor is that start-ups normally have limited resources (Barney et al., 2001) and limited access to capital, and thus they have limited control over the firm's growth process (Cressy, 2006). Davila et al. (2003) found that access to venture capital often leads both to economic growth and an increased in the number of employees. However, there are examples where too much capital may mislead the entrepreneur towards faster growth than the organisation is ready to handle (Bretteville and Solberg, 2009).

The principle goal should be to make money (i.e., through sales) before any money is spent. In the early phase of the start-up, costs need to be kept low while top competence needs to be available at the same time. A key challenge in technology ventures is often the balance between technology and business expertise in the team. The lean start-up organisation typically needs to hire services, whether complementary technological expertise, production capacity, administrative (like call centre services and accounting services) or others. A common pattern is to prioritise technologists early in the process and increases the management and marketing capacity later in the process. However, the emphasis on users' needs and a more proactive search for market opportunity supports including more business people earlier in the start-up process.

Later, when the firm starts growing and sales increase, its need to build the organisation is urgent. This is the time to hire people and build the organisation. In other words, once the company starts to make money, it is time to start spending money. The goal is not always to keep the "burn rate" low. Rather, it is to keep the burn rate low as long as possible, so when it is necessary to start spending money, it will be possible because the firm did not prematurely spend their resources. The point where most firms begin to spend significant resources is when the product is launched in the market on a large scale. Once the product or service is adjusted to the market conditions, the process of scaling up the firm may begin.

10.4.2   External Conditions for Growth

Start-ups will also meet different *external barriers to growth*. It may be hard to find a profitable position in the value chain (Dedrick et al., 2010), institutional conditions may be more or less supportive for business-growth (Fogel et al., 2006) and the company's network may be more or less able to provide access to resources and markets (e.g., distribution or access or certain customers, etc.) (Granovetter, 2000; Håkansson and Waluszewski, 2007). What can be done about this? Sarasvathy and Dew (2005) put emphasis on the entrepreneur's creativity and ability to develop new markets. By engaging with potential users during the innovation process, technology entrepreneurs are not only "finding" customers and markets but they are co-creating valuable products together with users, hence being part of shaping or developing markets.

When the technology venture starts growing, it will typically encounter a series of critical challenges and crises. A growth-oriented crisis may occur because the firm ran out of cash (which is why cash-flow management is so important in start-ups) or from a mismatch between market growth and organisational capacity (it is sometimes hard to build and train the organisation fast enough to handle rapid market growth). To avoid this, it is suggested to use scenarios to model the need for resources – employees, partners, facilities and cash – will develop over time. Typically, a set of scenarios are developed, either by varying a few critical factors to model the effects on the scenario, or simply by creating "worst", "best" and "most likely" cases to test the robustness of the company's business concept, organisation and strategy. An example of what to consider is, if the market is significantly smaller than expected, can the business still be made profitable? There is a vast amount of literature to explore in order to learn the art of scenario planning, such as Wade (2012). Sometimes unanticipated things happen that make planning difficult, and then the key issue is to learn and change quickly (see the "Learning" section below).

10.5   BUILDING THE TEAM

This part of the chapter discusses how to recruit and develop good teams. *Innovation management* is the process of managing innovation within an organisation. This includes managing people, ideas, information, initiatives, projects and all other aspects pertaining to innovation so that extra efficiency can be successfully added to a firm's activities and extra value can be added to the firm's value proposition for its customers. Misaligned expectations and interests, bad communication and conflicts within entrepreneurial teams frequently lead to low performance and even dissolution. However, with conscious facilitation of the team process, tensions may be exploited for creative problem solving. Research clearly shows that successful innovation teams are characterised by diversity and open discussion

(Van de Ven et al., 1999). This means managing entrepreneurial ventures is different from managing established and stable companies. This section provides advice on how to recruit and develop entrepreneurial teams and how to facilitate teamwork through a team's different phases. Motivational factors will be discussed, particularly how management emphasis on "inner motivation" may lead to high-performance and empowerment for skilful employees.

10.5.1 Composing Teams

Although different than a team working on a product/service at the mature phase, the team with the task of developing ideas into successful innovations is not very different whether in a start-up or an established company. *Entrepreneurial teams*, as well as teams in general, are often put together to solve complex tasks. As such, teams need to be composed of a variety of different competencies and experiences. The variety of expertise and skill sets is likely to create challenges and opportunities depending on where the right competence can be found. Variety is a key issue. The ability to analyse and tackle a problem from different angles provides the collective creativity that is needed. To facilitate collaboration, it is good for team members to have some degree of overlapping competencies. For example, it is not a coincidence that Silicon Valley – the global innovation hub related to information and communication technologies – collaborates with some of California's major universities for technology education and research (particularly Stanford, Berkeley and Caltech). Some areas in the world produce more human capital related to certain kinds of technology innovation and entrepreneurship than others, and different geographic regions thus provide different sets of opportunities.

In innovation teams, in addition to the variety of competences, there is a need for people to be able to move between multiple leadership roles. The top management of an entrepreneurial organisation needs to consist of actors able to take complementary roles (Van de Ven et al., 1999). Some need to support and nurture a creative climate and be sponsors to new ideas. Others, then, need to play the devil's advocate, to criticise the idea, to check whether it is robust enough, and whether it has taken into account the challenges that might come up. Therefore, a balanced variety of leadership roles and competences are required to encourage critical thinking and creativity to develop the best solutions. This team may be challenging both to compose and to develop.

Diverse teams are best for complex problem solving, and at the same time they tend to create tensions and conflicts. It will often be a challenge to understand each other across professions and experience. Technologists from different domains may attack a problem from very different angles and use different vocabularies to describe reality. Even more problematic is the common challenge to translate across the mindset of technologists and marketers. Their mindsets are made dissimilar by different education, different tasks and different time frames. For example, research and development (R&D) may take several years, while typically marketers' performance is measured weekly or monthly. The leadership skills needed to handle these conflicts constructively are the ability to facilitate good dialogue processes, create trust and clearly communicate the vision and the goals of the firm. At the same time, the entrepreneur needs to provide a lot of flexibility regarding the way to reach the end goal.

10.5.2 Recruiting/Composing

To recruit good teams is an interesting process of identifying talented people who are socially apt, display the right "entrepreneurial" attitudes to working pro-actively and flexibly, and have the right competence, experience and network. It is suggested that the priorities when recruiting should be kept in this order.

1. The team should be composed of talented people that are genuinely interested in the venture and their tasks. In this way, they will take responsibility for learning what they need to learn and to contribute in the best way possible.
2. When diverse teams are to solve complex problems, it sometimes represents a tough and stressful situation for the relationships between team members. Hence, it is important to have socially oriented people that are able to discuss and mediate interests along the way. This should not mean, however, that one puts together teams where all agree on everything, and look at things in too similar ways. Creative work in groups demands ability to view the challenge from different perspectives and angles.
3. Members of entrepreneurial teams need to show a clear entrepreneurial spirit, which means being prepared to work pro-actively and independently in finding ways to solve their tasks, as well as being learning-oriented in terms of not being afraid to explore issues and tasks that are unfamiliar.
4. Team members need a diverse set of competences. This may relate to their educational background, their work experience, and their social networks (see below). It may be difficult to analyse exactly what kinds of competences are needed when composing an entrepreneurial team. Therefore, it is important to analyse thoroughly what skills and competences are needed, while at the same time recruiting people that will be able to learn and take responsibility to solve a variety of tasks as they appear during the venturing process. The entrepreneur and the board should also consider changing team composition as the company's main challenges change over time.

10.5.3 Expectations and Agreements

Early in the team formation process, it is highly recommended to spend some time working together on clarifying expectations and ways of collaborating. Too many promising start-up teams failed or met severe collaboration problems because they did not do this properly. The entrepreneur should take responsibility to facilitate this process, where every participant needs to be actively involved in shaping the common work practice in the team. Even highly competent people are not providing much value without a good working climate. Central questions to discuss openly and create agreements on are, for example: How much time and effort is everyone expected to contribute? When tasks and roles are unclear, or when unexpected problems appear, how should it be tackled (and by whom)? When team members disagree, what are the routines for finding common ground or for making decisions? And, last, how are tasks delegated in the team?

Many technology entrepreneurs have problems delegating responsibility, as they want to keep in control of everything. However, this may have the effect that people stop taking responsibility and working pro-actively, because they expect the manager to intervene in every detail of their work. Skilled workers are also likely to get frustrated from detail-oriented management. Another source of frustration may be the need for making compromises on technological or business issues. Many technologists are driven by passion for technical problems (Knorr-Cetina, 2001) and may feel disappointed when decisions are made on business premises, while many business managers may feel frustrated and slowed down from "resistance" from technologists. Often there are important arguments on both sides, and the facilitation of good dialogue may provide the ground for better decisions. Through such discussions of team formation, the principles and expectations for working together should be agreed upon by the team members and documented. This will enable continuous evaluation and adaptation of the principles and expectations as the team process evolves.

In conclusion, the advice is to recruit good people, give them a degree of freedom and responsibility for solving their tasks, make agreements on how to work together, and facilitate regular arenas for evaluating, exchanging information and discussing the way forward.

10.6 TEAM ROLES

Related to the team formation, there is also the process of distributing and shaping team roles. This will normally happen whether one is aware of it or not, but it will be beneficial to be conscious about it in order to make sure important roles are covered, and to avoid role conflicts in the team. Ichak Adizes (2004) created a simple and useful framework of team roles to help assess and shape balanced teams.[4] He distinguishes between the need for doing things that work (effectiveness) and doing things without wasting resources (efficiency). He also distinguishes between the short-term needs and the long-term goals of the team. In this way, he comes up with four main team roles that fulfil complementary tasks: producing, administrating, entrepreneuring and integrating (PAEI).

The role of *entrepreneuring* in Adizes's framework (2004) means to identify opportunities in the environment of the firm. This is related to effectiveness and long-term goals. The entrepreneur will therefore also typically be the one to inspire the team toward the vision and to help focus resources towards achieving the longer term goals, even when short-term tasks feel urgent.

The role of *producing* is important, as entrepreneurs frequently need "doers" in their team; people that think practically about what could and should be done, and they do not hesitate in doing whatever it takes to move the venture towards its vision and goals. Similar to the entrepreneur, the producer aims for effectiveness, while focusing more on the short-term goals and results (Adizes, 2004).

The third team role, *administrating*, is more related to efficiency and short-term activities and goals. This is the role that typically will be concerned with how to solve the ongoing activities and will be instrumental in developing good routines and structure in the venture. It is easy to imagine how this role could come into conflict with the entrepreneur, as they are the most different: short- versus long-term goals, and efficiency versus effectiveness. When the entrepreneur has her mindset related to the vision of what is going to be achieved within the next one to five years, and the administrator feels strong responsibility for doing things right and without wasting resources, tensions may arise. Still, if the entrepreneur understands the importance of good coordination and efficient routines, and if the administrator does not forget why the company was started in the first place (the creativity and the vision), it is possible to balance and utilise the tensions in creative and constructive ways (Adizes, 2004).

The fourth team role, *integrating*, is often referred to as the most important role in many teams. They care for efficiency and mainly with a long-term mindset. While a start-up would be unthinkable without the entrepreneur, the integrator is the one taking particular responsibility for facilitating a good social climate. By making sure every team member feels valued and part of the collective while helping creation and coordinating collaboration, they are instrumental in creating and maintaining organisational culture and values. The integrator makes sure every team member has the best possible basis for doing a great job (Adizes, 2004).

It would be speculation to assume the typical pattern of technology entrepreneurs related to team roles. While some technology entrepreneurs are creative visionaries that enjoy the entrepreneurial role in a team, others may be more comfortable in the producing role having gotten into the entrepreneurial role out of necessity to mobilise resources or continue the technological exploration. Obviously, such considerations will have different implications for different start-up teams.

The PAEI and several other frameworks can be used to assess and form good and balanced teams. Many include questionnaires to test team members' understanding of the distribution of roles in their team (see *resources* below for references). However, it is important to be moderate in the interpretations of such assessment frameworks. It is not wise to categorise and lock people into roles. Rather, it seems as though people tend to choose team roles with partial attention to what is actually needed in the team at any given point. Hence, a person being the producer in one setting may turn out to be more of an entrepreneur or administrator in another where these roles are weak or lacking. In other words people are likely to have a repertoire of potential team roles they can play well. For the individual, this may vary from one team to another, and also in accordance with how a team and its tasks change over time. This may be good to keep in mind when working on developing the team during the start-up process.

10.6.1   Developing Teams

10.6.1.1   Team phases

Once the entrepreneurial team is assembled, it is important to remember that teamwork will benefit from paying attention to the team process throughout the development and stabilisation of the new venture. One can also expect the team dynamics and the team process to look rather different over time.

A common way of dividing a team process into stages is the *forming – storming – norming – performing framework* (Tuckman, 1977; Rickards and Moger, 2000). Team processes are never as tidy and linear as this framework. In fact, there is little evidence that teams have to go through stages in a particular order at all. Still, a framework like this can be useful to help reflect on and facilitate the development of the team. It may well be the case that a technology venture has to go through some or all of the stages several times, as the R&D activities often require different teams and team processes than the commercialisation activities.

The processes of composing the team and setting the stage for good teamwork as presented in the previous section resembles the *forming* stage in this model. Team members are often concerned with being accepted by the rest of the team and generally try to avoid things that may cause conflict or negative emotions. Instead, teams focus on the practical issues of forming the team and its tasks. Motivation and inspiration for starting the venture tend to be very high, but people will act relatively independently, and there is not yet a shared understanding of how to move forward. The entrepreneur will often need to be relatively directive in her leadership style in this stage (Tuckman, 1977; Rickards and Moger, 2000).

The next stage is the *storming* stage. This is the stage where people both have started becoming safer in the team, and at the same time frustrations may arise related to other team members. Different ideas and interests will be voiced and more competitive behaviour will be displayed. Some of the discussion will revolve around interpretations of what the task really is about. Team members may confront each other with discrepancies, and the boundaries between roles and functions may need re-negotiation. It may be good for the team members to know that this is perfectly normal and be prepared to deal with it openly and constructively. It is a time for letting the team grow together and prepare for tackling challenging tasks together. Teams that do not get through this stage may continue to struggle to produce results. Sometimes, the confrontations and discussions during this stage will reveal that team members' perspectives are too different for some topics. This makes it difficult to resolve conflicts and find common ground. Such teams will need reconfiguration. It is critical in this stage that the team establishes routines for collaboration and regular meeting points for evaluating both the business and the team process. Management needs to signal tolerance, acceptance and patience to team members in this stage, or else the team runs the risk of failing. A directive and accessible management style is common, hopefully leading the team members from tensions and arguments towards a stronger feeling of a joint project and purpose (Tuckman, 1977; Rickards and Moger, 2000).

The *norming* stage picks up on the clarification of expectations and goals in the first stage and takes this further. In the process of starting to work together and in exploring the entrepreneurial opportunity that was the basis for the start-up, the team members will now have gotten to know each other much more. They have become more aware of their own preferences and expectations, and they will develop more trusting relationships with their team mates. In this stage, it is important for the entrepreneur to maintain a strong focus toward shaping the culture and the values of the company, as well as to make sure that good social relationships develop. A mutual plan for the team, the settling of roles, and the taking of responsibility are desirable team goals to achieve in this stage (Tuckman, 1977; Rickards and Moger, 2000).

At this point, the team is likely to really start *performing*. Having gotten to know each other and having discussed roles and direction, it is now time to get the job done. Teams that positively progress to this stage are likely to become high performing. Team members know each other's strengths and weaknesses, are able to navigate and collaborate toward common goals and different opinions are aired and discussed mainly in constructive ways. Management now needs to become less directive and more concerned with facilitating and participating (Tuckman, 1977; Rickards and Moger, 2000).

For teamwork going on over a long period of time, such as a start-up process (often several years), teams may have to go through these stages several times as the main tasks and challenges change, as well as when the team composition changes over time (Tuckman, 1977; Rickards and Moger, 2000).

10.6.1.2 *Interdisciplinary team work*

We need to add a few notes related to interdisciplinary work. Most, if not all, technology innovation processes are characterised by being interdisciplinary (Mørk et al., 2006; 2010), and when the innovation is to be commercialised, the number of different expert areas to involve increases even more. The basis is, of course, knowledge. An inventor or entrepreneur needs to be aware that he cannot do everything alone. He does not have all the knowledge or the capacity he needs. A basic definition of entrepreneurship is "the pursuit of opportunity without regard to resources currently controlled" (Stevenson, 1983, p. 3). There is a shortage of knowledge and resources in almost all entrepreneurial ventures. Hence, there is a need to learn how to work across professions and organisations. The major resource of the technology entrepreneur for achieving the mobilisation of other resources towards realising the venture is the opportunity; the vision that sparks inspiration for different people to collaborate towards a common goal.

For instance, engineers' normal approach to their work is to go into an interesting problem, try to understand it, being fascinated by the technology or the technical problems needing to be solved. What typically happens then is that they tend to find a number of new problems that need to be solved. For every problem solved, ten new problems or alternative pathways may appear. Engineers are motivated by interesting problems and are very good at asking questions and challenging the status quo. This means that technology development tends to produce an increasing amount of alternative ways of solving things or alternative directions in projects (Hoholm, 2011). As discussed in Chapter 4, this may create tension with business processes where simplification and adaptation to user settings becomes important. As a leader, one needs to be able to translate knowledge across domains, across different work logics and languages. Engineers and scientists typically work over long time periods trying to solve complex problems, while marketers often need to sell their products within days or weeks.

10.7 LEADING THE ENTREPRENEURIAL ORGANISATION

To be an entrepreneur is to be a leader. Leadership is an art requiring vision, practice, relational skills and at least some level of self-reflection. As outlined in Table P4.1 above, the requirements of leadership and the organisational structure evolves with the entrepreneurial venture: (1) In the *inception stage*, the organisation structure is necessarily *unstructured,* as the team has to be involved in many different issues, of which many are related to creative and explorative work. Leadership is done in relatively small teams. Direct supervision works best, as everyone has to cooperate, and the entrepreneur should be able to keep good contact with all the others. (2) In the *growth stage*, the organisational structure needs development into more functional units/departments, while still executing centralised control, with the entrepreneur in contact with most of the team. Leadership is therefore moving towards more delegation and coordination work, while still having every unit report directly to the entrepreneur. (3) In the *expansion stage,* the organisational structure gets more complex, and hence, more decentralised control systems will emerge. Leadership, then, continues to delegate responsibility, but now in a more decentralised structure, meaning that indirect reporting and control will be developed. (4) Last, in the *maturity stage*, with a larger functional and decentralised organisation, leadership turns into a watchdog for the organisational culture and the overall vision and goals for the company.

We have seen many examples of entrepreneurs not being able to change leadership roles as the venture evolves over time. This tends to create a series of negative effects for the organisation, such as chaos, frustration, inefficiency and conflict. If, however, the entrepreneur understands this, it is clearly possible to be part of the growth, expansion and maturity stages and change along with the needs of the venture organisation: To go from doing "everything" yourself, via leading a small team, to representing the firm in external settings and taking part only in overall and strategic choices for the company.

There are some issues that are of particular importance for technology entrepreneurs as leaders, across all these stages. These are the shaping of organisational culture, the management of change, the handling of frustration and reflective leadership.

10.7.1 Shaping Culture

There is one point in the life of the organisation where it is clearly possible to shape and influence the culture of the organisation (Pettigrew, 1979). Management consultants tend to be overly optimistic related to the possibility of changing an established organisation's culture. In practice, this is very hard and may take several years. However, in the process of starting a new company, it is actually the entrepreneur and the team that are shaping the culture of the company, which will be there for years afterwards. The entrepreneur needs to be conscious about this and ask on what values and characteristics the culture should be based. Here are two principles to work from (adapted from Spinosa et al., 1997). First, there is the principle of matching leadership and organisation. The start-up team is modelling the organisational culture.

Case Box 10.1   Advanced Surgery[5]

Traditional surgery is in some settings falling out of practice due to the emergence of key-hole surgery (laparoscopy). The anatomy of the patient is the same, but the procedure is hugely different. Surgery is no longer a hand craft but rather is fully mediated through high-tech instruments, such as robots, cameras, etc. The skills of the surgeon must transform from the traditional methods of feeling and directly seeing the incision wound into the modern monitoring of 2D images on-screen while interpreting as if they were 3D. This change within the surgical industry created significant resistance from some traditional surgeons. As expected, the masters of the traditional practice resisted, because they are the best at performing the older surgical practices. And, they believe this is the best way. As a result, laparoscopic surgeons are becoming their own sub-profession within the medical industry.

Second, there is the principle of matching the organisational culture with the product (adapted from Spinosa et al., 1997). If we think about it, is it random what the culture of a fashion company should look like? Another example is to look at Apple. Apple was built as a rebellion against the bureaucratic way of working, which was strongly represented and supported by IBM and their huge mainframe computers. When Apple came up with the idea of having one computer per person, which could be put on the desktop, it allowed individuals to choose how to work, when to work and how to solve their problems, because they were in control of the technology themselves. It was a rebellion against the bureaucratic approach to work and organisation. To achieve this, it was important to build an organisational culture that could match that product. The Apple organisation themselves had to model the new way of working, the use of the new product and the values within which this product could have the highest use value. It was therefore connected with an informal, social working culture, where people would meet after work with a very friendly atmosphere while still being ambitious about achieving their goals. The leadership skills needed to achieve this goal were: to be consistent, to model the new practice (lead by example) and to have integrity to establish and to practise the values of the company in a trustworthy way. Innovation is about the recombination of resources and customers, always across boundaries. Entrepreneurial leadership requires the ability to see the world in different ways and to allow it to take on different perspectives.

10.7.2 Changing Practice

When developing an innovation, it often also requires changing user practices within which the innovation will be used. This is important to acknowledge, because innovating is to aim for changing social practice for one's own organisation, customers, or some other stakeholder. What the entrepreneur is then doing, without necessarily thinking about it, is challenging the existing ways of doing things, such as the established division of labour. Often such a new practice is both building on the established knowledge and practice, but it may also be destroying some of the established knowledge. While working with other disciplines, the product or service will be changed along the way. Many inventors have been frustrated and disappointed during such processes, as they see how interaction with other experts or users lead to changes in the product/service. Often this is necessary, so entrepreneurs need to be prepared to making compromises when their invention is changed as the result of encounters with other kinds of expertise. The leadership skills necessary to handle these possibly tense dynamics within teams are: conflict negotiation, the ability to make good compromises or synergies, meditation skills to create understanding, and motivation and inspiration to achieve the vision through a holistic picture of the project.

10.7.3 Frustrations as Source of Innovation

Gilder (1992, in Spinosa et al., 1997) researched the characteristics of successful entrepreneurs and found that they were characterised by three particular deeds: They showed humility, particularly to the fact that others could know more than themselves. They were generous, in the sense that they had a genuine wish to contribute with something positive with their business. And last, they were very committed to realising the venture, to the extent that they would invest a lot of their time and resources for an extended period of time. However, these are deeds we can find in many different people. Spinosa et al. (1997) asked what the more unique aspects to entrepreneurs were. They argue that it is the ability to *not settle with frustrations* that makes the difference. This is a rare ability. Everyday frustrations, as well as frustrating problems in their professional setting (e.g., technological problems), have thereby been the source of many successful innovations and ventures. This contrasts with what most people tend to do; when they meet barriers and other frustrating issues in their daily lives, people commonly start the process of normalising the problem – "it is just the way it is". Thereby, the problem gradually disappears from sight, as the individual gets used to it being there. In many cases the entrepreneur insists that what he experiences as frustrating should have been different. By insisting on this, keeping it in view, he will gradually start interacting with others around the problem, talk about it and often interesting and innovative solutions to the problem may emerge over some time. What one person experiences as frustrating often proves to be frustrating to others too; this may initiate the development of innovations and building a business around a value proposition that is truly valuable. At the same time, the challenge is to both focus on what is novel and different, while at the same time emphasise how it connects to what already exists, i.e., the more common and recognisable features of the innovation.

10.7.4 Reflective Leadership

The leadership requirements during the many stages of an entrepreneurial start-up are likely to change significantly over time. Entrepreneurs will therefore benefit from reflecting on their own role in the company from time to time. What is needed? What kind of leadership is needed at different points in time? We have seen many technology entrepreneurs being kicked out of the company after the start-up phase because the investors or the rest of the team are not satisfied with the entrepreneur and his nurturing of a creative chaos, not only in the beginning but also when the firm starts growing and gradually will need more structure. We have seen other entrepreneurs that are able to change according to the changing needs of the company, transform from being the creative entrepreneur living in a creative chaos where all team members need to contribute with many different tasks towards a more structured approach where he is the manager of a growing team. And then into a big corporation where there are other people to perform almost every task in the company, but the entrepreneur will still have to maintain the vision, in addition to representing the company externally – a "symbolic" leader. It is demanding to be able to handle all these different roles in a good way. It may therefore be sensible for some entrepreneurs to acknowledge that they are not good at everything, and at some point perhaps leave the CEO role to someone else. Hence, entrepreneurial leaders need to have a certain degree of self-reflection and ability to analyse what the situation demands. He needs to be open for feedback and criticism and find a good balance between flexibility and firmness.

10.8 ENTREPRENEURIAL NETWORK ORGANISING

10.8.1 Network Organisation

The entrepreneurial venture is often organised in a highly networked set of relationships. Hence, in most cases it is not relevant to delimit our understanding of the entrepreneurial organisation to the legal entity (the firm) that is registered with the government institutions. In practice the venturing process will move in and out of that setting, in and out of various networks; when mobilising resources, when developing the product, when exploring distribution channels and when investigating ways of financing the venture, everything happen not just within the company, it happens in networks.

The fact that the entrepreneurial venture consists of a number of relationships external to the legal entity of the firm means that the crucial question is not what is found within the firm, it is rather what kind of resources it is able to mobilise. So, it does not mean that the company has to own all important resources but that it is able to mobilise them in its network. The crucial questions, then, are: How to use others? What can partners contribute with (Håkansson and Waluszewski, 2007)? In social networks (between individuals) we can distinguish between strong and weak ties (Granovetter, 1983). Strong ties are relations to the people you know well, such as your friends, your family and your business partners. This is the kind of relationships where you can build efficiency, where you can have a high level of trust and you can really work well together. However, these may not be the relationships where you will get the more novel ideas, because they may be too similar to you, or too polite with you so that they are not able to criticise you when you need to be challenged. Weak ties are different – people that you just know a little, who you can relate to but more at a distance. You do normally not have close or formal relationships to them. This is where you can find people willing to challenge you, criticise your ideas and who are likely to provide innovative ideas for you because they have different kinds of experience and different competencies and networks. They can provide a fresh view.

We need to think about the organisation in a network view; we could call it an open organisational model, where the entrepreneur is managing the firm, as well as managing in networks. The leader needs to be good at building relationships, developing them, establishing trust, and also creating win-win situations in negotiations.

10.8.2 Why Networks are Superior for Start-ups

The good thing about networks is that when dealing with innovation, networks may enable both short-term and long-term work. In the beginning of a new venture it is difficult to know exactly what is needed of resources. This is why it sometimes is impossible to just go to an established market and ask for the best price to solve and innovation problem. If one knows exactly what she wants, then she can go to the market and ask for the best price, for the right quality. But this is generally not the case during innovation. The other thing that could be done is to integrate the resources, such as knowl-edge or people, into the firm, e.g., by hiring or partnering with people who are crucial for the business. But then again, it is expensive to pay full-time salaries if only needing them a third or half of the time. To build the organi-sation and integrate all the resources needed in the organisation might be very ineffective and very expensive. But, in a network one can build both long- and short-term relationships through contracts and agreements, as well as informal collaboration based on trust and knowledge of the other. Services can sometimes be mobilised for free, or exchanged, or bought. A variety of actors can be mobilised, such as universities, technology providers, market actors, user organisations, etc. The flexibility of using the network is often a necessary condition for succeeding with entrepreneurial ventures.

Wickham (2006) talks about two such open models. One is the "extended organization", where the suppliers, the associated companies, the non-com-petitors serving the same customers, and the distributors are included in the view of the venture. Formal and informal relationships are mobilised to solve the tasks according to needs. In such a model, it gets clear that the start-up not only mobilises resources from its network but also to some extent is dependent on this network – what can be done depends on the network. The second is the "hollow company", where all inputs to producing value is hired in strategic relationships according to what is needed. These strategic rela-tionships may be composed of owners (mother companies), or other partners through formalised agreements. After a while, when the value proposition is adjusted with the customers, and the company starts proving something in the market, then it can start hiring and building the formal organisation.

10.9 LEARNING FROM SUCCESS AND FAILURE

In this last part of the chapter, we will focus on the facilitation of entrepre-neurial/organisational learning, and how to manage crisis and change. It is easy to imagine that to lead a company during crisis may be challenging. But to lead a company during growth should, then, be a lot easier? It turns out both can be quite difficult, and moreover, growth tends to lead to crisis. To manage employees in a rapidly growing company, in a company hit by a crisis and a company that is on its way back to the top after a crisis provides different challenges.

10.9.1 Rapid Growth

To manage a company that is growing quickly tends to bring challenges such as:

> Prioritising between too many alternative opportunities. This relates both to alternative technological solutions, and to alternative market opportu-nities. Lack of strategy and routines for decision-making.

> Evaluating the use of financial resources because it starts becoming amply available. Problems with the cash-flow are often providing trouble for growing ventures, as costs tend to come before revenues.

Too much of the critical competence is with the entrepreneur, and there are too little routines and structure, making the firm vulnerable if the entrepreneur fails to delegate responsibility, recruit the right people or if he leaves the company.

Lack of preparation for the challenges of growth and expansion. Market growth creates pressure on the organisation, whether to scale up production and distribution, to develop a service organisation to keep customers happy or to engage in continuous innovation to keep ahead of competition.

10.9.2   Crisis

It is being said that the person that has not been thrown off a horse has never really ridden one. To lead a venture through crisis will provide valuable experience. But in the midst of the action it may be hard to acknowledge that a crisis might be on its way. To recognise and admit the crisis is very hard for many entrepreneurs. There are many reasons for problems in a venture such as political decisions, inflation, new competitors, etc. But these are not the most common reasons, according to Timmons and Spinelli (2009). The main reasons are often one of the following:

Weak strategic planning

General leadership problems

Weak economic understanding in management

Many people wonder whether it is possible to predict crises and hard times in advance, and hence, possibly avoid them. Many different models have been made to help with this. However, if this had been an easy task, we would not have seen so many companies having to close down.

The culture and the climate in a company are important through growth and crisis, and not least through the phase of rebuilding it after the crisis. Just like character is important for the behaviour and the choices of a person, the culture of an organisation will have implications for what is done during and after a crisis, and what outcome this will have. Organisational culture can be described along six basic dimensions (Timmons and Spinelli, 2009):

Clarity – the way they are organised and how they get the tasks done

Standards – to what extent the management expects and sets the standard for execution

Commitment – to what extent the employees feel committed to the goals of the venture

Responsibility – to what extent the employees feel and act responsibly

Encouraging – to what extent the employees feel recognition and encouragement for what they do well

Community – to what extent the employees thrive and work well together as a team

In general we can say that a strong culture along these dimensions will help the company survive and rebuild after a crisis. When the situation feels threatening and demoralising, the experience of community, and the proactive and responsible attitudes among the team members, will support joint re-orientation and action during the hard work of re-establishing the company.

10.10   ENTREPRENEURIAL LEARNING AND CHANGE

Investments towards innovation are not guaranteed certain returns; firms must always factor in high-risk factors when budgeting for innovation. Empirical data shows that research investments often do not meet the initial organisational goals. These high failure rates can have significant consequences on the organisation, not only in terms of financial loss (as many investments are not recuperated and do not result in any other organisational benefits) but failure can also negatively impact on the morale of the workforce. In turn, this can lead to an organisational culture, which rejects innovation attempts from the very beginning. This is why companies must accept failure as an integral part of the innovation process. Having policies and procedures in place will help in carefully assessing and screening ideas and give those involved the possibility to eliminate projects that are potential failures from the earlier stages in the process. Previous experience and encouraging open questioning of ideas can provide great insights in identifying possible failure causes.

10.10.1   How Do Entrepreneurial Teams Learn in Practice?

Start-ups must strive to identify threats before failure occurs. The major internal causes are either associated with the cultural infrastructure (e.g., poor leadership, poor communication, poor organisation etc.) or with the innovation process itself (e.g., poor definition of goal, poor alignment of actions to goals, poor monitoring of results, etc.) (O'Sullivan, 2002). This means that the team's capacity for continuous learning is crucial to success. Ucbasaran et al. (2009) identified how experience – even from failing start-ups – may lead to valuable learning to succeed in later activities.

Most executives are of the opinion that errors are undesirable. They put in a huge effort to make sure that the organisation learns from its mistakes (as well as the mistakes of others) but largely without results. The errors tend to pop up again and again. But the real problem is not that we make mistakes. The problem is that managers think incorrectly about failures! To deal constructively with failure one must, according to Amy Edmondson (2011) of Harvard Business School, divide them into different types: first, some errors may be bad and avoidable; second, some may be inevitable; and third, errors can be good and intelligent. We will in this section follow Edmondson's reasoning to flesh out how to learn more from failure.

Let us start with a mundane example: A 14-year-old boy played soccer on a good team. To get tough enough opposition, the team played a lot against older cohorts in series and cups. The point was to learn from making mistakes and from meeting stronger opponents – and hence losing games. When opponents are bigger, stronger and tougher, the underdog has to develop its technique and develop smart strategies. By losing game after game, they learned what worked and – importantly – what did not work against strong opponents. They had to learn from mistakes. And after a while they started winning games too. To learn from mistakes is not easy. Companies often lack both the ability to detect errors and to make good analysis of them. Furthermore, managers tend to underestimate the need for learning strategies that take into account the organisation's specific context. Thus, explanations of organisational failure end up as either superficial ("they did not follow the procedure") or based on self-interest ("the market was not ready", meaning "it was not our mistake").

10.10.2 Mistakes to Blame?

The biggest obstacle to learning from mistakes is the "blame game" being played in most organisations. To admit mistakes often means admitting being guilty and, therefore, also to be blamed. Managers feel they are faced with the following dilemma: How can we handle errors openly and constructively without simultaneously saying that "everything goes", which means to open up for mediocrity? Edmondson (2011) asked managers about how many of the flaws in their organisation were truly reprehensible. The answer was often low – between 2 and 5 per cent. Then she asked the same managers how many of the mistakes that are made were treated *as if* they are reprehensible. The answer was usually very high – between 70 and 90 per cent! The consequence of such a culture and leadership is that people avoid reporting errors if they can.

10.10.3 Errors Are Not Always Wrong

It is possible to combine the confidence to admit mistakes with expectations of good performance. The solution must start with differentiating more between different types of errors (Edmondson, 2011). *Avoidable errors* may occur during the performance of routine and predictable tasks. It may be, for example, operations on an assembly line, or the control of financial documents. Avoidable errors may be deliberate deviation from the instructions. This is perhaps one of the mistakes where the "offender" actually deserves to hear it clearly. However, inevitable errors may also happen due to inattention, or lack of competence. The solution to such errors is what we call continuous learning: Training, human resource development, improvement of working conditions, etc. For example, the "lean" approach to quality improvement is tailor-made to learn from these mistakes. Those who do the work helps with analysis and solutions, and thus to collective learning.

Inevitable errors are errors that occur in complex systems. Our society and our organisations are becoming more complex, composed of many different and specialised competencies and technologies. A consequence of the high complexity is the danger of accidental and unpredicted events. We are simply not able to have full knowledge of all the consequences of our systems. Such errors can occur because one follows the instructions, but this may prove to be inadequate. Or to solve the task can be so challenging that it cannot be resolved reliably every time. Furthermore, seemingly rational choices prove to have undesirable outcomes because no one knows the future. Complex processes sometimes break down, because they have not taken account of certain new interactions. Such errors are basically inevitable. The solution is therefore to detect errors as soon as possible and work actively and diligently to correct mistakes while they are small and manageable. The consequences of people not reporting errors can be fatal if the errors get to develop over time, or if many small errors add up to serious and threatening situations to the organisation.

The third category is *intelligent failures*. Innovative organisations are increasingly learning to design processes that "produce" error. By actively experimenting with various options and solutions, they can push the limits of what they can do, and discover the limits of what is working and not working in a quick, inexpensive and relatively low-risk way. Tolerance for error is a crucial prerequisite in such settings. According to author Eric Ries (2011) the start-up should actively try to disprove their own hypotheses as quickly as possible when developing new products and services. If the experiment process does not make it possible to find out that you are wrong, the risks of major errors and failed investments are clearly present. However, if you are dependent on a strong safety focus, it may be difficult to work very actively with these errors.

10.10.4 A Special Case: "High-Reliability Organizations"

There are some technology-based organisations where security or other kinds of reliability is particularly important, and where "intelligent" failures from experimentation error have their clear limitations. Aircraft carriers, nuclear power plants, passenger aircraft, hospitals and oil platforms are all examples of organisations in which reliability has to be more important than everything else. Karl Weick and colleagues (1999) have studied how such organisations learn and how they succeed so well in avoiding mistakes. It turns out that they are characterised by an intense focus on work processes, they are extremely mindful of the variation and the staff is very conscious when they interact with others at work. Such high-reliability organisations are characterised especially by the following:

- Highly concerned with errors
- Resisting simplistic explanations
- Sensitive to course of action and variety
- Concerned with coping in challenging conditions

– The structures are under-specified
– Good interaction across tasks

The last point is important; instead of organising everything in detail to ensure correct behaviour they have built space for local assessments of abnormal events. When unexpected events occur, it triggers individual and team-based decision-making, almost like anarchist mechanisms. This combination of thorough training, intense attention to work and manoeuvre in the face of the unexpected turns out to give a good ability to detect and handle unexpected events.

10.10.5 Good Strategies to Learn from Mistakes

Given that we have established an open climate to talk about mistakes in the team, and that we have a balanced view of different types of failure: What can we to do to learn from mistakes? How can we develop a learning culture? The manager's challenge in the effort to learn from mistakes is to develop an organisational culture where "the blame game" has no place. She should be comfortable with telling about – and learning from – mistakes. When raising children, parents will miss this point almost daily, as they ask "who did it" and thus exclude the possibility of an open and constructive process. Instead we should ask: What happened? Then we can trace the incident and explore learning potential. So, what are good strategies for learning from failure?

First, one should work on how to detect and report errors. It is said that Alan Mulally, when he took over as executive chair of Ford in 2006, confronted his management team on this (Edmondson, 2011). When they came to the management meetings with reports that everything is in perfect order, he had to remind them that the company had lost several billion dollars last year, before he asked: "Isn't anything not going well?" When he also applauded when the reports were honest about errors and problems, the organisation began to understand that he was serious about this. Many managers and employees are reluctant to report errors. The stigma of admitting error must be reduced, and the management is also shown to have a major impact on the degree of openness. The two major accidents of NASA space shuttles, in 1986 and 2003, show similar difficulties in reporting and assessing of errors (Starbuck and Hedberg, 2003; Edmondson, 2011). In both cases, the engineers discovered signs of possible danger well in advance. But the level of risk was toned down, and the pressure for more thorough research was rejected, thus it was not discovered that the problem was potentially large and dangerous. The outcome was tragic.

Second, start-ups should develop ways to analyse failure. To investigate reported errors can be uncomfortable. The organisation must reflect on its own practice and find out what really took place. This takes time and resources, and the work of identifying failure is not always a joyful task. Traditionally, determination and vigour have been rewarded at the expense of reflection and analysis. Furthermore, people largely prefer evidence that support their established beliefs. We downplay our responsibility and blame when we fail. A hospital doctor who had just switched workplace could tell about the dramatic cultural difference between his previous hospital, where talking openly about errors for learning was part of the daily routine, and the new workplace where mistakes were completely taboo to talk about at all. The risk of loss of prestige by admitting failure was imminent. Analysis of the "root causes" in continuous improvement (e.g., through lean tools), is an example of how to systematically unravel what led to the failure and thus develop good measures. Moreover, interdisciplinary teams may often have good success with complex learning and problem analysis.

Third, we can, as mentioned above, experiment with errors more pro-actively. One can strategically produce intelligent failures. In science and technology we know that errors, i.e., failed experiments, are a crucial part of the business that provides essential information. In other organisations, even when piloting a new solution, the purpose is that each pilot is perfect.

Case Box 10.2

In the telecom, cable TV and broadband markets we have seen some providers struggle with "chronic" growing pains. They have had severe trouble of matching their service organisations with their rate of growth. In this kind of companies, the service organisation is a particularly vulnerable part. They drive costs, which make it dangerous to scale up the organisation too early (without enough revenues). However, if scaled up too late, it may take months and even years to get up to date with all the waiting and increasingly frustrated customers. One such organisation told that they used the Balanced Scorecard as a "compass" for managing change in the face of a storming environment (customers, press) through two cycles of similar crises.

Thus, one is not able to create optimum conditions. But, when the new solution is meant to be used in daily practice, where conditions are often far less optimal, one can still experience failure. Instead, one should design processes with the aim to discover everything that can go wrong. This can often be done in a smart way, through small experiments, with low cost and limited/controlled injury. Sarasvathy and Dew (2005) have thoroughly documented how this is a main reason why talented serial entrepreneurs succeed time after time to develop innovative companies and products.

10.11 CHAPTER SUMMARY

In summary, we can thus say that the following are essential to develop culture and strategy for learning from mistakes:

- The courage to confront one's own and others' mistakes and short-comings
- Different attitudes to different types of errors (inevitable, unavoidable and intelligent failures)

- Employees need to feel safe to admit and report errors
- Top and middle management play key roles in the development of learning culture

Collins and Hansen (2011) argue that good results in successful businesses are produced through a combination of paranoia, discipline and creative analysis. Organisations can learn from both their own and others' mistakes. Strong focus on – and tolerance of – failure is critical. Different types of errors can and should be handled differently. Errors can often not be avoided anyway, so one should rather seek to include them as a strategic resource for learning and developing the company.

Case Study 10.1 Meltwater Ltd.

Written by Thomas Hoholm and Vibeke Isachsen, Business Development Executive in Meltwater Group.

In my experience culture beats strategy. We have seen how this principle works in practice. Jørn Lyseggen, one of the entrepreneurs and the CEO of Meltwater is sitting down with us at a café in downtown San Francisco. He refers to the famous expression, possibly coming from the mouth of Professor Peter Drucker, illustrating how a great strategy is useless without an organisation capable of putting it into practice.

Meltwater News (now Meltwater Group) was started in 2001 as a media monitoring company by two Norwegian IT entrepreneurs – Jørn Lyseggen and his partner. With a conscious aim to grow without external funding, they focused on creating a cost-conscious, down-to-earth, and sales-oriented culture. With the launch of Meltwater News in Norway, there were more than ten competitors – all of which were well funded – offering online media monitoring in the market. In the beginning, they developed and grew the company through bootstrapping; strictly providing their own hours and knowledge, as well as the resources available within their networks. Lyseggen have shown an uncompromising attitude to recruitment, by seeking to only hire people (sales people and engineers) with management potential and a commercial outlook.

Meltwater developed an unusually sales-focused organisation, building a customer base counting more than 20,000 corporate customers in 2013. Sales is one of the most undervalued functions in many technology ventures, but in Meltwater the ratio of engineers versus sales personnel has been approximately 30/70. To build a lean and commercially oriented company like this, it may be helpful to have a strong sales focus from the very start. Meltwater have created strong sales routines and methods. New employees are given ambitious sales goals from the start, while also getting good training and generous compensation for results during their training period. Because of this, new employees quickly move towards good performance, and Meltwater has won "great place to work" awards in several countries. Some recruits realise this is not what they want and therefore quit within the first few months. Still, Lyseggen believes talent is best developed by giving trust and responsibility while being in a supportive environment. When they hire sales people, their aim is not really to hire a good sales person, but rather to hire what may become one of their next managers. All managers have been recruited from within the Meltwater organisation to maintain the organisational culture. This means that they have developed their capacity to send out their own people to start-up new offices around the globe, which is one of the keys to their rapid growth: small sales-oriented offices (around 20 people) close to their customers.

Meltwater News quickly became the top online media monitoring solution in Norway. By the end of 2006, Meltwater News was the number one solution in Europe, and just two years later in 2008, the company grew to be one of the largest online media monitoring firms in the world, with branches on all continents. Building on the experience from growing Meltwater News globally, the entrepreneurs developed multiple, distinct product divisions providing solutions for online and social media monitoring, media contact databases, collaboration, talent management and search engine marketing. They use the dialog with their customers to understand what to develop next instead of waiting for what the competitors will come up with. Also the technology team has a strong sales orientation and will move quickly to respond to customer needs. The user friendly technology (an Internet based/software-as-a-service solution), the strategic pricing (setting the price at the level where the actual users of the data, such as PR managers, had the authority to make purchasing decisions), and the unusually commercially oriented way of building the organisation has brought rapid international growth to the company.

As the result of becoming a multinational company, Meltwater Inc. moved their headquarters to San Francisco, California in 2005. *We never know when Jørn shows up at our office*, a regional office manager told us. *Out of nowhere we might suddenly hear him whistle a tune down the hallway, and there he is. With more than 50 offices worldwide, he is travelling a lot to meet with all of them. He is very concerned with the culture, and he uses his visits to inspire for the vision and see that the Meltwater values are practiced.*

After having built the organisation and developed their customer base, Meltwater could go into the next phase of growth. By using their technology and customer base as a platform, they could develop a portfolio of new and related products to the same customers, such as social media monitoring and marketing (Meltwater Buzz) and media outreach (Meltwater Press). With such a powerful customer base, Meltwater realised it was very attractive to develop the business with existing clients further, in addition to continue acquiring new customers.

When it comes to organisational culture, Meltwater defined a set of organisational values: fun, number one, and respect. They try to nurture a balanced work culture. It should be fun to go to work, to meet colleagues and customers, to learn and improve, which is important when you have a very competitive and sales-oriented organisation ("number one"). This again, needs to be balanced with respect, in order to share the joy of others' success instead of competing in a negative way.

As emphasised in his opening statement, the entrepreneur for this company, Jørn Lyseggen, strongly emphasises how important the organisational culture, the values and the vision and maintaining the entrepreneurial drive in the company are. In his view, this is now one of his main tasks as the CEO of a growing multinational company with more than 950 employees.

Case Questions

1. Discuss whether "culture beats strategy". What does it mean? Do you agree?
2. What aspects of Meltwater's organising efforts have strengthened its success? What are the potential weaknesses of their way of organising?
3. Discuss how Lyseggen's role as entrepreneur and CEO may have evolved and transformed over time.

4. What problems may Meltwater's managers meet when moving to a new country to start-up new offices? What are the benefits of this growth strategy?
5. Can Meltwater's way of organising (in terms of recruitment, training, culture, growth) be maintained as the company matures?

Case References

The Meltwater Inc. website (www.meltwater.com). Accessed on 12 July 2013.

10.12 REVISION QUESTIONS

1. Identify and discuss the most important internal and external barriers to growth in technology ventures.
2. What characterises a well-composed team in a technology venture?
3. How may the team and its leadership requirements change throughout the entrepreneurial process?
4. Why is organisational culture particularly important and challenging for the leader?
5. To what extent – and how – is it possible to manage in networks?
6. "Fail fast!" has become a mantra for many technology entrepreneurs acknowledging they need to learn from failure. Discuss this statement in light of Edmondson's (2011) three types of error.

10.13 FURTHER READING

For a classic text on the performance of teams, please check out Katzenbach and Smith (1993/2006) *The Wisdom of Teams: Creating the High-Performance Organization*. New York: Harper Business.

For a good introduction to Sarasvathy's theory of effectuation, which is based on experimental research on successful serial entrepreneurs, check out Read, Sarasvathy, Due, Wiltbank and Ohlsson (2011) *Effectual Entrepreneurship*. London: Routledge.

10.14 RESOURCES

Team role frameworks, with instructions, explanations and assessment opportunities may be found at the websites of the Adizes Institute (www.adizes.com) and Belbin Associates (www.belbin.com).

10.15 NOTES

1. For further reading, see Chen et al. (2009); also identify "acquisition" as third growth strategy. See Gilbert et al. (2006).
2. See Churchill and Lewis (1983).
3. We have adapted Scott and Bruse (1987). This model has been recommended by Dr. Mark DeLessio and Dr S. Vyakarnam in their paper "Growing the Ven-

ture" for Enterprise Tuesday at the Centre for Entrepreneurial Learning, Judge School of Business, Cambridge University.
4. There are several team role frameworks available, often providing assessment tools and learning materials; one that is much used is Belbin's (www.belbin. com), which provides a more fine-grained set of nine different roles. We have chosen to present Adizes here because it is simpler while still being useful for discussing team roles in practice.
5. Adapted from Mørk et al., 2006; 2010.

10.16 REFERENCES

Adizes, I.K. (2004) *Management/Mismanagement Styles: How to Identify a Style and What To Do About It*. Santa Barbara, CA: The Adizes Institute Publishing.

Barney, J., Wright, M. and Ketchen, D.J. (2001) "The Resource-based View of the Firm: Ten Years After 1991", *Journal of Management*, 27(6): 275–641.

Bretteville, T. and Solberg, C.A. (2009) "Inside the Boardroom of the Born Global", Proceedings EIBA Conference, Valencia December.

Casson, M. (2005) "Entrepreneurship and the Theory of the Firm", *Journal of Economic Behavior & Organization*, 58: 327–348.

Collins, M. and Hansen, J. (2011) *Great by Choice*. New York: Harper Business.

Cressy, R. (2006) "Determinants of Small Firm Survival and Growth", in M. M. Casson, B. Yeung, A. Basu and N. Wadeson (eds), *The Oxford Handbook of Entrepreneurship*. Oxford: Oxford University Press.

Davila, A., Foster, G. and Gupta, M. (2003) "Venture Capital Financing and the Growth of Startup Firms," *Journal of Business Venturing*, 18(6): 689–708.

Dedrick, J., Kraemer, K.L. and Linden, G. (2010) "Who Profits from Innovation in Global Value Chains?: A Study of the iPod and Notebook PCs", *Industrial and Corporate Change*, 19(1): 81–116.

Edmonson, A. (2011) "Strategies of Learning from Failure", *Harvard Business Review*, 89(4): 48–55.

Fogel, K., Hawk, A., Morck, R. and Yeung, B. (2006) "Institutional Obstacles to Entrepreneurship", in M. Casson, B. Yeung, A. Basu and N. Wadeson (eds), *The Oxford Handbook of Entrepreneurship*. Oxford: Oxford University Press.

Gabrielsson, M., Kirpilani, M., Dimitratos, P., Solberg, C.A. and Zucchella, A. (2008) "Conceptualization to Advance Born Global Research: A Research Note", *International Business Review*, 17: 385–401.

Granovetter, M. (1995/2000) "The Economic Sociology of Firms and Entrepreneurs", in R. Swedberg (ed), *Entrepreneurship: The Social Science View*. Oxford: Oxford University Press.

Granovetter, M. (1983) "A Network Theory Revisited", *Sociological Theory*, 1: 201–233.

Hoholm, T. (2011) *The Contrary Forces of Innovation: An Ethnography of Innovation in the Food Industry*. London: Palgrave Macmillan.

Håkansson, H. and Waluszewski, A. (2007) *Knowledge and Innovation in Business and Industry: The Importance of Using Others*. Oxford: Routledge.

Knorr-Cetina, K. (2001) "Objectual Practice", in T.R. Schatzki, K. Knorr Cetina and E. von Savigny (eds), *The Practice Turn in Contemporary Theory*. London: Routledge.

Kor, Y.Y., Mahoney, J.T. and Michael, S.C. (2007) "Resources, Capabilities and Entrepreneurial Perceptions", *Journal of Management Studies*, 44(7): 1187–1212.

McDougall, P.P. and Oviatt, B.M. (1991) "Global Start-ups: New Ventures without Geographic Limits", *The Entrepreneurship Forum*, Winter, 1–5.

Mørk, B.E., Hoholm, T. and Aanestad, M. (2006) "Constructing, Enacting and Packaging Innovations: A Study of a Medical Technology Project", *European Journal of Innovation Management*, 9(4): 444–465.

Mørk, B.E., Hoholm, T., Ellingsen, G., Edwin, B. and Aanestad, M. (2010) "Challenging Expertise on Power Relations within and across Communities of Practice in Medical Innovation", *Management Learning*, 41(5): 575–592.

O'Sullivan, D. (2002) "Framework for Managing Business Development in the Networked Organization", *Computers in Industry*, 47(1): 77–88.

Pettigrew, A. (1979) "On Studying Organizational Cultures", *Qualitative Methodology*, 24(4): 570–581.

Rickards, T. and Moger, S. (2000) "Creative Leadership Processes in Project Team Development: An Alternative to Tuckman's Stage Model", *British Journal of Management*, 11: 273–283.

Ries, E. (2011) *The Lean Startup: How Today's Entrepreneurs Use Continuous Innovation to Create Radically Successful Businesses*. New York: Crown Publishing Group.

Sarasvathy, S.D. (2004) "The Questions We Ask and the Questions We Care About: Reformulating Some Problems in Entrepreneurship Research", *Journal of Business Venturing*, 19: 707–717.

Sarasvathy, S.D. and Dew, N. (2005) "New Market Creation through Transformation", *Journal of Evolutionary Economics*, 15: 533–565.

Siegel, R., Siegel, E. and MacMillan, I.C. (1993) "Characteristics Distinguishing High-growth Ventures", *Journal of Business Venturing*, 8(2): 169–180.

Spinosa, C., Flores, F. and Dreyfus, H.L. (1997) *Disclosing New Worlds: Entrepreneurship, Democratic Action, and the Cultivation of Solidarity*. Cambridge, MA: MIT Press.

Starbuck, W.H. and Hedberg, B. (2003) "How Organizations Learn from Success and Failure", in *Oxford Handbook of Organizational Learning and Knowledge*. Oxford: Oxford University Press.

Stevenson, H.H. (1983) "A Perspective on Entrepreneurship", working paper. Cambridge, MA: Harvard Business School.

Timmons, J.A. and Spinelli, S. Jr. (2009) *New Venture Creation* (int. ed.). New York: McGraw-Hill.

Tuckman, B.W. and Jensen, M.A.C. (1977) "Stages of Small-Group Development Revisited", *Group & Organization Management*, 2: 419.

Ucbasaran, D., Westhead, P., Wright, M. and Flores, M. (2010) "The Nature of Entrepreneurial Experience, Business Failure and Comparative Optimism", *Journal of Business Venturing*, 25: 541–555.

Van de Ven, A.H., Polley, D.E., Garud, R. and Venkataraman, S. (1999) *The Innovation Journey*. Oxford: Oxford University Press.

Wade, W. (2012) *Scenario Planning: A Field Guide to the Future.*, Hoboken, NJ: John Wiley and Sons, Inc.

Weick, K.E., Sutcliffe, K.M. and Obstfeld, D. in Sutton, R.S. and Staw, B.M. (eds), *Research in Organizational Behavior,* vol.1, Stanford: Jai Press, 81–123.

Wickham, P.A. (2006) *Strategic Entrepreneurship*, 4th edn. Harlow: Pearson Education Ltd.

10.17   GLOSSARY OF TERMS

Administrating: Related to efficiency and short-term activities and goals; typically will be concerned with how to solve the ongoing activities and will be instrumental in developing good routines and structure in the venture (Adizes, 2004).

Doers: People who think practically about what could and should be done, and they do not hesitate in doing whatever it takes to move the venture towards its vision and goals; aims for effectiveness, while focusing more on short-term goals and results (Adizes, 2004).

Entrepreneurial Teams: Groups with a variety of competences in order to challenge each other to develop a thoroughly designed and supported innovation.

Entrepreneuring: Identifying opportunities in the environment of the firm (Adizes, 2004).

External barriers to Growth: Items outside of the firm that limit the growth of the firm, such as access to funding.

Forming: The processes of composing the team and setting the stage for good teamwork (Tuckman, 1977; Rickards and Moger, 2000).

Forming – Storming – Norming – Performing Framework: A common way of dividing a team process into stages (Tuckman, 1977; Rickards and Moger, 2000).

Human Capital: The availability of skills, talent and know-how of employees that is required to perform the everyday tasks of the business.

Integrating: Caring for efficiency with a long-term mindset; often referred to as the most important role in many teams (Adizes, 2004).

Internal Barriers to Growth: Items within the firm that limit the growth of the firm, such as skill and capabilities of employees.

Innovation Management: The process of managing innovation within an organisation; this includes managing people, ideas, information, initiatives, projects and all other aspects pertaining to innovation so that extra efficiency can be successfully added to a firm's activities and extra value can be added to the firm's value proposition for its customers.

Norming: The stage when team members are most aware of their team interactions and are focused on the entrepreneurial undertaking; goals in this phase are the development of a mutual plan for the team, settlement of roles, and ownership of responsibility (Tuckman, 1977; Rickards and Moger, 2000).

Performing: The stage when it is time to get the job done, since team members know each other, understand their roles and the direction of the firm (Tuckman, 1977; Rickards and Moger, 2000).

Producing: Done by the *doers*, but aims for effectiveness, while focusing more on the short-term goals and results (Adizes, 2004).

Storming: The stage where people both have started becoming safer in the team, and at the same time frustrations may arise related to other team members (Tuckman, 1977; Rickards and Moger, 2000).

Chapter 11

INTERNATIONALISATION

11.1 LEARNING OBJECTIVES

After reading this chapter, you will be able to:

1. Understand the key decisions involved in firm internationalisation;
2. Define international entrepreneurship and identify the key drivers of high-tech venture internationalisation;
3. Define international market development as a key growth strategy;
4. Identify strategic options for international market coverage;
5. Assess the criteria for foreign market selection;
6. Describe and compare the foreign market entry strategies;
7. Understand the key strategic attributes for developing and sustaining international competitiveness of high-tech ventures; and
8. Appreciate the cultural implications for international business negotiations.

11.2 CHAPTER STRUCTURE

The core elements of this chapter are as follows:

- Introduction
- International Entrepreneurship
- Key Drivers of High-tech Venture Internationalisation
- Strategic Options for International Market Development
- Determining the Scale of International Market Activities (Coverage)
- Selecting which Foreign Markets to Enter and Segments to Serve
- Deciding on Foreign Market Entry Strategies (Modes)
- Developing and Sustaining International Competitiveness
- Cultural Considerations in International Business Negotiations
- Chapter Summary
- Case study – Aerogen Ltd.
- Revision Questions
- Further Reading and Resources
- References
- Glossary of Terms

11.3   INTRODUCTION

For many high-tech ventures, internationalisation has increasingly become a growth strategy to enable the pursuit of larger markets and exploitation of new innovations to full fruition (Dimitratos et al., 2004). This chapter introduces international entrepreneurship and presents an overview of how a new firm internationalises as a means for growth and expansion. The rapidly changing global business environment, economic integration and advances in technology and communications have created unprecedented opportunities for small firms looking to extend their sales activities beyond the domestic market. Cross-border business activity is of increasing interest to entrepreneurship researchers, and accelerated internationalisation is being observed in even the smallest and newest technology-orientated organisations. This chapter will provide students with the necessary knowledge, skills and techniques to gain an appreciation of the nature of and issues that affect international marketing decisions of new and growing high-tech ventures. It will equip the student with a cohesive and integrated understanding of how a firm can achieve and sustain international competitiveness in dynamic and globally driven high-tech markets through developing and managing strategic attributes. It further outlines the issues for conducting and managing business negotiations in a cross-cultural context.

11.4   INTERNATIONAL ENTREPRENEURSHIP

International entrepreneurship (IE) is described as "a process of creatively discovering and exploiting opportunities that lie outside a firm's domestic markets in the pursuit of competitive advantage" (Zahra and George, 2002, p. 11). Successfully internationalising high-tech ventures emulates a combination of innovative, proactive and risk-seeking behaviour that crosses national borders and is intended to create value in organisations (McDougall and Oviatt, 2000). Entrepreneurs can acquire new customers through the internationalisation of their venture. Pursuing an international market development strategy involves seeking new markets by selling its innovation to customers outside its own domestic market.

Firms that internationalise early in their life cycle are referred to as International New Ventures (INVs). INVs are defined as "business organisations that from inception seek to derive significant competitive advantage from the use of resources and the sale of outputs in multiple countries" (Oviatt and McDougall, 1994, p. 49). The term "born global" has also been used to describe these types of firms (Knight and Cavusgil, 1996). Such firms are globally market orientated from the outset and can be defined as "business organisations that have a global mindset from inception and aim to derive significant competitive advantages from the use of resources and the sale of outputs in multiple countries spanning the three economic trading blocs of NAFTA, EU and Asia-Pacific" (Andersson, Evers and Grigot, 2013).

For new firms operating in technological niches, the expansion into foreign markets is a commercial priority to generate revenues and thus to recuperate initial R&D sunk costs over a shorter time frame (Burgel and Murray, 2000). As discussed in Chapter 4, high-tech markets are characterised by a combination of factors such as market uncertainty, technological uncertainty and competitive volatility (Mohr et al., 2010). Insubstantial home markets, global niche opportunities and shorter product life cycle increase the pressure for new and small high-tech firms to develop sales internationally to appropriate the returns from their innovations. Hence, high-tech firms experience accelerated product life cycles and shorter opportunity windows. Sectors that are highly populated with INVs are typically characterised by technological innovations and high knowledge intensity as opposed to more mature or traditional sectors of the economy (Aspelund et al., 2007). They have an urgency to capitalise on their innovation, which often means going abroad (Jolly et al., 1992). One reason for this high density of INVs is due to the ease of transferability and mobility of competitive advantage tied to intangible assets such as unique knowledge and technology.

In small economies such as Denmark, Norway and Ireland, many high-tech ventures rely on internationalisation as a key path to growth, or may start off internationally orientated by default. This is typically due to their limited home markets. In particular, the dynamic nature of high-technology industries characterised by technological and short product life cycles coupled with high research and development (R&D) costs leads to early and rapid internationalisation (Johnson, 2004). Thus, it may be no coincidence that INVs have been studied in predominately high-technology and knowledge-intensive sectors, whereas a limited number of studies exist in traditional sectors (Evers, 2011a).

However, technological superiority is not a guarantee for high-tech firms' success. In fact, companies find it more and more difficult to gain international competitive advantage on the basis of state-of-the-art technology alone. High-tech firms will not prosper solely on the basis of outstanding R&D activities; these need to be complemented with marketing strategies and activities that successfully bring the innovation into the international marketplace. The manner in which companies choose to market themselves when exposed to competition, greater complexity, dynamism and uncertainty is critical to their survival (Evers, 2011b).

Case Box 11.1 OpenText: From a Canadian University Research Project to Global Internet Company[1]

Today Waterloo Canada based OpenText (www.opentext.com) is the world-leader in Enterprise Content Management software, taking the top spot in the Branham Group's annual ranking of the largest Canadian software firms, earning more than $CAD 1.2B in 2012.[2] OpenText's software helps large organisations search their intranets, manage documents and workflows, collaborate on projects and handle group scheduling. Its products also provide solutions for cataloguing data, library automation and group scheduling; specifically targeting firms in the financial services, legal services, media, energy and pharmaceuticals industries. However, 25 years ago this multinational was a fledgling spinout of a research project at the University of Waterloo. In the early 1980s, faculty members in the English Department, along with colleagues in Computer Science, won a bid to develop the full-text indexing and search technology that enabled the first digital version of the Oxford English Dictionary. The project developed valuable algorithms that could quickly search a large volume of unstructured textual data – the missing ingredient for distributing user-friendly data on CD ROM, and later through the Internet.

Recognising other potential uses for the program, University of Waterloo professors Frank Tompa, Timothy Bray and Gaston Gonnet secured the commercial rights to the algorithms and incorporated OpenText in 1991. By 1995 OpenText was adapting its algorithms to search the nascent World Wide Web and released its first web-based product, Latitude Web Server, which powered Yahoo! – the Web's first commercial search portal.[3] OpenText was international from inception – they targeted global data-rich organisations – and some of their first customers were headquartered in the UK, Switzerland and the United States. In its latest fiscal year, OpenText reported having more than 50,000 licensed users around the world; earned 53 per cent of its revenues from the Americas, 39 per cent from Europe and the Middle East and 8 per cent from the Asia-Pacific region; and had facilities in Canada, Germany, India, United States, UK and Australia.[4]

11.4.1 International Marketing

International marketing is a process of planning and conducting transactions across national borders to create exchanges that satisfy the objectives of individuals and organisations.

International marketing is the process by which individuals and companies:

- Identify needs and wants of customers across national boundaries
- Provide products, services and ideas competitively to satisfy needs and wants of different foreign market segments
- Communicate and promote information about products and services
- Distribute the technology products and services internationally using one or a combination of foreign entry strategies
- Design marketing programmes to satisfy the needs of target customers in foreign markets

Typically, the high venture would fully develop, commercialise and test its product in their home market before seeking out international customers/markets. Many nascent tech entrepreneurs are still trying to grasp the marketing and management of their ventures and typically would not have the required knowledge or experience of foreign market demands and customers. This can initially restrict international efforts until the venture can confidently serve domestic customers. As the firm grows, they can seek out international opportunities and acquire knowledge via desk research and network sources as discussed in Chapters 6 and 7 of this text-book. Valuable experience can be acquired in the local context and can be transferred to foreign context as a starting point. In the case of Internet business models, the Internet can render the venture international in the early stages of the business, when it may simply be a matter of customising the language and technical management of the website to capture international markets. It can overcome trade barriers particularly in the case of software products, information services, payment services, e.g., PayPal, and Search engines such as Google, etc.

There are four major strategic considerations for the internationalisation of high-tech ventures: (1) Deciding whether to go international; (2) assessing the strategic options and scope of activities; (3) selecting which foreign market segments to serve and deciding on foreign market entry strategies (or modes); and (4) developing, managing and sustaining international competitiveness in high-sector industries. Each of these considerations is discussed below.

11.5 KEY DRIVERS OF HIGH-TECH VENTURE INTERNATIONALISATION

The internationalisation of high-tech ventures can be influenced by a combination of forces, both internal and external to the firm. These can be classified under push and pull factors as illustrated in Figure 11.1. The factors specific to high tech ventures are described briefly below

11.5.1 Push, Pull and Intermediating Forces Influencing High-Tech Internationalisation

Essentially, push and pull forces direct the firm's strategy towards internationalisation by how they are mediated by the entrepreneurial mindset. As illustrated in Figure 11.1, pull forces can include both internal and external motives which motivate the firm to pursue foreign markets for revenue generation and growth. Push forces (or drivers) are internal to the firm and exert pressure on the firm (from the inside) to internationalise (See Figure 11.1). Proactively internationalising ventures tend to be entrepreneurial in nature and follow the Schumpterian pursuit for creating and exploiting opportunities, especially when the firm has "innovative combinations". Smaller knowledge-intensive firms are emerging in small home markets focusing on highly specialised global niches from the outset. Hence, a small home market and opportunities abroad render internationalisation a necessity for high-tech ventures rather than a choice (Evers, 2011a).

Further, firms may perceive that it possesses the capability of matching suppliers with the unique resources to meet the market demands abroad. This enhanced perception of a firm's resources and capabilities is due to the favourable contributions from both push and pull factors abroad. Also, the availability of resources in the form of knowledge and experience, as well

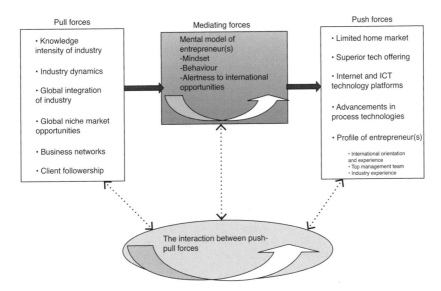

Figure 11.1 Dynamics of push, pull and mediating forces influencing high tech venture internationalisation

Source: Evers (2011a). Adapted from the *Irish Journal of Management*. Reproduced with kind permission of Orpen Press.

Note: For more detailed readings of Figure 11.1, please refer to Evers, 2011a; Johnson, 2004; Etemad, 2004.

as capital resources, can also be significant in the decision to exploit such opportunities for new firms. Hence, forces that push the firm out can be unique capabilities and competencies of the firm to overcome barriers such as shortage of finance (McDougall and Oviatt, 1991) and MNE adversaries.

The "mediating forces" are a third construct in this framework (Figure 11.1). These are "also referred to as the mental model of the entrepreneur" (Bell et al., 2003). The mediating factors refer to those forces that result from the interaction between dynamics of the push and pull forces bearing influence on the firm. It is a mediated impact, inasmuch as the entrepreneur's mindset vis-a-vis opportunity influences the strategic options for international market development. The combined impact of push and pull forces is also intermediated by the firm's assessment of its resources and capabilities at inception – in the case of new high-tech firms it is the entrepreneur as key decision-maker and a core intermediating force that lead to a decision to internationalise the new venture. The entrepreneur's mental model and mindset act as the intermediating forces at play with push and pull factors. The entrepreneur's perception of their external environment also impacts on the mindset in international decision-making and their characteristics are particularly relevant for deciding to internationalise (Evers, 2011a). This is discussed in the following section.

11.6   STRATEGIC OPTIONS FOR INTERNATIONAL MARKET DEVELOPMENT

When an entrepreneur decides to internationalise their innovation in foreign markets, a plan for building an international strategy needs to be mapped out. High-tech sectors are high globally driven industries, responsive to rapid technological developments resulting in short product life cycles and time frames in which to enter the market. A new venture must consider a global strategy, even if its initial strategy is to remain local. An international strategy involves transferring product capabilities and business model from the home market to foreign markets as a means to seek out ways of generating revenues from foreign markets to expand and grow the venture as well maximising the economic and value potential that the firm can add to its business.

As shown in Figure 11.2, Solberg (1997) suggests nine strategic options that an organisation can choose from. As high-tech ventures would typically be in the early and growth stages of the firm life cycle, they would typically fall into windows 1, 4 and 7 in Figure 11.2. As discussed earlier, high-tech industries tend to experience a high degree of industry globalisation and many high-tech ventures enter international markets by default. For example, as shown in Case Box 11.2, the medical device industry is a highly globalised industry and thus, many medical technology ventures from small economies would could opt for Window 4, targeting global market niches early in life cycle or prepare for global buy-out (Window 7).

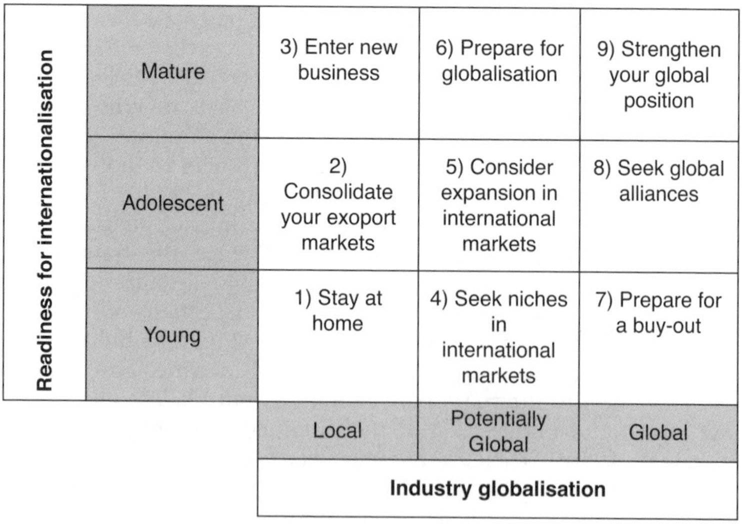

Readiness for internationalisation	Mature	3) Enter new business	6) Prepare for globalisation	9) Strengthen your global position
	Adolescent	2) Consolidate your exoport markets	5) Consider expansion in international markets	8) Seek global alliances
	Young	1) Stay at home	4) Seek niches in international markets	7) Prepare for a buy-out
		Local	Potentially Global	Global
		Industry globalisation		

Figure 11.2   Strategic options for internationalisation

Source: Adapted from Solberg (1997).

Case Box 11.2   The Global Integration of the Medtech Sector

The medtech sector is globally connected through multinational corporations (MNCs) and also highly populated by rapidly internationalising small- and medium-sized enterprises (SMEs) (Weigel, 2011). SMEs represent 80 per cent of Europe's medical device firms and have emerged the powerhouse of innovation in Europe (European Innovation 2006, p. 5). However, the medtech sector is highly regulated and its occupant firms are regularly exposed to factors that can both incentivise and restrain their international activities. For example, med tech firms are hampered by initial high costs of research and development (R&D), forcing early internationalisation to recuperate costs and gain first-mover advantage in their technologies. Foreign market entry can be also restricted by highly complex and diverse national regulatory systems. Such complexity involves different funding systems, national market regulation, distributions systems and many stakeholders in the sector influencing procurement decisions. For example, product regulations differ from one country to another, leading to expensive and complicated product compliance across diverse regulatory landscapes, with no certainty of product acceptance by the targeted foreign market. Many SMEs try to mitigate against such regulatory and cost pressures by partnering with, licensing their technology or being acquired by larger MNCs who already have an established international market base.

11.7   DETERMINING THE SCALE OF INTERNATIONAL MARKET ACTIVITIES

In general, a new or growing tech venture must select which international strategy it wishes to pursue and then determine which foreign markets to enter, market entry strategies used for selected markets and seek to obtain competitive advantage in those markets. Lynch (1994) identifies five territorial scales a firm can choose from to develop from a local market operation to various scales of international market coverage. The firm can evolve along the five scales illustrated in Table 11.1. Each route can incrementally lead into the next one or, depending on the strategic option discussed above, a born global venture can simply skip and operate at a global scale.[5]

11.8   SELECTING WHICH FOREIGN MARKETS TO ENTER AND SEGMENTS TO SERVE

A key question for the entrepreneur is: "Which foreign markets should I pursue and what are the potential customers I can target with my technology?" Entrepreneurs can target customer segments with their technologies in a foreign market. However, selling the same product into new foreign markets is a complex process, requiring a large degree of market research. In other words, the approach firms take for market validation in domestic markets is based on the same principles for new markets with different

Table 11.1   Scale of international activities and geographic coverage

Geographic scale	Description of activities
Local	Organisations supply to local nearby markets and within national boundaries where markets are large enough to sustain business growth.
National	Organisations supply into domestic markets but may engage in sporadic foreign sales through unsolicited customer inquiries and orders.
Regional	Organisations develop markets beyond their domestic market such as neighbouring regions or states, i.e., United States, Canada *or* countries neighbouring their own market as a national extension of their market, ie. Irish firm extending to UK or French firm developing its Spanish customer base and incrementally entering other European markets.
Continental	Organisations develop markets actively throughout the continent they reside in. For example many European-based organisations choose to develop markets actively in European countries. They may also re-locate some of their operations to European countries where it's most optimal for their business.
Global	Organisations with an already strong base can develop into other continents as part of their international market expansion activities. Many high-tech ventures operate from inception to be globally market-focused by the very nature of their product and the sector they operate in. These are more commonly known as "born globals".

economic, regulatory and customer landscapes. Some of the key factors that need to be considered that differentiate domestic and foreign markets are shown in Figure 11.3.

These factors include macro-factors such as language, social and cultural factors, market structures, customer and buyer needs, political economy, competitive landscape, economic product regulations and legal requirements and technological infrastructures. Figure 11.3 illustrates such factors as uncontrollable, which can necessitate firms to identify opportunities, adapt to foreign environment and address challenges in new foreign markets. Entrepreneurs can adopt a geocentric approach to international market development by seeking out and serving global segments of customers. This can enable them to operate within their capacity while helping to grow the business and particularly increasing the international business experience of operating a global venture.

11.8.1   Factors Influencing Foreign Market Selection

The next step for the entrepreneur is to decide which foreign markets to pursue. This process involves assessing foreign market potential and selecting target markets or segments within these foreign markets

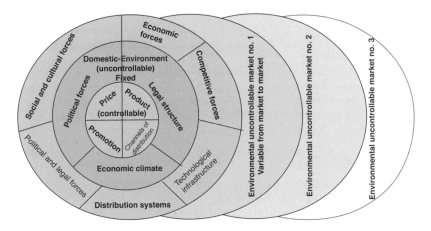

Figure 11.3 External analysis of foreign markets

into which it can deliver its innovation. In determining which foreign market to enter, there are eleven key factors (Baines et al., 2011) that must be considered to assess foreign market potential and target market attractiveness:

1. Assessment of current segment size and growth potential.
2. Industry and competitive analysis in target segment.
3. Pace of adoption in different markets, e.g., diffusion of innovation in developing economies can indicate a faster pace of adoption.
4. Assessment of company sales potential.
5. Ability to develop a competitive advantage in target segment. See Sections 9.5 and 9.6 in Chapter 9.
6. Psychic distance between home and target foreign market (i.e., cultural knowledge of doing business).
7. Costs and risks associated with operating in target segments.
8. Ability to overcome trade and government restrictions and product regulatory requirements.
9. Operational feasibility in accessing and delivering to customers in target segment.
10. Entrepreneur's experiential knowledge of the foreign market, resource availability and investment required.
11. Networks and contacts with access to foreign market and/or potential to develop networks in foreign market.

In terms of foreign market segmentation, the same principles and methods outlined in Chapter 9 used to segment and target foreign customers apply, yet with a larger degree of information required and costs associated with time spent researching foreign markets. As well as secondary desk research (see Chapter 7), government state agencies and industry networks can be valuable sources of market research and information. Leveraging and exhausting all channels of information sources are a critical part of screening each of the above factors to determine the overall foreign market potential and segment attractiveness in the foreign market. Foreign market selection is a critical decision for the venture particularly if the entrepreneur has no or limited international experience. Time and costs can be wasted if this process is not conducted rigorously and further with missed opportunities if this process is not done at all.

11.8.2 Standardisation and Adaptation of the Marketing Programme

Internationalising high-tech ventures must then decide to what extent that need to adapt (customise) their marketing strategy to local conditions and diverse needs across foreign customer segments.

As shown in Figure 11.4, at one extreme are companies that use a globally *standardized marketing programmes* worldwide (The components of the marketing programmes was discussed in Chapter 9). Standardisation of the product, advertising and distribution channels promises the lowest costs. At the other extreme is a *localized or adapted marketing mix*, where the producer adjusts the marketing mix elements (See Chapter 9) to each foreign target market.

Between the two extremes are hybrid options where the venture adopts a globalised marketing strategy, standardising its marketing programme where possible and adapting their programmes to foreign local environments and customers when necessary. For example, a high-tech venture offering technical services over the Internet may customise their webpages for their foreign markets or promotional materials may have to be translated into the language of the foreign market. Similarly, operating across diverse regulatory markets, means technology products need to be compliant to gain market acceptance, as well as fitting with customer needs irrespective of foreign territory.

Figure 11.4 Standardisation and adaptation in international marketing programmes

---

Case Box 11.3   Pocket Anatomy[6]

Pocket Anatomy (www.pocketanatomy.com) was initially established in 2006 as a service company providing high-quality 3D animations to the medical devices sector. In 2009, Pocket Anatomy entered into the Apple App Store, with the launch of Pocket Heart, a 3D medical application that promotes the anatomical understanding of the heart through its visualisation, along with quizzes and clinical cases. Since the introduction of Pocket Heart in 2009, Pocket Anatomy has gone on to develop an extended range of medical apps, including Pocket Anatomy and Pocket Brain. The App has No.1 ranking for paid Apps on the US iTunes Medical Store. The apps were initially developed with medical students in mind; however, an increasing number of groups and individuals are showing an interest in them, including healthcare professionals (doctors, nurses, EMTs), complementary therapists (yoga, acupuncture, massage) and people with a general interest in healthcare.

Adapting to Global Markets

As a developer of mobile software solutions, Pocket Anatomy relies solely on the Internet, and in particular the Apple App Store, to enter into foreign markets. The apps produced by Pocket Anatomy are potentially available in all of the countries worldwide in which Apple have an iTunes Store, providing them with access to a huge number of prospective clients. Currently the apps are only available in the English language. However, Pocket Anatomy acknowledges that translation and localisation are the next step in the distribution process and is addressing this challenge by working on providing market-specific product solutions. They have identified a number of countries in which there is a potentially high demand for their products in local languages, including France, China, Brazil and Japan. In order to fully penetrate these potentially valuable markets, Pocket Anatomy will have to adapt certain elements of their product, language being the main element. The core product will essentially remain the same in all countries; however it will be adapted to fit with local needs. Iconography, colour schemes and cultural sensitivities will all have to be considered alongside the adaptation of language to regional considerations. The Apple App Store provides Pocket Anatomy with a relatively low-risk and low-cost entry mode into international markets. Though not without its challenges and individual nuances, this distribution channel offers Pocket Anatomy access to potentially hundreds of millions of new customers across the globe.

11.9   DECIDING ON FOREIGN MARKET ENTRY STRATEGIES (MODES)

A foreign market entry strategy or mode is the channel or institutional arrangement that an organisation employs to gain entry to a new international market. High-technology organisations that are expanding into international markets can choose from a number of different entry strategies, depending on the risks they are willing to take, and the rewards which they wish to obtain. The higher the risk an organisation is willing to take, the higher the potential rewards There are five key modes of foreign market entry (as depicted in Figure 11.5 and detailed in Table 11.2): the Internet, exporting, licensing, joint venturing and direct investment. Each succeeding strategy involves more commitment and risk but also more control and higher potential profits. Figure 11.5 below identifies and defines some of

Table 11.2 Summary of foreign market entry strategies

Foreign market entry mode	Definition	Types	Advantages	Disadvantages	Example
Direct Exporting	Direct exporting involves a manufacturer selling directly to a buyer or importer in a foreign market.	Export through agents located in the foreign market. Export through distributors located in the foreign market.	Access to local market expertise. Higher level of control over the marketing mix compared to indirect exporting. Knowledge of the local market is gained by the home firm.	Loss of control over the market price due to local tariffs. Lack of control over distribution operations. Cultural differences can lead to communication difficulties.	Aerogen medtech company engage in direct exporting through intermediaries and direct to OEM customers (see case at end of this chapter).
Licensing	Licensing takes place when one organisation gives another something of value in return for payments and certain performance.		Licensing can increase the income generated by products that are already developed. It allows entry into otherwise closed markets. Very little investment is required. There is a high rate of return on investment. New products can be rapidly exploited. Patents are protected. The licensor gains access to the licensees existing customer base.	The licensee may not be as competent as previously expected which can result in high costs. It can be difficult to maintain quality. When the license expires the licensee will have acquired a high level of knowledge about the product/service and may become a competitor. The licensor has little control over operations. Negotiations to set up the licensing agreement are costly. License fees are just a fraction of what the company could earn if they were to enter the market on their own. Foreign governments often impose conditions on the transferral of royalties.	In 2007 Samsung and Sony Ericsson entered into a licensing agreement. The agreement allowed each company to use the others patents covering wireless technology. This licensing agreement involved numerous lawsuits and disagreements between the two companies.

	Description	Types	Advantages	Disadvantages	Example
Franchising	Franchising involves the franchisor giving the franchisee a right to use a business concept/system against payment and royalties.	Direct franchising Indirect franchising.	The franchisor has more control compared to other modes of entry such as licensing. Low-cost and low-risk entry mode. Creates new international markets easily. Generates economies of scale. Often leads to direct investment in the foreign market.	Identifying competent franchisees can be costly in terms of time and money. The franchisor has a lack of control over the franchisees operations. It can be costly to protect the brand name. If the franchisee runs the franchise badly, there is a risk that the franchisees' reputation could be damaged. Sharing business knowledge may create a competitor in the future.	Shield Security Systems is involved in the selling and instillation of burglar alarms, fire alarms and other electronic security devices. Through the use of franchising Shield Security Systems has expanded across the American market and entered into the Australian market.
Joint venture/ Strategic Alliance	A joint venture involves two organisations (parents) coming together and creating a third jointly owned organisation (child).	Contractual non-equity joint venture. Equity joint venture.	Provides access to local market expertise. Low levels of market and political risk. Sharing of knowledge and resources between the two organisations. Sharing of risk between the two organisations. Generates economies of scale. Avoids local tariffs and local government restrictions. Partners share the risk of failure.	Partners may have incompatible goals. Partners' contributions to the joint venture may be unequal resulting in tension between the two parties. Partners may lose control over foreign operations. The level of importance the two partners attach to the joint venture may diminish over time. Partners may become involved in long-term investments which are difficult to withdraw from. Partners have to share confidential information. Cultural differences between the home country and the foreign country may result in differences in management styles.	Trustwater is a high-technology firm involved in food and beverage, pharmaceutical and medical device manufacturing. Through joint ventures, Trustwater have successfully entered into the German market.

Continued

Table 11.2 Continued

Foreign market entry mode	Definition	Types	Advantages	Disadvantages	Example
Foreign Direct Investment (FDI)	FDI involves the home firm making an investment into foreign-based facilities.	Mergers. Acquisitions. Wholly owned subsidiaries.	Quick entry into new markets. Access to local expertise. Access to a qualified labour force. Established contacts in the local market. Recognised brand.	High-cost and high-risk entry mode. Potential communication and coordination issues between the home firm and the foreign firm. No integration with current operations.	When entering the American market Trustwater directly invested in the market setting up their own offices in Minneapolis.
The internet	The internet is a relatively new channel to enter into foreign markets. Using the Internet to enter into foreign markets involves the home country setting up a website in the foreign country where locals can buy their product/service.	Websites. Online App Stores.	Low-cost and low-risk entry mode. Quick and efficient way to enter the market. Organisations retain complete control. Creates new international markets easily.	No face-to-face interaction, which some customers may value. No access to local market expertise.	Pocket Anatomy produces medical education applications for medical students and those interested in learning about the human body. Through the online Apple app store, Pocket Anatomy has successfully entered into foreign markets such as the United States.

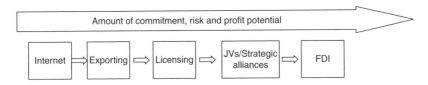

Figure 11.5 Foreign market entry strategies for hign tech ventures

the foreign market entry modes available to high-technology firms, as seen in Hollensen (2011).

Table 11.2 illustrates the advantages and disadvantages of each entry mode, as well as examples of companies who have successfully used these different modes to enter into foreign markets.[7]

The foreign market venture may choose one or a combination of ways to enter a new regional or national market outside its own. For technology products, exporting is a common method for new ventures. Also, licensing is a useful and less resource intensive way of generating revenue from foreign customers. It's inexpensive and allows the licensee to look after the manifesting and marketing of the technology in the new market in return for royalty payments to the inventor. The Internet has emerged as a highly cost effective and low-risk entry mode for information-based products and services that can easily be sold and distributed. It has immediate geographical reach, requiring adaptation of company website for large growth markets, e.g., the Chinese market would require the website in Chinese language, same for South American markets.

Another entry strategy that small firms use to initially enter a foreign market is through the more traditional mode of *exporting*. The company may passively export its surpluses from time to time, or it may make an active commitment to expand exports to a particular market. In either case, the company produces all of its goods in its home country. It may or may not modify them for the export market. Exporting involves the least change in the company's product lines, organisation, investments or mission. The venture can sell directly to customers or alternatively use foreign-based agents or/and distributors.

Agents are individuals or organisations that are contracted to your business and market on your behalf in a foreign market. They rarely take ownership of products and act as an external sales agent taking a commission on goods sold. Agents usually represent more than one organisation. Agents are a low-cost, but low-control, option. Agents might also represent your competitors – so beware of conflicts of interest. A key decision for the venture is finding the right agent. They tend to be expensive to recruit, retain and train if dealing in customised technologies. *Distributors* are similar to customers in that they take ownership and title of the products. Therefore, they have an incentive to market products and to make a profit from them.

A foreign market can also be penetrated through *joint venturing and strategic alliance* – joining with foreign companies to produce or market products or services. Unlike strategic alliances, a joint venture is an equity-based partnership. It differs from exporting in that the company joins with a host country partner to market technologies in host foreign market where partners reside. It differs from direct investment in that an association is formed with someone in the foreign market. Joint ventures to partner with indigenous Chinese firms are very much favoured by the Chinese government. Equally, as enforcement of IP laws are problematic in China, foreign firms consider it as an effective strategy to enter and exploit opportunities in China. The largest resource commitment to a foreign market is through *foreign direct investment* – through sales office or subsidiaries. If a company has gained experience in exporting and if the foreign market is large enough, locating foreign facilities offer many advantages. Generally, a firm develops a deeper relationship with government, customers, local suppliers and distributors, allowing it to adapt its products to the local market better. Finally, the firm keeps full control over the investment and therefore can develop manufacturing and marketing policies that serve its long-term international marketing objectives. The main disadvantage of direct investment is that the firm faces many risks, such as restricted or devalued currencies, falling markets or government changes.

11.9.1 Factors Influencing the Choice of Entry Mode

The choice of entry mode will be determined by a number of factors. The key factors can be divided into internal factors and external factors. Both are discussed below.

Internal factors

Firm Size: The size of an organisation indicates the resources it has available, larger firms will usually have more resources available to them than smaller firms. An increase in resource availability provides organisations with the opportunity to increase international business over time. SMEs are likely to enter foreign markets using export modes, as they do not have the resources available to utilise entry modes, which would give them more control. As larger firms often have more resources available, hierarchical modes are used when internationalising.

International Experience: International experience refers to the level of experience a firm has in operating in foreign markets. For example, the firm itself may have experience operating in international markets, or managers may have previous experience working in foreign countries. Organisations with international experience will be in a position to enter foreign markets with more certainty than firms with no international experience. International experience also reduces the costs and risks of entering into foreign markets. Firms with international experience favour direct investments in the form of hierarchical entry modes, such as wholly owned subsidiaries.

Product/Service Characteristics: The physical traits of a product or service, such as perishability, influence where the production area is situated, and therefore, the choice of entry mode. Products such as soft drinks and alcoholic drinks often use licensing agreements to enter into foreign markets as the cost of shipping to these markets is expensive. The complexity of a product also plays a role in choosing a foreign market entry strategy.

Products with a high level of complexity, such as technical products, may require service before and after the actual sale. The sales representatives must have a good knowledge of the product and as a result hierarchical modes where the organisation owns and controls the foreign organisation are used. In the case of services, where production and consumption cannot be separated, the organisation must be present in the foreign market from the beginning in order to interact with their customers. Hierarchical entry modes are advisable in this situation also as the organisation requires a high level of control.

External factors

Sociocultural Distance between Home Country and Foreign Market: Countries that are socioculturally distant do not have similar business and industry practices; they speak a different language and have very different cultural traits. For example, China is socioculturally distant to Ireland as there are language barriers, cultural differences and different business practices at play. When entering a market that is socioculturally distant from the home country, uncertainties may arise in relation to local business practices. Consequently, the level of perceived risk may be higher. Low-risk entry modes, such as agents and importers or joint ventures are preferred when there is a large perceived distance between the home country and the foreign market. These methods provide the home country with local knowledge of the foreign market, thus reducing the perceived level of uncertainty.

Country Risk/Demand Uncertainty: Foreign markets are often perceived as riskier than the home market. When entering foreign markets organisations may encounter both economic and political risks. When there is high economic or political risks associated with entering into a foreign market, organisations will not want to commit many resources to that country. Therefore, export modes, which require little resource commitment, are advisable.

Market Size and Growth: The size of a foreign market and the rate at which the market is growing play an important role in choosing an entry mode. For countries with a large market, which is experiencing high levels of growth, a high level of commitment and resources are required. Wholly owned sales subsidiaries or a majority-owned joint venture are advisable in this case. Smaller countries with smaller markets require less commitment and resources and may be served through licensing agreements or exporting.

Direct and Indirect Trade Barriers: Many countries place tariffs and quotas on the import of foreign goods. In order to overcome these barriers, firms wishing to enter such foreign markets often favour the creation of local production. Tendencies for foreign countries to "buy local" encourage the home country to set up joint ventures with local organisations. Such joint ventures can ensure that the organisation has a local image and locals would be more likely to buy these products.

Intensity of Competition: If the level of competition in a foreign market is high, the market will be less profitable and organisations are advised not to internationalise. If an organisation still wish to enter a saturated market, export modes are often used as they require little resource commitments.

11.10 DEVELOPING AND SUSTAINING INTERNATIONAL COMPETITIVENESS

As discussed in Chapter 6, in dynamic and competitive high-tech environments a firm's unique knowledge-intensive assets (in the form of technological offerings) and their ability to utilise technology effectively create the basis for competitive advantage. This can also accelerate early and successful internationalisation of new firms (Autio et al., 2000). High-tech ventures are challenged by the globalisation processes, such as rapid advancements in technology with increasing cost pressures, with many technologies being eventually replicated to a large extent by larger MNE competitors, resulting in poor performance or failure. However, entrepreneur-specific capabilities are important for international performance (Dimitratos et al., 2004; Ibeh, 2003), and can influence the strategic management and direction of the firm (Weerawardena et al., 2007). New firms can internationalise successfully to the entrepreneurs' specific capabilities (Knight and Cavusgil, 1996; Oviatt and McDougall, 1994). The owner-manager can be central to the development of dynamic capability for high-technology and knowledge-intensive firms.

As discussed earlier in Chapter 6, the dynamic capabilities of the firm suggest that organisations must become active generators of competitive resources by which entrepreneurs "integrate, build, and reconfigure internal and external competencies to address rapidly changing environments" (Teece et al., 1997, p. 380). Entrepreneurial orientated firms display capabilities like innovation and proactively seek the chance to recognise new opportunities (Lumpkin and Dess, 1996). What one conceives of entrepreneurship is a process, not just a status, and as such it requires dynamic attributes (Zucchella et al., 2005). It requires the entrepreneur to develop the organisation through capabilities reconfiguration (Montealegre, 2002) – the capacity of the entrepreneur to mobilise resources and develop and reconfigure dynamic capabilities in changing business environments for firm performance (Weerawardena et al., 2007). The dynamic capabilities view of the firm can also help explain an INVs adaptability and flexibility in managing, changing and diversifying markets, under the leadership and management of their founder-managers (Evers, 2011b).

Figure 11.6 identifies those attributes that can underpin a high INVs international competitiveness. Strategic attributes are defined as those resources and capabilities that enable the firm to develop and sustain competitiveness in international markets at an early stage in its life cycle. These are typically internal resources, and they provide the firm with a unique and sustainable advantage over competitors. Strategic attributes are identified at two levels: The Entrepreneur and The Firm (see Figure 11.6).

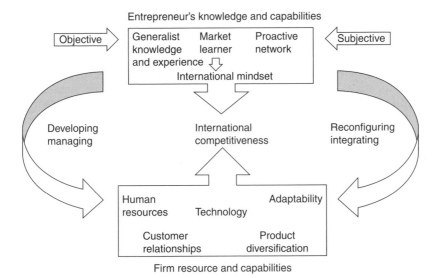

Entrepreneur's knowledge and capabilities

Objective ⇒

Generalist
knowledge
and experience ⬇

Market
learner

International mindset

Proactive
network

⇐ Subjective

Developing
managing

International
competitiveness

Reconfiguring
integrating

Human
resources   Technology

Customer
relationships

Adaptability

Product
diversification

Firm resource and capabilities

Figure 11.6 Strategic attributes for developing and sustaining international competitiveness in international new ventures

Source: Evers (2011) *Journal of Small Business and Enterprise Development*.

11.10.1   The Entrepreneur

The entrepreneur can possess strategic attributes and serve as a source of competitive advantage. Prior experience, knowledge and networking capabilities can help them strategically manage, develop and configure a firm's resources and capabilities for creating and sustaining competitiveness in the industrial and global sectors. In order to gain a competitive advantage and respond to the ever-fluctuating business environment, the entrepreneur's role is to re-organise the firm's external as well as internal organisational skills and resources. The INV entrepreneur's qualities can be categorised into the following: objective capabilities and subjective capabilities.

Objective Capabilities: Objective capabilities are described as the entrepreneur's prior technical, commercial (marketing) and start-up knowledge and experience. Such knowledge can give access to a network resource pool and valuable experience, which makes up unique human capital embedded in the founder-managers of the INV and hence a source of competitiveness (Loane and Bell, 2006). However, value for the firm will not be captured from these capabilities if the entrepreneur's effort and motivation are lacking or misaligned (Castanias and Helfat, 2001). Hence, we turn to other subjective capabilities of the entrepreneur.

Subjective Capabilities: Subjective capabilities are the entrepreneur's personal characteristics and competencies. The success of a firm, in relation to its competitors, is dependent on the INV entrepreneurs' personality as well as a proactive international mindset. An international market focus and global mindset refers to the INV founder's proactiveness and vision towards leading and managing their new ventures on international markets (Harveston et al., 2000). INV founder-managers require dynamic skills to drive the capability building process to ensure that the firm develops knowledge-intensive products competitively (Weerawardena et al., 2007, p. 299). A venture can develop competitiveness through the entrepreneurs "networking capabilities" for knowledge, relationship-building and resource acquisition. A market-focused learning capability is "the capacity of the firm, relative to its competitors, to acquire, disseminate, learn and integrate market information to create value activities" (Weerawardena et al., 2007, p. 300).

11.10.2   Firm Level

As illustrated in Figure 11.6, a firm's resources and capabilities enable the venture to deliver a value-added product and to respond to and adapt quickly to changes and developments in their market environments. At firm level, a number of key attributes emerge as the basis for competitive advantage for INVs (See Figure 11.6).

Human Capital and Technology: Previous studies highlight the fact that INVs use technological innovations to differentiate their products from competitors. Product differentiation can be broken down into quality and value, created through innovative technology and product design (Knight, 1997; Rennie, 1993). Quality is a distinct source of competitive advantage to the firm. A product's quality and uniqueness can be positively related to international competitiveness. Product differentiation can be a result of the unique knowledge possessed by the human capital of the firm embedded in product solutions.

Product Diversification: Product diversification is a vital component of a firm's internationalisation strategy (see Figure 11.6). It involves extending product lines, adding new product lines, and creating new customer markets in order to impact market expansion and penetration. Product diversification may be regarded as a strategic response to knowledge gained from the market regarding new developments and new customer channels. Product diversification can result in increased profits as the business targets foreign markets as well as new customer segments, such as the niche customer segments. In effect, international market growth by enabling the firm to build its resources base to further exploit new markets and penetrate current ones.

Organisational Adaptability: It is important that the INV has the ability to improvise, adapt and is also willing to find out what are the requirements of each customer, as well as the local distribution channels. The firm's ability to adapt accordingly is of vital importance in the market as firms may be hindered by unforeseen circumstances which require them to adapt accordingly. Therefore, a firm may require adaptable operational routines to serve all markets. International new ventures must have the ability to adapt quickly as survival renders adaptability as a dynamic capability (Teece et al., 1997) as well as a strategic attribute (see Figure 11.6).

Customer Relationships: As discussed in Chapters 6 and 9, customer relationships make up an important component of the venture's value-added network and marketing strategy. Ventures need to develop strategies to build strong relationships with their international buyers. Customer relationship-building and customer orientation is a well-founded capability in successful INVs (Loane and Bell, 2006). Customer service is also identified as a source of differentiation for the case firms. Following the successful targeting of the global niche customer segments, the firm must nurture and maintain a good working relationship with their international customers. The INVs' customer orientation, promoted by the founders close relationship-building and commitment to client satisfaction, needs to be embedded in the overall market offering for sustaining international competitiveness of the high-tech venture over time.

11.11 CULTURAL CONSIDERATIONS IN INTERNATIONAL BUSINESS NEGOTIATIONS

Despite the large volume of textbooks on international business, understanding the cultural background and context with whom the entrepreneur conducts business with is critical for successful business relationships and for the internationalisation of the venture. Cross-cultural negotiation is "when the parties involved belong to different cultures and therefore do not share the same ways of thinking, feeling and behaving" (Casse, 1981, p. 152). The ability to achieve mutually beneficial outcomes from cross-cultural sales negotiations is believed to be crucial to sales success internationally. The negotiation process is a complex process and is significantly influenced by the culture(s) within which the participants are socialised, educated and reinforced.

The cultural understanding of foreign partners needs to be considered at every stage of a sales negotiation process. INV entrepreneurs need to have a clear understanding of culture and work with the culture of the person they do business with. Hollensen (2011) states the following in relation to sales managers understanding culture, "managers with the skills to understand and adapt to different cultures are better positioned to succeed in these endeavours and to compete successfully in the world market." If managers are competent enough to understand different cultures that have a better advantage than those who do not fully understand it.

In order to conduct successful negotiations, each party must have some level of understanding in relation to the other party's culture. It may also result in the sales people adopting a negotiation strategy that in some levels aligns well with the other party's cultural system. Cultural readiness is required and this means research and training can be a close second to prior experience of working with different cultures. A common theory used to understand different cultural orientations is Hall's (1960, 1976) concept of low and high-context cultures.

11.11.1 Low and High-Context Cultures

The concept of high and low-context is suggested as a way to understand different cultural orientations and behaviours. Table 11.3 identifies the dimensions and how they are interpreted in low and high-context cultures. However, not all cultures can be stereotyped under this classification, there are expectations and variations. For example, relationship and trust building is very important in Ireland as it is in Morocco, yet these countries would fall into low and high-context respectively. Hall (1976) postulates that cultures fall along a high to low-context continuum, according to the role of context in communication. In high-context cultures, the context of communication is high because it includes a great deal of additional information, such as the individuals' background, associations, values and position in society (Keegan, 1989). High-context cultures include Japan, China,

Table 11.3   High- and low-context cultures

Characteristic	Low-context culture	High-context culture
Correspondence and language	Communication is clearly expressed and straightforward. Individuals depend on spoken and written language for meaning.	Communication is implied and indirect rather than clearly expressed. Individuals rely on aspects surrounding the verbal or written message for meaning.
Greetings	Casual handshakes.	Customary hugs, handshakes and bows.
Time management	Time is valued, punctuality is important. Time wasted leads to money being lost.	Time spent on relationships is valued.
Work approach	Individualist-Independence and youth are valued.	Collectivist-Respect for the elderly. Loyalty and responsibility are important.
Values and norms	Independent work. Conflict among individuals is confronted.	Group oriented, harmonious relations. Conflict is avoided.
Beliefs and disposition	Individuals and genders are treated equally. Those with power and control are challenged. Individuals are in charge of their own fate.	Individuals are treated differently depending on their status. Males and females are not treated equally and play different roles in society. Individuals with power and control are respected. Individuals accept their fate.
Mental process and learning	Lateral approach. Systems thinking. Individuals accept life's problems and realise they cannot solve everything.	Step-by-step approach. Individuals look to solve problems.
Business agreements and customs	Focused on making deals. Rewards are given based on performance and achievements.	Focused on building lasting relationships. Rewards are given based on seniority.

Source: Adapted from Hollensen (2011) *Global Marketing*, 5th edition, table 7.1, p. 238. © Pearson Education Limited 2001, 2011.

Brazil and Mexico and Middle Eastern Arab nations. Low-context cultures rely more on explicit information such as legal contracts to evaluate the business relationship at first hand. Low-context cultures include North America, UK, Ireland and Northern Europe.

11.12 CHAPTER SUMMARY

Internationalisation is a relevant strategic option for high-tech venture expansion and growth. This chapter introduces the relevance of international entrepreneurship for high-tech ventures and outlines key considerations for high-tech ventures pursuing the internationalisation route and internationally marketing their technology. First, high-tech ventures need to consider factors influencing the decision and enabling their venture to internationalise. Second, strategic options available are identified and scales of activities that can underpin the nature of the venture's geographic market scope are described. Third, selecting which foreign market segments to serve is a critical decision and the factors need to be evaluated carefully in this process. Fourth, the design and implementation of the marketing programme in foreign market segments must be considered in terms of standardisation and adaptation of the 4Ps. Fifth, the types of foreign market entry strategies available to the venture is presented. Using one or a combination of entry strategies will be determined by a number of factors, as well as ensuring a good fit into their international new venture's marketing strategy. Operating dynamic high-tech environments require the venture to be competitive in foreign markets but to sustain its competition. Using the Dynamic Capabilities perspective, Figure 11.6 depicts a framework identifying strategic attributes at entrepreneur and firm level to allow the venture to achieve and sustain international competitiveness in dynamic and globally driven high-tech markets. Finally, the chapter outlines the importance of and issues for conducting and managing business negotiations in a cross-cultural context.

Case Study 11.1 Aerogen Ltd.

Written by John Power – CEO and Founder of Aerogen Ltd.

Since its founder John Power first established a medical technology business in Galway in 1998 Aerogen (www.aerogen.com) has had an interesting corporate history. In 2000, the company merged with a US Silicon Valley–based Specialty Pharmaceutics company and went public on NASDAQ that same year. The company was acquired in a hostile takeover in 2005, and following an Management-Buy-Out (MBO) led by John Power in 2008, it again became an Irish-owned entity. Today the company successfully designs, manufactures (outsourced), markets and sells a range of patented drug delivery systems aimed at the critical care respiratory market. Its market leading electronic nebuliser products are used in acute care facilities in 65 countries throughout the world. It employs 55 people, 40 in its Irish facility and 15 internationally. It supplies an own-branded integrated product range to the all of the major Acute Care Respiratory

Original Equipment Manufacturers (OEM'S) as well as a stand-alone version of the nebulisers to Independent Distributors (IDs) in the larger internationally markets. These two channels account equally for 90 per cent of Aerogen's revenues with a further 10 per cent coming from non-acute care products.

The late business guru Peter Drucker stated: "Because the purpose of business is to create a customer, the business enterprise has two, and only two, basic functions: marketing and innovation." (Drucker, 1954, pp. 39–40) John Power is a firm believer in this approach and the company has effectively out-sourced both the manufacture and sales of his products, concentrating its resources to create competitive advantage in the key areas of Innovation and Marketing. To this end the company strategy is based on "Creating Value through Innovation", and adopts a Blue Ocean strategy through first-mover advantage with high-tech innovations in new markets. Aerogen has registered over 40 international product patents and its award winning nebuliser products are now widely regarded as "best in class", improving patient outcomes by giving superior drug deposition in the lung for respiratory compromised patients.

The company's international team is made of marketing and clinical support specialists (CSS) with nine people in United States, five in Europe and one in South-East Asia to support both its distributors and the end-user groups of medical and healthcare organisations in these markets. The CSS are not sales people per se but work alongside the Aerogen marketing team with the end-user stakeholder groups to assist in training and market development where they gather and evaluate latter experience and clinical needs of product. The team's collective remit is to create "pull" in the market of healthcare and medical organisations that are served by the ventilator companies.

Aerogen operate a very close business relationship with six of the world's largest OEM producers of mechanical (life-support) ventilation equipment for health care. The Aerogen nebuliser electronic drive circuitry is integrated into the OEM product and thus the marketing including product, product modification, promotion and intelligence is through partnership agreement with the onus on the OEM to sell the entire market offering to the end-user hospital. To both protect and develop its brand equity Aerogen insists that all the OEM-integrated products carry the Aerogen brand (similar to "Intel inside" strategy), and only Aerogen's range of disposable and re-usable nebulisers can be used in conjunction with its integrated systems as the founder says, "they [OEMs] sell the razor we follow up with blades". It is important to note that the integrated systems and stand-alone systems drive the same nebuliser products and that the Single Patient Use Solo nebulisers create a disposable revenue stream that accounts for 80 per cent of Aerogen's sales.

Up until Aerogen negotiated integration partnerships with the OEM's all its electronic control systems were discrete stand-alone products that could drive its range of nebulisers. As the OEM's have converted to integrated systems, the stand-alone products are now sold almost mainly through IDs. The main ID markets are North America, EU and Japan, although considerable sales are still made by both OEMs and IDs globally through supplying national health care tenders. For each country, Aerogen's IDs are carefully selected as they are expected not alone to make product sales but are trained to give clinical and technical support in the field and to gather important intelligence on public and group tendering in their markets.

Pull Approach towards End-users

Although its customers are B2B, OEMs and distributors, Aerogen's commercial team concentrate their core marketing activities on the end-user medical staff:

physicians, respiratory therapists and nurses working in ICUs. Increasingly though as health care economics play a greater role in product selection, Aerogen's commercial team needs to spend more time with other key influencers in the purchasing cycle. Department directors, Group Purchasing Organisations (GPOs) and pharmacy, all now have an influence on product adoption and acquisition and therefore unique selling propositions (USPs) need to be prepared for each influencer. The end-user medical staff remain however the most critical stakeholder group in its marketing strategy, and Aerogen implements a pull strategy in their marketing activities, focusing much of their promotions and market intelligence gathering activities on these actual end-users in medical and health organisations.

Case Questions
1. What type of factors do you think brought about John Power's decision to internationalise Aerogen's products?
2. What type of factors do you think Aerogen used to select its foreign markets and segments?
3. What type of foreign market entry mode(s) does Aerogen use to enter its foreign markets?
4. What is Aerogen's core competitive advantage on international markets? What type of strategic attributes characterise the firm to attain its competitive advantage in foreign markets?

11.13   REVISION QUESTIONS

1. Define International Entrepreneurship and its relevance to firms operating in high-tech sectors? Select examples of high-tech born globals that are less than seven years old.
2. Discuss the factors the venture needs to consider when selecting foreign markets to enter?
3. Drawing on relevant sources, discuss the Internet as an increasingly used foreign market entry strategy by high-tech ventures. Illustrate your answer with examples of companies who are dependent on the Internet for entering foreign markets.
4. Select a firm of your choice and assess the relevance of the Figure 11.6 framework for understanding how it develops and sustains its international competitiveness on foreign markets.

11.14   FURTHER READING AND RESOURCES

Baines, P., Fill, C. and Page, K. (2011) *Marketing*. New York: Oxford University Press.
Etemad, H. (2004) "Internationalization of Small and Medium-Sized Enterprises: A Grounded Theoretical Framework and an Overview", *Canadian Journal of Administrative Sciences*, 21(1): 1–21.

Evers, N., Andersson, S. and Hannibal, M. (2012) "Stakeholders and Marketing Capabilities in International New Ventures: Evidence from Ireland, Sweden and Denmark", *Journal of International Marketing*, 20(4): 46–71.

Evers, N. (2011a) "Factors Influencing New Venture Internationalisation: A Review of the Literature", *Irish Journal of Management*, 1.

Evers, N. (2011b) "International New Ventures in 'Low-Tech sectors' – A Dynamic Capabilities Perspective", *Journal of Small Business and Enterprise Development*, 18(3): 502–528.

Ghauri, P.N. and Cateora, P.R. (2010) *International Marketing*. New York: McGraw-Hill Higher Education.

Johnson, J.E. (2004) "Factors Influencing the Early Internationalisation of High-Technology Start-Ups: US and UK Evidence", *Journal of International Entrepreneurship*, 2: 139–154.

Hollensen, S. (2011) *Global Marketing A Decision Orientated Approach*, 5th edn. Essex: Pearson Education Limited.

11.15   NOTES

1. Case written by Prof. Rod B. McNaughton, University of Auckland Business School, New Zealand.
2. Top 25 Canadian Software Firms, http://www.branham300.com/index.php?year=2012&listing=5, Accessed on 23 June 2013.
3. OpenText's 20-year Journey of Innovation, http://www.opentext.com/2/global/company/2012-present.htm, Accessed on 23 June 2013.
4. OpenText Annual Report (2012), http://mimage.opentext.com/alt_content/binary/ot/investor/2012/2012-annual-report.pdf, Retrieved on 23 June 2013.
5. See also Baines at al. (2011).
6. Case written by Michelle Devaney, National University of Ireland, Galway.
7. For further reading on foreign market entry modes, see Hollensen (2011); Ghauri and Cateora (2010); and Baines et al. (2011).

11.16   REFERENCES

Andersson, S., Evers, N. and Grigot, C. (2013) "Local and International Networks in Small Firm Internationalisation: Cases from the Rhône-Alpes Medical Technology Regional Cluster", *Entrepreneurship and Regional Development: An International Journal.* DOI: 10.1080/08985626.2013.847975.

Aspelund, A. and Moen, Ø. (2001) "A generation Perspective on Small Firm Internationalization: From Traditional Exporters and Flexible Specialists to Born Globals", *Advances in International Marketing*, 11: 197–225.

Aspelund, A., Madsen, T.K. and Moen, Ø. (2007) "A Review of the Foundation, International Marketing Strategies, and Performance of International New Ventures", *European Journal of Marketing*, 41(11/12): 1423–1448.

Autio, E., Sapienza, H.J. and Almeida, J.G. (2000) "Effects of Age at Entry, Knowledge Intensity, and Imitability on International Growth", *Academy of Management Journal*, 43(5): 909–924.

Baines, P., Fill, C. and Page, K. (2011) *Marketing*. New York: Oxford University Press.

Bell, J., McNaughton, R. and Young, S. (2003) "Born-Again Global Firms: An Extension to the 'Born Global' Phenomenon", *Journal of International Management*, 7: 1–17.

Burgel, O. and Murray, G.C. (2000) "The International Market Entry Choices of Start-Up Companies in High-Technology Industries", *Journal of International Marketing*, 8(2): 33–62.

Casse, P. (1981) *Training for the Cross Cultural Mind*l, 2nd edn. Washington, DC: Society for Inter-cultural Education, Training and Research, Intercultural Press.

Castanias, R.P. and Helfat, C.E. (2001) "The Managerial Rents Model: Theory and Empirical Analysis", *Journal of Management*, 27(6): 661–678.

Dimitratos, P., Lioukas, S. and Carter, S. (2004) "The Relationship Between Entrepreneurship and International Performance: The Importance of Domestic Environment", *International Business Review*, 13(1): 19–41.

Drucker, P. (1954) *The Practice Of Management*. New York: Harper and Row Publishers.

Etemad, H. (2004) "Internationalization of Small and Medium-Sized Enterprises: A Grounded Theoretical Framework and an Overview", *Canadian Journal of Administrative Sciences*, 21(1): 1–21.

Etemad, H. "Globalization and Small and Medium-Sized Enterprises: Search for Potent Strategies", *Global Outlook* (formerly *Business and Contemporary World*), 11(3): (Forthcoming).

Etemad, H. "The Knowledge Network of International Entrepreneurship", *Global Outlook* (formerly *Business and Contemporary World*), 11(3): (Forthcoming).

European Commission (2006) *Reporting Intellectual Capital to Augment Research, Development and Innovation in SMEs*, Report to the Commission of the High Level Expert Group on RICARDIS, Eur22095.

Evers, N., Andersson, S. and Hannibal, M. (2012) "Stakeholders and Marketing Capabilities in International New Ventures: Evidence from Ireland, Sweden And Denmark", *Journal of International Marketing*, 20(4): 46–71.

Evers, N. (2011a) "Why Do New Ventures Internationalise? A Review of the Literature of Factors that Influence New Venture Internationalisation", *Irish Journal of Management*, 30(2): 17–46.

—— (2011b) "International New Ventures in 'Low Tech' Sectors: A Dynamic Capabilities Perspective", *Journal of Small Business and Enterprise Development*, 18(3): 502–528.

—— (2010) "Factors Influencing the Internationalization of New Ventures in the Irish Aquacultural Industry: An Exploratory Study", *Journal of International Entrepreneurship*, 8: 392–416.

Hall, E.T. (1960) *The Silent Language*. Garden City, NY: Doubleday.

—— (1976) *Beyond Culture*. Garden City, NY: Anchor Books.

Harveston, P.D., Kedia, B.L. and Davies, P.S. (2000) "Internationalization of Born Global and Gradual Globalizing Firms: The Impact of the Manager", *Advances in Competitiveness Research*, 8(1): 92–99.

Hollensen, S. (2010) *Global Marketing*, 4th edn. Essex: Pearson Education Limited.

Ibeh, K. (2003) "Toward a Contingency Framework of Export Entrepreneurship: Conceptualisations and Empirical Evidence", *Small Business Economics*, 20(1): 49–68.

Johnson, J.E. (2004) "Factors Influencing the Early Internationalisation of High-Technology Start-Ups: US and UK Evidence", *Journal of International Entrepreneurship*, 2: 139–154.

Jolly, V., Alahuhta, M. and Jeannet, J. (1992) "Challenging the Incumbents: How High-Technology Start-Ups Compete Globally", *Journal of Strategic Change*, 1: 71–82.

Keegan, W.J. (1989). *Global Marketing Management.* Englewood Cliffs, NJ: Prentice-Hall.

Knight, G.A. (1997) "Emerging Paradigm for International Marketing: The Born Global Firm", Ph.D. dissertation, Michigan State University.

Knight, G.A. and Cavusgil, S.T. (1996) "The Born Global Firm: A Challenge to Traditional Internationalization Theory", in S.T. Cavusgil and T. Madsen (eds), *Advances in International Marketing*, Vol. 8. Greenwich, CT: JAI Press, 11–26.

Loane, S. and Bell, J. (2006) "Rapid Internationalisation among Entrepreneurial Firms in Australia, Canada, Ireland and New Zealand: An Extension to the Network Approach", *International Marketing Review*, 23(5): 467–485.

Lumpkin, G.T. and Dess, G.G. (1996) "Clarifying the Entrepreneurial Orientation Construct and Linking It to Performance", *The Academy of Management Review*, 21(1): 135–172.

Lynch R., (1994) *European Business Strategies*, 2nd edn. London: Kogan Page.

McDougall, P.P. and Oviatt, B.M, (1991) "Toward a Theory of International New Ventures", *Journal of International Business Studies*, 25(1): 45–64.

McDougall, P.P. and Oviatt, B.M. (2000) "International Entrepreneurship: The Intersection of Two Research Paths", *Academy of Management Journal*, 43(5): 902–906.

Mohr, J., Sengupta, S. and Slater, S. (2010) *Marketing of High-Technology Products and Innovations,* 3rd edn. Englewood Cliffs, NJ: Pearson Prentice Hall.

Montealegre, R. (2002) "A Process Model of Capability Development: Lessons from the Electronic Commerce Strategy at Bolsa De Valores De Guayaquil", *Organization Science*, 13(5): 514–531.

Oviatt, B.M. and McDougall, P. (1994) "Toward a Theory of International New Ventures", *Journal of International Business Studies*, 25(1): 45–64.

Rennie, M. (1993) "Global Competitiveness: Born Global", *McKinsey Quarterly*, 4: 45–52.

Solberg, C.A., (1997) "Framework for Analysis of Strategy Development in Globalizing Markets", *Journal of International Marketing*, 5(1): 9–30.

Teece, D.J., Pisano, G. and Shuen, A. (1997) "Dynamic Capabilities and Strategic Management", *Strategic Management Journal*, 18(7): 509–533.

Weerawardena, J., Mort, G.S., Liesch, P.W. and Knight, G. (2007) "Conceptualizing Accelerated Internationalization in the Born Global Firm: A Dynamic Capabilities Perspective", *Journal of World Business*, 42(3): 294–306.

Weigel, S. (2011) "Medical Technology's Source of Innovation", *European Planning Studies,* 19(1): 43–61.

Zahra, S.A. and George, G. (2002), "International Entrepreneurship: The Current Status of the Field and Future Research Agenda", in M. Hitt, R. Ireland,

M. Camp and D. Sexton (eds), *Strategic Leadership: Creating a New Mindset*. London: Blackwell, 255–288.
Zucchella, A., Palamara, G. and Denicolai, S. (2005) "The Drivers of the Early Internationalization of the Firm", *Journal of World Business*, 42(3): 268–280.

11.17   GLOSSARY OF TERMS

Adaption or Localisation: A process whereby the organisation adjusts certain elements of the marketing mix in order to better meet customer needs.

Agents: Individuals or organisations that market your product on your behalf in foreign markets. They are a low-cost option; however, they may also represent your competitor so you need to be careful when choosing an agent.

Direct Exporting: A process whereby a manufacturer sells directly to a buyer or importer in a foreign market.

Distributors: Similar to agents. However, they take ownership of the product and, therefore, have a higher motive to market products and to make a profit from them.

Entrepreneur: An individual who possesses certain traits that allows him/her to successfully run an organisation. Entrepreneurs often have innovative business ideas that have not been seen before.

Foreign Direct Investment: When the home firm makes an investment into foreign-based facilities. This may be in the form of mergers, acquisitions or wholly owned subsidiaries.

Foreign Market Entry Strategies: The mode in which an organisation utilises in order to gain entry into a new foreign market. The choice of foreign market entry strategies is dependent on the amount or commitment, risks and potential profits the firm are willing to take.

Franchising: A process whereby the franchisor (in the home market) gives the franchisee (in the foreign market) the right to use a business concept or system in return for payment and royalties.

High-Context Cultures: Communications and building relationships is important to them. Examples of high-context cultures include Japan, China and Middle Eastern Arab nations.

Hybrid Options: The middle point between standardisation and adaption. With hybrid options some elements of the marketing mix are standardised, while others are adjusted.

International Entrepreneurship: A method in which an organisation can detect and exploit opportunities outside of their home market. By doing this, the firm may create a competitive advantage.

International Experience: Related to the amount of experience a firm has operating in foreign markets. The firm itself may have international experience, or its employees may have previous experience operating in foreign markets.

International Marketing: A process whereby an organisation identifies the needs and wants of customers in foreign markets, allowing them to conduct business outside of their home market.

International New Venture (INV): An organisation that from its inception has a global mindset. From the beginning, these organisations aim to create a competitive advantage through buying and selling into foreign markets.

Internet: A relatively new channel being used to penetrate foreign markets. Using the Internet as an entry mode into foreign markets involves the home firm setting up a website in the foreign market where locals can buy their products and services.

Joint Ventures (Strategic Alliances): Two organisations coming together in order to create a third jointly owned organisation (the child). There are two types of joint ventures: contractual non-equity joint ventures and equity joint ventures.

Licensing: When the home firm gives something of value to a firm in a foreign market in return for payments and certain performances.

Low-Context Cultures: Rely on explicit business information, such as legal contracts. Ireland, UK and Northern Europe are all examples of low-context cultures.

Mediating Factors: The mental mindset of the organisation. Mediating factors stem from the interaction between the dynamics of push and pull factors in the organisation.

Objective Capabilities: The entrepreneur's knowledge-related capabilities, such as prior experience in a firm's internationalisation process.

Organisational Adaptability: The process whereby INVs adapt and are willing to learn the needs of individual buyers and local ways of doing business.

Pull Factors: Internal or external to an organisation. Pull factors encourage the organisation to internationalise in order to increase profit and growth.

Push Factors: Forces within the organisation that drive them to internationalise.

Standardisation: A process whereby the marketing mix is identical in all foreign markets. This provides the organisation with the lowest cost for entry into foreign markets.

Strategic Attributes: Resources and capabilities that allow a firm to develop and sustain competitiveness in foreign markets at an early stage in their life cycle.

Strategic Options for Internationalisation: There are a number of options which a firm can choose from when considering internationalising. The options depend on the readiness of the firm to internationalise and the potential an organisation has to internationalise or to stay in the home market.

Subjective Capabilities: The entrepreneur's personal traits and capabilities which enable him to grow the venture.

Chapter 12
ENTREPRENEURIAL FINANCE

12.1 LEARNING OBJECTIVES

After reading this chapter, you will be able to:

1. Understand the centrality of maximising value to the entrepreneur in of entrepreneurial finance and recognise the terminology used in new venture financing;
2. Describe how finance and its sources are intrinsically linked to the new venturing process from inception of an idea to harvesting of the investment;
3. Appreciate the key operational imperatives for planning a new venture such as funding, cash-flow and profitability; and
4. Relate financial theory to the practice of new venturing, in a way that leads to better financing and investment decisions and a higher success rate for a new enterprise.

12.2 CHAPTER STRUCTURE

The core elements of this chapter are as follows:

- Introduction
- Application of Finance to the Entrepreneurial Context
- Funding: Debt or Equity?
- Staging of Finance to Development Milestones
- Sources of Finance in Different Stages of Development
- Negotiating a Deal with an Investor
- The Business Model
- Due Diligence
- Managing Cash-flow and Profitability
- Determining Financial Needs
- Valuation and Use of Real Options in Mitigating Risk
- Valuation Primer
- Harvesting and Exit Strategies
- Chapter Summary
- Case Study – Facebook
- Revision Questions

- Further Reading and Resources
- References
- Glossary of Terms

12.3 INTRODUCTION

This chapter aims to provide students, prospective entrepreneurs and investors with the tools to evaluate a new idea and to apply financial theory to the decision-making process in planning a new venture. While many textbooks on entrepreneurship focus on institutional financing issues, such as sources of finance and valuation, the focus of this chapter is on strategic decision-making, operations management and resource allocation.

While good ideas are a dime a dozen, it is much harder to find good people with the eye for detail to implement them. Entrepreneurs, therefore, need to have the financial literacy if they are to turn their visions into a reality. Entrepreneurs need to be comfortable with *investment decisions* and *financing decisions* (Smith and Smith, 2004) as well as *operations decisions* that affect cash-flow and profit. In the context of entrepreneurship, investment decisions focus on whether or not to pursue a new opportunity by investing time and money in the creation of a new asset. These decisions are based on the asset's ability to generate future cash-flows as well as the riskiness of those cash-flows. Given a decision to invest, e.g., acquire an asset, financing decisions, in contrast, focus on how best to finance the investment. Financing decisions relate to how best to acquire the funds, how to structure ownership of the new venture, how much money should the entrepreneur use compared to money from outside investors and the type of financial claim by outside investors, e.g., debt v. equity v. some hybrid, such as preferred stock or the timing of funding rounds.

Statistics on start-ups points to very low odds of success. Although it is difficult to define what is meant by "failure," proxy data indicates the risk to the both the entrepreneur and investor is very high. In the UK, for example, 75 per cent of start-ups fail within the first three years (Stark, 2001). A study of 128 UK start-up exits reported a highly skewed distribution of returns, with 34 per cent being a total loss, 13 per cent of the exits at break-even or a partial loss and 23 per cent of the investments having an internal rate of return of above 50 per cent (Mason and Harrison, 2002).

This is the backdrop against which seed investors select start-ups for their investment portfolio. Data from the Australian Bureau of Statistics (ABS) provide the following exit rates: of 316,850 new business entries during 2007–2008, 71.5 per cent were still operating in June 2009; 56.8 per cent were still going in June 2010; and 48.6 per cent were still going in June 2011 (ABS, 2012). Various studies over different periods and in different countries have found similar rates of failure. High failure rates have simply become accepted as the inevitable cost of entrepreneurship offset by wealth creation, jobs and socio-economic advancement.

This creates a funding gap as the risk associated becomes intolerable for many: the key problem being that most institutional investors, e.g., banks, are accustomed to investing in much lower risk investments (Table 12.1).

Table 12.1 Start-up risk versus requirements of institutional investors

Start-up characteristics	Banks and institutional investors prefer
• Business inexperience	• Track-record
• Fluctuation of cash-flows	• Steady cash-flow profiles
• New markets and complicated technology	• Easy to understand market
• High-growth rates	• Steady growth forecasts
• High debt ratios	• Low gearing

This funding gap (Figure 12.1) is often filled by risk-tolerant angel investors and government schemes that include a variety of supports linked intrinsically to structured programmes designed to de-risk start-ups for investor-readiness, such as accelerator programmes and prototyping schemes.

While outside investors tend to mitigate these risks through diversification, entrepreneurs many not have this option open to them. In choosing to launch a new business, first-time entrepreneurs, in particular, face the prospect of loss of salary, using their savings and mortgaging their homes to finance their business as they transition out of employment to focus on their new venture.

However, the angel and venture capital industry's modus operandi is premised on achieving a few exceptional returns among many failures or mediocre returns in each portfolio. Yet, there also legendary examples of trade sales of 10 times revenue or better, 100 times earnings or 50 times investment to know that such deals happen. There are also initial public offerings (IPOs) that point to staggering returns.

Case Box 12.1 Facebook's Millionaires[1]

With Facebook's initial IPO valuation close to $100nb, rock star U2's Bono is among a range of finance heavyweights, including Goldman Sachs tycoon Yuri Milner, tech hotshots Zynga co-founder Mark Pincus and PayPal co-founder Peter Thiel who became (if not already) billionaires overnight.

This does not include associates, friends and family members of Facebook founder Marc Zuckerberg with his 2.3 per cent stake now estimated to be worth $1.5bn.

This begs the question of how much Lady Luck plays? Did Zuckerberg, as the entrepreneur, and his early slew of investors happen to be in the right place at the right time? Possibly, yet there are underlying patterns in the few spectacular successes and the multitude of failures that may help to turn luck into a systematic process of optimising returns? Studies show that there are some good predictors of failure and success. Of course, not every entrepreneur makes the right financial decisions: Zuckerberg's co-founding partner, Eduardo Saverin, saw his 34 per cent share diluted to less than 5 per cent in an early funding round, and he was not the only one to miss out on a big payday. Ronald Wayne, who co-founded APPLE with Steve Wozniak

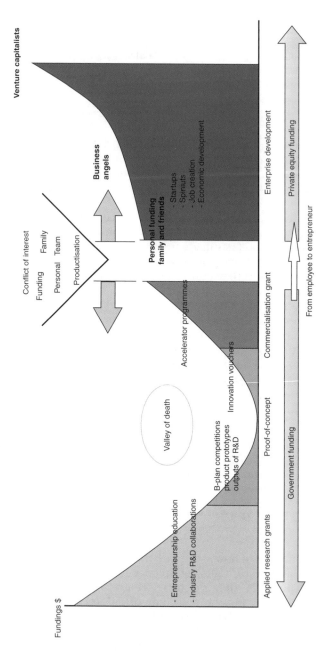

Figure 12.1 Common funding gaps often affect transition from employee to entrepreneur

and Steve Jobs in 1976, sold his 10 per cent share in the company for a total of $2,300: a position that would now be worth about $60 billion.

In summary, while we know that the failure rate of new ventures is high, we also know that many new ventures failure is due to poor implementation underpinned by poor financial decision-making. Many ventures that survive fail to meet up to expectations or, perhaps, never should have been undertaken in the first place. Sometimes, even when a new venture is successful, early financing mistakes prevent the entrepreneur from sharing in the rewards of the company.

The contemporary definition of entrepreneurship focuses on the pursuit of opportunity by galvanising resources outside the control of the entrepreneur. This definition suggests that entrepreneurship is a multi-stage activity (Figure 12.2).

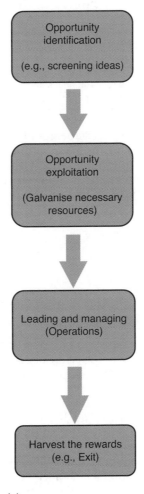

Figure 12.2 The entrepreneurial process

Opportunity identification (e.g., screening ideas)	The first step identifies opportunities to create value. Not all ideas will fall into this category, so the entrepreneur must use experience to assess the opportunity. This is, to a large extent, a cost-benefit analysis: to what extent do the potential awards exceed the opportunity cost forgone by pursuing something else? If the opportunity stacks up then the entrepreneur must devise a strategy to marshal resources, often outside his or her control, needed to realise the opportunity.
Opportunity exploitation (Galvanise necessary resources)	There are significant investment and financing decisions to be made at this point. Most new venture requires multiple injections of cash before they are sustainable. These usually come at a cost to the entrepreneur who may need to share equity in the business to acquire the resources needed.
Leading and managing (Operations)	The third stage requires execution of a plan to realise the opportunity. The common perception from investors is that while good opportunities are relatively easy to find, entrepreneurs with the management skills for execution are far less common.
Harvest the rewards (e.g., Exit)	Outside investors often bet on the *jockey as well as the horse*. The final stage of this process is where the entrepreneur "harvests" the rewards.

In May 2012, for example, Zuckerberg sold a tiny fraction of his shareholding in Facebook prior to the IPO, netting him $1.1bn. Of course, every new venture will not necessarily yield the expected rewards. Entrepreneurs needs to be aware of financial issues so that the appropriate strategic and implementation decisions can be taken to achieve the expected rewards.

12.4 APPLICATION OF FINANCE TO THE ENTREPRENEURIAL CONTEXT

The uncertainty of early-stage ventures requires an application of financial theory that differs considerably to that in more structured and mature contexts, such as investing large corporations.

1. In large corporations or institutions, risk reduction is premised on investors' ability to diversify their portfolios. Corporations, themselves, tend to have well-diversified businesses. So, a corporate decision to invest in a new venture is usually far less risky than an entrepreneur making a very specific decision to start the same venture from scratch. The un-diversified entrepreneur is, therefore, likely to have a different perception of risk and to arrive at a different valuation of the new if they agree on projected future earnings.
2. Corporate decision-making is usually vested in an executive team responsible for maximising shareholder value. Decision-making in a new venture setting primarily resides with the entrepreneur. However,

in the case where the entrepreneur raises capital by bringing in outside investors, the investor often insist in playing a role in decision-making. In some cases, they may even bring in a new CEO to replace the entrepreneur in this role.

3. Information problems between entrepreneurs and outside investors are likely to be much more acute than those between insiders and outsiders in corporations. Corporate shareholders tend not to get involved in its day-to-day project decisions. In a start-up scenario, the entrepreneur has to convince outside investors of the value of the project. Often the only way to do this is to prepare a well-thought-out business plan and to offer contract terms to outside investors that signal the entrepreneur's confidence in the venture.

4. Incentive schemes play an important role both in start-ups and corporations. In corporations, performance bonuses and stock options can align management and investor interests. Covenants can be used to discourage over-reliance on risky debt. In start-ups, contract terms between an outside investor and an entrepreneur are usually designed to incentivise the entrepreneur to develop the business quickly.

5. Uncertainty associated with new ventures is usually higher than that of corporations. Consequently, the use of options in contracts between investors and entrepreneurs can be advantageous to both parties hedging their bets on the likely outcomes of the venture. Traditional project valuation, involving forecasting cash-flows and discounting them back to the present (NPV), does not reflect the value of these options. Options that might be exercised include: staging of capital injections, linking them to milestones, abandonment, increasing the investment in the new venture, converting debt to equity, equity buy-back (Mason and Merton, 1985).

6. Shares in corporations are usually liquid, i.e., can be traded easily in the markets. Hence, investment decisions are based on the corporation's ability to generate free cash-flows and yield dividends. Investing in new ventures presents a different investment scenario. These investments are not liquid and often fail to generate free cash-flows for several years. Returns on investment are, therefore, harvested through liquidity events, such as public offering or trade sale. Because of the importance of liquidity events, their timings are usually built-in to the business plan (as an exit) and factored into the valuation of the investment.

The entrepreneur's priority in financial planning for a new venture is to balance retaining as much of the financial claims as the business grows with maximising the value created by the business. Different sources of finance are suited to the different stages of development.

12.5 FUNDING: DEBT OR EQUITY?

There are two basic options open to the entrepreneur for financing: debt or equity. Debt refers to borrowed money, secured in some way by an asset for collateral. However, equity is contributed capital, usually as a cash injection or as a contributed asset. New technology ventures often need long-term debt or equity capital to support anticipated rapid growth. Borrowing has the advantage in that it can be relatively quick to arrange and does not dilute equity ownership. However, debt subjects the venture to a long-term obligation and, therefore, increases risk. It is common for entrepreneurs to mix equity, debt, self-funding, and external funding.[2] The entrepreneur's personal assets, both equity and debt, as well as those of family and friends are most commonly used to finance concept or seed-stage companies. Banks and other institutional investors assess business plans for loan applications on the basis of whether or not the down-side risk is minimal enough so they are confident loans will be repaid. They are less concerned with upside potential and whether the new venture will exceed expectations. Cash-for-equity investors, however, will be more interested in the upside potential and the return on their investment.

The use of debt requires equity as a pre-requisite. A general rule of thumb is that for every dollar of early-stage equity, an entrepreneur could raise a dollar of debt, so long as there are additional assets to secure that debt. Lenders recognise that a start-up is usually unable to generate immediate sales or profits and, consequently, will seek to have the debt secured. This debt will most likely be short-term debt for working capital to be paid back from sales. Long-term borrowing is typically used to finance property or equipment, which in turn could be used to secure short-term debt. A big advantage of debt financing is that is does not dilute the entrepreneur's equity position. However, if credit costs rise or sales fail to meet targets, cash-flows really get pinched and bankruptcy can become reality. It is up to the entrepreneur to determine what blend of debt and equity is optimal for the particular stage of growth they are seeking to finance.

12.6 STAGING OF FINANCE TO DEVELOPMENT MILESTONES

The analogy is often drawn between undertaking a new venture and launching a rocket (Reis, 2011), the probability of success low and slight deviations can lead the venture way off target. The long journey proceeds in stages, at which there is the option to either terminate (abandon) or make minor adjustments. Early-stage ventures tend not to generate enough profit to support further growth. Hence, their development is fuelled by cash injections, just enough to get them to the next stage at which it is hoped that the venture will be able to raise more cash on more favourable terms. A new venture is essentially an experiment in which the assumption-to-knowledge ratio is high. Information about the potential of the business opportunity may be incomplete and asymmetric. The entrepreneur may have more accurate information about the product or technology whereas the investors may have more information about the market.

How does the investor test the ability of the entrepreneur and how can the entrepreneur avoid giving too much information about of the business idea away while convincing the outside investor that the opportunity is worth pursuing? Information problems are largely solved by staging finance to measurable performance milestones. Rather than committing funds up front, staging allows the investor to "wait and see" if the entrepreneur can deliver on key milestones, such as the development of a prototype or first sales.

Staging can also benefit the entrepreneur. Early funding can be costly as a large fraction of ownership would need to be exchanged for a small investment. Use of milestones not only allows the entrepreneur to retain more ownership but makes the investment more attractive. Staging is often event driven rather than time driven, each event validating or invalidating previous assumptions (Block and MacMillan, 1992). Achieving milestones allows the entrepreneur to de-risk the business.

12.7   SOURCES OF FINANCE IN DIFFERENT STAGES OF DEVELOPMENT

While each venture has a unique life cycle, there is a generally accepted model that outlines stages of business development, which require particular types of financing. Funding amounts required by a new venture generally increases as the entrepreneurial life cycle proceeds while risk reduces. Figure 12.3 outlines different sources of finance linked to the stages of development.

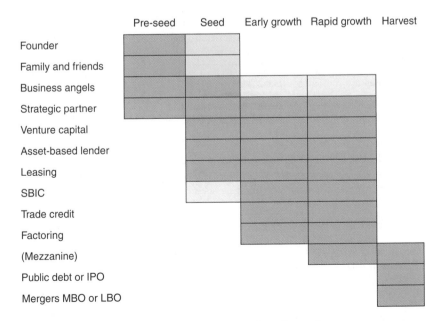

Figure 12.3   Sources of finance in different stages of development

Start-ups usually burn lots of cash in the early stages. Cash is the fuel that propels a start-up to sustainability. Start-ups are often limited by particular types of financing such as personal savings or personally secured debt. Conversely, businesses with a track-record find it easier to acquire financing with greater alternatives such as banks, angels and VCs. The challenge for start-ups is that institutional investors are used to investing in lower risk opportunities, and unless a new venture can generate positive cash-flows, it will not be able to obtain significant debt financing.

Friends, Family and Founders: It is important to point out that many SMEs (BDRC Continental, 2011) do not access formal sources of external finance. They, instead, tend to rely on trade credit from their suppliers or retained earnings. The most commonly used forms of external finance include: bank funding – either loans, credit cards or overdraft. Only a minority use equity finance from either venture capitalists or business angels. Start-ups also use personal finance to fund investment and growth or seek finance from informal sources like friends and family (Figure 12.4).

Data on the extent to which personal finances of founders, family and friends are used in new venturing varies but there are numerous examples of successful start-ups that bootstrapped or self-funded. Bootstrap start-ups have to find a way to attract sales quickly, so they are forced to develop a product that customers need and to find customers who are willing to pay for it.

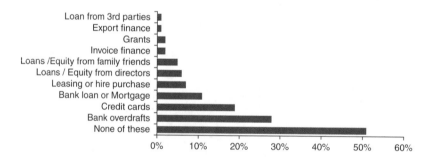

Figure 12.4 Use of external finance by SMES in UK 2011

Source: BDRC Continental (2011) *SME Finance Monitor: Q3 2011: Developing a Deeper Understanding* (November).

Case Box 12.2 Hewlett-Packard: An Example of Bootstrapping

As far back as the 1940s, two young graduates from Stanford University, Bill Hewlett and Dave Packard, with a mere $538 in start-up capital (Entrepreneur. com, 2008) begun their entrepreneurial endeavours in a garage in Palo Alto as they continued their collaboration with mentor Professor Frederick Terman. The professor watched his prime protégés graduate and three years later, Terman managed to entice them back with Stanford fellowships and part-time jobs (Jacobson, 1998). He suggested their first marketable product: an audio-oscillator based on a principle of negative feedback he had taught them at university. Soon after, the partners won their first big business! Disney ordered eight oscillators to fine-tune the soundtrack of Fantasia (Packard, 1995). This provided their first injection of working capital to move their premises and hire employees.

This genesis story of Hewlett-Packard, a $120bn company with over 300,000 employees and bell-weather of the DOW Jones, has inspired many engineer-entrepreneurs.

Note: 367 Addison Avenue Palo Alto, Hewlett-Packard Start-Up and Birth-Place of Silicon Valley

Angel Financing: With limited resources, it is very difficult for an entrepreneur to sustain growth through bootstrapping, in which case external financing must be pursued. Friends, family and founders (3Fs) can typically invest modest amounts of money, normally below $25,000. At the other extreme of the equity funding spectrum, most venture capital funds are currently investing a minimum of $500,000. Business angels are high-worth individuals, often experienced entrepreneurs, who provide financing and expertise to start-ups in exchange for an equity stake in the business. Business angels are often thought of as a bridge, filling the equity gap between the 3Fs, and venture capital that invest relatively small amounts in early-stage projects with high-growth potential. The most common exit point for an angel is a successful trade sale or IPO.

Case Box 12.3 Tenmou is Bahrain's First Business Angel Company

Tenmou provides relatively small amounts of funding, typically BD 20,000 ($53,000) for 20–40 per cent equity. More importantly, Tenmou's network of established entrepreneurs in the Middle East island kingdom offers a package of mentorship and funding to high-potential start-ups. Tenmou's investment fund is financed by some of Bahrain's best known businesses, including: Bahrain Development Bank and Bahrain's Aluminium giant, Alba (MacDonald, 2012). While angels have been a traditional source of financing for high growth ventures in the West, it is a new concept in the Middle East in which Tenmou hopes to contribute to the growing culture of entrepreneurship.

Venture Capital: Venture capital firms typically invest a large fund in a portfolio of high-growth ventures. Each fund is organised as a limited partnership, in which investors and the management team are partners. Investors tend to be institutional and well-diversified, such as pension funds, corporations, insurance companies and banks. The expertise of VC firms is in raising new funds every few years and identifying ventures with high-growth potential in which to invest. Not all ventures are suited to venture capital. VC investments are targeted at later-stage investments in which negative cash-flow early on is offset by very fast growth rates later (revenue of $0–$20m in four to five years) or opportunities with very large market potential ($50m–$100m in revenue).

VCs monitor the progress of their investees to the extent that they often have a hands-on approach to managing their investee ventures: they often sit on the board of directors, tie financing to strict milestones and appoint key managers. They often have industry-specific expertise and the majority of their investments are in the high-tech fields. Not all VC investments pay off. The failure rate can be quite high, and in fact, anywhere from 20 to 90 per cent of portfolio companies may fail to return on the VCs investment. However, if a VC does well, a fund can offer returns of 300 to 1,000 per cent (3X to 10X). Because the failure rate can be high, they often seek 10X returns on the capital invested with an understanding that extremely few of their investments are likely to hit that number. A 10X return sounds pretty spectacular but not necessarily to a VC or its limited partners. 10X on a $1.5 million investment would barely impact on a $800 million fund designed to return $2.4 billion. If the VC really wanted to impact on their reported returns to their limited partners then they would need several $5–10 million investments each returning a $50–100 million on exit.

If the dollar amount invested isn't enough of a constraint, the time-frame horizon for most planned VC investments constrains the pool of suitable investees even further. To ensure a decent return on the overall investment fund, a VC typically plans each individual investment over a maximum five- to seven-year horizon in order to return capital plus a return to their limited partners. VCs operate primarily in post-seed investments (Series A) where the amount of invested capital is significant and the timeline to exit is shorter. In these scenarios, the technology is developed and product has already been beta-tested. Customers like it and are prepared to pay real money for it.

Strategic Partner: The entrepreneur may consider a strategic partner in place of a VC or Angel. This could be a vendor, customer or other business partner with whom the venture is currently working, who might be interested in investing in the company. A strategic investor often has deeper pockets than an angel, but typically has a specific reason for investing so it's always important to know the reason behind the investment and to ensure interests are aligned. The investor may only want to leverage the venture's technology for its own purposes or may want a favourable licensing distribution agreement if the venture succeeds. Large corporations often provide venture funds as a vehicle for advancing their technology and product-market strategies. Some corporations invest in new ventures to develop them as strategic partners.

Government Sources: In many countries, provision of SME finance is seen an instrument of economic policy. Many governments, therefore, put in place appropriate interventions, often targeting the funding gaps left by private equity. In the United States, the federal government provides subsidies on financing through the Small Business Administration (SBA). Small Business Investment Companies (SBICs) access soft loans, guaranteed by the SBA and tend to invest it chunks between $250,000 and $5,000,000 in later-stage ventures (Klein, 2011). There are over 300 SBICs are in the United States with $16 billion in capital under management. In Europe, there are various schemes in place to foster technological innovation and deal with the gap between publicly funded research and technology spin-offs.

Case Box 12.4 Innovation vouchers a success story for firms and colleges[3]

FROZEN yoghurts for pets, portable sterilisers for babies' bottles, software, pharmaceuticals and chocolates are just some of the produces boosted in a wave of new links created between third-level researchers and innovative Irish companies.

So far, more than 1,000 small companies have availed of the Government's €5,000 "innovation vouchers" which allow them to link up with college researchers to solve business and technical problems. Enterprise Ireland manages the innovation vouchers.

One beneficiary has been Frozen Pet-Zerts in Rescommon, whose frozen organic yoghurts in banana, blueberry, peanut better and vanilla flavours, have been brought to market with the help of the St Angela's food research centre in Sligo.

Another is Shasta, an Athlone company that has developed a portable baby bottle steriliser. It use the vouchers to work with Athlone Institute of Technology on the prototype of the steriliser. Shasta is now working with the Irish operation of a global manufacturing company called Nypro Ireland, based in Bray, Co Wicklow, to manufacture this product. They have a patent pending in 144 countries.

Meanwhile, Waterford Institute of Technology (WIT) topped the list of third level institutes availing of the vouchers, bringing research support to 144 firms in all.

Tom Corcoren, research and innovation manager at WIT-based Arclabs, said: "The €5,000 voucher is only the key. In fact, researchers working with SMEs tend to keep going until they produce something concrete. The real gain has been to show companies that colleges are not some grand seat of learning. The business people sit down with the researchers and to talk about what can be achieved.

"I give a guide that the €5,000 gives them about eight to ten days of one researcher's time. In fact, these projects are often done by teams. The companies get great value for that money. These are often projects which previously simply couldn't have been done. That's the real gain."

Tom Corcoran's role is to match businesses with the best researcher for their goals – creating product prototypes, developing new markets, working on quality management systems, etc. The firms cover everything from IT, consumer goods and pharma. The brief also tends to vary considerable.

WIT has worked on quality processes for an anti-cancer drug with local pharma company Eirgen. In this case, the voucher has led on to further R&D work and deeper relations between the college and the company.

WIT has also worked on developing sales management strategies for hand-made chocolate producer, Gallweys Chocolates. The company has since expanded its product range and opened two cafes.

Minister for Science, Technology and Innovation, Conor Lemham, said that passing the milestone of 1,000 innovation vouchers suggests the scheme will continue to pay dividends for small Irish companies. He also paid tribute to WIT and presented awards to the top five knowledge providers.

"The vouchers are an important early bridge between firms and academic researchers. The scheme has helped small firms to explore how they can play their part in building the knowledge economy:" Mr. Lenihan said, "The vouchers have brought firms and researchers together in finding innovative ways to overcome challenges and give products a more competitive and commercial edge for the marketplace."

Small Irish firms are now working with research teams in more than 41 research institutions across the island.

WIT has completed 144 innovation voucher projects since the initiative's launch three years ago. IT Carlow has completed 70 projects; UCC, 68, Athone IT, 65 and CIT, 58. Enterprise Ireland executive director Feargal O Morlin said: "Enterprise Ireland is working with all the participating knowledge providers to ensure that small businesses in receipt of an innovation voucher get access to first-class human resources and equipment in 41 locations around Ireland."

The next call for vouchers applications will open on October 1. For more, see innovationvouchers.ie.

Innovation Vouchers (Public Funding Example for Innovation in Europe): Innovation vouchers are small lines of credit or lump-sum grants provided by governments to SMEs to purchase services from public knowledge providers, such as universities, R&D Labs, with a view to introducing innovations (new products or processes).[4] There has been some noted success with innovation voucher schemes in Ireland, Singapore, Belgium, Cyprus, Poland and the Czech Republic. The United States offers a similar scheme, called the small business technology transfer program (STTR).[5]

Although these schemes offer very small amounts of funding targets at seed and pre-seed stages, many governments offer larger funding schemes for high-tech companies who are further in their development.

Trade Credit: Trade credit is, perhaps the most common of short-term financing for SMEs. If, for example, a venture makes a purchase then receives the goods almost right away but does not need to pay for 30 days then this is equivalent to getting a 30-day interest-free loan. However, it can be costly as often discounts are offered to those who pay upfront or within a shorter time-frame. If, for example, a 2 per cent discount is offered for those who pay within 10 days but the venture chooses to pay on the 30th day then it is effectively borrowing the invoiced amount at 2 per cent for 20 days, which is equivalent to an annualised rate of 44 per cent per annum. Entrepreneurs must consider this in managing their cash-flow.

Factoring: When a venture offers trade credit to its customers, it generates accounts receivable. Factoring is a financial transaction whereby a business sells its accounts receivable to a third party (called a factor) at a discount. Similarly, invoice discounting is a cash-flow solution that releases the cash (up to 75–90 per cent of the value of the invoices) tied up in debtors. It can be a confidential facility, and it also allows the entrepreneur to control credit. When the full amount is collected, the factor remits to the venture the remaining 10–25 per cent and charges a 1–2 per cent fee.

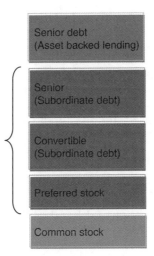

Figure 12.5 Mezzanine finance fills the gap between senior debt and equity

Mezzanine Finance: Mezzanine finance is a form debt used by companies that have positive cash-flows with revenues over $10 million. Mezzanine debt is a layer of financing rated between a company's senior debt and its equity. Structurally, it is subordinate to senior debt but senior to common stock or equity (Figure 12.5). Mezzanine debt usually takes the form of convertible debt, i.e., subordinate debt with a sweetener in the form of a call option (or warrant) to purchase equity. Although it is a more expensive source of funding than a straight-forward bank loan, mezzanine finance can be particularly helpful to fast growth companies.

Mezzanine capital is typically used to fund growth, such as an acquisition, new product line, new distribution channel or plant expansion or, in private business, for the company owners to take money out of the company or to enable a management buyout. With banks becoming more cautious and with equity finance being expensive (it dilutes ownership), mezzanine finance can be an attractive source of capital. In fact, many companies use an efficient combination of senior debt, mezzanine finance and equity to minimise the cost of capital.

Initial Public Offering (IPO): Private ventures may choose to "go public" for several reasons: the most common reason being that capital raised through an IPO does not have to be repaid, whereas debt securities must be repaid with interest. An IPO is essentially the offering of shares for sale to the wider public. It is seen as a convenient exit mechanism for VCs and early-stage investors to realise their investment gains, achieve liquidity and diversify. The majority of firms who chose to go public need additional capital to execute long-range business models, increase brand name and acquire funds for possible acquisitions. By converting to corporate status, a company can always return to the market and offer additional shares through a secondary offering. Getting an IPO right can be tricky: some recent IPOs, for example, have been associated with huge first-day gains following by flops in share price. This volatility often leads issuers and underwriters to time the IPO for market appreciation. The time and cost of compliance with the Securities and Exchange Commission (SEC) is also a critical factor as it can divert energies away from core business activities.

Public Debt: Later-stage ventures can, of course, seek to issue the bond market if they have a sufficient asset base and require significant amounts of capital.

12.8 NEGOTIATING A DEAL WITH AN INVESTOR

The deal defines the allocation of risk and returns to both the entrepreneur and investor and the details are usually documented in a term-sheet. Rather than get locked into detailed legal negotiations straight way, the term-sheet facilitates a non-binding agreement between the investor and entrepreneur with basic terms and conditions by setting out the amount to be invested and the ownership claims to which the investor is entitled.

Entrepreneur's main concerns	Investor's main concerns
• Loss of management control of the venture; • Dilution of personal stock; • Repurchase of your personal stock in the event of employment termination, retirement or resignation; • Adequate financing; • Future capital requirements and dilution of the entrepreneur's ownership; and • Leveraging indirect benefits of the investor, such as access to key contacts.	• Current and projected valuation; • Evaluating the risk associated with this investment; • Projected levels of return on investment; • Liquidity of investment and exit strategies (down-side protection); • Protection of the investor's ability to participate in future funding rounds if venture meets exceeds projections; and • Influence over decision-making.

Consider, for example a deal where a venture is seeking funding of $4 million to carry it to the next milestone. An investor is proposing to provide the capital in exchange for 2 million shares of common stock. It is agreed that the entrepreneur is to retain 8 million shares of common stock.

- The investor prices each share at $4m/2m shares = $2 per share
- The Post-Money Valuation is $2/share × 10 million shares = $20 million
- The Pre-Money Valuation is $20 – $4m = $16m

The *post-money valuation* is a measure of how much the outside investor believes the venture is worth. This becomes more complicated when the deal includes terms beyond a straight-forward cash for equity swap. Preferred stock, for example, has a higher claim on assets and earnings than common stock. Dividends must be paid to holders of preferred stock before being paid to ordinary shareholders. This makes preference shares more expensive. If, for example, the investor offers $4 million in exchange for 1.5 million shares of preferred stock convertible on a 1:1 basis to common stock then it would provide him or her with some down-side protection if the venture does not perform well, yet facilitate conversion to common stock if the venture does better than expected. This deal would also allow the entrepreneur to retain a reasonably high shareholding in parallel with downside protection and, therefore, a more valued position. In this case the valuationwould be:

- The investor prices each share at $4m/1.5m share = $2.67 per share
- The Post-Money Valuation is $2.67/share × 9.5 million shares = $25.3m
- The Pre-Money Valuation is $25.3m – $4m = $21.3m

It is important not to focus solely on the post-money valuation by the investor and to also assess the "sweeteners" promised to the investor that could affect that valuation. Due the uncertainty associated with investing in new ventures, the investor is likely to include a number of options, rights and contingencies as part of any detailed agreement. In the example above, the investor might insist on a warrant to acquire an additional 2 million shares if the venture fails to achieve a certain revenue threshold in two years. A common provision often used to protect investors in the event of a lower valuation in a subsequent funding round is a ratchet provision that prevents dilution of the investors shareholder value. This is usually provided by warrants to acquire additional shares at a set price or convertible stock with a floating conversion price. Other key provisions often included are:

- **Voting Trust:** Voting rights are assigned to the investor if the entrepreneur does not perform. It provides the investor with the ability to take control, even in a minority position.
- **Put Provision:** A put provision gives the investor the option to sell the business to the best bidder if there is no exit by a pre-defined date.
- **Piggyback Option:** This provides the investor with the right to sell its shares anytime the entrepreneur decides to sells shares either in a public offering or in a trade sale.
- **Drag Along:** This provides the investor with the right to force all other shareholders to sell if then it receives an acceptable price offer for its shares.
- **Tag-Along:** If an entrepreneur is offered a favourable deal for its shares then tag-along provides the investor with the option to notify the purchaser that it too may wish to its shares.
- **Unlocking Provision:** This provides the investor with the option of insisting that the entrepreneur buys him/her out if the entrepreneur receives an offer they don't wish to accept but the investor does.

12.9   THE BUSINESS MODEL

The business model and the business plan are addressed in Chapter 6. Business plans are commonly used to document an opportunity to potential investors and are often considered an intermediary step between strategy and implementation. There are plenty of web sites that will provide aspiring entrepreneurs with templates for business plans. From an investment perspective, it is much more common to assess the underlying principles that will lead to revenue growth. These principles are collectively enshrined in the business model (Chapter 6). Business plans for new ventures and start-ups differ considerably to those for established businesses. The main difference relates to the accuracy with which future projections can be made, the assumptions underlying established business plans tending to be much more reliable. Financial projections for established businesses can, for example, be based on prior experience whereas those for new ventures are often premised on macro-economic data, conjecture and performance of similar ventures. Planning is often based therefore on unproven assumptions such as:

1. How big is the market opportunity?
2. What market penetration can the new venture achieve?
3. What is the tie-to-market for a new product?

A business plan typically outlines a number of underlying assumptions about the new venture, e.g., time-to-market, product cost, pricing, first customers and sales targets. As the venture develops, these assumptions get tested as hypotheses, either de-risking the investment (if the hypotheses are proved) or triggering a re-evaluation of the venture (if the hypotheses are disproved). Milestones and financial projections are, therefore, critical to outside investors and if the entrepreneur needs to be able to articulate why a projection was not achieved and its implications for the business opportunity as the venture proceeds. Investors typically seek evidence in a business plan along three dimensions:

1. The Entrepreneurial team	2. Business idea merit	3. Evidence of commitment
• Qualification and reputation • Youth and experience • Track-record • Ability to implement the plan • Evidence of traction and partnerships • Ability to function as an effective team	• Technology risk • Alignment of product to market • Timing • Potential size of market opportunity • Route to market identified • No fatal flaws	• Time and capital already invested • salaries of start-up team • Equity buy-in for achieving key milestones • Investors protected against early exit by start-up team

A common problem for technology entrepreneurs is balancing the need articulate the merits of their business idea without disclosing critical aspects that could be appropriated by others. Providing evidence of intellectual property (IP) may signal to potential investors that the idea is based on deep-rooted know-how that cannot be copied easily, thereby avoiding the need to disclose unnecessary secrets. Where ideas are not protected by IP, the entrepreneur needs to be cautious in choosing a reputable investor or at least ensure that they have sufficient first-mover advantage that stealing their idea would not make much difference. There are differing views on what financial information to include in a business plan. However, it is commonly agreed that projecting financial performance of a new venture is as hard as forecasting the weather.[6] Investors often cite that prospective entrepreneurs over-state sales projections whereas entrepreneurs often believe this to be posturing so that investors can negotiate more a favourable deal. Yet financial projections provide the basis for entrepreneurs and outside investors to come to a common understanding about the potential value of a new venture. One common way to deal with this problem is to provide the investor with a long-term option, known as a warrant, to buy more shares at a nominal price if the venture fails to meet key sales targets. This not only signals the entrepreneur's confidence in the targets but de-risks the investor's investment and incentivises the entrepreneur to achieve the targets.

12.10   DUE DILIGENCE

Investors will always take reasonable steps to verify the accuracy of any business plan before pouring money into a new venture. Due diligence is a process in which all aspects of an investment decision are validated (Shontel, 2012). It can be expected that the investor will to conduct due diligence on all aspects of the business plan, including the entrepreneur's character and his or her team, recent financial performance of the fledgling business and its ability to grow, customers and partners, the current ownership structure of the business, validation of any IP and who has invested how much in the business to date, a review of all compliance and regulatory requirements and a review of any pending litigation, insurance or taxation claims. This process checks the integrity of the entrepreneur's business as well as provides a view on how it is managed.

The investor is likely to incur considerable costs during due diligence, and they will want to make sure that the entrepreneur's intentions are bone fide by acting in good faith during the negotiation period. For protection, the investor may request that the entrepreneur executes an exclusivity agreement whereby the entrepreneur agrees not to proceed with negotiations with any other party during the due diligence period.

Due diligence should work both ways, and entrepreneurs should also conduct due diligence on any potential investor. A common mistake made by entrepreneurs is to choose the investor who offers the lowest equity requirement for making the investment where, in reality, they me be better to choose an investor who can add greater value to the business. The entrepreneur should seek references from CEOs about what the investor was like to work with, assess the investor's credibility in the investment community as an enabler for future.

12.11   MANAGING CASH-FLOW AND PROFITABILITY

Managing cash-flow is critical in to a start-up's survival. Without cash in the bank, a new venture simply cannot pay the bills – wages, rent, raw materials, etc. Entrepreneurs often report that on paper their cash-flows seem positive with the venture appearing to make plenty of money but, in reality, they are cash-poor and struggling to our day-to-day operations. All too often cash inflows seem to be slower at coming in than the speed with which cash is being paid out and new business owners soon discover a simple truth: first, you pay for goods or services then eventually your customer pay you. This creates a drain on cash resources. The period between payment of cash and receipt of cash is called the "cash gap".

Cash-flow reflects how long your goods sit as inventory, how long it takes for your customers to pay and how long your suppliers give you to pay them. Cash-flow is best explained as a cycle. The cash you use in your business to acquire resources to sell products or services to your customers is then collected by way of customer payments. These payments are used to pay outstanding bills and to re-invest in more resources to sell additional products or services.

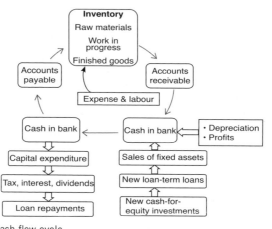

Figure 12.6   Cash-flow cycle

Source: After Walsh (2008) *Key Management Ratios*, 4th edition, © Pearson Education 2008.

The interval between interval between payment of cash and receipt of cash must be financed and the longer the time the more interest is paid on borrowings from a lender, consumer valuable working capital. Let's take the following illustrative example to how the cash-gap can drain financial resources. The summary below shows financial statements for a new venture.

12.11.1   Profit and Loss Accounts

	2012	2013
	€'000	€'000
Sales	1200	1400
Less cost of sales		
Opening stock	80	100
Purchases	700	800
Less closing stock	(100)	(150)
	680	750
Gross profit	520	650
Less expenses	(200)	(300)
Net profit	320	350

12.11.2 Balance Sheet at:

		31 December 2012		31 December 2012
		€'000		€'000
Fixed assets		1,000		1,000
Current assets				
Stock		100		150
Debtors		100		150
Bank		20		120
		220		420
Less current liabilities				
Creditors	80	140	80	340
		1,140		1,340
Financed by				
Capital at beginning of year		870		1,140
Add net profit		320		350
		1,190		1,490
Less drawings		50		150
		1,140		1,340

Let's assume that the interest rate being charged for a short-term facility in 2013 is 6 per cent. The calculations below illustrate the cost of poor cash-flow management. The cash-gap is essentially the average amount of days in which the business is relying on short-term credit, on which interest must be paid, to survive.

$$Cash\,Gap = Inventory\,Days + Days\,Receivable - Days\,Payable$$

$$Cash\,Gap = 365 / \frac{150}{1400} + \frac{150}{1400} - \frac{120}{1400} = 365 \frac{420}{1400} = 57\,Days$$

$$Daily\,Cost\,of\,Sales = \frac{€750,000}{365} = €2,054 \text{ each day}$$

∴ To cover the cash gap the company needs to borrow €2,054 each Day × 57 Days
= €117,85. At 6% the compay would need to pay €117,857 × 6%
= €7071 in annual interest.

This represents a small but not insignificant amount off the bottom-line.

Normally accountants recognise income at the time a sale is made irrespective if it is for cash or on credit. Using the accrual system, it is possible to record revenues before cash payments are actually received. Similarly accounting expenses do not necessary equate to negative cash-flows as the company may have purchased items but not yet paid for them. Depreciation, which is expensed against profit, does not affect cash-flow.

This partly explains why highly profitable ventures can have negative cash-flows. Common cash-flow problems include:

Reason	Solution
Volatility in critical business parameters	• Monitor for trends, e.g., slowing sales, rising costs. • Use risk management tools to reduce exposure to changing interest rates, commodity prices and exchange rates. • Use insurance to protect against loss of assets are income.
Excessive capital tied up in inventory and equipment	• Ensure Effective Raw Materials planning. • Reduce in work-in-progress (WIP). • Turn over excess stock, even at a discount. • Consider using leasing solutions for equipment instead of purchasing.
Long-term assets bought with cash	• Use longer term lending solutions for capital assets. • Match the length of the loan to the life of the asset.
Collecting accounts receivable too slowly	• Have a system in place to follow up overdue accounts. • Use electronic payment solutions. • Take post-dated cheques.

12.12   DETERMINING FINANCIAL NEEDS

Free Cash-Flow (FCF) is a more conservative description of cash-flow than Earnings Before Interest Depreciation Tax and Amortisation (EBIDTA). It represents the cash-flow after expenditure on maintaining and investing in new capital is made to support growth in the company.

$FCF = EBIT(1–TR) + Depreciation – \Delta\ Working\ Capital – Capex$

where

EBIT = Earnings before interest and tax
TR = Tax rate
Capex = Amount invested in new capital

12.13   VALUATION PRIMER

In corporate finance, the fundamental method of valuation is to calculate the net present value (NPV) of future cash-flows. In valuing shares, for example, the NPV calculation would include future dividends and capital appreciation. Similar the bond price is calculated using the NPV of future cash-flows, determined largely by its par value, the bond yield and time-to-maturity. Let's take simple example below in which a farmer is presented with a new business opportunity to plant willow as an energy crop. The following financial projections are given per acre.

	Yr1	Y2	Yr3	Yr4	Yr5	Yr6	Yr7	Yr8	Yr9	Yr10
	€	€	€	€	€	€	€	€	€	€
Costs										
Planting	600									
Purchase stock	1,600									
Pesticide spraying	200									
Fertiliser	100									
Cuttings	100									
Fencing wire	150									
Herbicide		75			50			50		
Harvesting				400			400			400
Drying cost				250			250			250
Operational costs	2,750	75	0	650	50	0	650	50	0	650
Grant aid	−1,031	−344	0	0	0	0	0	0	0	0
Costs before financing	**−1,719**	**269**	**0**	**−650**	**−50**	**0**	**−650**	**−50**	**0**	**−650**
Income										
Sale of harvest				2,880			2,880			2,880
Energy payment	125	125	125	125	125	125	125	125	125	125
Total income	125	125	125	3,005	125	125	3,005	125	125	3,005
Net income	**(1,594)**	**394**	**125**	**2,355**	**75**	**125**	**2,355**	**75**	**125**	**2,355**

The table below shows that the cumulative net income transitions from negative to positive in between Year 3 and Year 4.

	Year 1	Year 2	Year 3	Year 4
Income €	−1594	394	125	2355
Cumulative income €	−1592	−1200	−1075	1160

12.13.1 NPV Method

This simple break-even analysis does not discount the cash-flows hence does not take into account the time value of money and, therefore, under-reflects the need to maintain and replace capital. The table below shows the same cash-flows discounted at 30 and 40 per cent, respectively.

Year	1	2	3	4	5	6	7	8	9	10
Net income	−1594	394	125	2355	75	125	2355	75	125	2355
DCF@ 30%	−1226	233	56	824	20	25	375	9	11	170
DCF@ 40%	−1138	201	45	613	13	16	233	5	6	81

The net present value (NPV) is simply the summation of the discounted cash-flows.

$$NPV @ 30\% = \sum_{0}^{10} DCF = €501 \ per \ acre = €30,000 \ for \ 60 \ acre$$

$$NPV @ 40\% = \sum_{0}^{10} DCF = €67 \ per \ acre = €4,000 \ for \ 60 \ acres$$

The value placed on this venture ultimately depends on the discount rate used, which reflects the riskiness of the future cash-flow projections. The difficulty with this type of analysis is that it may simply be impossible to predict what future cash-flows might be. Furthermore, investors often use very high discount rates to reflect the risk of failure. The NPV method, therefore, can be difficult to apply to new venture valuations.

A very simple method often used is to use price-to-earnings (P/E) ratios. The investor, for example, could look at the net income predicted at a key milestone at some stage in the future and apply a *multiple*, typical of similar ventures, to it. This method is often used to arrive at a "ballpark" valuation. Firms that display similar "value characteristics" are selected. These value characteristics include risk, growth rate, capital structure and the size and timing of cash-flows. This valuation method is most useful when historical information about publicly comparable firms on and their capital structure, revenue, profit margins and net profit figures are known.

12.13.2   Venture Capital Method

The venture capital (VC) Method of valuation recognises that many investee start-ups tend have negative cash-flows for several years followed by highly uncertain but potentially substantial positive cash-flows. The NPV method, therefore, would not provide a meaningful valuation technique. The VC will also have an exit plan strategically linked to a key performance milestone at some stage in the future when a trade sale or IPO can take place. The steps in this method are:

1. Select the year for valuation and estimate the net income or free-cash-flow for that year.
2. Apply a P/E ratio to the net income and compute a valuation for that year.
3. Use a very high discount rate to calculate the present value (PV) of the valuation.
4. Using the PV calculate the fraction of ownership in exchange for the contributed investment.

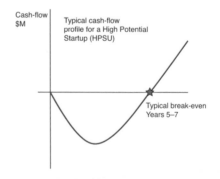

Figure 12.7   Cash-flow profile for HPSU

As an example, if a new venture can achieve free cash-flows of $5 million in the exit year (Year 5) and well-managed companies in this sector typically have a P/E ratio of 10 then we can calculate the terminal value in the fifth year at $50 million. If the VC uses a discount rate of 40 per cent, then the present value of this valuation is:

$$PV = \frac{FV}{(1+r)^r} = \frac{\$50m}{(1+0.4)^5} = \$9.3m$$

This is referred to as the **post-money** valuation. The required equity stake to meet the target rate of return is the amount to be invested by the venture capitalist divided by the present value of the terminal value of the company. If, for example, $4.3 million is being invested then the ownership percentage is:

$$Required\ Ownership\ by\ VC = \frac{\$4.3m}{\$9.3m} = 46\%$$

If the venture currently has 50,000 shares outstanding then it would need to issue a further 43,000 shares to the VC at a price of $100 per share. The pre-money valuation would be $5m.

12.13.3   First Chicago Method

The venture capital method is successful in many cases, but the discount rate applied is the determining variable that reflects many assumptions. A variation on the basic venture capital method, known as the *First Chicago Method*, compensates for the fact that subsequent performance of individual companies does not always match the projections contained in the original plans. This valuation method uses a lower discount rate applied to a cash-flow projection that is calculated as an average of three possible scenarios, with each scenario weighted according to its perceived probability.

12.13.4   Options

Investing in early-stage start-ups is high risk and often mirrors a game of poker in which the players (entrepreneur and investor) withhold information to convey a better hand than they actually have. One way to hedge against risk is to embed flexibility for the investor in any deal that allows them to either:

- increase their investment if the venture is going better than planned;
- decrease their investment if the venture is going poorer than planned;
- defer further investments (wait-and-see approach); or
- abandon the venture altogether.

These real options affect the value of the firm in a way that cannot be measured accurately using discounted cash-flow methods. New ventures backed by private equity companies often go through multiple funding rounds. Investors use this multi-stage approach to motivate the entrepreneur to perform better and limit their exposure by exercising their options. Applying the famous Black-Scholes formula (used for valuing financial options) to valuing new ventures as a portfolio of real options is a developing area of entrepreneurial finance.

$$C = SNd_1 - Ke^{-rT} Nd_2$$

Where

$$d_1 = \frac{\ln(s/k) + (r + \sigma^2/2)t}{\sigma\sqrt{t}}$$

And

$$d_2 = d_1 - \sigma\sqrt{t}$$

C = Call Option Price
S = Price of Underlying Stock
K = Option Exercises Price
N() = Area under normal Curve
r = risk-free rate
T = Time to Expiration
σ = Stock volatility (risk)

12.13.5 Factors Affecting Valuation

Value is the monetised priced agreed by buyer and seller, usually the entrepreneur and investor. Most entrepreneurs and investors have differing oblique points of view that do not intersect. In fact, often the two sides don't even speak the same investment language. There is a value divergence between the ideal valuation due to a venture's growth rate and the valuation of the investor's shares due to dilution by subsequent investors and other factors. Even in successful ventures, divergence, can be anywhere between 3x and 5x.

12.14 HARVESTING AND EXIT STRATEGIES

12.14.1 What Is Harvesting?

Harvesting can be considered to be the final stage in the entrepreneurial process, whereby investors reap the financial returns from their investments. Recall that unlike shares in a corporation traded over the stock exchange, shares in new ventures tend not to be very liquid. Outside investors value venture opportunities with an expectation of a liquidity event, often tied to a key milestone, that enables them to realise the return on their investment so that they can move on to other investments. Harvesting is a critical factor in the initial investment decision as valuation of the venture to both the entrepreneur and outside investor depends on the expected returns at the time of harvest. Despite the fact that entrepreneurs tend to focus their energies in enticing investors into investing in their ventures, investors will always look at potential exit strategies when assessing a business plan. While some entrepreneurs may wish to remain with the venture, harvesting can facilitate earnings on their human capital and opportunity costs associated with the start-up.

12.14.2   Initial Public Offerings (IPO)

There are many famous stories of Silicon Valley entrepreneurs making their fortunes in IPO's. Mark Zuckerberg sold about 30 million shares at a price of $38 when Facebook made its stock market debut. That's a staggering $1.14bn! The IPO has become the benchmark for many aspiring entrepreneurs as the ultimate exit for themselves and their investors. VC's for example, invest in ventures that they deem more likely to deliver an exit by IPO than by trade sale. Yet the percentage of angel investor exits by IPO remains relatively small. The table below shows some of the typical characteristics suited to an IPO.

Characteristic	Typical requirement for IPO.
Revenue	>$20 million.
EBIT	>$2 million. Company must be profitable for a number of years previous to IPO application.
Scope	Company has usually internationalised and entered global markets
Board	High profile board members with corporate experience.
Management	Management team with significant experience in large corporations.
Business portfolio	Range of products to sustain income stream.
Innovation	Pipeline of product development to ensure continued market leadership.
Cash reserves	Enough cash to meet growth requirements without further capital.
Brand	Strong public awareness of brand.
competition	Competitive advantage based on strong IP or business model that erects barriers to entry.

Few ventures in private ownership can meet these requirements. Generally, it will cost in excess of $500,000 in legal and accounting fees for even the smallest IPO. An IPO consumes significant time by senior management in the months leading up to event. The team must select an investment banker to advise on share issuance and to underwrite risk of share price fluctuations during the IPO.

The investment banker will act as intermediary between the venture and the market. It will conduct a full valuation of the company and due diligence. The IPO market is also very sensitive to prevailing economic conditions and timing is critical. High numbers of IPOs tend to coincide, for example, with breakthrough innovations with global potential – computing, silicon chips, the internet, genetics and green-tech. A venture also runs the risk of a post-IPO hangover as the markets tend to be much more wary of overvalued stock and misleading forecasts. Nor does a successful IPO guarantee a successful exit. In the aftermath of the Facebook IPO, its stock fell to its lowest price $19.69 as the initial lock-up expiration of 271 million shares kicked in. Zuckerberg decided not sell his shares for 12 months in order to dampen lock-up expirations and drive confidence. Lockups prevent entrepreneurs and key investors from selling shares for some period after the IPO. Failure to manage the post-IPO period can delay an exit or decrease the expected exit value. Notwithstanding these challenges, an investor can harvest from an IPO in a number of ways. First, they can sell a portion of their share in the IPO. Second, afterwards they can sell small volumes of shares from time to time on the stock exchange or make a private sale to another investor based on the market value of the share.

12.14.2 Trade Sale

In a private trade sale, an interested party can purchase equity in a venture for cash or share swap. The purchasing party will normally conduct due diligence and request warranties from the seller on the valuation. If the seller cannot warrant the value of the venture then the price is likely to be reduced. Angel investors and venture capitalists will always prefer selling their equity for cash. Any new investor will want to be reassured that value is not highly contingent on key members of the management team, such as the founding entrepreneurs. In such circumstances, they may insist in earn-out provisions that keep key personal within the business for a period of time or until agreed milestones are met.

Very few businesses pre-plan trades sales effectively. Many entrepreneurs and early-stage investors end up being forced into a fire-sale, often due to running out of cash reserves. The key to a successful sale is both parties arriving quickly at an agreed value to be acquired. It is important for both early-stage investors and the entrepreneurs to work proactively towards a best-case sale. The process (Figure 12.8) may enhance the locus of control over potential buyers.

12.14.3 The Challenges of High-Growth

The philosophical approach taken by the investment community to exits is extraordinarily one dimensional: invest in companies that have significant forecasted growth in sales and profits and sell out on a multiple of the profits. This one-size-fits-all approach fails to recognise some basic investment principles. First, high-growth in itself, as an investment strategy, is high risk (Garvin, 2004) and statistically produces far more failures than successes, and, second, the approach undervalues those ventures that can add strategic value to potential buyers.

The vast majority of existing businesses employ less than five people, and any that grow beyond a handful of employees are in the minority. In Australia, for example, 60 per cent of SMEs are non-employing; micro businesses (1–employees) account for less than 25 per cent; other small businesses (5–19 employees) account for less than 12 per cent; medium size businesses (20–199 employees) account for 4 per cent; and large companies employing over 200 employees account for about 0.3 per cent (Australian Government, 2011). Clearly if growing a business to the size of FACEBOOK was easy then there would be far more ventures making it to IPO.

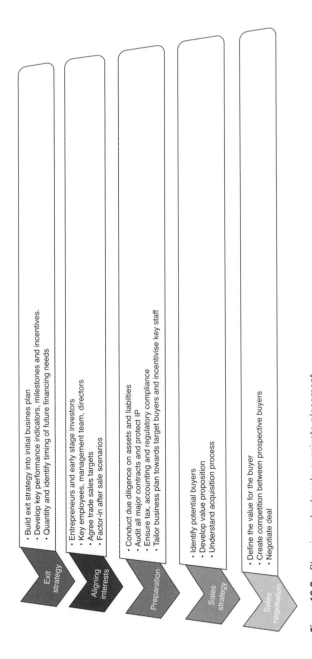

Exit strategy
- Build exit strategy into initial business plan
- Develop key performance indicators, milestones and incentives.
- Quantify and identify timing of future financing needs

Aligning interests
- Entrepreneurs and early stage investors
- Key employees, management team, directors
- Agree trade sales targets
- Factor-in after sale scenarios

Preparation
- Conduct due diligence on assets and liabilities
- Audit all major contracts and protect IP
- Ensure tax, accounting and regulatory compliance
- Tailor business plan towards target buyers and incentivise key staff

Sales strategy
- Identify potential buyers
- Develop value proposition
- Understand acquisition process

Sales negotiation
- Define the value for the buyer
- Create competition between prospective buyers
- Negotiate deal

Figure 12.8 Planning a trade sale or private placement

As a business grows, it has to cope with complexity and challenges associated with increasing in size. Its different stages of a development will reflect change to its business fundamentals. Complexity, for example, increases non-linearly with the number of staff. Too many entrepreneurs fail to cope with these changes.

During the pre-seed and start-up stages an entrepreneur is often able to drive the business through sheer energy and passion. Yet, as the business hires staff a management structures need to be put in place, job descriptions and reporting lines become fixed and performance targets become essential. Communications also become more challenging. These and many other challenges can undermine growth, so much so that extremely few companies manage to sustain double-digit growth for more than a few years. Therefore, although high exit values occur when growth is significant, ventures that pursue high-growth are more likely to stall than sustain their growth. Only rarely does a new venture achieve a size that allows an IPO or a good trade sale. Both investors and entrepreneurs should prioritise planning for an exit event as part of the business plan.

12.15 CHAPTER SUMMARY

The application of financial theory to new venturing has uniquely defining characteristics that differentiates it from classical corporate finance. New venturing (particularly for high-growth) is inherently high risk so financial strategies, such as use of real options, are required to mitigate that risk and to maximise the returns to the entrepreneur. New ventures are also inherently less liquid than corporate shares traded on the open market. Exit strategies for investors and entrepreneurs therefore need to take account of liquidity events such as IPOs and trade sales.

Valuation is particularly contingent on future cash-flow projection and the riskiness of those cash-flows. Traditional NPV methods of valuation do not necessarily apply as many new ventures have negative cash-flows in the early stages of their development. The "cash is king" cliché also has a particular relevance to new ventures in their early developmental stages. Without cash, it cannot survive and new ventures usually do not have the cushion of a large parental company if they run out of cash. Many new venture failures can attribute root-cause failure back to poor financial decision-making.

> **Case Study 12.1** The Facebook IPO
>
> Facebook filed its application for an IPO with the Securities and Exchange Commission in early 2012 and begun trading in May. Its initial valuation was estimated at $100 billion, four times that when Google went public in 2004, but the stock market has not been kind to the social networking company since. The share price dropped steadily from the first-day price of $38, and by August, it had fallen below $25.

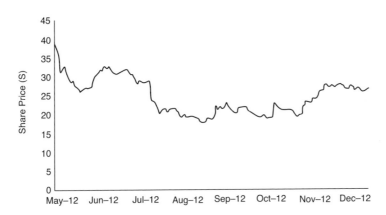

Figure 12.9 Fall in Facebook Share price post IPO

This, in part, is due to the increasing scepticism about how fast Facebook's profits and revenues can grow. It must make money from its users rather than simply add new ones, and it needs to find ways to do it from mobile devices where there is little space for ads. Yet, on its current share prices, Facebook is still valued at over $50 billion, which is staggering for a company only eight years old.

Zuckerberg began his project as a Harvard student, writing a program that allowed students to select the best-looking person from a choice of photos over the Internet.

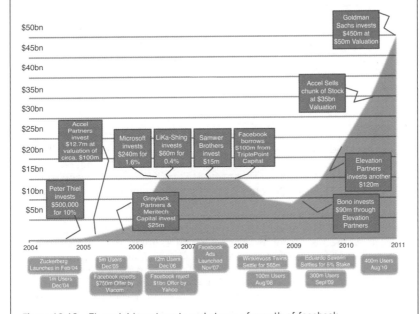

Figure 12.10 Financial investments and stages of growth of facebook

According to Zuckerberg's roommate at the time, Arie Hasit, "he built the site for fun." Needless to say Harvard's authorities were not impressed. "THE FACEBOOK" an online photo directory formally started in early 2004, with co-founder, Eduardo Saverin, providing the most of the initial capital – about $30k. Zuckerberg moved the business to California and bootstrapped his way through its first few months, spreading the website to other universities. It wasn't long into its early growth before it got its first investors.

Angel's Peter Thiel, Reid Hoffman and Mark Pincus invested $500,0000 for 10.2 per cent of the company, and Sean Parker, Napster founder, became Facebook's president. Even the office painter, David Chloe, got paid in shares and is now worth a staggering $240 million.

A year later, Facebook had over 5 million users and began to experience rapid growth, enticing Accel Partners, the venture capital firm headed by investor Jim Breyer, to invest $12.7 million in Facebook for a 15 per cent stake, valuing the company at almost US$ 100 million. At the same time, it rejected an offer from Viacom to buy the business for $75 million. Facebook continued near exponential growth for the next two years, and by 2008, a new round of investment, led by Microsoft implied a valuation of almost $15 billion, well over 30 time revenue.

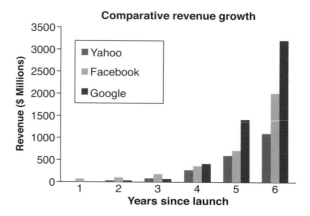

Figure 12.11 Facebook's revenue growth

Facebook did not focus on early revenue growth and did not become profitable until 2009. It made a modest $382,000 in revenue 2004; $9 million in 2005; $48 million in 2006; and in 2007, it made $153 million in revenue with reported $138 million loss; $272 million in 2008 with a $56 million loss; and was finally profitable in 2009 with a net income of $290 million[7] (Figure 12.11). This is not untypical for high-potential ventures. During the development stage, the entrepreneur is focused on product development and market feasibility and has not yet acquired the capacity for revenue generation. During start-up, a venture hires new employees, invests in equipment, etc. and, therefore, may start to generate revenue during this period. There is usually a significant negative cash-flow during this period that reflects investment in equipment, facilities, human capital and working capital. In the early growth stage, revenue begins to grow but profit and cash-flow remain negative. In many cases, revenue growth fizzles out, but, for some, there is an inflection point beyond which the slope of revenue growth increases. As in the case of Facebook, rapid growth requires significant logistical effort to garner external financing to support corresponding growths in working capital and fixed assets. By the time Microsoft invested $240m in Facebook, its revenue growth was 300 per cent p.a., but it was still generating a significant net loss and negative cash-flows. Its aim is to start generating profits and positive cash-flows and, therefore, make returns to debt and equity investors without the requirement for outside financing.

Case Questions

1. What milestones do you think would have been appropriate for Facebook to establish early on to help evaluate the merits of the venture and to attract outside funding?
2. How would you characterise the various stages of development that Facebook has gone through up to its IPO?
3. What stages of financing has Facebook gone through? How do the financing stages correspond to the milestones you identified in Question 1, and the development stages in question 2?
4. Explain how Facebook's valuation has evolved over time.
5. Consider the Facebook IPO in early 2012. Why do you think Zuckerberg decided to undertake an initial public offering at that time? In retrospect, do you think investors were receptive to the offering?
6. What do you think of the price of Facebook's shares in early 2012? What sorts of performance targets would the management need to achieve to maintain the price?

12.16   REVISION QUESTIONS

1. What do you believe are the main contextual differences between finance in a new venture setting and finance in a large corporation?
2. Classify the main types of options open to an investor and entrepreneur in structuring an investment deal. Why do you think "real" options are particularly useful in entrepreneurial finance?
3. Explain the concept to milestone financing, indicating why it might be beneficial to both the outside investor and to the entrepreneur. How can staging of finance reduce information and incentive problems facing a new venture?
4. Consider an investment deal in which the entrepreneur retains 800,000 shares. The investor is willing to contribute €2 million for an additional 400,000 shares. Calculate the "pre-money valuation" and "post-money valuation" and explain the difference in the concepts.
5. As a new entrepreneur with little track-record or credibility, how might you go about convincing an outside investor to invest in your business?
6. Explain what is meant by due diligence, and why it is important both for the investor and entrepreneur.
7. Explain the difference between profitability and cash-flow. Why is cash-flow particularly important for new ventures?
8. Explain how the valuation of a new venture can be conducted based on its projected future cash-flows. Even if an outside investor and entrepreneur agree about projections for future cash-flows why might their valuations differ?

9. Why do venture capital investment deals tend to provide the investor with convertible preferred stock than equity or debt?
10. Explain the concept of a ratchet as an anti-dilution mechanism. Why are ratchets common in financing new ventures?
11. What is a *business angel* and how does this type of investor differ from a professional (institutional) *venture capitalist*?
12. What are the main mechanisms by which an entrepreneur can exit (partially or fully) a business and harvest the rewards?
13. One option for financing a business is to seek credit from a bank. How might the business plan be prepared differently for a bank from one prepared for a cash-for-equity investor, such as a business angel?
14. What are the main challenges and benefits of taking a private company public?
15. Briefly outline what terms and conditions you would expect to see in the term-sheet.

12.17 FURTHER READING AND RESOURCES

- Adelman, P.J. and Marks, A.M. (2010) *Entrepreneurial Finance for Small Business.* Upper Saddle River, NJ: Prentice-Hall
- Leach, C. and Melicher R. (2011) *Entrepreneurial Finance.* Stamford, CT: Cengage Learning.
- McKaskill, T. (2009) *Raising Angel & Venture Capital Finance,* www.tommckaskill.com/ebooks.html.
- Smith, J. and Smith, R.L. (2011) *Entrepreneurial Finance, Strategy, Valuation & Deal Structure.* Hoboken, NJ: Wiley and Sons.

12.18 NOTES

1. From Timmons and Spinelli, 2008.
2. http://www.businesspartners.com/DebtVsEquity.html.
3. *Irish Examiner,* 03/09/2010.
4. http://www.oecd.org/dataoecd/53/42/48135973.pdf.
5. http://sbir.gsfc.nasa.gov/SBIR/nasasbir.htm.
6. Ministry of Small business and Economic Development, British Colombia; *Business Planning & Financial Forecasting: A small business start-up Guide;* www.smallbusinessbc.ca.
7. http://techcrunch.com/2012/02/01/facebook-ipo-facebook-ipo-facebook-ipo/.

12.19 REFERENCES

http://www.businesspartners.com/DebtVsEquity.html.
http://www.oecd.org/dataoecd/53/42/48135973.pdf.
http://sbir.gsfc.nasa.gov/SBIR/nasasbir.htm.
ABS (2012) *Counts of Australian Businesses including Entries and Exits, Jun 2007 to Jun 2011,* Australian Bureau of Statistics.

Australian Government (2011) *Key Statistics on Australian Small Businesses*, Department of innovation, Industry, Science and Research.

Block, Z. and MacMillan, I. (1992) "Milestones in Successful Venture Planning", *Harvard Business Review*, 63(5): 184–197.

BDRC Continental (2011) *SME Finance Monitor: Q3 2011: Developing a Deeper Understanding*, (November), http://www.bdrc-continental.com/EasysiteWeb/get-resource.axd?AssetID=4201&servicetype=Attachment.

Entrepreneur.com (2008) "William Hewlett & David Packard: Maverick Managers", *Entrepreneur Magazine*, October.

Garvin, D. (2004) "What Every CEO Should Know About Creating New Businesses", *Harvard Business Review*, July–August 2004: 18–20.

Jacobson, D. (1998) "Cover Story: Founding Fathers", *Stanford Alumni Magazine*, July– August.

Klein, K.E. (2011) "Small Business investment Companies Explained", *Bloomberg Business Week*, 4 January.

MacDonald, A. (2012) "Tenmou Offering Key Investment", *Gulf Daily News*, 12 April: 19.

Mason, C.M. and Harrison, R.T. (2002) "Is It Worth It? The Rates of Return from Informal Venture Capital Investments", *Journal of Business Venturing*, 17: 211–236.

Mason, S. and Merton, R. (1985) "The Role of Contingent Claims Analysis in Corporate Finance", in *Recent Advances in Corporate Finance*, Edward Altman and Marti Subrahmanyan (eds). Homewood IL: Richard D. Irwin, 7–54.

Ministry of Small Business and Economic Development, British Colombia, *Business Planning & Financial Forecasting: A Small Business Start-up Guide*, www.smallbusinessbc.ca.

Packard, D. (1995) *The HP Way: How Bill Hewlett and I Built our Company*, New York: HarperBusiness.

Reis, E. (2011) *The Lean Start-Up: How Today's Entrepreneurs Use Continuous Innovation to Create Radically Successful Businesses*. Crown Business.

Shontel, A. (2012) *What to Expect from Investors during the Due diligence Phase?* www.businessinsider.com.

Smith, J. and Smith, R. (2004) *Entrepreneurial Finance*, 2nd edn. New York: Wiley, 4.

Stark, Antony. (2001) *SME Support in Britain*, www.adb.org/Documents/Reports/PRC-SME/App5-UK.pdf.

Timmons, J. and Spinelli, S. (2008) *New Venture Creation: Entrepreneurship for the 21st Century*.

12.20   GLOSSARY OF TERMS

3X: A colloquial term in the investment community. A 3X return equates to 300 per cent. A 5X return equates to 500 per cent.

Black-scholes formula: A mathematical formula that provides a theoretical calculation for pricing financial options.

Business angel: An investor (often a wealthy individual or network of individuals) who provides revenue to small start-up firms or entrepreneurs. Business angels are often successful entrepreneurs themselves. They are usually investing in the person rather than the firm.

Collateral: Property or assets that a borrower gives to a lender in order to secure a loan.

Common stock: Shareholders with common stock are at the bottom of the priority ladder for ownership structure. If a company goes bankrupt, common shareholders will only receive their money after creditors and preferred shareholders have received their share of the leftover assets.

Convertible stock: A type of preferred stock that can be exchanged into shares of common stock.

Covenant: A promise in a financial contract that certain activities will or will not be carried out. Covenants are often requested, in the form of debt-to-asset ratios, by lenders to protect them from borrowers defaulting on their obligations due to financial actions detrimental to themselves or the business.

Debt: An amount of money borrowed by one party from another. Debt can come in a number of forms, including bonds and loans.

Due diligence: The care and thought that an investor should take prior to entering into an agreement/transaction with another party.

Equity: The ownership of any asset after all debts associated with that asset are paid off.

Factoring: A financing method that involves a business owner trading their accounts receivable to a third party at a discount in order to raise capital.

First-mover advantage: A type of competitive advantage that a company acquires by being the first to enter a new market.

Free cash-flow: The money that an organisation can generate after putting aside the money needed to maintain or grow its asset base. Free cash-flow allows organisations to pursue new opportunities, such as the development of new products.

Initial Public Offering (IPO): When a privately owned company becomes publicly traded on the stock exchange, giving the right or members of the public to buy shares. IPOs are often issued by young companies seeking the large amounts of capital to expand.

Innovation voucher: Provide organisations in their early stages with funding in order to overcome challenges relating to innovation.

Leveraged Buyout (LBO): The acquisition of another company using a large portion of borrowed money. The purpose of leveraged buyouts is to allow organisations to make large acquisitions without having to commit a large amount of revenue.

Liquidity event: Investment start-up companies are said to be "illiquid" because its shares are not traded in a public stock exchange and, therefore, not easily sold. A liquidity event is an exit strategy for an illiquid investment. It allows the initial investors to cash in some or all of their ownership shares.

Management Buyout (MBO): A situation where the management of a firm buys a controlling interest in the firm from the existing majority shareholders.

New Present Value (NPV): The difference between the present value of cash inflows and the present value outflows. If the NPV is positive, cash-flows will also be positive, if the NPV is negative, cash-flows will also be negative.

Preferred stock: Preferred stock shareholders have a higher claim on assets and earnings than common stock shareholders. Preferred stock must be paid out prior to dividends to common stockholders.

Profit: The amount of money an organisation makes from a business activity after paying all of the expenses incurred.

P/E ratio: Price-to-Earnings ratio is a multiple used to value equity in a company. For example, if stock is trading at $16 and the earnings per share for the most recent 12-month period is $4 then the stock has a P/E ratio of 16/4 or 4.

Ratchet: An anti-dilution provision that gives the investor protection from dilution of value in the event of subsequent financing at a lower valuation.

Senior debt: The borrowed money or loans that a company must repay first if it goes bankrupt.

SBIC: Small business investing companies are privately owned investing companies that provide small businesses with financing.

Stock option: A right sold by one party to another that gives the buyer the right to buy or sell stock at an agreed upon price within a certain time-frame or on a certain date.

Subordinate debt: The borrowed money or loan that ranks below other loans. Subordinate debt will be paid only after senior debt has been paid in full.

Term-sheet: A template outlining the basic terms and conditions under which an investment will be made. It provides a basis for a legally binding agreement.

Trade sale: The selling of a new venture total assets or part of its assets to another organisation.

Valuation: The method of estimating net worth of an asset or a company.

Venture Capital (VC): Money supplied to start-up firms and small businesses by institutional investors with perceived long-term growth potential.

Warrant: Similar to an option, a warrant is a security that gives the owner the right to buy the underlying stock of the issuing company at a fixed exercise price until the expiry date. Warrants are frequently attached to preference shares as a sweetener, allowing the issuer to offer lower interest rates or dividends.

Index